The Last Ottoman Generation and the Making of the Modern Middle East

T0372718

The modern Middle East emerged out of the collapse of the Ottoman Empire, when Britain and France partitioned the Ottoman Arab lands into several new colonial states. The following period was a charged and transformative time of unrest. Insurgent leaders, trained in Ottoman military tactics and with everything to lose from the fall of the empire, challenged the mandatory powers in a number of armed revolts. This is a study of this crucial period in Middle Eastern history, tracing the period through popular political movements and the experience of colonial rule. In doing so, Provence emphasizes the continuity between the late Ottoman and Colonial era, explaining how national identities emerged, and how the seeds were sown for many of the conflicts which have defined the Middle East in the late twentieth and early twenty-first centuries. This is a valuable read for students of Middle Eastern history and politics.

Michael Provence teaches Middle East history at the Department of History at the University of California, San Diego. He is the author of *The Great Syrian Revolt and the Rise of Arab Nationalism* (2005).

Advance praise for *The Last Ottoman Generation and the Making of the Modern Middle East*

The Last Ottoman Generation and the Making of the Modern Middle East

Michael Provence

University of California, San Diego

CAMBRIDGE
UNIVERSITY PRESS

CAMBRIDGE
UNIVERSITY PRESS

University Printing House, Cambridge CB2 8BS, United Kingdom

One Liberty Plaza, 20th Floor, New York, NY 10006, USA

477 Williamstown Road, Port Melbourne, VIC 3207, Australia

314-321, 3rd Floor, Plot 3, Splendor Forum, Jasola District Centre,
New Delhi – 110025, India

79 Anson Road, #06-04/06, Singapore 079906

Cambridge University Press is part of the University of Cambridge.

It furthers the University's mission by disseminating knowledge in the pursuit of
education, learning, and research at the highest international levels of excellence.

www.cambridge.org
Information on this title: www.cambridge.org/9780521761178
DOI: 10.1017/9781139049221

© Michael Provence 2017

First published 2017
5th printing 2019

Printed in the United Kingdom by TJ International Ltd. Padstow Cornwall

A catalogue record for this publication is available from the British Library.

Library of Congress Cataloging-in-Publication Data

Names: Provence, Michael, 1966– author.
Title: The last Ottoman generation and the making of the modern
    Middle East / Michael Provence.
Description: Cambridge, United Kingdom : Cambridge
    University Press, 2017. | Includes bibliographical references and index.
Identifiers: LCCN 2017006688 | ISBN 9780521761178 (hardback : alk.
    paper)
Subjects: LCSH: Middle East—History—20th century. | Turkey—History—
    20th century.
Classification: LCC DS62.8 .P76 2017 | DDC 956/.03—dc23 LC record
available at https://lccn.loc.gov/2017006688

ISBN 978-0-521-76117-8 Hardback
ISBN 978-0-521-74751-6 Paperback

Contents

Figures

Maps

ix

Tables

Acknowledgements

This book got its start during a year spent in Beirut in 2005–6 supported by the Fulbright Program and AUB. The year ended with a war that caused me, my travel and life companion Lor Wood, and our then two-year-old son, August, to flee for Damascus. That July 2006, we briefly joined, in far better circumstances than most, thousands of Lebanese refugees moving east toward Damascus, where there were already a million Iraqi refugees from the invasion and occupation of Iraq. On the streets of Damascus, our old friend Adel Samara shouted a greeting, jumped out of a taxi, ran across six lanes of traffic, swept us up, and restored our faith in humanity and the endlessly restorative properties of Syrian cooking. We traveled on to Aleppo, Adana, and Istanbul, generously helped by everyone we met along the way. Many old and new friends had embraced us warmly in that year. Abdul-Rahim Abu Husayn, Stefan Weber, John Meloy, Clare Leader, Helen Sadr, Samir Seikaly, Jamal Wakim, Martha Mundy, Max Weiss, Mary Wilson, Cyrus Schayegh, Karim Makdisi, and Hala Dimechkie, Kirstin Scheid, Tariq Tell, Jocelyn De Jong, Nadia Maria el Cheikh, and Amelie Beyhum all helped make Beirut, like Damascus before it, the home I always want to return to. I was lucky to enjoy memorable lunches with the late Kamal Salibi.

Back in San Diego, at the University of California, Hasan Kayalı, then and now, is the dear friend I turn to for every kind of counsel and encouragement. He was also the first reader of this book, and saved me (and readers!) from countless errors. The late UCSD History Chair John Marino was always tremendously supportive. Joseph Esherick, Frank Biess, Eric Van Young, and Pamela Radcliff have been inspiring colleagues. A memorable graduate seminar in 2011 and the detective work of the late and deeply missed Patrick Otis Healy, laid bare the earliest traces of the connection between Salah al-Din and General Gouraud. Ben Smuin took time from his own research at Nantes to excavate French documents on the exile of Yasin al-Hashimi. Reem Bailony and Nir Shafir helped in the final stage. Suzanne Weissman was an early and enthusiastic reader. Comrade of two decades, Joe Logan, introduced me to Mesut Uyar, who knows more about the education of late Ottoman officers than anyone alive, and always shares his knowledge graciously. Mary Wilson insisted I meet Laila Parsons, who became my accomplice in the study of post-Ottoman rebels. Mary also introduced me to Ziad Muna, who published my last book in Arabic despite his initial misgivings. Talal Kamal Rizk and Gilberto Conde helped keep memories of Damascus alive for me.

This book was mostly written in Berlin, a city destroyed by the folly and wickedness of the wars of the 20th century, rebuilt, and now home to thousands of refugees from the Middle Eastern wars of the early 21st century. The Zentrum Moderner Orient (ZMO), under the directorship of Ulrike Freitag, with its amiably bustling communal kitchen, tranquility, and wonderful library, was the perfect place to work. Thomas Ripper always helped me in the library. Nora Lafi has kindly shared her office, and leafy view, with me during two long stays. Somehow she tolerated me at an adjoining desk for at least fifteen months. The support of the Alexander von Humboldt foundation made my stay possible; an experience no amount of acknowledgement can repay. Stefan Weber, Salam Said, Astrid Meier, Jens Hannsen, and the late Thomas Philipp, encouraged me at every turn.

Cambridge editors Marigold Acland and Maria Marsh cheerfully tolerated my delays when I expected to be told to get lost. I suspect Eugene Rogan's good word saved me at least a few times. Matt Sweeney designed the book with more skill and understanding than I could hope for. Sarah Turner improved the manuscript with endless patience.

Most of the photos came from the private archive, long collected and generously shared, of Wolf-Dieter Lemke. A spring 2016 invitation to AUB and a wonderful meeting with the grandson of Yasin al-Hashimi, Mazin Ali Mumtaz al-Daftari, and May Ziwar al-Daftari, helped bring the final pieces together and provided an intimate portrait of Yasin Paşa.

At the earlier stages, great teachers Peter Sluglett, Nadine Meouchy, the late Khariyya Qasimiyya, Abdallah Hanna, and Rashid Khalidi guided me patiently. Perhaps not so innocently, Philip Khoury asked, "Why don't you write about all the revolts?" More than ten years on, every page reflects the help of these dear people along the way. I hope they will approve but I'm surely the one to blame if they don't.

Notes on Transliteration

Transliteration of words, names, and places is a vexing problem in a work such as this, dealing as it does, with Arabic, Ottoman, and modern Turkish, and a variety of states and institutions, many of which imposed, and changed, their own names, spellings, and even alphabets. Names, titles, and places I have rendered in the fashion most common to English speakers. Villages and towns not widely known outside the region, I have rendered in Modern Turkish or a simplified Arabic transliteration according to post-WWII borders. Names of individuals I have rendered into modern Turkish or Arabic transliteration based mostly upon the place they ended up after 1918, which is to say the Turkish Republic or various Arab countries. The names of Ottoman schools, institutions, ranks, and titles I have rendered in modern Turkish wherever they happened to be. I have also made some possibly quixotic choices that may seem logical only to me. A case in point is Yasin Paşa al-Hashimi, in which I give the Arabic transliteration of his name, and the modern Turkish rendering of his Ottoman-bestowed title. I have followed my ear in using Arabic given and family names: usually complete (Fawzi al-Qawuqji), sometimes with the definite article (al-Qawuqji) and occasionally without (Qawuqji), or with the given name only (Fawzi).

List of Abbreviations

AUB   American University of Beirut
BNA   British National Archives
CO   British Colonial Office
FO   British Foreign Office
IFEAD   Institut Française d'Études Arabes de Damas
IJMES   *International Journal of Middle Eastern Studies*
MAE   French Ministère des Affaires Etrangères
MWT   Markaz al-Watha'iq al-Tarikhiyya (Syrian National Archives)
SHAT   Service Historique de l'Armée Terre
LN   League of Nations Archives
IU   Istanbul University Archival Collection

Maps

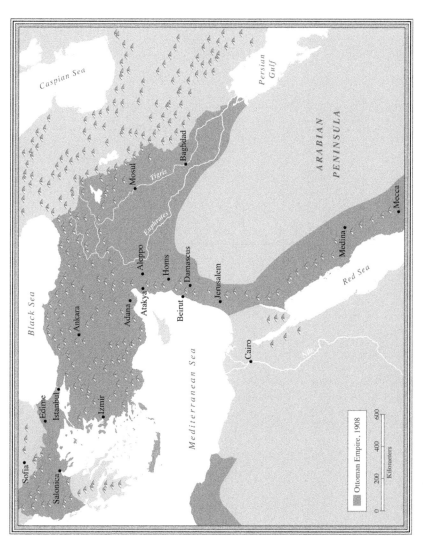

Map 1. Ottoman Empire in 1908

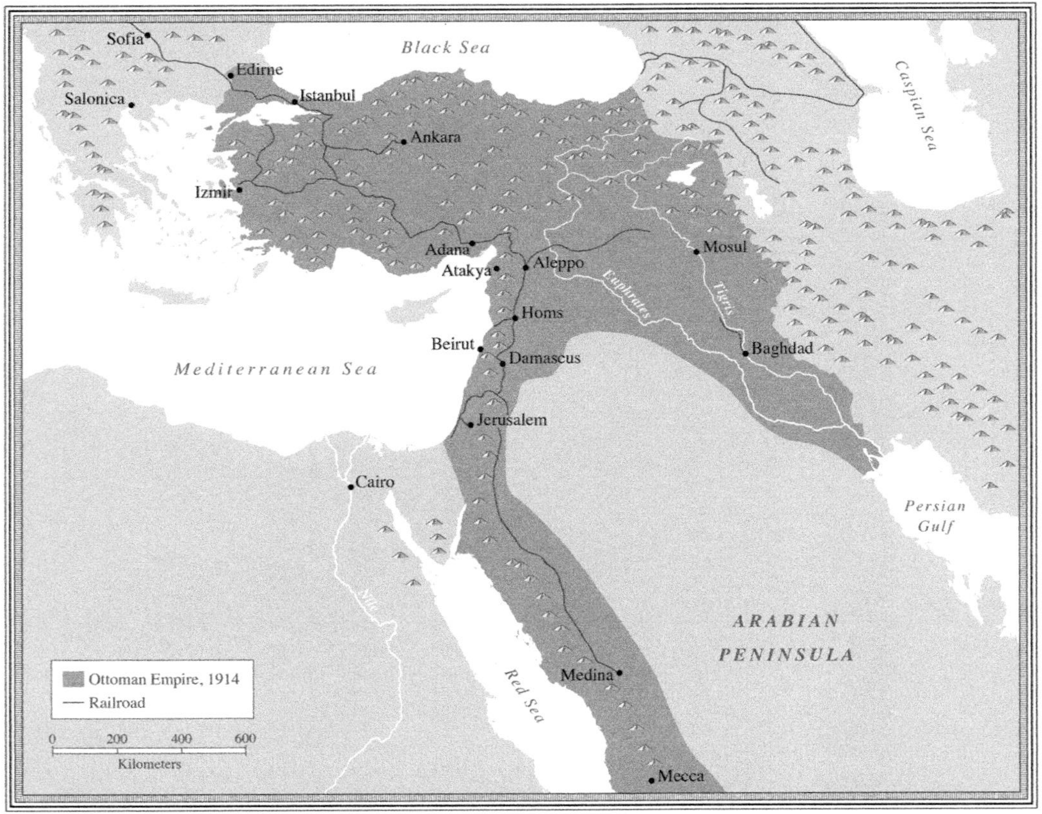

Map 2. Ottoman Empire in 1914

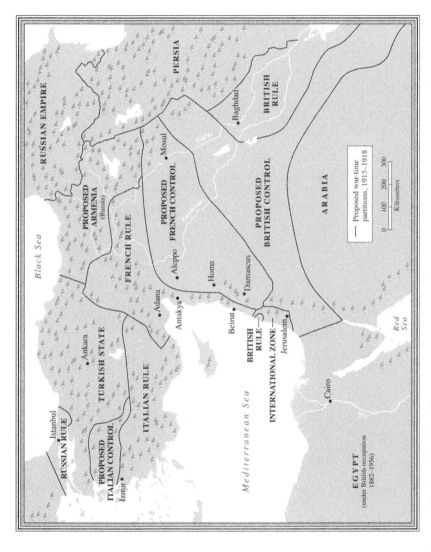

Map 3. Wartime Partition Plans

xvii

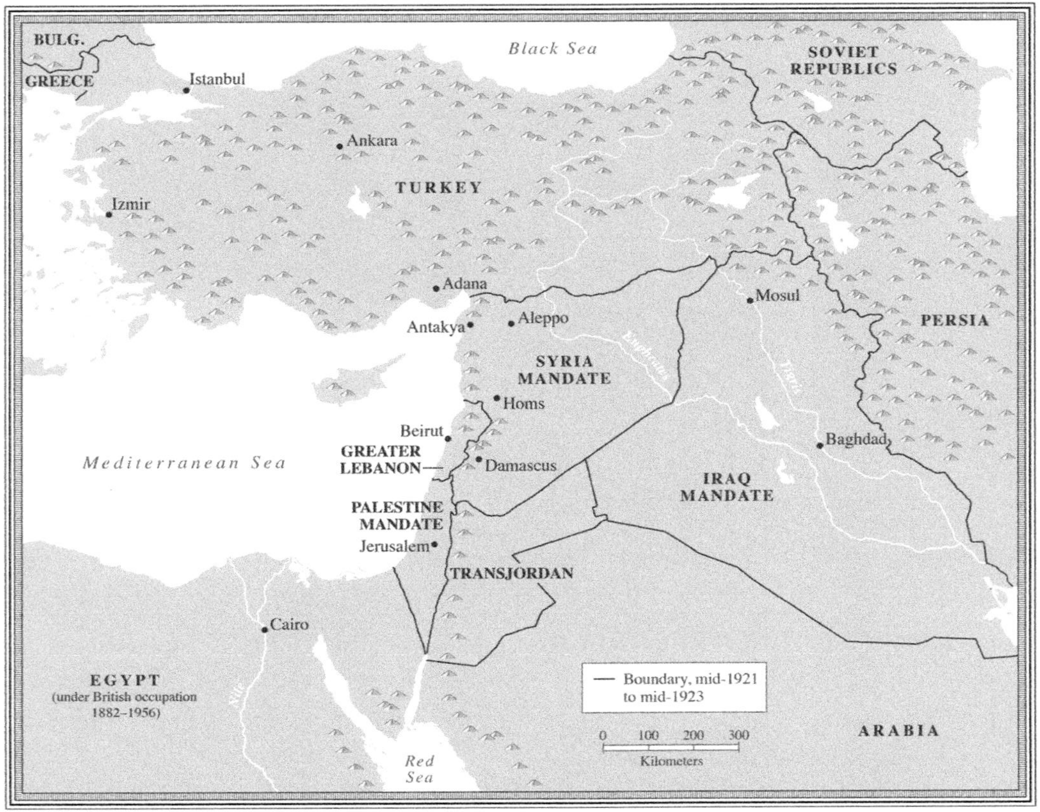

xviii

Map 4. Post-Ottoman Middle East, 1921–3

Political and Military Figures of the Last Ottoman Generation

Ottoman State education was divided between civil and military systems. At the pinnacle of the military system was the staff college (Erkân-i Harbiyye Askeriyye), which accepted no more than 10 percent of military-academy (Mekteb-i Ulūm-i Harbiyye) graduates, most of whom had received ten or more years of intensive state schooling. The Mülkiye (Mekteb-i Mülkiye-i Şahane) was similarly the pinnacle of the civil system, though less selective than the staff college. Both were intended to train high civil and military functionaries. Some Mülkiye graduates continued to the law college (Mekteb-i Hukuk-i Şahane), and some transferred from one system to the other.

Table 1. *Military Officers*

Name	Place and birth date	Education	Position, Nov. 1918	Post-war vocation	Death
Saʿid al-ʿAs	Hama, 1889	Staff College, Istanbul	Jailed middle-rank Ottoman staff officer	Insurgent leader, policeman	In battle, Palestine, 1936
Yusuf al-ʿAzma	Damascus, 1883	Staff College, Istanbul; Kriegsakademie, Berlin	Senior Ottoman staff officer	Politician	In battle, Syria, 1920
Bakr Sidqi	Kirkuk, 1890	Staff College, Istanbul; Britain, India	Middle-rank Ottoman staff officer	Senior officer, politician	Assassinated, Mosul, 1937
Jaʿfar al-ʿAskari	1885, Mosul	Military academy, Istanbul; Kriegsakademie, Berlin	Captured middle-rank Ottoman officer	Politician	Assassinated, Baghdad, 1936
Yasin al-Hashimi	Baghdad, 1884	Staff College, Istanbul	Senior Ottoman staff officer	Politician	Alleged heart attack, 1937
Taha al-Hashimi	Baghdad, 1888	Staff College, Istanbul	Senior Ottoman staff officer	Senior officer, politician	London, 1961
Ramadan Shallash	Zur province, 1879	Tribal School; military academy, Istanbul	Middle-rank Ottoman officer	Insurgent leader	Alive in 1950
Mustafa Kemal	Salonika, 1881	Staff College, Istanbul	Senior Ottoman staff officer	Politician	Istanbul, 1938
Mustafa İsmet (İnönü)	Izmir/Malatya, 1888	Staff College, Istanbul	Middle-rank Ottoman staff officer	Politician	Ankara, 1973
Fawzi al-Qawuqji	Tripoli, 1890	Military academy, Istanbul; St Cyr, France	Middle-rank Ottoman officer	Insurgent	Beirut, 1977
Nuri al-Saʿid	Baghdad, 1888	Military academy, Istanbul	Captured middle-rank Ottoman officer	Politician	Assassinated, Baghdad, 1958
Mahmud Şevket Paşa,	Baghdad, 1856	Staff college, Istanbul; Kriegsakademie, Berlin	Assassinated as Grand Vizir Istanbul 1913	Dead in 1913	Assassinated, Istanbul, 1913

Table 2. *Civilians*

Name	Place and birth date	Education	Position, Nov. 1918	Post-war vocation	Death
(Muhammad) Amin al-Husayni	Jerusalem, 1895	Al-Azhar, Cairo, Mülkiye, Istanbul	Ottoman reserve officer	Politician, Mufti	1974, Beirut
Ibrahim Hananu	Near Aleppo, 1869	Mülkiye; Mekteb-i Hukuk, Istanbul	Senior Ottoman governor and administrator. Aleppo municipal council	Politician, lawyer, insurgent	Tuberculosis, Aleppo, 1935
Musa Kazim al-Husayni	Jerusalem, 1853	Mülkiye, Istanbul	Retired Ottoman governor and administrator	Politician	Police beating/old age, Jerusalem, 1934
Shakib Arslan	Mount Lebanon, 1869	Beirut Sultani	Member of Ottoman parliament, envoy to Berlin	Journalist, activist	Beirut, 1946
Ihsan al-Jabiri					
Rashid ʿAli al-Kaylani	Baghdad, 1892	Mülkiye Mekteb-i Hukuk, Istanbul	Lawyer and judge, Baghdad	Politician, lawyer	Beirut, 1965
Muhammad Kurd ʿAli	Damascus, 1876	Idadiye Damascus (Maktab ʿAnbar)	Journalist and publisher	Literary scholar, journalist	Damascus, 1953
Jamil Mardam Bey	Damascus, 1894	Sorbonne, Paris	Spent war years in France	Politician	Cairo, 1960
ʿAbd al-Rahman Shahbandar	Damascus, 1880	Syrian Protestant College (AUB)	Physician, exiled ex-Ottoman politician. Joined and left Unionist Party. Fled Damascus during World War I.	Politician, physician, exiled 1925–37	Assassinated, Damascus, 1940
(Muhammad) Rashid Rida	Tripoli (Qalamun), 1865	Tripoli and al-Azhar, Cairo with Muhammad ʿAbduh	Damascus after 1908. Returned to Cairo before 1914, and returned to Damascus in 1918.	Scholar, cleric, journalist/ publisher	Cairo, 1935

(continued)

Table 2. (*cont.*)

Name	Place and birth date	Education	Position, Nov. 1918	Post-war vocation	Death
Shukri al-Quwatli	Damascus, 1891	Mülkiye, Istanbul	Prison in Damascus	Politician, prime minister	Beirut, 1967
Rustum Haydar	Baalbak, 1889	Mülkiye, Istanbul Sorbonne, Paris	Fled Ottoman Damascus to join Faysal, August 1918.	Politician, lawyer	Assassinated, Baghdad, 1940
Saʿid Haydar	Baalbak, 1890	Mekteb-i Hukuk, Istanbul	Lawyer, professor of law, Damascus University	Lawyer, politician, exiled 1925–37	Damascus, 1957
Hashim al-Atasi	Homs, 1875	Mülkiye, Istanbul	Serving Ottoman governor and administrator	Politician, prime minister	Homs, 1960
Jamal al-Husayni	Jerusalem, 1894	Syrian Protestant College (AUB)	Ottoman reserve (conscript) officer	Activist, politician	Saudi Arabia, 1982

Table 3. *Non-Ottoman Figures*

Name	Place and birth date	Education	Position, Nov. 1918	Post-war vocation	Death
Edmund Allenby	England, 1861	Staff College, Camberley	Senior staff officer, Occupied Enemy Territory Administration (OETA)	1917–20	London, 1936
Léon Blum	France, 1872	École normale supérieure, Sorbonne, Paris	Official of the French Socialist Party	Prime Minister, 1936–7, briefly 1938	Paris, 1950
Robert de Caix	France, 1869	École Libre des Sciences Politiques, Paris	Journalist and editor, leader *parti colonial*	Mandate 1920–3. PMC 1924–39	Paris, 1970
Kinahan Cornwallis	USA, 1883	Oxford	1916–20 Director, Arab Bureau	Advisor, Iraqi Interior Ministry	Hampshire, England, 1959
David Lloyd George	England, 1863	Local church and home school	British prime minister, 1916–22	Politician, retired	Wales, 1945
Henri Gouraud	France, 1867	Military academy, St. Cyr	Senior staff officer, 4th Army	First French Mandate HC, 1920–3	Paris, 1946
Georges Clemenceau	France, 1841	Lycée, Nantes	French prime minister, 1917–20	retired	Paris, 1929
Henry de Jouvenel	France, 1876	Collège Stanislas de Paris	Journalist, reserve officer, western front	High Commissioner Syria, 1925–6	Paris, 1935
T.E. Lawrence	Wales, 1888	Oxford	Middle-rank reserve officer	Various	England, 1935
William Rappard	New York, 1883	Harvard, Vienna	Professor, University of Geneva	League of Nations PMC Director	Geneva, 1958
Maurice Sarrail	France, 1856	Military academy, St. Cyr	Senior staff officer, dismissed	Mandate HC 1924–5	Paris, 1929
Herbert Samuel	England, 1870	Oxford	Politician	First British Palestine Mandate HC 1920–5	London, 1963

Introduction

Saladin's Pilgrims and the War to End Wars

In 1898, as part of a grand tour of the realms of his Ottoman brother monarch, German Kaiser Wilhelm II visited the great Ottoman city of Damascus. To Wilhelm, Damascus was a city of Roman antiquity, of Saint Paul, and of Saladin. Especially Saladin. Salah al-Din Ibn Ayyub as he had been known in the Middle East, was the medieval sultan who had defeated and expelled the Crusaders from Jerusalem in 1187. Saladin's memory had been revived in a number of eighteenth- and nineteenth-century works of popular literature published in German and English, satisfying a romantic thirst for stories of Oriental fantasy and adventure. Wilhelm II, perhaps more than other contemporary heads of state, crafted a self-consciously romantic public image and visual representation of his rule.[1] His visit to the Ottoman realms glamorized his notions of Roman imperial antiquity, medieval chivalry, the Crusades, and German imperial ascendance within a parade of romantic evocations.

Unlike Wilhelm, the Ottoman citizens of Damascus were not thinking of the ancient past, but of a promising future for their city and empire. Saladin's memory (and his modest tomb) was probably foremost among many, sometimes dimly, remembered sultans and princes. But for the citizens of the city, Wilhelm's visit represented their arrival on the world stage, and underscored the respect and importance, the city, its elite cosmopolitan citizens, and the Ottoman state under its sultan, hoped to enjoy. By all accounts they threw a party and reception for the ages to welcome Wilhelm. A century later the memory of the party survives in oral history among Damascenes. The following decades of revolution and war, culminating in the Great War of 1914–18, dashed the optimistic hopes of the dawn of the twentieth century.

The visit to the Ottoman realms so impressed Kaiser Wilhelm that he commissioned a number of lavish gifts for his friend Sultan AbdulHamid II and the Ottoman people. The gifts include the splendid gilded tile fountain still prominent in Istanbul's historic imperial center, a large

1

marble plaque in the Baalbek Roman temple in today's Lebanon, and finally a beautiful gilded bronze wreath, almost one meter in diameter, made by the best German jewelers and metal smiths, which was sent to adorn the modest tomb of Saladin. The wreath read, in Arabic, "This crown was presented by His Majesty, the Emperor of Germany, eminence Wilhelm the Second in commemoration of his pilgrimage to the tomb of eminence Salah al-Din al-Ayyubi." For his part, Abdul-Hamid gave archeological gifts to Wilhelm that form the core of the collection of Berlin's Pergamum Museum, which, a century later, is Germany's most visited museum.

The Great War of 1914–18 ended the Ottoman state after seven centuries and ended the German monarchy of Wilhelm after forty-seven years. It also ended centuries of Russian and Hapsburg monarchy. In Damascus, the War brought the end of 402 years of mostly peaceful and prosperous Ottoman rule. Immediately after the fall of Damascus, another famous European visited Saladin's tomb. In the days after the British entry into the city and the retreat of the Ottoman army north toward Aleppo, and today's Turkish border, Colonel T.E. Lawrence, later known as Lawrence of Arabia, visited the site in the garden just outside the Umayyad Mosque in the old city. Lawrence had long been an enthusiast for the history of the Crusades and had visited the city, its monuments, and the tomb before, in summer 1909, as an Oxford undergraduate, when he spent three months on foot visiting the Crusader castles of Ottoman Syria. Lawrence titled the resulting thesis, "The Influence of the Crusades on European Military Architecture – to the End of the 12th Century," for which he received first-class honors.

On October 31, 1918 Lawrence returned not as a student, or as an archeologist, which he had been in 1912 and 1913, but as a new conqueror of an ancient, fabled city and empire. He seems to have envisioned himself a crusader or desert knight. Lawrence proceeded directly to the tomb of Saladin, where he took the heavy gilded bronze wreath and silk sash, carried it to his billet, and took it with him when he returned to England by ship a few days later. Back in London, Lawrence brought the trophy to the newly established Imperial War Museum, where it remains today. He attached a handwritten note with the donation, reading "as Saladin no longer required it."[2]

A month or so later, British Prime Minister David Lloyd George consented to the wish of his wartime counterpart French Premier Clemenceau for south eastern Anatolia, and the northern parts of Ottoman Syria including Beirut, Damascus, and Aleppo. By mid 1920 a French army marched east from Beirut to conquer and occupy the great city of Damascus and expel the once-British sponsored Arab government

Lawrence and Amir Faysal had set up in 1918. Immediately after claim- ing the city, another famous European soldier visited the tomb of Saladin.

In July 1920, French general and first High Commissioner for the French Mandates of Syria and Greater Lebanon, Henri Gouraud, made his first visit to the newly occupied city. Once in Damascus Gouraud went directly to the tomb of Saladin. In the garden outside the small tomb building, Gouraud delivered a speech in which he ignored the small crowd of anxious Damascene onlookers before him, and instead addressed Saladin directly, proclaiming, "arise Saladin, we have returned, and my presence here consecrates the victory of the Cross over the Crescent."[3]

No less than Wilhelm, or Lawrence, General Gouraud was an impor- tant figure in the history of the Middle East in the century since the Great War and the end of the Ottoman state. General Gouraud, along with his secretary general, Robert de Caix, were the original colonial architects of political, legal, and governmental structures that still exert constant influence on the daily lives of millions of people of Syria and Lebanon. They, more than anyone, were the inventors of the states of Lebanon and Syria, as they exist today, and in a sense, the originators of conflicts that continue to afflict the people of the region.

Gouraud, Lawrence, or Wilhelm are not the focus of this book but their dreams and visions figure in it. It is instead the story of a collision, with effects that still reverberate, between an imperial fantasy world they shared, which melded ambitious, shifting imperial strategies and dreams of world domination, with fantasies of the past and present and a frequently outsized self-regard for their wisdom, abilities, and culture. Such fantastic visions collided with the forces and structures of an Ottoman authoritarian modernity, little different from ideologies of modernity, state patriotism and militarism that dominated all European Great War powers and roiled Europe's twentieth century. This is the story of the late Ottoman vanguard who gambled and lost. It is also the story of a tradition of Great Power politics in the Middle East, and the pervasive habit of the Great Powers to occupy a Middle East fantasy world of their own invention, with predictably tragic consequences. The three victorious powers that emerged from the war, Britain, France, and the United States, conspired to deny the political agency of Ottoman Muslims, and instead resolved to emphasize something then called the "national idea," which endeavored to fragment the world into a multitude of small and manageable national states, arranged hier- archically and accorded rights of self-representation according to their level of "civilization," or national development. The former Ottoman peoples occupied an intermediate place above Africans and well below

Eastern European and Balkan Christians formerly part of the Austro-Hungarian Empire.

Middle Eastern historians have long been preoccupied with national histories and the rise of individual nationalisms. Modernity, ethnic nationalism, and the Middle East post-colonial nation-state are understood to be intertwined; a perspective that also lay behind the League of Nations and various post-World War I settlements.[4] This book does not follow this pattern. It tries to imagine the viewpoint of many former Ottoman citizens who argued that the divisions of and governing arrangements of the post-Ottoman, colonial period were inferior, less free, and less representative than what had come before. Many protested that Ottoman rule had been better, more just, and perhaps more modern, than what we take to be the modern nation-state system of the Middle East. Their voices have been silenced by a hundred years of colonial and nationalist historiography, but if we want to know what was lost and what the world looked like in 1920, such voices are important. This book tells the story of the slow demise of a system of ordering the world that spanned centuries and regions and how people tried to survive this personal and political cataclysm. Obviously, many did not survive. The book takes as its frame of reference not the birth of something new, but the death of something old and evolving, and asks how did the old things, patterns, habits, cultures, ways of thinking, and possibilities affect what came after.

Loss from the collapse of the state and trauma from a decade of total war were the dominant experiences of the period. The modernizing Ottoman state, its system, its culture, and institutions had been increasingly present as backdrop in the lives of the people who lived through the decades surrounding the World War I. But by the early 1920s the state had disappeared from all its realms. Just as loss and disorientation were common experiences, so too was trauma and cataclysm that accompanied the decade of war at the end of the Ottoman years. In greater Syria as much as twenty-five percent of the population perished from war, famine, and disease between 1915 and 1919. These common experiences were shared and thus required little explicit explanation or discussion. Decades later we take this silence for inconsequence. This book argues the opposite; the cataclysm of war and the demise of the Ottoman state was so great it went without mention because of the ubiquitousness of the experience. No one escaped the suffering and no one needed to explain it.

This book is a history of an end, and a collapse so immense it has been forgotten and erased by near universal consensus. The book tries to re-imagine the world of the Middle East as it might have seemed to a formerly optimistic and privileged person at the moment of its collapse into something different and all together less optimistic. For a hundred years, historians have interpreted the history of the twentieth century in the Middle East as the birth of this or that nation, the emergence of this or that state, the rise of this or that idea. By contrast, this is the story of the end of plans, hope, prospects, and horizons, and how people survived, and made sense of the events that had overtaken them. It is the story of the collapse of a state and its institutions and the certainties that had ordered life for millions for centuries, albeit certainly with constant change, but also with hope, occasional optimism, and collective effort. The book tries to tell this story in a way which I hope would have been familiar to those most affected, and in a modest way, to take a step toward settling some long overdue accounts.

Modernity, Militarism, and Colonialism in the Making of the Middle East

The modernizing Ottoman State had touched the lives of all within its domains in the years immediately before the war. Those who lived through the period shared a range of experiences common to all the major combatant states. The nineteenth-century European state had evolved in the century after the French revolution to become a state that educated, taxed, counted, conscripted, trained, and claimed to act in the name of, and derive its legitimacy from, the collective will and spirit of its population.[5] The combatant states fostered a range of public rituals, origin stories, and invented traditions intended to cement loyalty, allegiance, and compliance with the state. In the Ottoman state these centered around Islam, the person and office of the Sultan-Caliph, or successor to the Prophet Muhammad as titular head of the Muslim community. The state also claimed to provide justice and representation to its non-Muslim population, who received quotas for representation in various elected Ottoman bodies. Like other states in Europe, state legitimation included a sometimes contradictory mix of majority religious appeals, claims of popular sovereignty, and claims of legal equality before the law for all religious communities. In this way the state sought to harness the loyalty of its majorities, while attempting more fitfully to insure the compliance of its religious minorities. The appeals to equality were often more theoretical than actual, as France's Dreyfus Affair of 1894, and the repression and mass killings of Ottoman Armenians about the same time demonstrate.

The colonial legacy of today's Middle East is no better understood than the Ottoman legacy, and has often been ignored for similar reasons. The Great Powers, and various regional client states planned and discussed the partition of the Ottoman Empire long before the Balkan and Ottoman crises of 1911–13, and World War I. The partition plans, maneuvers, and negotiations were inevitably accompanied by a range of racial, religious, cultural, and civilizational oppositions. Put another way, a host of essential positive attributes claimed to characterize the British and French nations were arrayed against negative attributes claimed to characterize Ottoman Muslims; rationality against fanaticism, civilization against barbarism, evolutionism against timeless primitivism, modern against backward, and Christian against Muslim. These assumptions and preconceptions were not always openly expressed but they underlay all aspects of the post-world war settlement, and in fact made possible the kind of breathtaking hubris the settlement displayed. Notably, as Ottoman intellectuals pointed out at the time, such partitions and colonial arrangements were not contemplated or replicated in the conquered territories of the Hapsburg or German empires in central Europe. The difference was mostly religion, though so-called Oriental Christians, including Greeks and Armenians, were also considered unworthy of full self-rule.

Legacies

This book makes three central arguments: First, the common legacy of the late Ottoman modernization project is second only to the colonial legacy in shaping the history of the region and its peoples. Second, the colonial legacy on the Middle East is a common experience, whether in Palestine, Iraq, Syria, or Turkey, without which the history of the region is incomprehensible. And finally, the durable tendency to view the history of the region through the lens of national histories of Turkey, Syria, Lebanon, Palestine, etc. obscures commonalities that were clear to all until at least the 1940s.

The book begins with a chapter examining the common structures, themes, and experiences of late Ottoman life. It focuses on the formative experience of military school, and follows the life experiences and adventures of several late Ottoman figures who began life as provincial children, of mostly modest background, and attended subsidized elite state schools. As members of a self-conscious, meritocratic, state elite, together they experienced privilege and responsibility for the fate of the state, war and trauma, followed by defeat, unemployment, prison, and worse, and went on to emerge as statesmen, nation builders, activists, or revolutionaries. The chapter shows that late Ottoman attitudes and structures were formative on the decades that followed, despite the collapse and disappearance of the state. The modernizing Ottoman state broadly shared similar institutions and attitudes with other modernizing European powers, and the Ottoman state and its fate deserves a more central place in the history of Europe and World War I than it customarily receives.

The second chapter examines the theories and practices of post-world war colonialism, as practiced by the victorious powers on the territories of the vanquished. It examines the legal and racial structures and theories that legitimated colonial rule over formerly independent peoples. Part of the effort to colonize the Ottoman realms required a rhetorical removal of the Ottoman state from the story of Europe, and the tacit placement of Ottoman Muslims into racially deficient non-European categories that demanded colonial tutelage. The resulting inconsistencies at the core of the colonial and League of Nations mandate system had consequences for the post-Ottoman region and its people that are still unfolding one hundred years later. The chapter introduces readers to the general themes and narrative of interwar Middle Eastern colonialism, which are explored in more detail in subsequent sections.

The remaining chapters follow the adventures and struggles of the last Ottoman generation through the interwar decades. These chapters make the central argument that for those who lived through them, the borders, states, and national histories that characterize the usual framework for understanding the region would have made no sense. The book attempts to re-imagine a post-Ottoman Middle East of great cities, and rural and pastoral hinterlands, interconnected through modern infrastructure, and institutions, undivided by borders, ruling arrangements, or the constructed barriers of human consciousness.

A century later, the poisonous fruit of the Middle East colonial settlement is still in the headlines. Almost one hundred years after the end of the Great War, one of the Middle Eastern states created in its wake, Syria, where this book was first conceived, is in an advanced state of civil war and social and political disintegration. The conflict is widely claimed to be the gravest humanitarian and refugee crisis since World War II. The roots of the conflict in Syria today, like many other regional conflicts, reach directly into the polluted soil sown by the post-War settlement, and my only optimistic hope is that the reader may discern the shadows of these roots, and know that the suffering of today did not come from nowhere, but from the conviction, still nurtured widely, that some people were more deserving of life and liberty than others simply by the accident of their birth, and that the people who have suffered most from this conviction, now and in the past, did nothing to deserve their awful inheritance.

Notes

1. Peter Schamoni makes this argument in his documentary based on historical footage of Wilhelm's reign in his *Majestät brauchen Sonne: Kaiser Wilhelm II.-der erste deutsche Medienstar*, 2000.
2. Lowell Thomas, *With Lawrence in Arabia* (New York: Garden City Publishing, 1924), p. 291, www.iwm.org.uk/collections/item/object/30083872, accessed July 1, 2015, and correspondence with Mrs. Jane Furlong, Imperial War Museums.
3. Pierre La Mazière, *Partant pour la Syrie* (Paris: Audinière, 1928), p. 191.
4. The excellent recent book, Michael A Reynolds, *Shattering Empires: the Clash and Collapse of the Ottoman and Russian Empires, 1908–1918* (Cambridge University Press, 2011), pp. 17–18, makes this point well.
5. Eric Hobsbawm, *The Age of Empire: 1875–1914* (New York: Vintage, 1987), Selim Deringil, *The Well-Protected Domains: Ideology and the Legitimation of Power in the Ottoman Empire, 1876–1909* (London: I.B. Tauris, 1998).

1   Ottoman Modernity in the Long Nineteenth Century: Training State Servants and Making Citizens

Events in the Final Ottoman Decades

1839–76	Ottoman legal and governmental reforms, including legal equality, state education, local, and provincial elections, etc.
1876	Ottoman Constitution
1876–1909	Sultan Abdul-Hamid II
1877	Sultan Abdul-Hamid II dissolves constitutional assembly
1877–8	Russo-Ottoman War in Balkans
1878	Congress of Berlin introduces the "national idea" to international settlements and partition plans. Great Power sponsorship of client "nations" was thought to limit the possibility of direct Great Power annexations, and direct conflict
1882–1956	British invasion and occupation of Ottoman Egypt
1870s–1890s	Mass expansion of Ottoman state education
1908	Ottoman army forces Ottoman Constitutional Restoration
1909	Failed Counter-Revolution causes abdication of Sultan Abdul-Hamid
1911	Italian invasion of Tripoli province (Libya)
1912–13	First and Second Balkan Wars
June 28, 1914	Heir to Hapsburg throne assassinated in former-Ottoman provincial capital Sarajevo. Resulting ultimatums start World War I

Modern Education and a Late Ottoman Childhood

At the end of the nineteenth century a 10-year-old boy began a long walk away from home. He kissed his mother, perhaps for the last time, cried a little, and left, carrying some belongings, carefully packed for the journey, accompanied by his father, an uncle, or older brother. They soon passed beyond beloved and familiar sights, through unfamiliar villages, or neighborhoods, over the passage of hours, or even days. Finally they reached the grand doorway of a large stone building, with an inscription neither could likely read, bearing the signature of the Ottoman sultan, and reading "Imperial Military Middle School." The boy kissed his father, perhaps cried a bit more, but furtively, and passed through the doorway into the seemingly durable embrace of the modernizing state.

Attending a state middle school was an experience of anxiety and wonder for children in the nineteenth-century Ottoman Empire. In Damascus, Beirut, Adana, Salonica, and other provincial capitals, the journey to school started by leaving the family home. The path might have taken the parent and child through olive groves, fruit orchards, or wheat fields, and neighboring villages, and down the mountains, toward a town nestled on the shores of the Mediterranean, or along a large river. It would surely have been the largest town, and probably the largest building, the boy had ever seen. Anxiety and dread gave way to excitement and pride when the boy received his splendid new woolen uniform, complete with brass buttons bearing the imperial coat of arms, and a crimson fez.

In the nineteenth century in Europe and the Mediterranean basin, most people were peasants and most died not far from their birthplace. It would not have taken the child long to realize that his life was about to change in a way different from the lives of his parents or grandparents. Education and association with the state would indeed open new vistas on a world beyond the village or neighborhood. School would be jarring, eased by new friends, and a dormitory full of boys just as alone and disoriented. Teachers spoke unfamiliar languages and new words, and there would surely be a huge and frightening quantity of things to learn. Military or civil middle school would, however, be the first real step in becoming part of a late Ottoman elite, and children would meet peers with whom they would share experiences and outlook over the coming decades. Everything they learned and did conditioned them to believe they were the foremost guardians of the Ottoman state, its sultan, and its Muslim people. They came to form a self-conscious elite and expected to assume leading roles in the army and politics. Similarly conditioned men played singular roles in all the countries that marched to war in 1914. In the former Ottoman lands, they continued their central role after the defeat in 1918.

Modernizing the State

In 1874 Benjamin Disraeli's Conservatives defeated British Liberal Party Prime Minister William Gladstone. In defeat and opposition, Gladstone turned to pamphleteering to attack his rival's government and prepare his return to power. His pamphlet, *Bulgarian Horrors and the Question of the East*, was a fierce attack on the Ottoman Empire, Ottoman policy in the Balkans, and by extension, the claimed friendly inaction of Disraeli's government.[1] Ottoman Sultan Abdul-Hamid II came to power the same year, 1876, advanced and selected by the leaders of a constitutional revolution in the Ottoman capital.

In Istanbul the leaders of the constitutional movement had forced the abdication of the previous sultan. The constitutionalists advanced Abdul-Hamid II as the first monarch intended to rule under the limits of a basic law. All major dynastic powers underwent similar nineteenth-century processes of constitutional challenge to royal prerogative. Gladstone's screed dripped racist contempt and stung modernizing Ottoman elites. Sultan Abdul-Hamid II was a disaster for the constitutionalists, and under cover from war and the international crisis, he dismissed the assembly and ruled without constitutional oversight. Most of his European royal contemporaries tried, and sometimes succeeded, in reinstituting royal autocracy in the late nineteenth century.

The end of war in the Balkans, and the division of South Eastern Europe between the Russian and Ottoman spheres, was negotiated and concluded at Bismarck's Congress of Berlin in 1878. The sting of the British denunciation and betrayal and the occupation of Ottoman Cyprus helped move modernizing Ottoman elites into the emerging camp of unified imperial Germany. Gladstone rode populist outrage and nationalist fervor against the "Tyrannical Turk" back to power in 1880, and within eighteen months had bombarded, invaded and occupied the autonomous Ottoman province of Egypt. Gladstonian contempt for the Ottoman state was long lived, and endless discussion of the "Sick Man of Europe" predisposed Gladstone's admiring successors, like Winston Churchill, to repeatedly underestimate Ottoman resilience and vitality on the battlefields of the World War I. Gladstone was remembered in the Ottoman lands too, and almost fifty years later, and decades after his death, he was still reflexively cursed by Ottoman elites.[2]

In 1884 Prussian General Colmar Von der Goltz, author of the seminal book on the militarized nation, *Das Volk in Waffen* [*The Nation in Arms*], became the leader of the new German military mission to the Ottoman state. Three years earlier Sultan Abdul-Hamid had made a personal request to Bismarck to send a military mission. Bismarck proceeded slowly and informed both British and Austrian embassies of the request. When Bismarck finally sent several officers, followed by Von der Goltz, he insured they would be under formal contract to the Ottoman staff command, and be on leave as serving German officers. Von der Goltz stayed in Istanbul for twelve years until 1896. He retired an honored Prussian general in the early years of the new century, but he stayed in touch with his admiring former students among the Ottoman general staff, who wrote frequent letters to their old teacher and friend. Baghdad-born Mahmud Şevket Paşa was Goltz Paşa's closest friend and ally among Ottoman staff officers, and spent several years in Germany in the 1890s. Mahmud Şevket wrote, translated, and published prolifically on military topics, between 1890 and 1910 including at least two training and theory manuals in collaboration with Goltz Paşa. The two agreed, and transmitted to their students and disciples, the conviction that elite army officers should be the leading vanguard of modern, self-confident, militarized nations.[3]

Career officers were divided into two broad groups: a usually illiterate majority promoted through the ranks, called *alaylı*, and a smaller elite called *mektebli* who had experienced an intensive, decade-long, cadet-education process. In outlook, culture, and socialization, the two groups could scarcely have been more different. Tensions between these two groups played out on the streets and barracks of the capital in the period between 1908–13, and were arguably central to late Ottoman internal conflict.[4] When the *alaylı* officers launched the counter-revolution in April 1909, the young *mektebli* officers considered Mahmud Şevket Paşa the savior of the revolution and their intellectual godfather, and he served as Grand Vezir between 1909 and his assassination in 1913. A large display in today's Turkish Military Museum, in the old military academy in Istanbul, remains a shrine to Mahmud Şevket Paşa. Kaiser Wilhelm II recalled Von der Goltz from retirement in 1914 and he returned to Ottoman service soon after. Goltz Paşa died of typhus near Baghdad in April 1916, at the age of 72, a week before General Townsend's surrender of a British army division to the Ottoman force that had been under his command, at nearby al-Kut. The surrender is sometimes considered the gravest British defeat of the Great War. Goltz was buried in Istanbul.

The Ottoman modernization project long predated Von der Goltz's mission, and owed far more to processes of nineteenth-century transformation common to all the Great Powers of Europe, than to the actions of any one individual. Indeed, there was nothing unusual about military missions and consultation between powers in the period, and while Von der Goltz's book was immediately translated to Ottoman Turkish, and became a basic textbook in the rapidly expanding Ottoman State school system, it was widely influential in France, Britain, and America – where it was translated and read somewhat later than in Istanbul. The Prussian military example and Bismarck's unification of Germany gained admirers far and wide in the final decades of the nineteenth century. Like many state elites in Europe and America, Sultan Abdul-Hamid himself likely read Von der Goltz's book, and sought to fashion a strong and authoritarian Ottoman-Islamic "nation in arms," albeit with the officer class subordinate to royal authority.[5]

Ottoman modernity was part of a universal discourse of nineteenth-century modernization, militarism, and progress, and was fully integrated into and inseparable from wider European trends and processes. Indeed, the Ottoman project could be denounced and intervention, imperial annexation, or partition justified for domestic political gain in Britain and Russia by Czarist and Gladstonian invocation of the "Sick Man of Europe," but not apparently the "Sick Man of Asia." The Ottoman state remained part of the story of Europe. The features of nineteenth-century modernity were similar in all the eventual belligerents of the Great War of 1914: mass standing armies, conscription, state education, census-taking, state networks of communication and mobilization, mass collective ritual and participation, the notion of popular sovereignty, and more-or-less willing, and sometimes eager, collective sacrifice for God, king and country and the living body of the nation.

Yet the Ottoman Middle East has long been considered apart from the story of nineteenth-century modernization, militarism, nationalism, and the eventual cataclysm of the Great War. In common with other countries, devastated in the Great War, the central feature of the nineteenth century was a re-negotiation and codification of the contract between the state and its subjects or citizens. The Tanzimat decrees began the process in 1839, declaring the equality of imperial subjects before the law, and introducing the idea that the sovereign's right to govern flowed, at least in part, from the fulfillment of a contract with, and eventually from the consent of, the governed. Much of the Ottoman modernization project has been considered in isolation from the wider world of ideas of the time. Likewise, influential scholars since the mid-twentieth century have argued that the essential character of Ottoman modernity was reactive, imitative, defensive, and ultimately defective relative to the presumably more successful modernization projects of Germany, Britain, France, the Soviet Union, and America, which while exemplifying and eventually monopolizing claims to modernity, also brought two world wars, the Holocaust, the nuclear immolation of Japanese cities, and the Cold War, among other worldwide cataclysms.[6]

Ottoman and Middle Eastern modernization is usually characterized as a failed project. It has usually been styled as "westernization," secularization, and defensive modernization. Lost in this story is both the universal character of nineteenth-century modernization and the culturally unique elements of the Ottoman modernization project. Just as French, Prussian, and Russian nineteenth-century modernization efforts borrowed heavily from one another, each had many features that were unique and often culturally specific "invented traditions," in Eric Hobsbawm's evocative phrase.[7] For the Ottoman state, these elements of common state culture and invented traditions focused on Islam, the sultan and caliph, the glories of the Ottoman and Islamic past, and the anxiously hoped-for return to splendor and worldly power.

Ute Frevert, in studying Prussian conscription, identified a series of common themes among the major states of post-Napoleonic Europe. All states recognized the need for standing armies and all reluctantly embraced mass conscription. The imperative to conscript soldiers forced monarchs and war ministers to slowly concede to changes in the relation between state and subject. Through the middle decades of the nineteenth century, state builders as diverse as Napoleon, Muhammad ᶜAli of Egypt, Friedrich Wilhelm III of Prussia, and Ottoman Sultan Mahmud II, confronted the limits of armies made up of aristocratic and often uneducated officers, paid and often unreliable professional soldiers, and press-ganged and often absent recruits. For most aspiring reformers, Napoleon's revolutionary army was the demonstration case. But mass conscript armies required a change in relations between the state and its subjects, ultimately creating citizens and eventually producing demands for limits on the power of the sovereign. Friedrich Willhelm's minister of war had great difficulty convincing him to accept what he considered the revolutionary potential of universal conscription. The threat of Napoleon decided the issue, but Friedrich Willhelm did not welcome the notion of "turning everyone into a soldier."[8] It was only when the survival of the state itself seemed to hang in the balance that the monarchs of Europe accepted conscript armies.

The Ottoman state, too, followed this path. State elites throughout Europe worried ceaselessly that conscription and the creation of citizen–soldiers would lead to demands on the state for constitutional limits on the power of the sovereign. They had good reason to fear the revolutionary potential of armed, trained citizen-soldiers. It is noteworthy that when a mass conflict finally engulfed Europe in 1914, the monarchs of every combatant state except Britain were among the casualties. The royal houses of Russia, Imperial Germany (Prussia), Austro-Hungary (Habsburg), and the Ottomans, all succumbed to the forces unleashed by nineteenth-century modernization.

Mass conscription required mass identification with the state and its official narratives. In the Ottoman realms, famous mid-century Ottoman statesmen like ᶜAli Paşa, Rashid Paşa, Fuad Paşa, and Midhat Paşa expected that mass identification with the state would eventually come to mean wide participation in the state in the form of constitutional and representative government. In this they, like their counterparts throughout Europe in wake of the 1848 revolutions, were disappointed. The Ottoman State did experience a constitutional revolution, but the constitutional assembly only governed for a year, until new Sultan Abdul-Hamid II dissolved it in 1877. While sanction for rule had once been seen as a contract with God for the care of the flock, it was evolving to become a constitutional contract between ruler and ruled.

The centerpiece of Ottoman modernization, as in every other European power after the French Revolution, was military conscription and state education. Armies of citizen–conscripts frightened monarchs and state elites with their revolutionary potential, and state education and state nationalism were the two prongs of the approach to acculturate the citizen-soldier to conservative ruling-class hegemony. In the Ottoman realms this took the effect of a state education law in 1869, and after Abdul-Hamid's ascension to the sultanate in 1876, a state identity based on Islam, anti-imperialism, and a series of invented traditions intended to cement loyalty to the state and its sovereign. Like every other European power, by mid century the Ottomans had devised a national flag, anthem, and costume. Like all his fellow monarchs, Sultan Abdul-Hamid feared citizen-conscripts, politicized military officers, and constitutional government. His fears were well founded.

Conscription

Organized Ottoman conscription began in theory in 1834. The Tanzimat edicts promised orderly conscription, applied equally on all Ottoman subjects, without regard for religion – a clear indication that previous practice had been neither orderly, nor equitable, and based on arbitrary capture and servitude of Muslim youth. In 1843 a new recruitment law established a lottery based on census registration, and reverted to the customary exclusion of non-Muslims from military service. The new system established a five-year term of service, followed by seven years of reserve service.[9]

The new system resembled closely those established by the other European powers, and answered both the needs of the modernizing state, and the demands of the population for equitable regularity in conscripting sons, husbands, and fathers. Conscription was not popular anywhere, and while occasional patriotic fervor infected some men and boys, wives, mothers, and fathers almost inevitably opposed the demands of the state for young men. State education and indoctrination fostered patriotism and nationalism and increased the romantic and manly appeal of military service in the Ottoman realms, as elsewhere.

But such romanticism was almost always short-lived and various forms of compulsion became necessary. Uncounted thousands of deserters and draft resisters were executed, sometimes after trials, by all combatant powers during World War I. Even though the Italian invasion of Libya, and the Balkan wars in 1911 and 1912, brought forth enthusiastic Ottoman volunteers, the supply dried up when young men got wind of the conditions of service.[10] Similar stories of initial enthusiasm and ensuing dread existed in all other states at war.

Most national armies maintained various types of exemptions, which often involved paying the state directly, paying and sending a substitute, or being a member of a social class, vocation, or minority exempted from service. In Ottoman practice, substitutions were called *bedel i-şahsi*, and eventually it was possible to pay the government for a conscription exemption, though the fee was very high. Opposition to the inclusion of non-Muslims in the military was widespread among Ottoman Muslims, including the army command, and non-Muslims were exempted, or excluded, depending on perspective, until the Second Constitutional Revolution period, after 1909. Other, less cosmopolitan states, conscripted sectarian minorities, and so while the Prussian officer corps was similarly unenthusiastic about the inclusion of German Jews in the military lottery, Jewish men eagerly signed up for inclusion in the rituals and obligations of full civic participation.[11]

Ottoman Christians, like other Ottoman subjects, avoided army service whenever possible. Christians were generally exempted from conscription, though they paid an exemption. Muslims who wished to buy an exemption from conscription, usually for a son, paid far more than Christians and Jews. Christian and Jewish Ottomans did, however, serve in the army and were occasionally commissioned as officers, most often as army physicians. After the 1908 Constitutional Revolution most exemptions were abolished, and non-Muslims were conscripted and eventually served alongside their Muslim fellow soldiers, though not often at the front lines. The Ottoman conscription law in 1909 was one impetus for emigration to North and South America for Ottoman Christians. The U.S. and Canadian governments called the immigrants Turks, and they mostly called themselves Greeks or Syrians, and later Lebanese.

Ottoman military reformers faced more difficult challenges than those confronted by their French, German, or Austrian contemporaries. The vast geographical expanses, relatively low population density, and human diversity of the empire made mobilization nearly impossible and imposed great financial burdens on the state. In the 1840s the state realms were divided into command regions, each of which comprised an army corps, theoretically complete with administration, conscription, training, and education. Istanbul and a handful of provincial capitals like Damascus opened military high schools (*askeri idadi* schools), where staff officers taught the cadets. The government also organized provincial military commands, alongside the existing provincial government, and began to regularize conscription. But the theoretical comprehensiveness of the system existed mostly on paper until the late 1870s, when the catastrophic defeat in the Russo-Turkish war made military capability crucial to the survival of the state.

By the final decade of the nineteenth century, Ottoman conscription was beginning to conform to its theoretical function: to quickly and smoothly supply large numbers of recruits from one end of the country to the other. Modern communications of telegraph, train, and steamship were important to this effort, but there were other factors too. An increasing percentage of officers were now educated and literate, and staff officers could speak German with allied officers, Turkish among themselves whatever their regional origin, and Turkish, Greek, Arabic, or Kurdish to conscript troops.

In the period before the Great War, regional army corps administered conscription by district. Regional staff officers consulted population records and compiled lists from registered young men. All eligible men, including those presenting exemptions, were ordered to appear in the central square of the district (*qada'*) capital, generally defined as a town of at least 500 houses. Conscription officers were required to set up a table, and place two large canvas bags upon it; one with names, one with slips of paper, corresponding to the number of recruits required, reading "*asker oldum*," or "I have become a soldier." Names were drawn along with their opposite slips of paper, until all the needed slots had been filled. Some men returned home, while others reported immediately for service. The registration lists were altered accordingly.[12]

Orderly conscription and improved mobilization infrastructure did not mean improved conditions of service. And in all of the final Ottoman wars, including World War I, it seemed that feeding, resupplying, and caring for injured soldiers was an afterthought. The hardships and misery of WWI conscription continues to occupy a place of trauma and horror in popular memory throughout the Middle East. Conditions for officers were nearly as bad, and Goltz himself succumbed to typhus in Iraq. Three million men eventually served in the Ottoman army during the Great War, and it is certain that many thousands among those had also fought in Libya, the Balkan Wars, and perhaps in the many insurgencies after the 1918 armistice. Given the pre-industrial conditions of the Ottoman realms, the lack of food and medical care, the vast distances over thousands of kilometers they covered, often on foot, the repeated defeats they brought to better-equipped and -trained British and allied forces is worthy of historical note.[13]

In most of their engagements, Ottoman forces defeated larger and better-equipped and -fed British forces. And yet, in each of the Ottoman wars of the early twentieth century, the number of soldiers who perished from disease, poor medical care, malnutrition, and starvation exceeded the numbers killed in battle.[14] The resilience and effectiveness of the Ottoman army astonished and embittered its enemies, but as historian and former Turkish military academy archivist Mesut Uyar has noted, by 1914 the Ottoman army had been the focal point of more than a century of reform, self-criticism, and educational refinement. It should be obvious that such a massive state mobilization project would have lasting consequences on the post-Ottoman Middle East.

State Military Education and Elite Civil Education

Patriotism in uniform could bring its social rewards. In Germany it provided the potential status as reserve officer for boys who had undergone secondary education to the age of sixteen, even if they went no further. In Britain, as the war was to show, even clerks and salesmen in the service of the nation could become officers, and in the brutally frank terminology of the British upper class, "temporary gentlemen."[15]

Military education deserves, but has never received, a major explanatory role in the modern history of the region. As the largest state education project undertaken in the Middle East, and as a self-conscious engine of social leveling, the military education project had results that continue to unfold in Turkey and the Arab Middle East. And yet, despite the influence of people such as Mustafa Kemal, Enver Paşa, Cemal Paşa, İsmet İnönü, Nuri al-Saᶜid and uncounted others, all produced by the late Ottoman military system, military schools have only rarely attracted the attention of historians. Modern education also introduced army officers to politics, a legacy that has continued to affect the region.

Modern Ottoman State education began with military academies in the imperial capital. The Ottoman military academy (Mekteb-i Ulum-i Harbiye) opened in 1834. Military preparatory schools in the capital soon followed.[16] Preparatory schools were intended to prepare cadets for the central military academy, but their organization and coordination were haphazard and unsystematic. By 1850 there were three or four military high schools including Istanbul, and the Damascus military school.[17]

Ottoman reformers systematized state education with the education law of 1869. The military and civil educational systems both came to be based around a similar set of assumptions and goals. The military system, however, despite the minimal attention of historians, predated the civil system and was always better funded and more carefully organized. The law called for a primary school, or *ibtidaiye* school, in each village, a middle, or *rüşdiye* school in each town, and an *idadiye* or *sultani* preparatory school in each provincial capital. At the middle-school level (*rüşdiye*) and above, the schools were divided into either military (*askeriye*) or civil (*mülkiye*) systems.[18]

The primary and middle schools were often combined to provide a total of six years of instruction. The next step, the preparatory school, provided an additional three years. The preparatory schools, which boarded students in the important cities, like the Damascus military school, or prestigious and expensive civil (Sultani) schools like Beirut's Sultani, Damascus' Maktab ʿAnbar, and Istanbul's Galatasaray school, were sometimes combined with middle schools to provide up to seven years of instruction. The most promising students would continue their studies in an imperial service academy, either the military academy (or Mekteb-i Ulûm-ı Harbiye), or the Imperial Civil Service School (or Mekteb-i Mülkiye-i Şahane), or imperial medical school, or law school.[19]

Ottoman State schools attracted the sons and sometimes daughters of the ambitious rural and urban lower-middle classes. By 1890 thousands of children attended many hundreds of local village or urban primary schools, which would have differed slightly from less widespread earlier educational models. Some of the state elementary schools enrolled boys and girls together, and there were a smaller number of schools exclusively for girls. Boys were supposed to attend primary school from ages seven to eleven, girls from ages six to ten.[20] The new state primary schools had a slightly fuller curriculum than more traditional Qur'an schools, and they also gained a reputation for more progressive, gentler methods and less corporal punishment.

Parents would take children to school in their quarter or village, and choose the schools based on what was available, their appreciation for the possibilities offered by education, and their hopes for their children. Urban areas, particularly the larger cities, always had more, and probably better, schools. Modern state primary schools existed alongside Qur'an schools, and schools run by churches and synagogues. Parents hoping for further education for their children, and perhaps careers in the government, would have chosen state primary schools, while other parents, both in towns and the countryside, followed the more common practice of arranging no formal education for their children.

Many families expected children to work from a young age, and needed their labor to help provide for the family. Other parents felt that the only purpose for formal education was to learn correct religious practice and read a holy book, and consequently sent their children to local Qur'an or church schools. Many parents probably did not appreciate the difference between state and religious primary schooling in the nineteenth and early twentieth century. The value of education was not always self-evident, and certainly parents feared that the absence of their children in distant government employment might doom them to destitution in old age. As times changed, many parents designated one child for schooling, and the others for work or trade. This was an obvious strategy to spread the risk of a child not returning to help the family, on the one hand, and limiting the direct expense of school, and the indirect expense of lost labor, on the other. Such calculations featured in all modernizing states, and among many families today.

Children attended state primary school six days a week, four hours per day. They began their three years of instruction by learning the Arabic alphabet, the rudiments of religion, Qur'anic verses, reading and writing. There was still time for work or play at home or in the neighborhood, and the schools were nearby and not particularly large. The number of such schools ranged from as high as 50 to 20 schools per district (*Qada*: an administrative district smaller than a county or *Sanjaq*) in the region of Istanbul, Bursa, Sinop, Izmir, Jerusalem, Damascus, and Beirut. (See Figure 1.1.)

Figure 1.1. Ottoman-Arab School Kids, *c.*1900 (collection of Dr. Wolf-Dieter Lemke)

Children started with letters and basic reading, most often from the Qur'an. The primary-school curriculum expanded in the second and third years, as subjects and additional hours were added. In the second year students began to learn counting and numbers. In the third and final year of primary school, they were expected to have two hours weekly of Ottoman history, along with reading, math, religion and morality. Directed readings on prescribed topics took three hours per week and included morality, geography, and agriculture.[21]

Primary-school teachers were in short supply and were often employed under apparently casual circumstances, based on local need and with the minimal qualification of basic literacy in Ottoman Turkish or Arabic. Many teachers were non-Muslims. The practice of both casual employment and loose qualifications was identified as a problem, and teacher-training academies were established in Istanbul and provincial capitals including Damascus, Baghdad, and elsewhere by the first decade of the twentieth century, when there were at least sixteen such academies training primary-school teachers.[22]

After three years at a state primary school, students graduated to middle school (*rüşdiye*). Middle schools were divided into state civil and military schools, though each comprised three years of instruction and a similar curriculum. As in other modernizing states, students wore military-type uniforms, with distinctions between the civil and military garb. Uniforms were dark blue woolen coats and trousers, with a red tarbush (fez) for headgear. Civil-school students had one row of embossed brass buttons, military school students had two rows in an open V shape.[23]

Middle schools were far more widely separated than primary schools and students often had to travel and board to attend. As government schools opened, villagers and townspeople learned of the new schools the way they learned most of their news, by word of mouth from people traveling beyond the village or quarter, or from people passing by. Family members would enquire with local officials or perhaps travel to enroll children in new middle schools. Despite suspicion of the government and its taxation, registration, and conscription, state schools became popular within a short period of time. (See Figures 1.2 and 1.3.)

Attending a military or civil middle school was probably a matter of resources for most families. Military middle schools were always completely free, including uniforms and books, and unlike civil schools, military middle schools sometimes had lodging and board facilities.[24] Civil schools usually charged tuition, on a sliding scale based on the wealth of the child's family. Children who did not already live in a regional or provincial center (*sanjaq* or *wilayat*), and who did not have

Figure 1.2. Beirut Rüşdiye, *c.*1895 (Library of Congress, Abdul-Hamid Photo Collection)

extended family to move in with, and who did not have money for tuition, were forced to attend military schools or curtail their education. In this way, the state reinforced a tendency for military-school students to hail from rural areas and more modest families than those educated within the civil system.

Curricula followed the pattern established in primary school. Studies focused on reading, writing, math, and religion, though students began to learn written and spoken Turkish, or Arabic depending on the native language of the region. In the later years Persian, Greek, or French was added. History, geography, and practical hygiene and comportment were also added. Each town of 500 houses was supposed to warrant a middle school, a goal that was generally met in the final Ottoman decades. After three years, students graduated to the preparatory school. The average student was now twelve or thirteen years old, and those who had lived in the same town as the middle school would be leaving their native village or town, and family house, for the

Figure 1.3. Rüşdiye Students. *c.*1895 (Library of Congress, Abdul-Hamid Photo Collection)

provincial capital to continue their studies. In this their experience was similar to children in modernizing states in Europe and America. Ambitious families accepted the absence of a child for education or immigration, in hopes of future prosperity.

Ottoman preparatory schools enforced the division between civil and military education. Ottoman Ministry of Education documents did not differentiate military-school students by religion, perhaps adopting an official state fiction that they were all Muslims. In practice, however, military schools seem to have enrolled a small number of non-Muslim students, particularly in regions where there were significant non-Muslim populations like Damascus, Baghdad, and Beirut.[25]

Civil schools were intended to compete directly with missionary education, and statistics listed students by religion and obviously enrolled non-Muslim students. Civil-school students paid high tuition and were exempted from legally required military service. Christians were also exempt until after the re-introduction of the Ottoman Constitution in 1908. Sultan Abdul-Hamid had evidently vetoed a recommendation early in his reign to conscript non-Muslims into the Ottoman military.[26]

The Galatasaray Lycée, founded in 1868 in Istanbul, was the prototype elite civil preparatory school. In its emphasis on French education, it was intended to attract the sons of Ottoman elites and compete directly with foreign missionary schools, many of which had been established by French Catholics, and American Presbyterian missionaries. The Galatasaray School, once also known as the *Mekteb-i Sultanî*, eventually became a twelve-year preparatory school, and in the final Ottoman decades often sent its graduates to the Imperial Civil Service School. The Mülkiye School was older, having been founded in 1859, and was in competition with the Galatasaray School in the 1880s. The Galatasaray School, probably because of its emphasis on French instruction, produced a majority of high officials in the Foreign Ministry, while the Mülkiye produced a majority of the high officials in the Interior Ministry.[27] After 1909, the Mülkiye became a special university faculty, attracting graduating students from the Galatasaray School and other Sultani schools.[28]

Midhat Paşa was the leading late-Tanzimat-era Ottoman reformist statesman. Midhat is most famous for leading the Ottoman constitutional movement of 1876, an achievement that led to his execution on the presumed orders of Sultan Abdul-Hamid. But Midhat was also the leading figure of Ottoman educational and provincial reform. Claims of Ottoman decline notwithstanding, the stunning catalog of his innovations predate similar reforms in any number of European countries. Midhat was governor of Baghdad province from 1869–72, Grand Vezir under Sultan Abdul-Hamid from 1876 to early 1877, and governor of Syria between late 1878 and 1880, after which time he was tried, exiled to Arabia, placed in prison, and strangled.[29] He ordered the construction of schools, roads, bridges, and markets all over the Ottoman lands. Many still stand and some, like the famous Midhat Paşa (Basha) suq in Damascus, still bear his name.

Midhat Paşa arrived in Baghdad in 1869 with an imperial *firman* that listed a primary goal "to reorganize and improve the Sixth Imperial Army of Iraq."[30] He opened the military middle school in the year of his arrival, 1869, and he opened the military preparatory school in 1871, in time to accept the first class to complete the middle-school curriculum. Serving staff officers of the Ottoman 6th Army taught at both schools, and both schools offered free tuition to qualified students. The Baghdad middle civil preparatory school opened in 1871 and the civil preparatory, or high school (*mekteb-i sultani*) opened in 1873.[31] By 1900, however, the number of students attending the Sultani School had reached only ninety-six students, up from sixty-eight in 1898.[32] By contrast, the Baghdad military preparatory school enrolled 256 boys. The Baghdad military middle school enrolled 846 boys in the same year, a number only slightly lower than the combined total of all middle and preparatory schools, private, missionary, and state-run, in all of Baghdad, Mosul, and Basrah provinces.[33] Over three-quarters of the Iraqi prime ministers from 1920 to 1958 were graduates of the Baghdad military preparatory school.

Damascus already had a preparatory military school and in 1875 military middle schools opened in Beirut and Damascus in new and impressive buildings. According to the Ottoman ministry of military education documents, the state, then on the verge of bankruptcy and insolvency, opened nine major provincial military middle schools in 1875 alone. School administrators found that students needed additional work to prepare for the preparatory schools. Consequently, the government used scarce resources to open an unprecedented number of middle military schools over the course of a single year.

When Midhat arrived in Beirut as new governor in 1878, he was pleased to find that a number of the city's most prominent Muslim citizens had formed a charitable association for the development of civil education. With big ideas but a minuscule budget, Midhat Paşa made the association a centerpiece of his education reforms, and encouraged the establishment of similar associations in Damascus and elsewhere. The Jamᶜiyyat al-Maqasid al-Khayriyya al-Islamiyya, or the Makkased Society, helped to fund and establish a number of schools, but the society's fondest wish was the establishment of a Sultani Lycée on the model of the Galatasaray School in the imperial capital.[34]

Prominent families in provincial capitals like Baghdad, Beirut, and Damascus lobbied tirelessly for elite state civil educational institutions. In each city, however, the state built and opened military schools before the civil schools. In Damascus, the military preparatory school had been in operation since 1850, and in 1875, at least ten years before the civil preparatory (Maktab ᶜAnbar) opened, the Damascus middle military school opened near the preparatory school in Damascus' Marja quarter.[35]

Sultan Abdul-Hamid judged Midhat and the independent educational societies a threat. And as Midhat was removed and exiled, the Makassed Society was dissolved and a state-controlled educational board took its place. State funding followed and the Beirut Sultani Lycée (Mekteb-i Sultani) opened in 1883. The Beirut Sultani moved into a splendid new building in the Basta quarter outside central Beirut. The school soon enrolled the sons of the most prominent and wealthy

Beiruti families.[36] The teachers were important scholars and tuition was expensive. The Egyptian scholar-activist Muhammad ʿAbduh taught there briefly during his exile from British-occupied Egypt.

Students could board at the school or attend during the day, and fees were expensive; upwards of 15 gold Ottoman lira for board and tuition.[37] By sultanic decree, students were exempted from military service – a valuable benefit considering the low regard Ottoman-Arab elites held for military careers. Prominent families supported elite civil education as an "escape from the military careers they dreaded for their children."[38]

The Damascus Sultani Lycée opened two years later in 1885. It was established in a beautiful mansion built by Damascene Jewish merchant Yusuf ʿAnbar, who had gone bankrupt building the huge house. After his bankruptcy, ownership reverted to the state. The mansion proved a perfect place to establish a large school, and the two schools, in Beirut and Damascus, soon enrolled close to a thousand boys between them. The curriculum lasted six years, and a sizable proportion of boys were boarders from other parts of the realm.[39]

Missionary education and Ottoman civil education were important in the late empire and in the formation of the modern Middle East. The growth of foreign and missionary education posed a challenge to Ottoman officials, and they intended elite civil preparatory schools to help counter the influence of foreign education. Ottoman elites worried ceaselessly about the activities of the missionaries, concerned that they sought to convert Muslims and subvert non-Muslim Ottoman subjects.[40] The prospect that prominent Ottomans, especially Muslims, might send their children to be educated by missionaries was troubling. The missionary colleges opened in the mid 1860s, and in direct response, the Galatasaray Lycée opened in 1868.[41] Provincial civil preparatory schools were supposed to follow, but money was always short and implementation was slow. The schools eventually enjoyed the prominence their advocates envisaged, and many Ottoman intellectuals and politicians attended and taught at the schools. Former students fondly chronicled their experiences in memoirs that further lifted the civil schools to a remembered prominence beyond that of the more numerous military schools.

Military Culture and Late Ottoman Society

In comparison with civil schools, military schools opened earlier, got better buildings and more funding direct from the state treasury, enrolled more students, and did not charge tuition. By contrast, schools opened in the civil system, under the Ministry of State Education, opened more slowly, were built and operated with a greater concentration of local funds, and charged very high tuition fees.

The civil schools were prestigious and drew their students from the families of established Ottoman elites. Tuition was expensive and the schools existed in direct competition to the foreign missionary schools, which the state and its elites saw as a threat. Military education, by contrast, was designed to draw the sons of notable rural and provincial families into the state system, and was an important tool of state integration. Prussia, France, and the Austro-Hungarian Empire also drew military cadets from the rural and provincial middle classes and educated them at minimal expense to their families. By 1900 there were scores of Ottoman military middle and preparatory schools in operation, enrolling tens of thousands of students from Yemen to the Balkans.

People in many rural and pastoral regions had violently opposed the demands of the state for revenue, registration, census-taking, and conscription, but provincial schools became quickly popular and oversubscribed. The policy of attracting the children of influential local families enjoyed rapid success, and by 1897, there were eight provincial military preparatory schools (*idadiye*), with 2,764 students. Three times as many boys were simultaneously enrolled in military middle schools (*rüşdiye*) throughout the empire.[42] By 1899 over 25 percent of the Ottoman Officer corps of 18,000 had been educated and commissioned through the military educational system.[43]

The Imperial Military Academy in Istanbul was the final educational destination for young men from the provinces. But the military preparatory schools were not the only path to the imperial academies. There was also the *Aşiret Mekteb-i Hümayun*, or the Tribal School, in Istanbul, which recruited the sons of influential nomadic and rural families. The school boarded boys from the provinces and provided a more highly structured curriculum than the provincial schools. The larger provincial schools also boarded students, but the Tribal School operated in the imperial capital and virtually imprisoned students within the school compound. Boys from the ungoverned frontier regions would attend by nomination and once at the school they would undergo a "civilizing" process to turn them into loyal Ottomans. The journey from Iraq, Yemen, the Syrian desert, Hijaz, or Libya to the Tribal School might take more than a month, by land and steamship, after which boys were normally greeted in a special ceremony attended by imperial dignitaries.[44] Tribal School students received a heavier dosage of religion, and various types of behavioral conditioning, than students in the regular preparatory schools.[45] They received remedial-level basic skills in reading, writing, and languages, to compensate for their lack of preparation relative to other provincial students.

School administrators expected Tribal School students to be illiterate at the time of arrival in Istanbul. And though they began their studies about the age of 12, the first-year curriculum resembled that of a state primary school for 6-year-olds. Most of the provincial middle schools and some preparatory schools also offered remedial courses of study – an obvious nod to their function as laboratories of state integration and social leveling. Both Tribal School and provincial school graduates usually matriculated to the Imperial Military Academy in Istanbul. By the time students arrived in the capital they had spent up to nine years in the Ottoman military education system without expense to their families. The increase continued during the last fifteen years of the Ottoman State, as ever more officers came from the military education system, rather than up through the ranks. After the 1908 revolution, and especially after the unsuccessful counter-revolution of 1909, many illiterate senior officers were pensioned off and retired from service. In the period after 1908, educated military officers took their place as a self-conscious and unchallenged state elite.[46]

The Military Academy and Staff College

Successful graduates of state preparatory schools made the journey to Istanbul to continue their studies in the imperial capital. Travel in the Ottoman realms was rigorous; the long journey presaged government careers spent in often grueling travel from one far-flung imperial outpost to another. For students from the Ottoman Arab provinces the trip often involved weeks of land travel on foot to a sea port, perhaps Alexandretta, or Beirut, and then by steamship to Istanbul.[47] By the first decade of the twentieth century, student cadets could travel part of the distance by train. The Ottoman state placed great emphasis on train construction and efficient communication, but faced greater difficulties than other European powers in the relative absence of navigable rivers, and the many mountains and deserts. Students finally arrived at the military academy, where cadets from the Balkans, Anatolia, Libya, Yemen, Syria, Iraq, or Kurdistan lived and studied together. During the final Ottoman decades, the military academy, *Mekteb-i Ulum-i Harbiye*, admitted and graduated about 500 students a year, for a total enrollment of about 1,500.[48]

Cadets began an intensive three-year education culminating in their commission as Ottoman military officers. The academy curriculum followed and refined the secular and practical scientific character of the *idadiye* and *rüşdiye* schools. Military drills, field medicine, surveying, fortifications, reconnaissance, and communications were added to the study of French, German, and Russian, geography, and math.[49] Ottoman and some world history was taught, but no religious instruction was offered, though students prayed together. 60 to 70 percent of the students came from the Anatolian and Balkan regions, but Sultan Abdul-Hamid was anxious to increase representation of the non-Turkish and non-European provinces and actively recruited young men from the Arab and Kurdish regions. Decades later, retired officers described the policy as part of the Sultan's efforts to "draw the people closer to himself."[50] By all accounts, the imperial academies comprised a rarefied and politicized atmosphere, and students took a keen interest in the affairs of state, and organized secret political organizations to debate political topics they could not discuss in their classes. Goltz Paşa, Mahmud Şevket Paşa, and their successors convinced generations of Ottoman officer-cadets that they should be the rightful leaders of a militarized nation.

Modern Infrastructure

The Ottoman telegraph network was inaugurated during the Crimean war in the 1850s. Within twenty years the Ottoman network was among the largest in the world and for a time carried the bulk of transmission between India and London. Sultan Abdul-Hamid II extended the wires still further until no town was beyond telegraphic reach. The state telegraph company employed an army of technicians and specialists who transmitted messages in Ottoman, Arabic, French, English, and other languages. The telegraph was a powerful tool of governance, and led to better coordination of provincial and central government, revenue collection, improved news and information dissemination, and most notoriously during the Hamidian period, more government surveillance of political dissidents, particularly within government and military service.

Modern communications technology cut both ways. The sultan used the system to monitor the state's employees, and dismiss or exile potential or actual troublemakers at a moment's notice when he chose, but political activists used the telegraph to organize opposition to the government. It is noteworthy that after the armistice that ended the Great War, the Ottoman army retained control of the telegraphic communication system in Anatolia, but not in greater Syria. Thousands of Ottoman subject-citizens used the new technology to address grievances to the state in the form of petitions. Ottoman and post-Ottoman State archives contain uncounted thousands of telegraphic petitions protesting everything from official corruption and police brutality, to bad service at the state telegraph office.[51]

Fast communications alone was not enough without the fast movement of people and goods, and trains, roads, and government building construction came to consume a huge share of Ottoman revenue. All the cities of the former Ottoman realms are full of nineteenth-century buildings and structures still standing, still in use, and unnoticed as late Ottoman structures by almost everyone. In cities from Iraq, Yemen and Libya, to Anatolia and the Balkans, these structures include roads, electrical generating plants, water and sewer systems, hundreds of commercial and governmental buildings, hundreds of schools, and hundreds of railway stations, almost all built in the final thirty years of Ottoman rule. Klaus Kreiser has noted that when Abdul-Hamid's court architect, Raimondo d'Aronco, designed and built the colossal and famous iron monolith telegraph monument at Marja Square in Damascus, the inscription proclaimed that today the sultan-caliph alone makes the decisions about highways, railroads, and telegraph lines, and such decisions are no longer in the hands of the foreigners.[52] Modernity meant independence, dignity, and survival for the Ottomans.

Ottoman railway builders had tremendous disadvantages relative to their western European contemporaries, but by 1918 there were more than 10,000 kilometers of railway lines, many of which crossed rivers, difficult desert terrain, and mountains. The railway lines ran from Istanbul through western Anatolia, to Aleppo in northern Syria. Both the Anatolian railway and the Baghdad railway beyond Aleppo were German concessions. The Hijaz railway, from Aleppo to Damascus, Medina, and intended to reach Mecca, was built entirely with Ottoman funding by a worldwide subscription of Muslims. Neither the Baghdad line nor the Hijaz line had reached its final planned destination by 1914, ending at Nusaybin and Medina respectively.

For most of the final Ottoman decades, foreign bankers controlled much of the state treasury, and the empire was generally unindustrialized. There were comparatively few industrial factories capable of sophisticated manufacturing of the type coming to dominate the economies of North America and a few of the countries of Europe. Railway locomotives, industrial machine tools, and all manner of heavy machinery had to be imported. Even things such as the steel railway rails and nails had to be imported at first. Labor for bridge-making and road-laying was in relatively short supply, owing to low population density. Conscript soldiers often supplied railroad and construction labor. And while expertise developed quickly, the chief engineers and technicians were likewise foreign concessionaires or contractors.

Modern development was a comprehensive project, however, and while railways were built with foreign expertise and materials, the government embarked on a program to build major maintenance and manufacturing facilities in proximity to the centers of rail travel. In a village south of Damascus an entire industrial military suburb was designed and built from scratch to provide support for the Hijaz railroad. The suburb, called al-Qadam, comprised a mainline train station, a sprawling maintenance yard with forges, iron casting facilities, and machining and engineering facilities sufficient to rebuild and manufacture spare parts for any locomotive of the time. The complex was based upon, and resembled closely, a state-of-the-art German rail yard and factory of the late nineteenth century, but in striking contrast, the entire complex was constructed from native black basalt stone. Machinery, tools, locomotives, and rolling stock were imported from Germany and Switzerland, but even before the completion of the rail line and maintenance complex, industrial training schools had been opened with great fanfare in Beirut and a number of other Ottoman cities.[53]

The al-Qadam suburb also held a range of barracks and military facilities built both to safeguard the security and take advantage of the mobility afforded by train travel and the new facility. The Hijaz railway was thus a complicated and variegated project blending Islamic and imperial legitimacy and prestige, industrial and infrastructural investment and development, and long-term military and security strategy. The effort and its crucial importance cannot be called a failure since the Syrian national train system, like the Turkish, Jordanian, Iraqi, and Israeli state train systems, are based on Ottoman infrastructure. The infrastructure included rail lines, cars, and engines, stations, and maintenance facilities. But it also includes a legacy of modern industrial policy that still extends to education and culture today. The state built a large apparatus to support industrial development, most particularly technical academies and workshops. These institutions have had lasting effects in the post-Ottoman Middle East. In Turkey, Kemalist industrial statism did not represent a break, but rather a continuation of an evolving policy. In Syria, the al-Qadam rail yard and its maintenance machinery have been maintained and remain in daily use more than a century later.

State industrial facilities required trained workers. Technical and vocational schools were built to train Ottoman technicians and engineers to build and maintain the structures of the industrial state. One year before the opening of the Hijaz railway in September 1908, the Beirut al-Maktab al-San'i[c] opened in a large and beautiful new building in August 1907. (See Figure 1.4.) The school was intended to board

Figure 1.4. al-Maktab al-San'i^c Inauguration, Beirut (Lemke Collection)

and educate a hundred students in the latest arts and industrial skills. Practical craft and trade schools had already opened in other Ottoman cities, and as was the usual case, had opened first in the capital, probably in the 1870s. Such a school opened in Damascus in the 1880s, though in the early years it emphasized artisanal trades more than industrial trades.[54] The Damascus industrial trade (al-Maktab al-San'i^c) school opened in Qadam, next to the Hijaz railway workshops in 1910. A modern state needed modern leaders, and Ottoman schools produced young men who expected to assume positions of leadership in their Ottoman State and nation.

Ottoman Sons Become Saviors of the Nation

By 1914 Ottoman military academy graduates formed a highly educated, multilingual, cosmopolitan, corps who shared the abiding conviction that the future survival of the state properly lay in their hands. As in Germany, France, and Britain, army officers saw themselves as an elite national vanguard. Their collective failure in late 1918 must have been unimaginably bitter.

Yasin al-Hashimi was born in 1884, the son of a neighborhood headman (*mukhtar*) in Baghdad. Neighborhood headmen, then and now, are the bottom rank of local officials. A headman would, however, be well acquainted with the potential benefits of government education and higher employment, and al-Hashimi senior enrolled all three of his sons in subsidized, tuition-free local military schools. He also had two daughters, Shafiqa and Zaynab, who seemed to have attended school. The family was fortunate to reside in a major Ottoman city and provincial capital, which had enjoyed significant state investment in educational institutions. The distance between their neighborhood, family home, and state schools was a matter of a few minutes' walk. Like his older brother Da'ud, and his younger brother Taha, Yasin attended military middle and preparatory schools in his native city, and after eight or nine years, at the age of 15 or 16, he traveled to the imperial capital of Istanbul, over two thousand kilometers west, to begin study at the military academy.[55]

Yasin completed his studies near the top of his class after three years around 1902. He was immediately selected to attend the general staff college (Erkan-i Harbiye Askeriye) for a further three years, an honor accorded to the top cadets. While the military academy enrolled over 1,000 and yearly graduated 500 or more cadets, the staff college enrolled fewer than fifty students at any given time. Among al-Hashimi's classmates in a class of fewer than twenty officers, was Mustafa Kemal, who graduated from the staff college in the same year of 1905, and eventual Arab nationalist exemplar ᶜAziz ᶜAli al-Misri who had graduated at the top of his class the year before, and had been posted to Macedonia.[56] Syrian national hero Yusuf al-ᶜAzma graduated from the staff college the following year in 1906. All were secret members of the Committee of Union and Progress (Committee of Union and Progress).[57] Al-Hashimi was sent to Mosul, and Kemal was sent to Damascus, where he started the first CUP-affiliated secret society in that city. Al-Hashimi shortly went to Damascus also, where both he and Kemal would have been teaching in the military preparatory school as staff captains. Yusuf al-ᶜAzma was sent to Germany for further training.

Yasin al-Hashimi was married around 1910 at the age of 26 to Rafiqa ᶜAbd al-Majid. Married Ottoman officers lived with their families, who moved with them to different postings, if transportation over the vast distances was available and practical. In the frequent case of arduous journeys and long distances, they lived in barracks with other officers, in which case they visited their families during infrequent home leaves. Yasin and Rafiqa had four children; three daughters, and a son who died in childhood. The daughters were Madiha, born 1911, Sabiha, born 1913, and Niᶜmat, born 1915. As a young man of modest background, whose life and prospects were transformed by modern education, Yasin al-Hashimi insured his daughters received the best education available.[58]

Yasin al-Hashimi began the Great War a major (*binbaşı*) and ended it a Major General (*Mirliva*) on the Palestine Front. In 1914, al-Hashimi shared command of a division in Syria, and then received a promotion to lieutenant colonel (*Kayamakam*) in 1915. He served with distinction in the defense of Gallipoli, as chief of staff under his comrade Kemal, who had been promoted to lieutenant colonel in March 1914, months before the outbreak of the war.[59] Yasin al-Hashimi met Amir Faysal at Damascus in 1915, but considered Faysal's proposal for the Arab Revolt foolish and its prospects counterproductive; a view seemingly shared by a majority of Ottoman Arab officers. Al-Hashimi was repeatedly promoted and received a host of Ottoman and German decorations during the war. He played an important role in Central Europe in 1917 in the last campaign against the Russians before the Russian Revolution, and was decorated by the Kaiser himself. In a war with few heroes, his reputation survived the defeat. In September 1918 he was in command of the Fourth Ottoman army corps in Palestine. His old comrade and sometime rival Mustafa Kemal Paşa arrived to command the Seventh Army Corps on September 1, 1918, immediately before the defeat at the Battle of Nablus and just in time for the final retreat north.[60] Yasin ended the war at the same senior rank as Kemal, but he was younger and had begun the war one promotion behind, meaning Yasin was promoted faster between 1914–18 than Kemal.

Yusuf al-ᶜAzma is famous in Syrian historiography, but his fame is based partly on error. Al-ᶜAzma was killed leading the defense of Syria against French invasion and occupation in July 1920. He has long been considered the first hero of the Syrian nation. Syrian schoolbooks and nationalist legend maintain that he joined Faysal's Arab revolt and fought both the "Turks" and the French. Along with Saladin, and Hafez al-Asad, al-ᶜAzma is one of the only Syrian heroes honored with a statue and square bearing his name in Damascus. But part of Yusuf al-ᶜAzma's legend is fiction. He was educated in the Ottoman system and spent most of his life in the Ottoman army far from his birthplace in Damascus, including at least two years in advanced training in Germany. He was a graduate of both the military academy and the Ottoman staff college. In education, culture, politics, and language, Yusuf al-ᶜAzma died as he had lived: part of a highly educated Ottoman elite. His widow and children returned to Istanbul after his death.

Yusuf al-ᶜAzma hailed from a notable Damascus family originating in the Maydan quarter and was born in 1884.[61] By the time of his birth the family had moved to a large courtyard house in central Damascus in the Suq al-Qutn neighborhood. He attended primary, military middle, and military preparatory school in al-Marja quarter, the new nineteenth-century Ottoman administrative quarter, a few hundred meters from his family home. The ͨAzmas often chose military careers for their sons, and apparently did not possess the traditional Damascus notable distaste for martial vocations. Yusuf was accepted and traveled to Istanbul for training at the military academy around 1899. He clearly distinguished himself, and upon graduation, he continued directly to the staff college (Erkân-ı Harbiye Askeriye). Graduates from the normal three-year military academy course received commissions as third lieutenants (*Piyade Mülazım*), but most staff college graduates, like Yusuf, received commissions as staff captains (*Yüzbaşı*).

Yusuf al-ͨAzma seems to have surpassed his staff-officer comrades in early distinction and official favor. Like his fellows, he received an immediate posting to Damascus, but unlike Mustafa Kemal and Yasin al-Hashimi, he escaped the unglamorous duty of teaching in a provincial military preparatory school, and within months, he was sent to Berlin. There he spent a further two years of service and study in the Prussian *Kriegsakademie*, which in 1907 would probably have been considered the world's foremost military academy.[62] While at the *Kriegsakademie* he translated and published at least one textbook on military training from German into Ottoman Turkish.[63] From there, he returned to Istanbul and became chief secretary of the Ottoman Legation in Egypt. At the outbreak of the Great War, al-ͨAzma hurriedly returned to Istanbul where he received a posting as chief of staff to the twentieth Ottoman infantry division, and then to the twenty-fifth division in action in Thrace.[64] He was next detailed an aide to Ottoman war minister Enver Paşa and accompanied him on a tour of Anatolia, Syria, and Iraq. He thereafter served with distinction on the Caucasus front. At the end of the war he was a 34-year-old staff colonel – a very high rank among Ottoman officers of his generation.

After the armistice, Yusuf al-ͨAzma went home to Damascus. But he was a stranger in his native city, and apart from a brief posting in 1907, he had not lived in Damascus for almost two decades, during which time both he and the city had changed tremendously. Damascus was a city under British army military occupation, in concert with its Arab allies, few of whom were Syrians. In defeat, his friends and comrades from twenty years of Ottoman army service had scattered to the winds, some like Enver, under threat of arrest by allied occupation forces, some in Istanbul, and he found himself in a city he no longer knew, occupied and dominated by the enemy he had fought. He probably felt more at home in Istanbul, speaking Turkish, a language he spoke at home with his Istanbul-born wife and children. Like Yasin al-Hashimi, his brother officer of twenty years, former fellow student at the staff college, al-ͨAzma accepted an offer of employment in the nascent government of Amir Faysal, and requested official release from Ottoman service, which was duly granted and recorded in December 1919.[65] Within eighteen months he was dead, and destined to become the pre-eminent heroic martyr of the Syrian nation.

Yasin al-Hashimi's younger brother, Taha al-Hashimi, was born in Baghdad in 1888, and educated there at the same military middle and preparatory schools as his two older brothers. He completed his preparatory-school studies and traveled to Istanbul to enroll in the military academy in 1903. Taha graduated a second lieutenant in 1906, and immediately entered the staff college and graduated first in his class in 1909. He was appointed a staff captain to the Fifth Ottoman Army in Syria, and participated in the Hawran repression operations south of Damascus with General Sami Paşa al-Faruqi in 1910. By late 1910 he was chief of staff to the 8th brigade at Damascus. He served as a staff officer during the Balkan wars, and in 1913 requested permission to go to Yemen to organize the Ottoman defense of the province. The journey took two-and-a-half months during peacetime, and he traveled by ship from Istanbul to Beirut, by train to Damascus, and Aleppo, overland to Mosul, and by riverboat to Baghdad and Basra, and by ship between Basra and Yemen. He arrived in Yemen in March of 1914, in time to engage British forces probably even before the Ottoman state officially entered the war. Taha spent the entire war a staff officer of the seventh Ottoman brigade, in numerous engagements against British forces in southern Yemen. At the time of the armistice in late 1918, he was a lieutenant colonel. Taha al-Hashimi began a year-long journey north with remnants of his force, to report to the imperial capital, which he reached after an arduous journey in late October 1919.[66]

Fawzi al-Qawuqji may be the most famous perennial rebel of the last Ottoman generation.[67] His fame stems not from his forgotten two decades in Ottoman school and military service, but from his quixotic and unsuccessful role as a tragic hero of Arab nationalism and the struggle for Palestine. Qawuqji was born in Tripoli, in today's Lebanon, in 1890. Tripoli was an important Ottoman Mediterranean sea port, on par with Haifa to the south and Alexandretta to the north. Inland trading and agricultural export towns had their seaports, and Tripoli served the Syrian towns of Homs and Hama.

Tripoli was a stunningly beautiful city at the turn of the last century. The town nestled at the bottom of a hill capped with an ancient stone castle predating the Crusades, and renovated in the 16th century with an inscribed gate in the name of Ottoman Sultan Sulayman. The Abu ʿAli river flowed down from snow-covered peaks due east and cleaved the hill between castle and foothills to the east. The Ottoman city covered the plain below the castle to the west, and the city was separated from its Roman and Phoenician harbor by a mile-long road running through verdant orange groves. The town had been important for millennia and was well endowed with clean, cold water, brilliant sunlight, and Mediterranean breezes. It had several Mamluk public baths, many mosques and churches, and a strong and growing central government presence in the form of state schools and administration buildings.

The town had received a significant amount of state investment, and by 1900 had a broad central square and municipal garden surrounded by modern buildings, shops, a hotel, and a government office of post and telegraphs. When Qawuqji was ten years old, he would have witnessed the construction and inauguration of the grand Hamidian clock tower in the square that remains a city landmark today. (See Figure 1.5.) Shortly before the war in 1911, the rail line linking Tripoli to Homs, and the Ottoman rail network, was completed. Ottoman citizens like Qawuqji were acculturated to the benefits and symbols of Ottoman modernity.

Qawuqji attended elementary school in his neighborhood. Six days a week over the course of three years, he walked the short distance along the ancient lanes of the city, and spent his days learning the kind of basic skills state elementary schools around the globe instilled in the

Figure 1.5. Hamidian Clock Tower, Jaffa (Lemke Collection)

final decades of the nineteenth century. He went home in the afternoon
and had a big lunch and spent the late afternoon playing in the neighborhood with other children. At nine or ten years of age, Young Fawzi
would have begun his studies at the state middle school. There was a
state civil middle school established at Tripoli by 1897, but his family
probably did not possess the financial resources to pay the expensive
tuition, and Fawzi would have left his family behind to attend school in
Damascus or Beirut as a boarder at the tuition-free military middle
school. Decades later, Qawuqji began his memoir with the words, "I
opened my eyes on the world and found myself in the Ottoman school
system."[68] After middle school and perhaps a summer spent at home in
Tripoli at the age of 12 or 13, Fawzi continued at the Damascus military secondary school. He graduated from the preparatory school at the
age of 17 or 18 and made the long trip to the imperial capital.

Qawuqji graduated from the Ottoman imperial military academy a
second lieutenant of cavalry in 1912. He seems to have been a fairly
indifferent student, and did not attend the staff college. Like his brother
officers, Qawuqji was posted to a far-flung province, in his case to
Mosul. He then traveled west to fight in the Balkan wars. In the months
after the entry of the Ottoman Empire into the Great War in late
October 1914, Qawuqji traveled to Baghdad as part of the first
Ottoman reinforcements to arrive in January 1915 under the command
of Süleyman Askeri Bey. The counteroffensive against British-occupied
Basra failed after an extraordinarily difficult battle and both Qawuqji
and Süleyman Askeri Bey were evacuated to hospital in Baghdad.
Despondent over the defeat, and already a famous army officer,
Süleyman Askeri shot himself with his sidearm in the hospital.[69]

Qawuqji spent months recovering from his wounds, and finally persuaded the Ottoman military doctors to allow his return to active service. He did not rejoin his unit, but opted to travel west to join the
defense of his native region. He first sailed upriver to Mosul, and then,
with an officer companion, rode for twenty days on horseback between
Mosul and Aleppo in early summer 1915. He took the train south from
Aleppo to Homs and Tripoli and reported to the summer headquarters
of Cemal Paşa at ʿAlayh in Mount Lebanon above Beirut. Qawuqji
noted that the cool heights of Mount Lebanon were his first real rest in
years, but he also noted with disapproval the luxurious circumstances
enjoyed by Cemal Paşa and his favorites.

Fawzi found much to complain about, including his observation that
Cemal was busy imprisoning notable Arab leaders and intellectuals and
sending Arab officers and conscripts to Anatolia, while he imported
non-Arab officers to defend Syria. Fawzi enjoyed his stay and struck up

a passionate friendship with a local Christian woman during his time in the mountains. Despite the complaints of his memoirs, which seem to bear the stamp of mid-twentieth Arab nationalist claims about "Turkish tyranny," Fawzi enjoyed good relations with Cemal and was allowed to remain in greater Syria. He claimed without irony that, "Cemal sent the Arabs to Galipoli while Syria was emptied of quality defenders."[70]

In 1916 Qawuqji received orders to travel to Jerusalem and report to the garrison town of Beersheba on the Palestine front. He traveled by train from Mount Lebanon to Damascus and from there to Palestine. His female friend accompanied him to the ᶜAlayh train station, and rode with him on his train journey. From Damascus they traveled south by train, and enjoyed a long holiday in the Roman town of Sabastia near Nablus in today's West Bank. He was pleased his unnamed lady friend was able to accompany him on this part of his journey.

In his off-duty activities Qawuqji was like many other officers of his generation. Ottoman officers considered themselves an educated modern elite. They commanded mostly illiterate conscripts, and were outnumbered by career officers who had risen through the ranks and were often barely literate. The educated officers, by contrast often of modest background, had received years of schooling, possessed skills in multiple languages (in Qawuqji's case, Turkish, Arabic, French, and German), and had often spent time abroad posted in Germany. They had traveled the empire itself, which in the closing decade of the nineteenth century was still breathtakingly cosmopolitan and diverse. Their education in the Ottoman school system emphasized the sacred duty to serve as the vanguard defenders of the Ottoman sultan, caliph, Muslim people, and the Islamic religion, but displays of outward religious piety were hardly expected. Part of their modern cosmopolitanism often seemed to instill an enthusiastic appreciation for the company of liberated women and drinking alcohol.[71]

In the first few months of 1916, Qawuqji arrived at Beersheba. Despite its Biblical antiquity, Beersheba was built as a late nineteenth-century Ottoman garrison town and administrative center. The town resembled a cavalry outpost in the American West, surrounded as it was by desert and barren hills. It existed to extend central and provincial government presence into the nomadic and rural frontier regions. The town comprised a central square and municipal garden laid out in front of the government Saray, office of posts and telegraph, army office, and after 1915, a train station for a spur line of the Hijaz railroad. With the coming of the war to the Ottoman realms, Beersheba became the last outpost separating Ottoman greater Syria from British-occupied Egypt and the Sinai. While the town had been built from scratch with Ottoman State investment, it was a small settlement, and the garrison was mostly billeted in tents.

From Beersheba, Qawuqji participated in long-range mounted reconnaissance patrols into Sinai, to probe the British lines to the south.[72] Qawuqji was decorated for his service in the campaign, and developed an appreciation for the German chief of staff of the Eighth Ottoman Army, Kress von Kressenstein. Decades later, Qawuqji remained proud of the trust von Kressenstein had placed in him. He fought in the first battle of Gaza in March 1917 and the second battle of Gaza in April 1917. Like many Ottoman officers of his generation, Qawuqji viewed the German military with admiration and fondness, especially when contrasted with what he, and many others among his fellow Ottoman officers, considered the continual perfidy of the British.[73]

Qawuqji continued to command long-range mounted reconnaissance units during the Ottoman defense of Palestine and Syria. He took orders from Mustafa Kemal, ranged through Palestine and the Hawran region, and learned well the topography of the area between Damascus and Jerusalem. He was present at the final defeat at the battle of Nablus, and the retreat north. Qawuqji was in Damascus at the moment of the British entry to the city. Officers who had not retreated north with Mustafa Kemal Paşa hastened to doff their army uniforms and put on civilian clothes. Scattered remnants of the army tried to escape the city, but found they were tracked and fired on by British aircraft. Qawuqji followed the railroad track on horseback, traveling by night to avoid airplanes, and went first to Rayaq, the rail junction and Ottoman airbase town in the Biqaᶜ. He made his way to Homs, where Kemal planned and then aborted an attempted regroup and defense of the city.

At Homs, Qawuqji had a final meeting with Mustafa Kemal Paşa. Kemal lamented the certain defeat due to the relentless harassment by British aircraft and cavalry, and sadly admitted that now was the time for all to return to, and defend, their native regions. Qawuqji claimed Kemal wished the Arabs freedom and success, and when Qawuqji requested dismissal from the Ottoman force and return to Tripoli, Kemal granted permission. The remaining defenders retreated to Aleppo. Qawuqji noted that Homs fell on 17 October 1918, the same day he arrived in Tripoli. He had returned to his native city after an absence of more than a decade, a defeated officer of a defeated empire.[74]

Necessity dictated similar arrangements among many less prominent former Ottoman officers. Saᶜid al-ᶜAs had been born in modest circumstances in 1889 in the central Syrian town of Hama. He attended the Damascus military middle and preparatory schools and went to Istanbul, where he graduated from the military academy as a second lieutenant in 1907. He was immediately posted to Damascus, where he taught a year in the military preparatory school he had attended. There he would have known Mustafa Kemal, who was posted to the school and Fifth Army headquarters between 1905 and 1907. As noted, Kemal also took part in the first Damascus chapter of the secret society *Watan*, later merged with the Committee of Union and Progress.

In 1908, al-ᶜAs was accepted to the staff college and returned to Istanbul. In the imperial capital he witnessed the 1908 Constitutional Revolution and graduated a staff captain in 1910. (See Figures 1.6a and 1.6b.) Between 1911 and 1913 he fought in the Balkan wars, first against guerrilla forces, under the command of ᶜAziz ᶜAli al-Misri, and finally against the regular armies of the Balkan states. Al-ᶜAs later noted that his views on the effectiveness of guerrilla warfare were formed in this period. In 1913 he became the Director of the military preparatory school at Damascus under the command of Yasin al-Hashimi.[75] During the war al-ᶜAs fought the Russians in eastern Anatolia, and took part in the defense of Galipoli in 1915.[76] The following year he was posted to Syria and in 1917 he was tried and convicted for his political activities, which included writing pseudonymous articles critical of the wartime Ottoman leadership in Syria. The court martial took place at

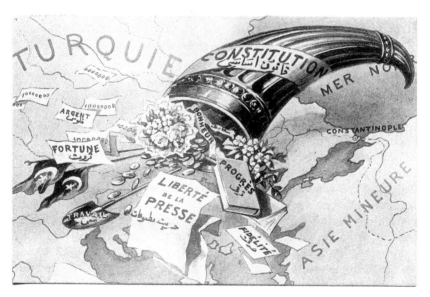

Figure 1.6a. Two Views of the Ottoman Constitutional Restoration, 1908–9 (Lemke Collection)

Figure 1.6b.   Two Views of the Ottoman Constitutional Restoration, 1908–9 (Lemke Collection)

the summer headquarters of Cemal Paşa at ʿAlayh in Mount Lebanon. He was initially sentenced to hang, like the others tried at ʿAlayh, but his sentence was commuted and he spent six months in prison in ʿAlayh, and the final year of the war imprisoned in the citadel at Aleppo. As a highly educated and seasoned staff officer, he was probably a major or perhaps a colonel at the time of his sentence and imprisonment. He was released the day Faysal arrived in Aleppo on 26 October 1918.

Late Ottoman military education often included a measure of social engineering. Ramadan Shallash was born around 1879, a son of the shaykh of the upper Euphrates tribe al-Bu-Saraya. His father sent Ramadan to attend the first class at the Ottoman Imperial Tribal School, from which he graduated in 1898, and entered the military academy. Shallash certainly would have needed the specialized remedial curriculum of the Tribal School. After his five-year course of study, with its emphasis on religion, Ottoman history and culture, and basic reading and writing skills, he may still have had difficulty competing on an equal footing with military academy students, many of whom were younger than he, and who had already received eight or nine years of intensive elite schooling to his five years.[77] Imperial affirmative-action policy may have played a role in insuring students like Ramadan graduated, though nearly 10 percent of students washed out of the Imperial Military Academy.[78]

The experience of the Tribal School or military academy did not embitter him and Shallash served the Ottoman army well into the Great War. He composed an autobiographical entry fifty years later and continued to use by then deeply unfashionable lofty honorific titles to refer to the Ottoman state and its sultan.[79] He eventually graduated and was commissioned a captain in the Ottoman army, probably in some special cavalry unit. Shallash may have benefited from sultanic favor or imperial policy favoring the sons of rural shaykhs. The average graduate would be a 20-year-old second lieutenant, while Shallash claimed to be commissioned as a captain at graduation. Shallash went to Libya in 1911 to fight the Italian invasion of that Ottoman province. There he met, or become reacquainted with, the three most prominent commanders of the defense, all provincial products of the Ottoman education system, ᶜAziz ᶜAli al-Misri, Enver Paşa, and Mustafa Kemal Paşa.[80] Other young officers like Saᶜid al-ᶜAs, Fawzi al-Qawuqji, Yasin al-Hashimi, and Jaᶜfar al-ᶜAskari also saw action in Libya, and experienced the consequences of European designs on the Ottoman homeland they had been trained to defend.

Jaᶜfar al-ᶜAskari was born in Baghdad in 1885. He attended Ottoman primary and military middle school in Mosul and then traveled to the Baghdad military preparatory school in 1897.[81] Around this time the Baghdad military preparatory school enrolled 551 boys. In 1901, he graduated and embarked on a 44-day journey to Aleppo on foot with a pack donkey, after which he continued by ship to Istanbul.[82] In Istanbul, al-ᶜAskari spent three years in the Imperial Military Academy, from which he graduated a second or third lieutenant of infantry in 1904. He was sent back to the Euphrates and Syrian desert region, where he served in various internal campaigns for the next six years. For eighteen months he taught at the Baghdad military middle school, an assignment he considered marginally better than the endless campaigns against recalcitrant rural shaykhs and various tax-evaders, who, Jaᶜfar claimed, thought bribes would solve their problem with the Ottoman authorities.

Al-ᶜAskari considered such corruption emblematic of the autocracy of Sultan Abdul-Hamid and welcomed his deposition in 1909. Al-ᶜAskari apparently benefited from the new regime, led as it was by another alumnus of the Baghdad military preparatory school, Mahmud Şevket Paşa, because he was quickly selected to take part in a mission to Germany in 1910. In Berlin he met Enver Bey, the new Ottoman military attaché to Germany, who impressed him greatly. Berlin and the

German army was a source of constant wonder to al-ᶜAskari, but he spent only a few months in Berlin before he was detailed to a German Grenadier regiment in Karlsruhe. He cherished the comradeship of his German brother officers and especially enjoyed "beer night" at the rustic officer's lodge.

Al-ᶜAskari stayed in Germany for three memorable years, and only returned when he was ordered to report for duty at the beginning of the Balkan wars in October 1912. He was appalled by the state of the Ottoman forces he encountered during the wars in 1912 and 1913, but he served with distinction, and seems likely to have been on the cusp of being promoted to captain. At the end of 1913 he was appointed an instructor of military tactics at the Aleppo military preparatory school. In mid-summer 1914, al-ᶜAskari finally passed the entrance examination for the Ottoman staff college at Istanbul, but was unfortunately denied his opportunity by the Ottoman entry into the war; instead of school, he reported for immediate front-line duty at Gallipoli.

Early in 1915 al-ᶜAskari went to the Libyan–Egyptian border region around Benghazi, where he helped organize a guerrilla campaign against the British, as had his more senior comrades, Enver, Mustafa Kemal, and ᶜAziz ᶜAli al-Misri against Italy in 1911. A year of incredible adventures followed, during which Cemal Paşa, military governor of Syria, and commander of the Fourth Ottoman Army, upon hearing al-ᶜAskari's scheme to return to Libya by a small ship carrying munitions, replied, "I have no one under my command crazy enough for such a mission."[83] Al-ᶜAskari purchased a dilapidated freighter in Beirut, raised money, and purchased weapons in Aleppo and Damascus and waited in Beirut to run the Anglo-French sea blockade with ᶜAdil Arslan, younger brother of Shakib Arslan. In Libya they joined up with Nuri Paşa, the brother of Ottoman war minister Enver Paşa, who al-ᶜAskari had met in Berlin.

In February of 1916 he was wounded in close combat by a sword-wielding English cavalryman, and was taken prisoner to Cairo. Al-ᶜAskari was probably a captain, or perhaps a major, and after recovering from his wounds and several months in a prison camp, his brother-in-law, Lieutenant Nuri al-Saᶜid, persuaded him to defect to the British side of the war. Nuri al-Saᶜid later claimed to have deserted the Ottoman army before the war while he was still a student at the staff college, and after the outbreak of the war, he was captured and held in a prison camp in Basra in southern Iraq, from which British intelligence officers recruited him to switch sides. The defection was a difficult decision for al-ᶜAskari. His memoir is at pains to emphasize his wish to help the "Arab cause" of Sharif Husayn, but he also makes clear that many of his imprisoned brother officers considered him a traitor to the Ottoman state.[84]

Jaᶜfar al-ᶜAskari's memoirs show no Ottoman officers freely deserted the Ottoman army service to join the Arab Revolt. All were recruited from British prison camps, or intercepted while fleeing Cemal Paşa's dragnet in Syria, and all appear to have been recruited through the intervention, and personal touch, of a handful of British intelligence officers. Once recruited, Jaᶜfar attempted to persuade his fellow captured officers to switch sides at the various prison camps around Cairo.

Officers born in the late 1880s and 1890s comprise the last Ottoman generation. Such men finished the war as mid-ranking officers and were likely to have seen more direct combat than older, more senior officers. They were consequently both less likely to have survived the war, and more likely to have taken part in the various insurgencies that followed the armistice. They were well represented in all the Ottoman successor states and independence movements into the 1940s. The Arab Revolt, made famous by T.E. Lawrence, and a century of disproportionate attention, relative to other aspects of the Great War, included a small number of such mid-level ex-Ottoman officers. The vast majority of younger Ottoman officers, whatever their origins, remained in Ottoman service throughout the war, and most who survived probably fought in the Anatolian insurgency, and became citizens, and pensioners, of the Turkish Republic, whether or not their birthplaces were within the borders of the Turkish Republic. The handful of Arab officers who joined the British-sponsored revolt of Sharif Husayn and his sons, appear to have been generally lower-ranking, less distinguished, and exclusively recruited from allied prison camps. None seem to have freely abandoned their Ottoman posts and joined the Arab Revolt.

Arab and Turkish nationalist historiography has claimed Turkish or Arab ethnic nationalism, and territorial ambitions for ethnically defined Turkish or Arab states predated the Great War. Later nationalist myth, probably originating with George Antonius, claimed the CUP was a "Turkish" club and that al-ᶜAhd was an "Arab" club, and that both served as the seedbed for Turkish and Arab nationalist movements. Both organizations, however, had Arab, Turkish, Kurdish, Bulgar, Albanian, Circassian, and Muslim–Greek military students and young officers among their ranks, and none of the secret societies had the doctrinal and ideological rigidity or the ethnic chauvinism later claimed for them. ᶜAziz ᶜAli al-Misri, founder of al-ᶜAhd, later reported that the aim of al-ᶜAhd was to foster Ottoman unity and *heal* rifts between Arab, Anatolian, and Balkan officers.[85]

Civilian Politicians and Civil-School Graduates

The Ottoman constitutional revolution of 1908 and 1909 brought military officers of mostly modest background into Ottoman politics. As the influence and power of officers increased, the influence of civilian politicians waned. Such people were often members of famous Ottoman service families, some of which had produced provincial and central state functionaries for generations, or even centuries. The many crises of the last Ottoman decade, and the post-Great War period only hastened the process of militarizing Ottoman society. In the broadest sweep, Ottoman and post-Ottoman history of the Middle East in the twentieth century is the story of the gradual eclipse of aristocratic families and the rise of military officers of mostly modest background in politics. And yet, civilian elites struggled mightily in their way to retain their influence and their claims to speak for society. Like the officers, the sons of such families experienced elite Ottoman education, though in their case, it was usually elite Ottoman civil education.

Musa Kazim Paşa al-Husayni came from a distinguished Ottoman provincial family. He was born in 1853 in Jerusalem and in 1918, when he was 65 years old, he had already had an illustrious career in Ottoman service. He possessed formidable communication skills in Ottoman and Arabic as well as perhaps German or French. He had graduated from the school of civil service (Mektab-i Mülkiye) in Istanbul, which trained a majority of high officials of the imperial civil administration in the second half of the nineteenth century. He served as district commissioner (*qa'immaqam*) throughout Ottoman Syria, Anatolia, and had most recently been governor (*mutassarif*) in Yemen, and Bitlis, in eastern Anatolia. At the outbreak of the war Musa Kazim was retired from his administrative career. His younger brother, Jerusalem major Husayn al-Husayni, surrendered the city to British General Allenby in December 1917, and died a month later, at which point Musa Kazim became mayor of Jerusalem, under British army occupation.[86]

ᶜAbd al-Rahman Shahbandar was the son of a successful, but not prominent, Damascene merchant, born in 1880. His parents made the unusual choice to send him to the Syrian Protestant College (American University of Beirut since 1920), where he completed his studies as a physician and married into a Damascus family far more prominent than his own. In Beirut he also became a political activist, joining the Committee of Union and Progress, and an instructor in the SPC medical school, organizing Muslim and non-Protestant college students to oppose mandatory chapel, thereby edging the college toward its eventual secularism.[87]

Student activism revealed that Shahbandar possessed a gift for oratory and political mobilization. He was an enthusiastic member of the Unionist Party between the 1908 revolution and 1912, but back in Damascus he became critical of the centralizing and dictatorial tendencies of the Ottoman Unionist leadership. Along with a handful of other politicized intellectuals, he organized a group called the *Hizb al-lamarkaziyya al-idariyya al-ʿUthmani*, or the Ottoman Administrative decentralization party, calling for greater autonomy and self-representation in 1913. Criticism of the Ottoman government became dangerous with the coming of World War I, and he fled to Cairo ahead of Ottoman governor Cemal Paşa's police, in 1916, passing briefly though the village of a Druze shaykh named Sultan al-Atrash, south of Damascus. Shahbandar spent the war years practicing medicine in Cairo. After the end of the war, in 1919, he returned to Damascus, and in the next year, became briefly the Foreign Minister of the short-lived Arab government.

Shakib Arslan was a tireless advocate for the dignity and independence of the Ottoman state and its people, though events throughout his life forced him to adjust the focus of his advocacy. He was born in 1869 in a village in Mount Lebanon where his family enjoyed historic prominence and close ties to the Ottoman authorities. He received at birth the hereditary title of prince, which he used throughout his life, often modified as *Amir al-Bayan*, "the prince of eloquence," in tribute to his rhetorical skills in Arabic.[88] His father was a sub-district chief, and his uncle, Amir Mustafa, was district administrative head or *qa'immaqam*. His family sent him to Beirut for his education, which was the finest locally available, first in Maronite schools run by priests and finally in the Sultani state preparatory school in Beirut. The Beirut Sultani school was part of the same late Ottoman system of elite civil preparatory schools that included the Galatasaray Lycée in the capital and Maktab ʿAnbar in Damascus.

At the Sultani school, Shakib met and studied with famous Egyptian activist-scholar Muhammad ʿAbduh. The shaykh made a deep and lasting impression on the young Druze man, and Shakib remained his lifelong disciple, and he maintained his conviction, instilled at ʿAbduh's feet, that Europe was a threat and a potential enemy to the Muslim people and the Ottoman state.[89] While a student Arslan began to publish poetry, essays, and journalism; he was a prolific writer to the end of his life. After completing his studies at the Sultani school, he assumed his hereditary duties as a local political and dynastic leader. Local politics was unsatisfying, though, and he soon departed for Egypt for further study with ʿAbduh, and then to Istanbul where he was received into lofty literary and political circles. He returned to Lebanon after a tour of Europe, and assumed his role as an astute, and increasingly renowned, Ottoman-Arabic literary figure and provincial politician.

Arslan successfully weathered the deposition of Sultan Abdul-Hamid in 1909, and the rise of the Unionists, with his influence and access intact. He reacted angrily to the Italian invasion of Ottoman Libya in 1911, and resolved to join other Ottoman volunteers. After some ill-fated attempts, he arrived in Libya in 1912, where he met Enver, Mustafa Kemal, and ʿAziz ʿAli al-Misri, who were all young staff majors and emerging rivals. Arslan stayed for two months, chronicling the defense, writing a series of rousing calls for Ottoman patriotism, and forming a close and admiring relationship with Enver.[90]

Early in 1914 he was elected a delegate to the Ottoman parliament for the district of Hawran, south of Damascus. He spent the war enjoying close and trusting relations with both Enver and Cemal, and defending the wartime policies of the Ottoman state vociferously and with conviction. Arslan traveled between Syria and Istanbul repeatedly and put his literary skills at the service of the Ottoman government. At the time of the armistice in late 1918, he was in Berlin as a special envoy to the German government from Enver Paşa.[91] Before his departure in summer 1918 Enver promised casually that the mission should only take a month or even less. "After that you can return here and travel to Syria." But Arslan noted sadly years later, "I have been in Europe since that time, now more than five years away from my home." [92] His exile would last almost thirty years, and he would not return to Syria till the last years of his life. Of course, the state and sovereign he had sought to serve had disappeared almost three decades before, too.

Conclusions

In the closing decade of the nineteenth century, thousands of young men and women entered modern Ottoman State schools determined to succeed within a state and system they pledged to protect and preserve. Their convictions, expectations, and efforts were shared by state elites in every European Great War combatant state. The Ottoman State schools and institutions that shaped them gave meaning to their lives and their struggles even after the state they had sworn to serve had disappeared. The story of their times, lives, and struggles properly begins, not with the Turkish or Arab nationalism they may have eventually espoused, but with the experiences they shared as self-identified protectors and servants of a doomed empire.

Notes

1. W.E. Gladstone, *Bulgarian Horrors and the Question of the East* (London: J. Murray, 1876), partly reproduced with commentary from Nazan Çiçek, in Camron Amin, Benjamin Fortna, and Elizabeth Frierson (eds.), *The Modern Middle East: A Sourcebook for History* (Oxford University Press, 2006), pp. 416–22.
2. See for example Mustafa Kemal's "Letter to the Syrians," British National Archives [BNA], FO 406/41 no. 191, December 2, 1919. Many early Kemalist proclamations mention Gladstone.
3. Colmar von der Goltz, *Das Volk in Waffen: ein Buch über Heerwesen und Kriegführung unserer Zeit* (Berlin: R. V. Decker, 1884), *Millet-i Müsellaha: Asrımızın Usül ve Ahval-i Askeriyesi* (Istanbul: Matbaa-ı Abüzziya, 1305 [1887]).
4. Victor R. Swenson, "The Military Rising in Istanbul 1909," *Journal of Contemporary History*, 5:n4 (1970), 171–84.
5. Şükrü Hanioğlu, *Atatürk: An Intellectual Biography* (Princeton University Press, 2013), pp. 34–5.
6. Works of Bernard Lewis, Hamilton Gibb, and Harold Bowen, among many others.
7. Selim Deringil was first to put the Ottoman state in Hobsbawm's story of the nineteenth century. "The Invention of Tradition as Public Image in the Late Ottoman Empire, 1808 to 1908," in *Comparative Studies in Society and History*, 35 (1993), 3–29.
8. Quoted in Ute Frevert, *A Nation in Barracks: Modern Germany, Military Conscription, and Civil Society*, trans. Andrew Boreham (Oxford: Berg, 2004), p. 47. Ottoman Sultan Abdul-Hamid II shared this fear. Merwin Griffiths, "The Reorganization of the Ottoman Army under Abdül-Hamid II 1880–1907," unpublished PhD dissertation, UCLA, 1966, pp. 111–12. Griffiths' extraordinary thesis was written with the help and input of living Ottoman officer veterans in the 1950s and 1960s.
9. Erik Jan Zürcher, "The Ottoman Conscription System in Theory and Practice, 1844–1918," International Review of Social History 43 (1998), 83–4, and Abdallah Hanna, "The First World War According to the Memories of 'Commoners' in the Bilād al-Shām," in Heike Liebau, Katrin Bromber, Katharina Lange, Dyala Hamzah, and Ravi Ahuja (eds.), *The World in World Wars: Experiences, Perceptions and Perspectives from Africa and Asia* (Leiden: Brill, 2010), pp. 299–311.
10. BNA, FO 195/2445, December 7, 1912, Consular Report.
11. Frevert, *Nation in Barracks*, pp. 65–6.
12. I have drawn this description from Erik-Jan Zürcher, "The Ottoman Conscription System in Theory and Practice, 1844–1918," *International Review of Social History*, 43 (1998), 83–4.
13. The Ottoman army is beginning to get the attention it deserves. See especially Eugene Rogan, *The Fall of the Ottomans: The Great War in the Middle East, 1914–1920* (New York: Basic Books, 2015), and the works of Edward Ericson, Mesut Uyar, Mustafa Aksakal, and Yücel Yanıkdağ.

14. Hikmet Özdemir, *The Ottoman Army 1914–1918: Disease and Death on the Battlefield*, trans. Saban Kardaş (University of Utah Press, 2008).
15. Eric Hobsbawm, *The Age of Empire: 1875–1914* (New York: Vintage, 1987), p. 161.
16. Major works in Ottoman education include Benjamin Fortna, *Imperial Classroom: Islam, the State, and Education in the Late Ottoman Empire* (Oxford University Press, 2002), Selçuk Akşin Somel, *The Modernization of Public Education in the Ottoman Empire, 1839–1908: Islamization, Autocracy and Discipline* (Leiden: Brill, 2001), pp. 24–9. Somel and Fortna's works on Ottoman education are outstanding and comprehensive, but neither investigates deeply military or provincial schools. Emine O. Evered, *Empire and Education under the Ottomans: Politics, Reform and Resistance from the Tanzimat to the Young Turks* (London: I.B. Tauris, 2012), makes a valuable contribution toward understanding military and provincial education.
17. Library of Congress, [LC], Abdul-Hamid collection, "Statistical Abstract of Third Year Military High Schools for Adolescents." This is actually a list with enrollments and opening dates of provincial *idadi askeriyye* schools in 1893, LOT 9519, no. 4, LC-USZ62-81073 (b&w film copy neg.) www.loc.gov/pictures/collection/ahii/item/2003673270/
18. My reconstruction of the school system relies on a variety of sources including Selçuk Akşin Somel, the Library of Congress Abdul-Hamid collection, the Ottoman Ministry of Education year books, *Salname-i Nezaret-i Maarif-i Umumiye* (Istanbul: various dates), ᶜAbd al-ᶜAziz Muhammad ᶜAwad, *al-Idara al-ᶜuthmaniyya fi wilayat suriyya, 1864–1914* (Cairo: Dar al-maᶜruf, 1969), and surveys of existing school buildings in Damascus, Beirut, Aleppo, Tripoli, Ankara, Edirne, and Istanbul between 1999 and 2014.
19. Somel, *The Modernization of Public Education*, Appendices 4–6, curricula of İbtidâî, Rüşdiye, and İdâdî schools 1904, pp. 297–309. Tahsin ᶜAli, *Mudhakkirat Tahsin ᶜAli 1890–1980* (Beirut: al-Mu'asasa al-ᶜarabiyya lil-darasat wal-nashar, 2003), p. 15.
20. Somel, *The Modernization of Public Education*, p. 110.
21. Somel, *The Modernization of Public Education*, App. 4, p. 299.
22. See Stefan Weber, *Damascus: Ottoman Modernity and Urban Transformation, 1808–1918* (Aarhus University Press, 2009), vol. II, p. 150. According to the Syrian provincial yearbook, *Sâlnâme-yi vilâyet-i Sûriye. Def'a 27* (1311 [1894]), the Damascus teacher-training college opened in 1892. The building today houses the Syrian Ministry of Tourism. Weber's remarkable book about Damascus is the most important scholarly work ever published on a late Ottoman provincial capital.
23. For details on uniforms, see Mahmud Şevket Paşa, *Osmanlı Teşkilât ve Kıyafetler-i Askeri* (Istanbul: Mekteb-i Harbiye Matbaasi, 1907).
24. Istanbul University Archival Collection, IU, *Mekâtibi Askeriye Şakirdanının*, 1318 (1901). military-school Gazette and student log books, indicating all enrolled students, their cadet grade level, class standing, and marks in individual courses. The Istanbul University collection is based on the contents of the personal library of Sultan Abdül-Hamid in the Yıldız Palace. The materials were transferred in the 1950s.

25. IU, *Mekâtibi Askeriye Şakirdanının Umumi, Imtihanlarının neticelerini*, Istanbul, 1318 (1901). I base the argument that non-Muslim students may have been enrolled on an analysis of names, which are listed, complete with course grades, class standing, and town or region of origin, in the cadet books. At least a few of the listed students have names typically associated with Arab Christians.

26. Merwin Griffiths, "The Reorganization of the Ottoman Army under Abdül-Hamid II 1880–1907," unpublished PhD dissertation, UCLA, 1966," pp. 151–2. Erik-Jan Zürcher, "The Ottoman Conscription System in Theory and Practice, 1844–1918," *International Review of Social History*, 43 (1998), 437–49. Salim Tamari, "The Short Life of Private Ihsan, Jerusalem 1915," *Jerusalem Quarterly*, 30 (Spring 2007).

27. Carter Findley, *Ottoman Civil Officialdom: A Social History* (Princeton University Press, 1989), pp. 154–7.

28. Findley, *Civil Officialdom*, p. 154.

29. Ali Haydar Midhat, *The Life of Midhat Paşa* (London: John Murray, 1903), p. 176.

30. *al-Zawra* (Baghdad newspaper), no. 1, 5 rabi^c al-awwal, AH 1286, quoted in Abdul-Wahhab Abbas al-Qaysi, "The Impact of Modernization on Iraqi Society During the Ottoman Era: A Study of Intellectual Development in Iraq, 1869–1917," unpublished PhD dissertation, University of Michigan, 1958, p. 34.

31. Qaysi, "The Impact of Modernization," pp. 58–9.

32. IU, *Maarif Nezareti Salnamesi* (Istanbul, 1316 [1898]).

33. IU, *Maarif Nezareti Salnamesi* (Istanbul, 1318 [1901]).

34. Jens Hanssen, "The Birth of an Educational Quarter," in Hans Gebhardt, Dorothée Sack, Ralph Bodenstein, Andreas Fritz, Jens Hanssen, Bernhard Hillenkamp, Oliver Kögler, Anne Mollenhauer, and Friederike Stolleis (eds.), *History, Space and Social Conflict in Beirut* (Wuerzburg: Orient-Institute Beirut, 2005), pp. 158–9; Donald Cioeta, "Islamic Benevolent Societies and Public Education in Ottoman Syria, 1875–1882," *Islamic Quarterly*, 26 (1982), 46–7.

35. LC, Abdul-Hamid collection, "Statistical Abstract of Fourth Year Military High Schools for Adolescents Rusdiyye." This is actually a list of *rüşdiye askeriye* schools in 1893 LOT 9519, no. 1, LC-USZ62-81070 (b&w film, copy neg.).

36. Sawsan Agha Kassab and Omar Tadmori, *Beirut and the Sultan: 200 Photographs from the Albums of Abdul Hamid II (1876–1909)* (Beirut: Éditions Terre du Liban, 2002), p. 60. Since 1926, the old Sultani School has been the Makkased Society girls' college and the Society educates thousands of Lebanese children.

37. *Thamarat al-Fanun*, year 13, no. 630, July 6 and 19, 1887. Quoted in Kassab and Tadmori, *Beirut and the Sultan*, note 44, p. 195.

38. Kassab and Tadmori, *Beirut and the Sultan*, p. 60, and George Antonius, *The Arab Awakening: The Story of the Arab National Movement* (London: H. Hamilton, 1938) p. 41. ^cAbd al-Aziz Muhammad ^cAwad notes in *al-Idara al-^cuthmaniyya fi wilayat suriyya* that tuition was 20 to 30 gold pounds, for non-boarding or boarding students.

39. Nadia von Maltzahn, "Education in Late Ottoman Damascus," unpublished MA thesis, Oxford University, 2005, p. 25.

40. Deringil, *The Well-Protected Domains*, pp. 104–6.

41. ʿAwad, *al-Idara al-ʿuthmaniyya fi wilayat suriyya*, pp. 254–6.

42. LC, Abdul-Hamid collection, "Statistical Abstract of Third Year Military High Schools for Adolescents," LOT 9519, no. 4 [item] [P&P], and Griffiths, table: "Graduates of the Military Schools by Year, 1898," p. 105.

43. Griffiths, "The Reorganization of the Ottoman Army," p. 115.

44. Eugene Rogan, "Aşiret Mektebi Abdülhamid II's School for Tribes (1892–1907)," *IJMES* 28 (1996), 83–107. Rogan's article is the best investigation of the Tribal School.

45. IU, *Mekātibi Askeriyye Şakirdanının Umumi, Imtihanlarının neticelerini*, Istanbul, 1318 (1901), p. 35.

46. Swenson, "Military Rising," pp. 171–84.

47. ʿAli, *Mudhakkirrat Tahsin ʿAli*, p. 15. Jaʿfar al-ʿAskari, *Mudhakkirat Jaʿfar al-ʿAskari* (Surrey, UK: Laam Publishing, 1988), pp. 25–6.

48. From statistics compiled by Merwin Griffiths in "The Reorganization of the Ottoman Army," p. 105. See also Mahmud Şevket Paşa, *Osmanlı Teşkilāt*.

49. IU, *Mekâtibi Askeriyye Şakirdanının Umumi, Imtihanlarının neticelerini*, (Istanbul, 1318 [1901]).

50. Griffiths, "Reorganization of the Ottoman Army," Annex I, pp. 175–7.

51. Yuval Ben-Bassat, *Petitioning the Sultan: Protests and Justice in Late Ottoman Palestine* (London: I.B. Tauris, 2013). See Eugene Rogan, "Instant Communications: The Impact of the Telegraph in Ottoman Syria," in Thomas Philipp and Birgit Schäbler (eds.), *The Syrian Land: Processes of Integration and Fragmentation: Bilād Al-Shām from the 18th to the 20th Centuries* (Stuttgart: F. Steiner, 1998), pp. 113–28.

52. Klaus Kreiser, "Public Monuments in Turkey and Egypt," *Muqarnas*, 14 (1997), 111. See Eugene Rogan, "Bringing the State Back: The Limits of Ottoman Rule in Jordan, 1840–1910," in Eugene Rogan and Tariq Tell (eds.), *Village, Steppe and State: The Social Origins of Modern Jordan* (London: British Academic Press, 1994).

53. William Ochsenwald, *The Hijaz Railroad* (Charlottesville: University Press of Virginia, 1980). Ochsenwald writes that Hijaz railway archives are unavailable in Damascus, which I confirmed in many conversations with Syrian state railway employees in 2006. I visited, surveyed, and documented the Qadam yard, and interviewed five or six senior employees in 2006.

54. *Sâlnâme-yi vilâyet-i Sûriye. defʿa 13* (1298/1880-81), p. 128, and *al-Muqtabas*, 3 April 1910. Quoted in Weber, *Damascus*, vol. II, p. 150.

55. Family detail from an interview with grandson Mazin Ali Mumtaz al-Daftari and May Ziwar al-Daftari, London, May 8, 2016, and May al-Daftari's forthcoming book, *Yasin al-Hashimi: Sira wa dhikrayat*, and Phebe Marr, "Yāsīn al-Hāshimī: The Rise and Fall of a Nationalist (A Study of the Nationalist Leadership in Iraq, 1920–1936)," unpublished PhD dissertation, Harvard University, 1966, p. 54.

56. The cadet books show class standing and marks or individual cadets. IU, *Mekatıb-i Askeriyye*, h1318 (1901). ᶜAziz ᶜAli was at the top of the class. Cemal Paşa mentions him with admiration but also exasperation in his memoir. Djemal Paşa, *Memories of a Turkish Statesman, 1913–1919* (New York: George H. Doran, 1922), pp. 60–1.
57. Phebe Marr interviewed Taha al-Hashimi in 1959. Marr, "Yāsīn al-Hāshimī," p. 63. Majid Khadduri interviewed al-Misri in the 1950s in Cairo. Al-Misri confirmed his Unionist membership. See Majid Khadduri, "ᶜAziz ᶜAli al-Misri and the Arab Nationalist Movement," in Albert Hourani (ed.), *Middle Eastern Affairs*, 4 (London: St. Antony's Papers, no. 17, 1965), pp. 140–63, and for Kemal, see Ernest E. Ramsaur, *The Young Turks: Prelude to the Revolution of 1908* (Princeton University Press, 1957), p. 95. For ᶜAzma, see Adham al-Jundi, *Tarikh al-Thawrat al-Suriyya fi ᶜAhd al-Intidab al-Fransi* (Damascus: Matbaᶜat al-Ittihad, 1960), p. 168.
58. Interview with grandson Mazin Ali Mumtaz al-Dafatari and May Ziwar al-Dafatari, London, May 8, 2016, and May al-Daftari's forthcoming book, *Yasin al-Hashimi: Sira wa dhikrayat*.
59. *Türk İstiklal Harbine katılan tümen ve daha üst kademelerdeki komutanların biyografileri* (Ankara: TC Genelkurmay Harp Tarihi Başkanlığı Ya Yayın Yeri, 1989), pp. 1–2.
60. Piecing together Hashimi's service record has been challenging. See Khayr al-Din al-Zirikli, *al-Aᶜlam: Qamus Tarajim li-Aashar al-Rijal wa al-Nisa' min ᶜArab wa al-Mustaᶜribin al-Mustashriqin* (Beirut: Dar al-ᶜIlm li-al-Malayin, 1990), vol. VIII, p. 128. Marr, "Yāsīn al-Hāshimī," pp. 71–2, and Hanioğlu, *Atatürk*, pp. 82–3.
61. Zirikli, *al -Aᶜlam: Qamus Tarajim*, vol. VIII, p. 213, and Linda Schilcher, *Families in Politics: Damascene Factions and Estates of the Eighteenth and Nineteenth Centuries* (Stuttgart, F. Steiner, 1985), pp. 144–6.
62. Zirikli, *al -Aᶜlam: Qamus Tarajim*, vol. VIII, p. 213.
63. Yusuf al-ᶜAzma, trans. *Piyade Acemi Neferi Nasıl Yetiştirilir* (İstanbul: Mahmud Bey Matbaası, 1325 [1909]), Wilhelm Rücker, *Praktische Winke für die Ausbildung des Infanterie-Rekruten* (Berlin: Mittler, 1909). Thanks to Mesut Uyar for this citation.
64. Zirikli, *al -Aᶜlam: Qamus Tarajim*, vol. VIII, p. 213. And Adham al-Jundi, *Târîkh al-thawrât al-sûriyya fî ᶜahd al-intidâb al-fransî* (Damascus, 1960), p. 168.
65. Binbaşı Yusuf Bey, Mesut Uyar Private Collection, Zat İşleri, Erkân-ı Harbiye Ümera ve Zabitan Künye Defteri, no. 3. I record my thanks to Professor Mesut Uyar for the document.
66. Taha al-Hashimi, *Mudhakkirat Taha al-Hashimi* (Beirut: Dar al-Ta'liᶜa, 1967–78), pp. 6–8.
67. Laila Parson's much-anticipated book on Qawuqji's life, *The Commander: Fawzi al-Qawuqji and the Fight for Arab Independence 1914–1948* (New York: Hill and Wang, 2016), is the last word on his extraordinary story.
68. Fawzi al-Qawuqji, *Mudhakkirat Fawzi al-Qawuqji*, reprint of both volumes of 1975 edition, edited by Khayriyya Qasimiyya (Damascus: Dar al-Numayr, 1995), p. 15.

69. al-Qawuqji, *Mudhakkirat Fawzi al-Qawuqji*, p. 28.
70. Qawuqji, *Mudhakkirat Fawzi al-Qawuqji*, p. 29.
71. Mustafa Kemal Atatürk is obviously the most famous example of this tendency. The late and lamented Professor Khayriyya Qasimiyya in numerous conversations with me noted wryly that Qawuqji never lost his enthusiasm for the company of young women.
72. Fawzi al-Qawuqji, *Mudhakkirat Fawzi al-Qawuqji*, p. 31.
73. Kress von Kressenstein, "The Campaign in Palestine from the Enemy's Side," *Royal United Services Institution Journal*, 67:467 (1922).
74. Qawuqji, *Mudhakkirat Fawzi al-Qawuqji*, pp. 70–1.
75. Jundi, *Tarikh*, pp. 253–4. BNA CO 730/150/6, "Profiles and Assessments," YASIN Paşa AL HASHIMI.
76. Fayiz Sara, *Saᶜid al-ᶜAs, 1889–1936: Hayatahu-Kifahahu* (Damascus: manshurat wazara al-thaqafa, 1993), p. 35.
77. Rogan notes in his article that most students entered the Tribal School between the ages of 12 and 16. Shallash's self-reported birth date of 1869, and his appearance in the first class (1892–8), make him 23 years old at the beginning of his eight-year Istanbul education. It is likely that his biographical dictionary entry contains a misprint and that he was born in 1879, or later. Jurj Faris, *Man hum fi ᶜalam al-ᶜArabi* (Damascus: Maktab al-Dirasat al-Suriyya wa-al-ᶜarabiyya, 1957), p. 344, and Rogan, "Aşiret Mektebi," p. 86.
78. IU, *Mekatıb-i Askeriyye*, h1318 (1901). 74 entering students out of a class of 811 failed and washed out.
79. Faris, *Man hum*, p. 345.
80. Ahmad Djemal Paşa, *Memories of a Turkish Statesman, 1913–1919* (New York: George H. Doran, 1922), p. 63.
81. "Statistical Abstract of Third-Year Military High Schools," LOT 9519, no. 4, LC-USZ62-81073 (b&w film copy neg.).
82. Jaʿfar 'Askari, et al., *A Soldier's Story: From Ottoman Rule to Independent Iraq* (London: Arabian Publishing, 2003), p. 18. Translated from an edited Arabic manuscript memoir. Also Zirikli, *al -Aᶜlam: Qamus Tarajim*, vol. II, pp. 129–30.
83. Al-ᶜAskari, *Mudhakkirat*, p. 62. My translation.
84. Al-ᶜAskari, *Soldier's Story*, p. 100.
85. Khadurri, "ᶜAziz ᶜAli al-Misri," p. 149. From a different perspective, see Djemal Pasha, *Memoirs of a Turkish Statesman: 1913–1919* (London: Hutchison, 1922), pp. 6–64.
86. Al-Ziriklī, *al -Aᶜlam: Qamus Tarajim*, vol. VII, p. 326.
87. Philip Khoury, "'Abd al-Rahman Shahbandar: An Independence Leader of Interwar Syria," in Camille Mansour and Leila Fawaz (eds.), *Transformed Landscapes: Essays on Palestine and the Middle East in Honor of Walid Khalidi* (New York: American University in Cairo Press, 2009), pp. 31–5, and Zirikli, *al -Aᶜlam: Qamus Tarajim*, vol. III, p. 308.
88. William L. Cleveland, *Islam Against The West: Shakib Arslan and the Campaign for Islamic Nationalism* (Austin, TX: University of Texas Press, 1985), pp. 8–9, and Zirikli, *al -Aᶜlam: Qamus Tarajim*, vol. III, pp. 173–74.
89. Cleveland, *Islam Against The West*, p. 9.

90. Cleveland pays relatively little attention to this episode, though it was evidently important to Arslan. See Cleveland, p. 20, and Shakib Arslan, *Sira Dhatiyya* (Beirut: Dar al-Ṭaliᶜa, 1969). He included a photo of them together as the second illustration in his memoir.
91. Cleveland, *Islam Against The West*, p. 39.
92. Arslan, *Sira Dhatiyya*, p. 262. Quoted in Cleveland, *Islam Against The West*, p. 40.

2 The Theory and Practice of Colonialism in the Post-Ottoman Middle East

Events in the Formation of the Colonial Middle East

May 1916	British and French diplomats Mark Sykes and François Georges-Picot meet in Paris to negotiate partition of the Ottoman realms
October 30, 1918	Armistice of Mudros (Ottoman)
November 3, 1918	Armistice of Villa Giusti (Austro-Hungarian)
November 11, 1918	Armistice of Compiègne (German)
December 1918	Clemenceau visits Lloyd George in London; they agree on Ottoman partition
January–April 1919	Paris Peace Conference formally ends the war; proposes League of Nations, and Mandates
February 1919	British evacuate Cilicia in advance of French occupation
June–August 1919	King–Crane Commission and report (suppressed)
February 1920	London Conference (UK, France, and Italy secretly prepare for San Remo)
April 1920	San Remo Conference proposes and formally apportions 'A' mandates between Britain and France
August 1920	Treaty of Sevres (formalized at San Remo Conference) maps out full partition of the Ottoman realms
March 1921	Colonial Secretary Churchill's Cairo Conference resolves to appoint Faysal and ᶜAbdallah King and Prince of Iraq and Transjordan
April 1921	Prince ᶜAbdallah b. Husayn of Transjordan
August 1921	King Faysal b. Husayn of Iraq
October 1921	First League of Nation Permanent Mandates Commission meeting
October 1922–July 1923	Treaty of Lausanne renegotiated terms of Ottoman surrender and signaled the emergence of the Turkish Republic as sole independent Ottoman successor state

56

Ottoman politicians had considered Great Power imperialism the gravest danger to their state in the years before the world war. The war, the defeat, and the accompanying disasters cut millions adrift from the certainties and hopes that had ordered life. Lives, plans, and careers were cut short and altered in ways unforeseen and unwanted. In Berlin, news of the fall of Damascus sent Shakib Arslan rushing to return to Istanbul. He boarded a train and traveled east until he reached the Ukrainian port of Nikolaev on the Black Sea coast. While waiting for a ship, he met some Ottoman Arabs fleeing the capital, from whom he learned that Istanbul was under British occupation and that he, as a member of the wartime government, would likely face prison or worse. Arslan joined his comrades in an arduous return journey to Berlin and to what would become permanent exile.[1]

Yasin al-Hashimi was in hiding, seriously wounded, in Damascus. Years earlier, Amir Faysal himself had tried to convince al-Hashimi to join the nascent Arab Revolt. But Yasin al-Hashimi refused this and later appeals, and never wavered in his belief that Britain would not be a friend to the Ottomans or the Arabs. By the end of the war, he had spent twenty-five years as an Ottoman officer and cadet. He was a 34-year-old major general in command of an army corps in Palestine, and among the highest-ranking and most distinguished young staff commanders in the Ottoman army.[2] Al-Hashimi escaped the British capture of Dar\u0000a, near today's Syrian–Jordanian border at the end of September 1918, and led a retreat north. He was wounded in combat on the 100-kilometer retreat to Damascus, and, unable to continue, took refuge at the house of the al-Na\u0000iama family near Damascus' Suq al-Hamidiyya.

Yasin al-Hashimi's wounds forced him to remain behind while Kemal retreated north toward Aleppo. Former comrades among Faysal's forces got wind of his presence in the city. Nuri al-Sa\u0000id, \u0000Ali al-Jawdat, and Jamil al-Midfa\u0000i were junior Ottoman officers from Iraq who had been captured by British forces and had joined Faysal's Revolt after their internment in prisoner-of-war camps in Egypt. When they learned Yasin al-Hashimi was wounded and hiding in Damascus, they searched until they found him and beseeched him to join the new government of Amir Faysal.

Yasin al-Hashimi had no wish to abandon his responsibilities as an Ottoman staff officer. In October of 1918, though, there seemed to be no Ottoman state left to serve, and left behind on the retreat to Anatolia he had few options. Having found al-Hashimi, his old comrades and adversaries still had difficulty persuading him to join them.[3]

Al-Hashimi sought assurances that their entreaties were not part of a British plot to gain his surrender. Eventually they convinced him, and Faysal immediately named al-Hashimi military chief of staff above the handful of ex-Ottoman officers who had joined his revolt. The improvement in his prospects did not last long and by the end of the following year, General Allenby ordered him jailed in Palestine. Uncounted thousands of other Ottoman State employees faced similar peril, uncertainty, and desperate circumstances in 1918 and 1919.

World War I is remembered for senseless carnage in Europe over now-obscure European power struggles. But the war engulfed the globe, and affected millions of soldiers and civilians, only a minority of whom were full citizens of France, Britain, or Germany. Tens of millions of conscript soldiers from the Ottoman lands, the far-flung Russian and Hapsburg empires, and British and French colonial empires fought and suffered in the cataclysm. Many returned home embittered to find the justice and prosperity they had been promised did not come to pass. The memory of the war became a touchstone for disillusionment and lost innocence in Europe. In Turkey and post-colonial countries from North Africa to Burma, less complicated, and more plainly heroic independence struggles supplanted the popular memory of the Great War.

Europeans and North Americans remember the battlefields of France and Flanders. But France and Belgium were not the only battlegrounds, and their prominence in memory comes from the European monopoly on the story and meaning of the war. Also forgotten is much of the underlying struggle for global domination between Britain, Germany, France, and Russia. Seen from a less common perspective, the war sprang from British anxiety over the German–Ottoman alliance, and access to India, Egypt, and the newly exploited oil resources surrounding the Persian Gulf. It was a reactionary struggle between the British *world-dominating present*, and the feared German *world-dominating future*. British war planners laid out a secret invasion plan for southern Mesopotamia and Abadan, the refinery town at the head of the Persian Gulf, in late summer 1914, months before the Ottoman Empire had entered the war. The Ottoman State officially entered the war on October 29, 1914, by which time the British force had already landed and was ready to begin the offensive. One week later, on the day of the British declaration of war, the British Army Indian Expeditionary Force launched the Mesopotamia campaign on the Ottoman province of Basra at the head of the Persian Gulf. It took two-and-a-half years to finally capture Baghdad. The disastrous Gallipoli campaign followed the Mesopotamia campaign a few months later. Colonial soldiers from India and Australia in the hundreds of thousands fought in these campaigns.[4]

For Ottoman citizens, summer 1914 was a continuation of war, beginning when Italy invaded Ottoman Libya in 1911, sparking a scramble among smaller European powers for Ottoman territory. World War I emerged from this contest and should be considered a part of it. The first Balkan War began in 1912. As the Balkan League alliance of Bulgaria, Serbia, Greece, and Montenegro formed and attacked the Ottoman provinces in Europe in 1912, the Great Powers stood officially aloof. Behind the scenes, however, tensions and ambitions leading to the 1914 outbreak had already emerged. Russia supported the Balkan League's moves against the Ottoman state. Austro-Hungary discouraged the war, fearing disorder on the border and its recently annexed province of Bosnia-Herzegovina, with its cosmopolitan former Ottoman provincial capital of Sarajevo. France encouraged Serbian truculence, and Britain claimed officially to oppose the war while encouraging Greek and Bulgarian expansion against both the Ottomans and Russia. Germany, sensitive to Ottoman lack of preparedness, opposed the war and urged its Ottoman ally to assume a defensive line near Adrianople (Edirne).[5]

The Ottoman army was swept from the Balkans and in the wake of its retreat came another flood of Muslim refugees to Istanbul. In mid 1913, the Balkan League alliance fell apart when Bulgaria attacked its former allies Serbia and Greece, and the Ottoman army counterattacked and recaptured some Balkan territory. In London, the cabinet of Liberal Party Prime Minister Herbert Asquith was already preoccupied with what Balkan conflict, Ottoman retrenchment, and German involvement would mean for the security of British oil fields in Persia, and the eventual partition of "Asiatic Turkey."[6]

By 1914 the Ottoman East had been the object of British, French, and Russian imperialist expansion for more than a century. The rising industrial and military power of Germany frightened French, and especially British, politicians. If Britain could lose its export markets to competition from Germany, eventually it could lose the empire itself. Before and during the war, a consensus emerged among British policy-makers: the aim of the war would be the retention and protection of the empire, and the empire could only be protected by expelling the Germans, and thus the Ottomans, from proximity to the Suez Canal and the Persian Gulf. Suez and the Gulf were the lifelines to India and to the new British-controlled oil fields of Persia, and the corridor between the Mediterranean and the Gulf would have to be under British control.[7] Customary disdain for the

Ottoman State became especially bitter on the part of British generals and politicians after the defeats of 1915. The Russian exit from the war against Germany in 1917 made the prospect of German control of the Balkans a terrifying possibility also. The war in the East was a disaster for the allies until the very end.

For France the extension of empire to the Eastern Mediterranean was less a matter of protection than historical destiny: the fulfillment of the civilizing mission (*mission civilisatrice*) to bring Francophone enlightenment and civilization to the less developed peoples of the world, and strike a blow for the supremacy of French power, prestige, and culture. French colonialists were particularly concerned to be the "Protector of the Oriental Christians" and a potent popular historical narrative combining mythic Frankish Crusaders, Catholic missionaries, the right-wing cadres of the colonial army, and provincial textile magnates from Lyon and elsewhere, evolved to advocate a French Mediterranean empire. French merchants and industrialists had a long association with silk and cotton producers on the eastern Mediterranean coast of Syria and Cilicia, and coveted petroleum resources also. But the Great War had nearly destroyed France and expansion of empire could only take place in uneasy partnership with the wartime ally and longtime rival, Great Britain.

To protect the empire, Britain had to control the Middle East, and defeat the Ottoman Empire. Despite a century of propaganda centered on the decay, decadence, and "rot" at the heart of the Ottoman realms, the Ottoman state had not collapsed, and had to be defeated; a process that arguably was incomplete in October 1918, and proved to be far more challenging than anyone expected. British politicians and generals underestimated both the strength of the Ottoman military and the vitality and legitimacy of the state itself. That its demise had been so long anticipated, made the staggering cost of its defeat all the more bitter. British forces everywhere proclaimed their intention to liberate newly occupied peoples from tyranny and the "Turkish yoke." Few indeed had desired such liberation. (See Figure 2.1.)

Wartime Arrangements and Proclamations

British and French diplomats and strategists began the partition well before the end of the war with a series of secret agreements, and short-term policy initiatives intended to guard varying objectives and preclude dissent over the post-war negotiations. The British government was in a stronger position than France or Russia, since the Western Front engulfed much of France, and Egypt and the Trucial States of the Persian Gulf

FOUR des
BALKANS

LES ALLIÉS :
On va donc partager le Croissant

Figure 2.1.   Balkan War Cartoon, 1912 (Lemke Collection)

were already British colonial possessions. The map of the region today remains much as it was plotted and penciled in by French and British diplomats in 1916. No one among the region's millions of inhabitants was consulted.

The pledges began with the Constantinople Agreement of March 1915, in which the British government, then planning the assault at Gallipoli, promised the Ottoman capital and the control of the straits between the Mediterranean and Black Sea to Czarist Russia. British policymakers, led by Secretary of State for War Herbert Kitchener and Lord of the Admiralty Winston Churchill, sought to deliver a rapid defeat to the Ottoman Empire by naval assault and invasion of Gallipoli, and a short march and quick capture of the Ottoman capital at Istanbul. British forces could then re-supply Russia through the straits, and the agreement over Istanbul and the straits would induce the Russian government to remain in the war. Churchill hoped the easy victory over the Ottomans in early 1915 would allow a subsequent march on Austro-Hungary, isolating and allowing attack on Germany from the south, ending the stalemate on the Western Front.

Short-term objectives and fanciful hopes dictated action. Great Britain had opposed Russian desires for a Mediterranean presence for a century, and the Crimean War, one of the most destructive wars ever before the Great War, had been fought to frustrate Russian moves toward the sea. In the event, the Gallipoli Campaign was a humiliating defeat for Britain and for Churchill personally. 400,000 mostly colonial soldiers were killed and wounded. A commission convened to investigate the defeats against the Ottomans determined that poor planning and persistent under-appreciation of the enemy caused the defeats.[8]

In Cairo the British High Commissioner, Henry McMahon, wrote to the Ottoman religious governor of Hijaz, Sharif al-Husayn, promising an independent kingdom if Husayn would lead a revolt against the Ottoman state. Sultan Abdul-Hamid II had appointed Husayn in early 1908 shortly before the restoration of the Ottoman constitution. Like most of Abdul-Hamid's supporters, Husayn feared the Unionist government in Istanbul would imprison or force him into exile.[9] Husayn sought British support to carve out some kind of guarantee against the new army officer leaders of the Ottoman government. Meanwhile, British colonial civil servants were haunted by creeping fears of the suddenly formidable "Turks," and the appeal of Ottoman propaganda and victories on colonial Muslims. Tens of millions of Indian Muslims lived under British rule, and the night terrors of Ottoman victories and mass colonial disorder in India and Egypt in the midst of a world war, fused seamlessly with orientalist fantasies of a reborn Arabian-nights-style caliphate under British sponsorship.[10]

Meanwhile, similar orientalist fantasies of the German intelligence service had been responsible for the Ottoman call to worldwide jihad for the sultan-caliph against the Entente Powers. Ottoman war minister Enver Paşa reminded an enthusiastic Kaiser Wilhelm II that a "holy war" against infidels would necessarily include Germany too.[11] Wilhelm, like the British, was undeterred by such details, and the message was slightly altered to a jihad against the Entente. McMahon and his fellow colonial functionaries, seized by similar dreams, resolved that the Arab revolt would provide the Entente Powers an "Arab" Caliph to counter the Central Powers' "Turkish" Caliph. Husayn would be king and caliph of a new British-Entente-aligned Muslim nation, in opposition to the Central Powers German-aligned Ottoman-Muslim nation.[12]

Husayn wrote McMahon that his kingdom would include the area from the eastern Mediterranean coast and Sinai east of Egypt, to the frontier with Persia, and to the Taurus mountains north of Aleppo. McMahon replied that "the districts of Mersina and Alexandretta, and portions of Syria lying to the west of the districts of Damascus, Homs, Hama and Aleppo, cannot be said to be purely Arab, and must on that account be excepted from the proposed limits and boundaries."[13] McMahon knew that the region of coastal Mount Lebanon was a long-standing zone of French influence, and exempted it from his agreement with Husayn.[14] He did not know or care about Palestine and so did not mention it in his correspondence, and was apparently unconcerned about the border between British-occupied Egypt and what he expected, if he expected anything, would be a British-aligned kingdom adjoining the British-aligned kingdom of Egypt stretching toward the Persian Gulf. Neither did he concern himself with the question of how or why he, or Husayn, were qualified or empowered to dispose of any portion of the territory of a sovereign state. By mid 1917 the control of Palestine had come to seem important.

McMahon and others in the colonial service of the empire were concerned to keep the various colonies quiet while the soldiers, metropolitan and colonial, of the British army were being annihilated in their hundreds of thousands on the Western Front. Husayn's sons did raise a revolt and participate in fighting the Ottoman army in Palestine and Syria between 1916 and 1918; in the meanwhile, however, other parts of the British army continued to gravely and disastrously underestimate the Ottoman foe. In April 1916 a British army division made up of colonial troops from India and British officers surrendered in Iraq. Goltz Paşa himself had commanded the Ottoman forces, but he died of typhus at the age of 72 two weeks before the surrender.

Shortly before the British surrender a secret delegation including T.E. Lawrence (of Arabia) tried to negotiate a payment of ransom to allow for the flight of the besieged army, offering to pay two million British pounds sterling and pledging not to attack Ottoman forces anywhere in the region. The Ottoman high command refused any negotiation and the entire force of some 13,000 surrendered. A similar number had perished during the siege. British military and colonial functionaries had reason for bitter feelings toward their Ottoman enemies.

The month following, in May 1916, diplomats Mark Sykes and François George-Picot met in Paris. Whether by accident or design, the agreement they reached in secret was in direct contradiction to the pledges between Sykes' colleague Henry McMahon and Husayn, so while Husayn had been promised a contiguous kingdom, France and Britain agreed to partition the entire region between themselves into French and British zones of direct and indirect rule. The Sykes–Picot agreement

Figure 2.2.   Yasin al-Hashimi and Kaiser Wilhelm, at Galician Front, July 1917 (IWM, w/permission)

remained secret till late 1917, when the new Bolshevik government published the secret wartime treaties of the Entente allies and the Czarist government it had overthrown. Today the map of the region still resembles the lines Sykes and George-Picot drew together in 1916.

By early 1917 the Ottoman army had defeated and humiliated two major British offensives and remained undefeated in battle. (See Figure 2.2.) British war aims were under dire threat if greater Syria and Iraq could not be conquered, held, and detached from the Ottoman realms. If Britain was defeated, or made peace without decisive victory in the Middle East, the Ottomans and Germans could be reasonably expected to expand the rail lines and gain effective control over the Suez Canal, Egypt, and the Persian Gulf at Kuwait.[15] British-initiated peace negotiations took place in Switzerland during 1917 and 1918, but both sides were unenthusiastic about a negotiated settlement: the Ottomans because they were undefeated in the east and expected a German victory in France, and the British because the situation on the Western Front was not sufficiently desperate to abandon the hope of conquering Greater Syria and Iraq.[16] Negotiating a settlement to detach the Ottomans from Germany would have required giving up the dream of an empire from the Mediterranean to the Gulf, and accepting a growing German role in the region.

When a British army finally conquered and occupied Baghdad in April 1917, Prime Minister Lloyd George's War Cabinet in London instructed its commander to declare:

Our armies do not come into your cities and lands as conquerors or enemies, but as liberators. Since the days of Midhat, the Turks have talked of reforms, yet do not the ruins and wastes of today testify the vanity of those promises?

The Germans and the Turks, who have despoiled you and yours, have for 20 years made Baghdad a centre of power from which to assail the power of the British and the Allies of the British in Persia and Arabia. Therefore the British Government cannot remain indifferent as to what takes place in your country now or in the future, for in duty to the interests of the British people and their Allies, the British Government cannot risk that being done in Baghdad again which has been done by the Turks and Germans during the war ...

Many noble Arabs have perished in the cause of Arab freedom, at the hands of those alien rulers, the Turks, who oppressed them. It is the determination of the Government of Great Britain and the Great Powers allied to Great Britain that these noble Arabs shall not have suffered in vain. It is the hope and desire of the British people and the nations in alliance with them that the Arab race may rise once more to greatness and renown among the peoples of the earth, and that it shall bind itself together to this end in unity and concord.[17]

The proclamation illustrates the attitudes and aims of the British empire in the Middle East and anticipates the central trope of mid-twentieth-century Arab nationalism. Like later Arab nationalist histories, the statement claims an oppressive ethnic identity for the Ottoman State it never claimed for itself. The statement argues that Ottoman rule had brought nothing but "ruins and wastes," never mind the fact that General Maude commanded the army that had just finished an invasion of the province and a siege of the city, and that the battle involved all the modern technology of warfare including airplanes, machine guns, trains and telegraphic communication on both sides. Trains and steamships supplied both armies. The presentation appears less disingenuous and more illuminating of imperial policy when it admits that Baghdad in Turkish/German hands was a nightmarish prospect for Britain. General Maude died of cholera a month later in the same Baghdad house in which Goltz Paşa had died of typhus a year earlier.

In late October 1917 Bolshevik leader Lenin issued his "Decree on Peace," demanding an end to the war, to imperialism, and to secret diplomacy. It and similar speeches were widely reported in newspapers around the world. Lenin pointed out that the "wearied, tormented, and war-exhausted toilers and laboring classes of all belligerent countries thirsted for peace." And that the peace he proposed would be immediate, without colonial annexations and without indemnities.

The government considers that to continue this war simply to decide how to divide the weak nationalities among the powerful and rich nations which had seized them would be the greatest crime against humanity, and it solemnly announces its readiness to sign at once the terms of peace which will end this war on the indicated conditions, equally just for all nationalities without exception ...

The government abolishes secret diplomacy, expressing, for its part, the firm determination to carry on all negotiations absolutely openly and in view of all the people. It will proceed at once to publish all secret treaties ratified or concluded by the government of landlords and capitalists from March to November 7, 1917.[18]

One week later, Foreign Secretary Balfour issued his declaration in support of Zionism. For the British cabinet the victory in Baghdad and prospect of victories in Palestine brought new confidence. There would be no more contemplation of a negotiated settlement with Istanbul, and the improvisational pledge to support the territorial ambitions of the Jewish nationalist movement in Europe seemed to make sense. The Balfour Declaration was a public relations move intended to gain support for the British war effort on the part of Jewish populations in America, Russia, and Germany and facilitate British control after the war.[19] The Sykes–Picot accord with France in 1916 had made Palestine more strategically important and Balfour's declaration corresponded with successes in the Palestine Campaign under the command of General Allenby. The Balfour Declaration represented an attempt to walk back some of the expansive promises made to France in the Sykes–Picot accord the year before under more desperate circumstances. Allenby captured Beersheba on 8 November, meaning that the Balfour Declaration appeared in the press the same day as the news of the first British victories on the Palestine front.[20]

Like the effort to draft Husayn as an anti-Ottoman Arab caliph, the Balfour Declaration was based on a simple-minded impression of the political consciousness of American and European Jews. In other words, as British policy-makers hoped Ottoman Syrians could be peeled off from their loyalty to the Ottoman state, by sponsorship of an alternate caliph of the "true race," Russian Bolshevik Jews, German Jews, and American Jews were imagined to owe allegiance to their religion above all else.[21] As a wartime policy to convince Trotsky to keep Russia in the war, or to urge Jewish–German soldiers to desert their units on the Western Front, the Balfour Declaration was a failure. But as a policy securing Palestine for Britain, and enabling the implantation of a reliable immigrant client population into a colonial territory, support for Zionism held promise, and appeared for a decade or so anyway, to be a qualified success. Zionist leaders, and probably Husayn also, actively manipulated British prejudice and ignorance in pursuing their political goals.

Two months after the Balfour Declaration, in early January 1918, in direct response and as an attempt to co-opt the Bolshevik position, American President Woodrow Wilson issued his famous "Fourteen Points" speech to a joint session of congress. For perhaps the first time, an American president addressed a mass audience outside the United States, in invoking the language of universal rights and equality of nations and peoples. But Wilson failed to understand the implications of his words on popular aspirations in the colonial world.

What we demand in this war is nothing peculiar to ourselves. It is that the world be made fit and safe to live in; and particularly that it be made safe for every peace-loving nation which, like our own, wishes to live its own life, determine its own institutions, be assured of justice and fair dealing by the other peoples of the world, as against force and selfish aggression.

All the peoples of the world are in effect partners in this interest, and for our own part we see very clearly that unless justice be done to others it will not be done to us ...

Open covenants of peace must be arrived at, after which there will surely be no private international action or rulings of any kind, but diplomacy shall proceed always frankly and in the public view ...

A free, open-minded, and absolutely impartial adjustment of all colonial claims, based upon a strict observance of the principle that in determining all such questions of sovereignty the interests of the population concerned must have equal weight with the equitable claims of the government whose title is to be determined ...

The Turkish portions of the present Ottoman Empire should be assured a secure sovereignty, but the other nationalities which are now under Turkish rule should be assured an undoubted security of life and an absolutely unmolested opportunity of autonomous development, and the Dardanelles should be permanently opened as a free passage to the ships and commerce of all nations under international guarantees ...

We have spoken now, surely, in terms too concrete to admit of any further doubt or question. An evident principle runs through the whole program I have outlined. It is the principle of justice to all peoples and nationalities, and their right to live on equal terms of liberty and safety with one another, whether they be strong or weak.[22]

Debate continues over the contradictions of the wartime pledges. And while the tangle of promises, counter-promises, agreements, and faithful or faithless intentions, bureaucratic feuds, and shadowy rivalries have now flummoxed and fascinated generations of historians, the authors of each agreement made their decisions casually and based on expediency. The pledges were mostly intended to achieve some now obscure short-term wartime goal, often without regard for any other previous promise or agreement. The agreements and pledges were not usually binding, and those claims that eventually took precedence were based on the preponderance of political, financial, and military power at the end of the war. Put another way, Britain achieved its aims and other parties achieved theirs to the extent that they were in a position to demand them without compromise, as in the case of France, or to the extent that they appeared to correspond with short-term British policy objectives, as in the case of the Zionists, or the Hashimites of Iraq and Transjordan.

The Paris Peace Conference and Post-War Negotiations

The war ended in late 1918 and brought a long series of peace conferences and treaty conventions. Lenin and Wilson had laid down a challenge to the victorious Great Powers, and their popular idealism threatened to upset the terms of the settlement and the distribution of the spoils of the French and British victory. As historian Erez Manela has shown, Wilson soon recoiled from the anti-imperialist hopes his speeches and proclamations had provoked, but the news of the "Fourteen Points" and the dawn of a new world of justice and freedom animated discussion, hope, and protest throughout the world.[23]

Before the Paris Peace conference had convened, and before Wilson had arrived in Europe, French Prime Minister Georges Clemenceu paid a four-day-long victory visit to his British counterpart, David Lloyd George. Clemenceu and Lloyd George drove together through wildly cheering crowds from the train station. Clemenceu was touched by the outpouring, and Lloyd George, with an artful instinct for negotiation, picked this moment to strike. Upon reaching the French Embassy, Lloyd George convinced Clemenceu to concede Palestine and oil-rich Mosul to Britain despite the Sykes–Picot lines. For his part, Clemenceu claimed Syria, Cilicia, Alexandretta, and a percentage of Mosul oil for France. The deal was struck. Over the next twelve months, Clemenceu came to fear that the slippery Lloyd George and his Hashemite client Faysal would deny him Syria, but both powers ended up with what they privately apportioned in December 1918.[24] Lloyd George eventually exclaimed to Clemenceu, "the friendship of France is worth ten Syrias."[25] By the time the Paris Peace Conference convened the next month, in January 1919, the partition of the Ottoman realms had already been decided secretly between Clemenceu and Lloyd George. If Wilson did not know, he soon suspected a backroom arrangement had been made.

The Paris Conference dealt principally with the terms of peace in Europe. In keeping with Wilson's "Fourteen Points," however, the Conference did take up the partition of the Ottoman Empire, ostensibly in keeping with the principal of self-determination for Ottoman citizens and Zionists. The Conference delegates endorsed Wilson's proposal to create an international body to help keep the peace, adjudicate disputes, and safeguard the interests of people subject to the military occupation of the victorious powers. Wilson's proposed League of Nations would assume the legal trusteeship of territories separated from the Ottoman Empire or Germany, and which would be administered for the League of Nations by the mandatory powers, Britain or France. The League of Nations and the populations of the mandated territories thus assumed all the responsibilities and none of the benefits of national sovereignty.

The Peace Conference produced the Charter of the League of Nations. Article 22 dealt directly with those parts of the Ottoman state under Allied military occupation and expected to remain under some form of French or British rule.

To those colonies and territories which as a consequence of the late war have ceased to be under the sovereignty of the States which formerly governed them and which are inhabited by peoples not yet able to stand by themselves under the strenuous conditions of the modern world, there should be applied the principle that the well-being and development of such peoples form a sacred trust of civilisation and that securities for the performance of this trust should be embodied in this Covenant.

The tutelage of such peoples should be entrusted to advanced nations who can best undertake this responsibility, and who are willing to accept it, and that this tutelage should be exercised by them as Mandatories on behalf of the League.

Certain communities formerly belonging to the Turkish Empire have reached a stage of development where their existence as independent nations can be provisionally recognised subject to the rendering of administrative advice and assistance by a Mandatory until such time as they are able to stand alone. The wishes of these communities must be a principal consideration in the selection of the Mandatory.

The text of the League charter, much of which had been written by Wilson himself, was already a grave disappointment to the inhabitants of the regions under discussion. Wilson had raised hopes he could not and would not satisfy. Telegrams arrived in Paris, Washington, and London, arguing forcefully for independence and the application of the principles of self-determination and consent of the governed.

Rustum Haydar, Faysal's advisor, pointedly asked the delegates of the peace conference

What does the word mandate mean? We do not exactly know. I only wish to say that the nations in whose name I speak intend to remain free to choose the Power whose advice they will ask. Their right to decide their fate in the future has been recognized in principal. Very well! But you will allow me to say,

Gentlemen, that a secret agreement to dispose of these nations has been prepared, about which we have not been consulted. I ask the Assembly whether this state of things ought to exist or not. [26]

Clemenceau, sitting at the end of the table with Wilson at his right, ignored Rustum Haydar, and instead addressed a matter of mundane procedure before calling the day's session to a close. Rustum Haydar had quickly grasped that independence was out of the question and the matter of defining the meaning of mandate would fall to the mandatory power itself. Wilson, who also witnessed the speech, was a product of the segregated American South, and was perfectly accustomed to a colonialist hierarchy of humanity in which men who traced their lineage to the states of northern Europe would decide the destinies and best interests of less-evolved peoples.

Rustum Haydar, by contrast, hailed from a cosmopolitan Ottoman background and had been born in 1889 in Baalbak, near Damascus, in the shadow of the world's largest Roman temple. Haydar had received an elite Ottoman civil education starting with the state middle school in Baalbak, continuing at Maktab 'Anbar at Damascus, and the Mülkiye civil service academy at Istanbul. From there he had proceeded to Paris, where he attended the Sorbonne. Educated in Damascus, Istanbul, and Paris, fluent and cultured in Ottoman Turkish, Arabic, and French, he delivered his speech in French, which, like Arabic or Ottoman, Wilson would not have understood without the aid of an interpreter. [27]

Claims of "self-determination" for smaller nations, a principal Wilson and Lloyd George had adopted, perhaps unconsciously, perhaps cynically, from the speeches of Trotsky, was to form a core of justification for the peace settlement. Before it was decided how the regions placed under League of Nations mandate were to be guided and governed, their population should be surveyed to determine their level of political consciousness and aspirations. Wilson appointed a commission to query the wishes of the populations under discussion in Ottoman Syria. His British and French counterparts worked quietly to avoid any public consideration of the wishes of colonial subject populations, and considered the commission an example of Wilsonian foolishness. The British occupation forces were apparently successful in preventing a commission from visiting Iraq or Egypt, but in spring 1919 two prominent Americans embarked on a commission of enquiry in Ottoman Syria.

Henry King and Charles Crane arrived by steamship at Jaffa in June 1919. They spent the next forty-two days traveling through the region. Their itinerary is almost incomprehensibly nostalgic since they traversed without hindrance or delay, by car, train, and motor yacht, through what would become, under the colonial settlement, six separate states or entities, including Turkey, Syria, Israel, the Israeli-occupied West Bank, Gaza, Golan Heights, Lebanon, and Jordan. Despite the end of the Great War only months before, and the attending destruction and famine, the commission was able to drive by car in a period of two days from Haifa, to Acre, and Tyre, on to Nazereth, around Lake Tiberias, the Golan, and on to Damascus. The roads, ports, and rail lines were evidently in good and serviceable condition despite the official claim that the region was so undeveloped as to be "unable to stand on its own." Due to fortified national borders, resulting from the 1920 settlement, the Arab–Israeli conflict, and a long series of wars, no one has made such a trip for almost seven decades. Everywhere, the commission interviewed leading citizens. The commission visited thirty towns, meeting and interviewing prominent citizens, and received 1,863 petitions, many of which were duplicates in whole or in part. The majority (70–80 percent) of the petitions called for the territorial unity of greater Syria, absolute independence, and opposition to Zionism. Much smaller percentages indicated support for some form of mandate "assistance," and low single digits indicated support for direct mandates in Lebanon. Slightly less than 1 percent supported Zionism.[28]

British and French officials blocked the King–Crane commission report. The commission was not allowed to enter Iraq, and when its comprehensive report, complete with statistics, maps, and various analyses, was completed in August 1919, both governments ignored it and managed to convince Wilson to temporarily suppress it. Wilson had resolved to publish the report once the Senate had ratified the Paris Peace Treaty and joined the League of Nations. One of Wilson's advisors claimed the president had "clean forgotten" he had sent the commission in the first place, and a few weeks after the completion of the report, in late September and October, a series of strokes incapacitated Wilson, and neither the Peace Treaty nor membership in the League was ever ratified.[29] By the time the King–Crane report was finally published, more than three years later, France and Britain were fully entrenched and acknowledged as the League of Nations mandatory powers over Syria, Greater Lebanon, Iraq, Transjordan, and Palestine.[30]

The San Remo Conference and the Treaty of Sèvres

After the Paris Peace Conference Lloyd George changed his mind, and then changed his mind again. Though Clemenceau had conceded Mosul and Palestine, he understood Lloyd George had agreed to France's wish to receive coastal Syria and Cilicia up to the central Anatolian plateau in the region of Sivas. Lloyd George, meanwhile, had told Clemenceau that

those areas allotted to France would be handed over by the British occupation forces. Lloyd George wavered on whether, or how, he would
withdraw British forces from the French zone north of the Taurus
Mountains in the region of Adana and east toward the Euphrates.

Support for Faysal in Damascus was also contentious, and though
Lloyd George had promised Syria to Clemenceau, his government had
also promised it to Faysal, who was present in Damascus at the head of
the Arab government, supported by a British subsidy. Lloyd George and
the British government more generally refused to intervene on Faysal's
behalf with France, and Allenby urged Faysal to negotiate with the
French directly. Clemenceau and the colonial lobby in France would not
accept Faysal, and General Gouraud in Beirut refused to talk with him.
Robert de Caix wrote articles accusing Britain of cheating France out of
Syria, and paying undue attention to a "native government whose whole
endeavour is to provoke demonstrations" against France.[31] Lloyd George
decided Britain would leave Syria and Faysal would be on his own.

General Allenby, commander of the British occupation forces in
Ottoman, Greater Syria, decided to withdraw from those areas promised to France before French forces could arrive. Allenby expected
that nationalist forces and remnants of the Ottoman army would return
to the field, and that the only way to avoid being drawn into a resumption of war alongside the French forces would be to evacuate quickly
with no formal handover of authority.[32] Allenby decided to leave
Faysal, the Anatolian insurgents, and the French to themselves, and to
cut ties with all parties in order to hold Palestine. He imprisoned
Faysal's chief of staff Yasin al-Hashimi in Ramla in Palestine as a pre-
ventative measure, since al-Hashimi was the leading ex-Ottoman military figure in Syria, and the obvious leader of any serious movement of
armed opposition. Allenby ended Faysal's subsidy and removed the last
British personnel from Damascus in September 1919. At the end of
1919 Clemenceau had argued forcefully that if a peace with the
Ottomans was made in London, and if France remained in a subordinate position to Britain in the East, French prestige would shrink to
that of a power of the second rank, and his government could not retain
the confidence of the country. He would sooner resign.[33]

At San Remo, in April 1920, France and Britain assumed the League
of Nations mandates for Syria, Palestine, and Iraq respectively. The
borders of the mandate territories were still undefined, and had to
remain so until the final terms of the Ottoman surrender was negotiated. Two months before, however, in February, British troops had
evacuated Cilicia and French forces had occupied their positions. As
Allenby anticipated, various groups of renegade Ottoman soldiers in

Cilicia and coastal Syria engaged in combat against French forces. By the opening of the Treaty of Sèvres in August, a few months later, French forces had been defeated in Cilicia. A French army had defeated Faysal's forces outside Damascus and occupied the city.

The Treaty of Sèvres was intended to formalize the Ottoman surrender to Britain and France. The treaty would codify the arrangements between Britain and France made at San Remo and transfer legal title to the territories to be held as League of Nations mandates. But by the time the treaty convention met, France had been defeated and expelled from Cilicia, and had made an evacuation agreement with a renegade Anatolian government led by Mustafa Kemal Paşa and not recognized by the government in Istanbul, which had signed the armistice in 1918.

In Damascus during 1919, Ottoman generals Yasin al-Hashimi and Yusuf al-ᶜAzma had advised would-be British client King Faysal to prepare for military confrontation with France and Britain. Instead, Faysal visited Allenby and placed his hopes on the good will of Lloyd George while Allenby put Yasin al-Hashimi in jail. In May and June 1920, the upper Euphrates region of Iraq, claimed, but not occupied, by Britain, exploded in a major uprising, capturing several towns and defeating British garrisons. French General Gouraud sent an army east from Beirut and defeated Faysal's hastily prepared forces outside Damascus and forced him into exile in July 1920, ten months after Lloyd George abandoned him. The Anglo-French settlement was unraveling before it had been finalized.

The League of Nations and Anglo-French Colonialism in the Middle East

The public have misunderstood the powers of the League of Nations regarding mandates. Mandates were not the creation of the League, and they could not be altered by the League. The League's duties were confined to seeing that the terms of the mandates were in accordance with the decisions taken by the Allied Powers, and that in carrying out these mandates the Mandatory Powers should be under the supervision – not under the control – of the League.

A mandate was a self-imposed limitation by the conquerors on the sovereignty which they exercised over the conquered territory.

Arthur Lord Balfour, speech to the Council of the
League of Nations, June 1922[34]

The League of Nations moved to its new home in Geneva's Hôtel National in November 1920. The headquarters was in a central location on the alpine shores of Lake Geneva, and in sight of the perpetually snow-covered peaks of Mont Blanc. After President Wilson's death in 1924, the Hôtel National was renamed Palais Wilson, and in the late

1920s work began on the eventual home of the League of Nations on a donated park above the city and lake and across from Mont Blanc. The location, in a breathtakingly lovely place in the most tranquil and picturesque city, in the most important neutral European country, lent an air of peaceful, civilized, and optimistic industriousness to the work of the various commissions and councils.

Geneva was a fitting and appropriate home for an organization of such high hopes and fine idealistic principals. It is also sadly symbolic that the long-planned League of Nations headquarters, the *Palais des Nations*, high above the shores of the lake, surrounded by a vast park full of ancient trees, including many Lebanon cedars, was finally completed in 1936 in time for the Great Palestine Revolt, the Spanish Civil War, the Italian invasion of Ethiopia, and the German occupation of Central Europe, all of which conspired to doom the League of Nations to final irrelevance and oblivion. The grand building was nearly empty through the World War II, and eventually became the headquarters of the United Nations in Europe. The League of Nations library, a gift to the League from John D. Rockefeller Jr., serves today as the archives.

Woodrow Wilson had made the phrase "Consent of the Governed" the centerpiece of his political career and philosophy. Wilson had adopted the more radical-sounding phrase "self-determination" from Lloyd George, who borrowed it from Trotsky.[35] In declaring war on Germany in 1917 Wilson proclaimed "The world must be made safe for democracy. Its peace must be planted upon the tested foundations of political liberty." Wilson had opted not to include Austro-Hungary or the Ottoman State in his war declaration since neither state had menaced the US, but he had chosen, self-consciously and against wide criticism, to place his finger on the scale of the European balance of power, guaranteeing an eventual British and French victory in Europe. Wilson's politics exemplified the idea of consent and of popular sovereignty as the basis of all state legitimacy. As his own experience in denying rights to African-Americans in the American south demonstrated, however, the practice was more complicated than the theory. Rarely was the gap between liberal theory and political practice wider than in the League of Nations Middle East mandates.

British and French policy-makers worried the new League of Nations mandatory regime would place limits on their rule in the new territories. British diplomats negotiating the San Remo Conference in April 1920 agreed that the best situation would be for the League to draft the mandate treaties for each country, and submit the drafts to the mandatory powers for approval. If the League of Nations drafted the treaties it would avoid the perception that colonial powers were drafting their own colonial treaties, to be merely rubber-stamped by the new League of Nations

Mandates Commission. "If the Allies in conference distribute the mandates among themselves and then draft the conditions on which they will take them, it will enhance the impression (current already in some quarters) that mandates are merely 'whitewashed' annexation," noted a British diplomat.[36] French diplomats by contrast, were worried that they would be somehow tricked or out-maneuvered by the Mandates Commission, and perhaps by the British, and that ceding control of the treaty-drafting process would damage the admittedly tenuous French position.[37] The result was stasis, and it took eighteen months for the mandatory governments to finally submit their mandate treaties to the League of Nations. Once the treaties were submitted, the Mandate Section scheduled the first Mandates Commission meeting for October 1921.[38]

The Mandate Section was organized in early 1920, but the small staff of typists, secretaries, and translators had to wait to convene the first meeting of the permanent Mandates Commission. William Rappard took the job as director of the Mandate Section and member of the Mandate Commission. (See Figure 2.3.) The Commission comprised

Figure 2.3. Mandates Section Staff. William Rappard at right, *c*.1922 (League of Nations Archive, w/permission)

Figure 2.4. Mandates Commission, *c.*1922 (League of Nations Archive, w/permission)

nine appointed members, one each from Britain and France, and other countries occupying mandates. The Mandate Commission members from mandatory countries were called "accredited representatives." (See Figure 2.4.) The Commission was supposed to review and comment on the treaties and reports submitted by the powers, but at first neither Britain nor France was in a hurry to provide the treaty or reports. Meanwhile, petitions in their hundreds streamed into the mail room at Geneva.

Rappard was a Harvard-trained political economist who, though belonging to an old Geneva family, was born and grew up partly in New York. He had served as a member of the Swiss delegation to the Peace Conference and had met Wilson there. Wilson so admired Rappard that their personal relationship influenced the decision to base the new League of Nations at Geneva. Rappard was equally at home in the two official languages of the League, French and English, and as a Swiss citizen, he had not served in the government of any of the Great Powers, though he was an international lawyer and academic of increasing renown. He approached the work of the League of Nations with critical neutrality that his British and French colleagues rarely shared.

In January 1920, as the Mandate Section began its work, the *Manchester Guardian* published a report titled "The Problem of the Mandates." The article was read, annotated, discussed, and preserved in the first archives of the Mandate Section. The article identified the flaws of the mandate regime before its launch, and its annotations show Rappard was aware of the pitfalls that eventually doomed the mandatory arrangement. The article noted that collisions between the Great Powers over their desires to dominate weaker countries were a central cause of the war, and that the League of Nations should limit these conflicts. The League of Nations could mark an advance from an atmosphere of competitive predation between strong and weak countries to one of protection. In contrast to old imperialism, perhaps the strong could work together to protect the weak. But why, the report asked, should the new "international protectorates," or mandates, not be under the impartial and international control of the League itself, instead of the old imperial powers, and why do the former territories of the Ottoman Empire require any tutelage at all except for the most informal and disinterested advice?

The writer blamed President Wilson for what seemed likely to be a miscarriage of justice and missed opportunity. The writer noted that Britain and France had a long history of rivalry and tangled interests in the region of their mandates, and that the League of Nations could do nothing to dull the competition. "The Anglo-French Agreement of 1916 (Sykes–Picot) is still extant and neither government has had the courage to denounce it, and its ugly but precise features." Claims of disinterested altruism notwithstanding, the writer noted, "Mesopotamia is an outpost for the defense of India, and the Admiralty covets its untapped oil. As for Palestine, Lord Curzon declared in a speech a few weeks ago that we could not give up Egypt (a protectorate) because it was necessary for the defense of Palestine (a mandate), and that he considered Palestine in the strategic system of the British Empire." France also had interests in railways and silk, and the church in its mandates.

The *Guardian* noted the wishes of the populations had never been considered, despite mandate language requiring this consideration. Mandates would succeed only if the relationship between mandatory and citizens was precisely defined, and if the League of Nations had oversight and the ability to challenge or end the mandate. Secretary General Sir Eric Drummond's office noted that the proposal for a regularized inspection regime was "alarming," and sure to provoke opposition.[39]

Despite the refusal to allow mandatory citizens to take part in League of Nations discussions, hundreds of petitions, letters, and telegrams began to arrive before anyone had considered what to do with them.

The accredited representatives of Britain and France at Geneva considered such correspondence from their mandatory charges a great nuisance and made clear their wish to dispose of petitions unread and unconsidered. In this hope they were unsuccessful, and though many considered the written protests deeply irritating, it was a singular feature of the mandate regime that they could not be simply thrown away. The presence of an ever-growing number of protests brought the gap between mandate theory and practice into immediate and stark relief.

Both mandate and League of Nations officials knew little about Ottoman governance and were apparently unaware of the historical role of petitions in the Ottoman state. But Ottoman subjects had been interacting with their government by petition for centuries. In the early modern period the Ottoman sultan, in common with most monarchs, legitimated his rule by claiming a divine dispensation. The state, like earlier Islamic kingdoms, based the dispensation on the sovereign's role as guarantor of justice. The Ottoman "Circle of Justice" spelled out societal obligations in a comprehensive theory of state. The state dispensed and guaranteed justice to the state's subjects, thereby assuring security and prosperity.

Petitioners routinely made reference to the role and importance of justice in the relation between sovereign and subject, and commonly called upon the sultan to be aware that this or that official was denying or degrading the justice the state guaranteed. After 1908, petitions were often couched in terms of constitutional rights, parliament, and citizenship, and the scope of possible complaints and expectations of redress, expanded dramatically.[40] In 1920, bags of petitions took the mandates' new masters by unpleasant surprise.

The earliest petitions to the League of Nations were in opposition to Zionism, the Balfour Declaration, and the assignment of French and British mandates in Syria and Palestine. The leading Ottoman politician of Jerusalem, Musa Kazim al-Husayni, wrote in December 1920, and repeatedly over the following months. He identified himself as "the legal representative of all classes and communities of the Palestinian Arab People." He wished to remind Great Britain of the pledges given to Sharif Husayn, and emphasized his people's opposition to the establishment of a Jewish national home in Palestine. Al-Husayni protested for the rights of Palestinians to determine the destiny and direction of their own country.[41] His letters were polite, and dignified, but his expression in English left something to be desired.

Musa Kazim al-Husayni was a distinguished veteran Ottoman statesman, a former provincial governor, and parliamentary representative, and mayor of Jerusalem. When al-Husayni addressed protestors at a demonstration in Jerusalem against the San Remo Conference in April 1920, he was fired as mayor and briefly imprisoned. Forcibly retired, he turned to full-time international political advocacy for the cause of Palestine. Musa Kazim made many trips to London and Geneva, as chairman of the Arab Executive Committee in Palestine.[42]

The Executive Committee of the Syrian–Palestinian Congress formed the main exile advocacy group for the population of Syria and Palestine. From exile in Europe Shakib Arslan had become the congress' leading figure. After fleeing the allied occupation of Istanbul in November 1918, he stayed in Berlin in the company of a handful of other exiled Ottoman politicians. He spent the next few years a mostly homeless exile, living in hotels in Berlin, Switzerland, and for a time in Moscow, and eventually back to Istanbul, where he learned he had few friends and fewer options left. The French occupation made it impossible for him to return to Syria or Lebanon, and French authorities explicitly barred him. Between early 1924 and 1925 he lived sporadically with his family in exile in Mersin in Turkey near the northern border with the Syrian mandate. He collected petitions and wrote an endless stream of Arabic and French articles, letters, and editorials. He also tried to arouse Mustafa Kemal to support opposition to the Anglo-French settlement and possible reattachment of the mandate territories to Anatolia. Kemal was unmoved.[43] Arslan traveled repeatedly to Geneva after 1919, and lived there in exile for two decades after 1925, often in difficult financial and personal circumstances.

Rappard was unsure how to deal with the seemingly endless protests. Rustum Haydar had identified the problem during the Paris Peace Conference: the League of Nations charter defined a mandate loosely, but neither the rights of the mandatory citizens nor the limits on the power of the mandatory power were defined. Rappard wrote League of Nations Secretary General Sir Eric Drummond for guidance. Drummond, a veteran of the British Foreign Office and a member of the Liberal Party, was not interested in the protests from the new mandates, and ignored repeated requests from Rappard for clarification over the space of two years. Rappard proposed that letters and petitions be formally acknowledged and forwarded to the Mandates Commission.

I cannot bring myself to feel that we are doing our full duty toward the inhabitants of these territories. Their protests are certainly often naïve and badly worded, but I do feel that they can make out a strong case against the way in which they have been and are being treated by France and Great Britain, as well as against the League of Nations ... I think that we should not forget that in the course of the war these populations were promised national independence and that the Covenant recognizes their right to be consulted.[44]

Figure 2.5.   Syrian–Palestinian Congress, August 1921, Arslan at right
(League of Nations Archive, w/permission)

Drummond replied with irritation. The number of petitions was in
the hundreds, and they had become increasingly pointed in their rea-
soning and charges. "The *wishes of the inhabitants* is only the concern of
the mandatory power and not the council. I have continually stated that
I do not think that documents such as these, which contain absurd alle-
gations should be circulated." [45]

In August 1921 Shakib Arslan organized and convened the first
Syrian–Palestinian Congress with a group of ten Arab Ottoman intellectuals at a Geneva hotel. (See Figure 2.5.) Arslan timed the congress to
correspond with the first meeting of the Mandate Commission in
October. The ten comprised a cross-section of Ottoman Arab elites in
their education, backgrounds, and sectarian diversity, including prominent Muslim religious scholars, Christian financiers, and Arslan, a politician and professional essayist. The group elected Arslan secretary, and
resident representative in Geneva. The congress was funded by wealthy
landowner Michael Lutfallah, and included in the Executive Rashid
Rida, Ihsan al-Jabiri, Suleyman al-Kinᶜan, and a variable list of other
prominent Syrians, most of whom lived in exile in Cairo or Europe.

The 1921 meeting produced a detailed pamphlet intended for discussion at the Mandate Commission meeting. The pamphlet argued that the actions of the mandatory powers had proved the League of Nations was powerless to protect the rights of mandatory citizens, and that the mandatory states had prevented citizens from travel to attend international meetings, and placed insurmountable barriers to the free movement of information about conditions within the countries.

If the League is unable to cancel these mandates, to declare us independent and to accept us into its body as it accepted Georgia, Estonia, Lithuania, Latvia, Albania, and Armenia, which are neither more developed nor more important than we are, all we ask is to not subscribe to mandates.[46]

Arslan recognized that the justification for mandates was based on an unspoken racial and religious hierarchy, which qualified Christian Europeans for independence, and Muslim Arabs for rule by mandate. Yet racial hierarchies were subordinate to imperial strategy. The racialized theories of mandatory rule were ideologically calibrated to advance the policies and strategic imperatives of empire. The will to power came first, and the racial hierarchy was devised to legitimate it.

Shortly before the Syrian–Palestinian Congress opened its conference, a delegation visited Permanent Mandates section head William Rappard. Prominent Islamic jurist and intellectual Rashid Rida led the group and did the talking but needed translation. Rappard knew the League of Nations General Secretary Eric Drummond had denied their request to address the commission, and that their pamphlet would not be read or discussed by the Mandates Council. Rappard drafted a report on the discussion, which was included in the file for the members of the Mandates Commission.

The Syrian people had great confidence in the League of Nations. The attitude of the mandatory powers in Syria and Palestine is intolerable and tends to undermine this confidence. The League of Nations should send an impartial Commission of Enquiry to the country. A representative congress of Syrians should be allowed to meet officially to discuss a form of government, and to choose the mandatory power and the content of the mandate. Otherwise the Syrian people will never be satisfied and their faith in the Covenant will disappear.

The main grievances presented were that the mandatory powers, far from seeking to establish the Syrian people as an independent nation, oppressed them in every way. They had never been consulted about the choice of the mandatory, and it would soon become evident to every impartial visitor that the attitude of the mandatory powers in Syria and Palestine was most exasperating to the great majority of the inhabitants. France was treating Syria absolutely as if she were one of her North African colonies, abrogating old laws and promulgating new ordinances without any regard for the wishes of the people ...

Great Britain was carrying out the Balfour Declaration and pursuing a land policy which was contrary to the wishes, rights, and interests of the Arab population.

The delegation insisted they deserved and could be satisfied with
nothing but independence. Rappard asked why, in that case, should
they present their case before the League of Nations rather than before
the Powers? They claimed the "League of Nations stood for political
honesty and justice." As political exiles they had been unable to receive
any kind of meaningful hearing from the mandate authorities, banned
as they were, or in Paris or London. Telegrams arrived from America
and elsewhere in hopeful support of the delegation. "Thousands of
Syrians respectfully request your worthy support to the Syrian conference now at Geneva, Syrian national Society, Boston."[47]

The first Mandates Commission meeting finally took place in
October 1921. The Mandates Commission comprised nine appointees,
all Europeans except for a Japanese diplomat, and all experts in colonial administration.[48] Rappard's Mandates Section was in charge of
day-to-day correspondence and management at Geneva. The Mandates
Commission met twice a year to review the annual mandatory reports
and hear and question the "accredited representatives."[49] Drummond's
position on petitions prevailed and a detailed and tremendously complicated procedure was devised to limit petitions and curtail the ability of
mandatory citizens to challenge the mandatory power or represent their
countries at Geneva. Rappard's protests went in vain, but he continued
to write reports on petitions and interviews, which were entered into
the Mandates Commission record and discussed.

In order to be considered worthy of submission to the Mandates
Commission, petitions had to be deemed "receivable." Receivable petitions could not contain complaints incompatible with the provisions of
the mandate, be anonymous, or repeat charges covered in any other
petition. Finally all petitions from inside the territory had to be submitted first to the mandate authorities. Petitions from outside could be
sent directly to the League of Nations. The secretary general would
acknowledge all petitions. Even if a petition was deemed "receivable,"
the Mandate Commission could do no more than ask for a reply from
the mandate power accredited representative on the Commission. The
Mandate Commission did not have the power to investigate complaints,
or require any action on the mandatory power.[50]

The system was designed to make self-representation by mandate
citizens impossible. The requirement that petitions be submitted first
to local mandate officials caused a sharp decline in correspondence.
Petitioners would receive a form letter informing them that "all

petitions emanating from inhabitants of mandated territories must be forwarded to the Secretariat of the League through the intermediary of the mandate Power."[51] Petitions from outside continued to arrive, however, and the Mandate Commission, and more often than not, Rappard himself, continued to ask the accredited representatives to reply to them.[52] The possibility that mandate authorities would fail to forward complaints about their own administrations went unmentioned.

For most of the next two decades the system functioned and the two accredited representatives remained constant. Lord Frederick Lugard represented Britain and Count Robert de Caix represented France. Both de Caix and Lugard were experienced colonial administrators. Lugard was the architect and theorist of cost-controlled indirect colonial rule innovated in Africa, which also came to dominate in Iraq. De Caix was the secretary general of the first French Mandate regime and the architect of the French strategy of separating Syria and Lebanon into sectarian cantons or statelets, limiting the possibility of unified nationalist movements, and sponsoring Christian minorities over Muslim majorities. De Caix is mostly forgotten, but he was the single most important French colonial policy-maker during the mandate.

In mid 1922 Jamal al-Husayni, the young nephew of Musa Kazim al-Husayni, sent a lengthy petition under the imprint of the Palestinian Arab Congress. Jamal al-Husayni had attended the Syrian Protestant College (American University of Beirut since 1920), and had been educated in English. Husayni's letter was well-written and researched and carefully argued in form and content, and made several points: The Palestine Mandate was overwhelmingly inhabited by a Muslim and Christian Arab majority. Many among the population could trace their local ancestry back centuries, and it had been an Arab country for at least 1,500 years. The population had lived under the authority of the Ottoman State for four centuries, with a high degree of local autonomy, and what Husayni termed perfect harmony and total freedom of faith, practice, and education. "The inhabitants of all races and religious beliefs participated on a basis of equality in the election of local officials and representatives."

Jamal al-Husayni quoted from the Husayn–McMahon correspondence, and argued that the British pledge to Sharif Husayn, which clearly included Palestine, preceded the Balfour Declaration, and was therefore legally binding over the Balfour Declaration. He cited the Covenant of the League of Nations, and pointed out that the Balfour Declaration was in clear contradiction to the terms of the League of Nations mandate. The mandatory power sponsored Zionist colonization against the wishes of the native inhabitants whose rights it pledged to uphold as legal guardian, in what the League charter called a "sacred trust of civilization."[53] Rappard acknowledged the letter, but it is unlikely anyone else on the Mandate Commission read the petition, since coming directly from Jerusalem, within the mandate, it would not have been "receivable."

The petition procedure placed the indigenous inhabitants of Syria, Lebanon, Palestine, and Iraq at a disadvantage since they had few international advocates, while the Zionist movement, which was led by influential Europeans, had a great advantage in its ability to lobby the League and make its voice heard. And yet, a small number of former Ottoman Arabs, led over the decades by Shakib Arslan, managed a sustained effort to lobby the League of Nations from exile in Europe and elsewhere.

Mandate Governance in Practice

Colonial functionaries in Britain and France envisioned their mandates as colonies and conquered territory. They conceded little to the League of Nations Permanent Mandates Commission, and even less to indigenous political leaders. When concessions were granted, they were invariably cosmetic and calculated to win praise in metropolitan newspapers and Geneva. The British government had specific goals in Transjordan and Iraq (and Egypt) having to do with military bases, secure communications, and oil concessions. These priorities were eventually obtained by treaty. The contradictions of the Palestine Mandate were more difficult to reconcile and placed greater, and eventually unsustainable, demands on the British Mandate administration and the treasury. France's mandates in Syria and Lebanon were also more complicated, troublesome, and expensive, tangled up as they were in various strands of French national myth-making and nationalist ideology.

Acceptance of the modest demands of the Mandates Commission varied. British functionaries immediately understood the bureaucratic appetite for reports, and flooded Geneva with an endless stream of paper in response to every query, however minor. French functionaries were less self-confident and refused requests for specific information or replies to petitions for nearly a decade. The annual reports for Syria and Lebanon for 1920 through 1926 under-reported every kind of disorder and repression. Under the pressure of international opprobrium surrounding the Syrian revolt of 1925–7, French reports became gradually more comprehensive. Persistent negative press coverage tainted the British in Iraq in 1920, France in Syria in 1920 and 1925, and Britain in Palestine in the 1920s and through the 1930s. Such negative publicity came at a price that British and French politicians were often reluctant to pay.

The tactics, goals, and intentions of colonial rule changed over time. All of the mandate states began their existence under some form of military occupation and direct rule. Only Palestine functioned as a settler colony, where an indigenous majority was marginalized and disenfranchised in favor of the immigrant minority. Despite optimistic initial intentions, direct rule was too expensive, and too unpopular – both in the imperial capital and in the colony, and the other four mandates developed varieties of indirect rule, albeit with ultimate authority resting with colonial officials in most areas involving security, politics, and law.

Lebanon and Syria eventually became indirectly ruled colonial-constitutional republics, while Iraq and Transjordan quickly became indirectly ruled colonial-constitutional monarchies. British officials secured their durable interests in petroleum, access to military installations, imperial security, and communications by a series of unpopular treaties imposed on the ruling monarch and parliament in both countries, as they had also done in Egypt. King Faysal in Iraq, Prince ʿAbadallah in Transjordan, and King Fuad in Egypt thus owed their positions to a delicate balance between imperial power and popular support, generally tilted toward serving British interests. France was more ambitious and less successful in securing its interests by treaty, due in part to the more ideological character of what constituted French interests.

Indirect rule in Palestine and Greater Lebanon was based on the expectation that Zionists and Lebanese Christians would prove loyal and reliable colonial subjects. The mandate granted Zionists and Maronite Christians economic and political domination and conditional possession of states of their own, literally carved out of the territory of the majority indigenous population. In return, the colonial client populations served as instruments of policy for the colonial state. But metropolitan colonial advocates did not describe the colonial patron–client relationship between metropole and colony as one based on common interests, but in self-affirming ideological terms: the Zionists in Palestine and the Christians in Lebanon supported the colonial power not because their interests dictated, but because their racial, cultural, and civilizational status was superior to that of the majority populations. Bluntly stated, they were more "civilized," and thus higher on the racial hierarchy than other colonial subjects. In a perverse twist, the influx of Jewish refugees from Germany after 1933 brought fiscal solvency to the Palestine Mandate administration, and probably temporarily postponed an official British disengagement from Palestine.

The Mandates Commission had no power to influence events or dictate policy, but always received blame for the distasteful consequences of colonial policing, counter insurgency, and policy generally. Crises demanded changes in mandate governance, and revolts in Iraq in 1920, and Syria in the mid 1920s, brought a shift toward indirect rule. But changes in governance came in response to various types of political pressure, and not in answer to any advocacy on the part of the League of Nations. British and French politicians and colonial functionaries were never compelled to take the League seriously or change policy at its behest.

On the other hand, the Mandates Commission and international attention compelled the creation of quasi-representative institutions not previously associated with colonial rule. In keeping with the racial and cultural paternalism of the time, the mandates were styled as educational operations between master nations and student nations. The mandatory state derived its legitimacy from the idea that it was a representative state of a "national people" in formation. The definition of the "national people" was contentious from the outset as the British Mandate identified European Jewish immigrants as a "nation" in their newly formed homeland under the Balfour Declaration, and the French Mandate identified Arab Christians as the preferred "nation" in formation. The Great Power effort to fragment and indirectly annex Ottoman territory through the manipulation of the "national question" had its origin in the period between the Crimean War in the 1850s and the Congress of Berlin in 1878.

Both British and French mandates claimed to foster representative government for those ex-Ottoman populations most receptive to mandate rule. The Mandates Commission applied modest pressure on the mandatory states to provide evidence of tutelage. Mandate governments decreed constitutions, elections, and supposedly representative institutions, always making the deceptive claim that such innovations were unprecedented in the region.

The representative character of such institutions was defective relative to the previous Ottoman system. Moreover, mandate functionaries rarely acknowledged the existence of previous Ottoman representative institutions. No functionary of the mandate system, or metropolitan politician, could admit the fact that Ottoman citizens had drafted constitutions, elected local and parliamentary representatives, negotiated laws, and state policies, and addressed petitions and grievances to the state's representatives for decades before League of Nations mandatory tutelage arrived on the scene. Where Ottoman governors and institutions of state had been accessible, at least to some citizens, the office of mandate High Commissioner was designed to remotely control every aspect of the state and to be completely inaccessible.

Consequently, High Commissioners in British Palestine, and Iraq, and French Syria and Lebanon, canceled and voided elections, dismissed and

jailed politicians, and had veto power over all laws, including every constitutional draft law. The office of the High Commissioner decided and
implemented administrative divisions, and election districts. The colonial
archives are mostly silent on the shadowy aspects of mandatory rule such
as extra-judicial detention, torture, collective punishment, assassinations,
and executions of critics and challengers of the mandatory regimes.
Uncounted thousands of petitions alleging such abuses were dispatched
to the Mandates Commission, but serious investigations could not take
place without the cooperation of the Mandate authorities. The Mandate
Commission had little appetite for such investigations anyway. The application of martial law, detention without charge, trials, prison sentences,
and executions could all be ordered or commuted at the whim of the
High Commissioner, habits that have continued as a feature of Middle
East legal regimes since the colonial period. The League of Nations performed the unenviable service of shrouding such practices in a façade of
international legalism and phony representative government.

The Mandate in Palestine

Herbert Samuel was the first British High Commissioner in Palestine.
Samuel arrived in Palestine even before the Treaty of Sèvres formally
transferred title for the Palestine Mandate from the Ottoman state to
the mandate power and League of Nations in mid-summer 1920.
Samuel had been a successful British politician and had advocated
British sponsorship of Zionism in the years before the Balfour
Declaration. Samuel envisioned and designed an indirectly ruled colonial state, run and policed by an integrated Zionist–Arab civilian
administration and overseen by British colonial officials and police.
    The problem with the conception was its unrepresentative bifurcated
structure. The two communities within the colonial state were to take
part in native rule on a supposedly equal footing. This despite the fact
that the indigenous majority comprised 85 percent of the population,
and the immigrant minority was of European origin and was officially
recognized both by the Balfour Declaration and the League of Nations
as possessing special rights to the colonial territory. The mandate charter
codified these special rights in July 1922, and named the Zionist Agency
official representative of the Jews of Palestine. In influence, access, and
internationally acknowledged rights, there was thus a basic asymmetry
between the Arabs and Zionists in Palestine.[54] British colonial functionaries envisioned Zionist settlers as a loyal colonial client population.
    British military and colonial officials had already worked to hobble
Arab political opposition to British rule. In the months before the

inauguration of the mandate and the arrival of Samuel, British military governor Ronald Storrs dismissed the mayor of Jerusalem, Musa Kazim al-Husayni. Husayni was the senior and most distinguished Ottoman civil servant of the most prominent Jerusalem family. Storrs immediately placed his finger on the scale of Palestinian politics when he appointed Raghib al-Nashshashibi, a member of a rival Jerusalem family, mayor to succeed Musa Kazim.

Herbert Samuel intended to forestall the Zionist dream of an independent Jewish state, and deny Palestinians their wish for an unpartitioned independent regional state. Zionist leaders insisted on equal representation with Arabs in every state institution, in spite of their comparatively tiny numbers. The Zionists, disappointed as they were in Samuel's intentions, endorsed the mandatory regime and participated fully in governing the mandate. The World Zionist Organization was born as a European lobbying movement, and in 1921 formed the Zionist Executive (later the Jewish Agency) to lead the Zionist National Assembly and represent the Zionist movement and population in the Palestine Mandate. In this form the Zionist Agency was accepted by the League of Nations and the mandate authority as the legitimate representative of the Jewish population of Palestine.

By contrast, neither the Palestinian Arab Congress, nor the Arab Executive it formed, were ever recognized as representative bodies by the mandate or the League of Nations. Shortly after his dismissal as mayor of Jerusalem, Musa Kazim al-Husayni was elected chairman of the nine member Arab Executive committee. The Arab leadership, almost entirely educated under, and acculturated to, the Ottoman system, was at a disadvantage from the outset. Samuel and succeeding officials never recognized the right of self-representation, and the mandate government refused to accept Palestinian governing bodies unless they first endorsed both the mandate and the Balfour Declaration – a pattern that has prevailed till this day in relations between Zionists and Palestinians.

Palestinian leaders, including Musa Kazim al-Husayni himself, traveled to London and Geneva to present their case to the British government and the League of Nations. Inevitably they found that their interlocutors did not accept their basic right of self-representation, and that advocates for the Zionist state had been there first. While ex-Ottoman statesmen traveled to European capitals to press their case, supporters of Zionism like US Supreme Court Justice Louis Brandeis and Albert Einstein, among many others, made passionate appeals on behalf of Zionist colonization. Shakib Arslan knew better than most that success in lobbying depended on access.

The Mandate in Syria and Lebanon

French colonialism in the Middle East began and ended as a military affair. The first High Commissioner, General Henri Gouraud, appointed in October 1919, was also the commander of the Army of the Levant. Generals Maxime Weygand and Maurice Sarrail followed Gouraud between 1923 and late 1925, when in the midst of the Syrian Revolt, Sarrail was removed, and Henry de Jouvenel, a civilian politician and journalist, stepped in to salvage the mandate. Civilian diplomat Henri Ponsot succeeded de Jouvenel in 1926, and was the longest-serving High Commissioner, between 1926 and 1933. The last civilian diplomat High Commissioner, Damian de Martel, arrived in late 1933, negotiated a never-ratified treaty with Syrian politicians in 1936, and left Syria after the beginning of the World War II in October 1939. His successor, military intelligence officer Henri Dentz, who was pressed into service as Vichy High Commissioner, allowed German access to mandate ports and airfields, and was eventually sentenced to death for collaboration with the Nazis.

Gouraud and his General Secretary and chief strategist Robert de Caix established the principal patterns of the French mandatory regime in Syria and Lebanon. As noted above, de Caix served as the accredited representative to the League of Nations for the French Mandate between 1924 and 1939. The mandate government identified educated Ottoman Muslim Arabs of the cities as its main enemies, and sectarian minorities and rural populations as its potential allies, in subduing and ruling the country. The members of the minorities were arranged in a hierarchy with Lebanese Maronite Christians in alliance with Jesuit priests at the top, followed by the other Christian rites, ᶜAlawite, and Druze Muslims, and Bedouin.

Two months after the conquest of Damascus, in September 1920, General Gouraud announced the formation of the State of Greater Lebanon with its capital at Beirut. The state would take its place as the Maronite homeland, based on an expansion of the Ottoman autonomous governate of Mount Lebanon (*mutasarrifiyya Jabal Lubnan*) from about 5,000 to 10,450 square kilometers.[55] The Ottoman State had formed the governate of Mount Lebanon in 1860 after the Druze-Maronite war that brought unwelcome French and British intervention. Famous mid-century Ottoman statesman Fuad Paşa intended to create a semi-autonomous Maronite state in order to limit potential sectarian conflict and keep France out of Ottoman affairs. Gouraud and de Caix considered the Maronite clergy France's greatest local allies, and so consulted them about the new arrangement. They desired a larger

Lebanon, under Christian domination, to include Beirut, the fertile plain of Biqa^c and the mountains surrounding it to the north, east, and south. The problem with this territorial dream was the dilution of a Maronite majority in an expanded territory. Gouraud and De Caix placed Maronites in a dominant position despite their numbers.

When General Gouraud declared the existence of Greater Lebanon he also announced a fifteen-member Administrative Council organized by sect, and 66 percent dominated by Christians. The council was organized by religion and locale and Gouraud appointed its members. When General Gouraud selected his Administrative Council, he ignored the existing Ottoman Administrative Council. The Ottoman administration had included a Christian governor, always originating from outside Lebanon, and a loose representative structure in which each district was supposed to be represented on the Administrative Council by a member of the "dominant sect." Modifications could be made, and in practice the representative usually came from the leading family of the districts, with less regard for religion than status and position.[56] The Ottoman pre-war council resented their exclusion and objected strongly to the mandate. Seven of the twelve members wrote a petition to the League of Nations, and protested the expansion of Lebanon, the French Mandate, and the denial of the full independence they felt they deserved. Among the signatories were the most prominent Christians in the country, including Saad Allah Hoyek, the brother of the Maronite Patriarch, the leading pro-French figure and supporter of General Gouraud's plan.[57] They pointed out that under Ottoman rule they had enjoyed great autonomy.

How could the colonial power assure its Christian clients political domination as a sectarian minority? A doctored census and sectarian electoral roles followed shortly, but the acknowledged result was a Muslim majority colonial state under the control of indigenous Christians with a colonial sponsor.[58] The system of sectarian proportional representation and the division of Lebanon into seventeen separate and legally defined sectarian communities was an invention of Robert de Caix and has prevailed in Lebanon until the present. Lebanese of all religions regularly denounce sectarian proportional representation, but the country seems to be stuck with it, along with many other lesser-known colonial institutions.

Having defeated Faysal's army, conquered Syria, occupied Damascus, and invented Lebanon during summer 1920, Gouraud and de Caix turned their attention to arranging Syria's regions and religions. The colonial idea of protecting eastern Christians from the imagined savagery of their Arab Muslim neighbors was more complicated in inland Syria. Damascus, Aleppo, Hama, and Homs all had large, cultured, multi-religious elite families who expected to exert their influence on local and regional politics as they had done as Ottoman provincial elites. People like Shakib Arslan, Musa Kazim al-Husayni, Yusuf al-ʿAzma, Faris al-Khuri, and Rustum Haydar were representatives of such families. A strategy emerged of separating the troublesome cities from rural areas, which were expected to be more quiescent and more easily convinced of the benefits of French rule.

Robert de Caix designed the partition of the Syrian Mandate into five separate micro-states, each with a specific sectarian majority, beginning after the occupation of Damascus and Aleppo in summer 1920.[59] First the two major cities were separated and governed separately by an appointed native governor with French military advisors. In 1922 the State of Jabal Druze was formed in a mostly Druze region south of Damascus, and the coastal mountain area north of Greater Lebanon was declared the territory (later state) of the Alawites. Later that same year, the major cities of Damascus, Aleppo, Homs and Hama were brought back together in an entity called the Syrian Federation, mostly for reasons of economizing on direct rule.

Under Ottoman rule both Damascus and Aleppo had been separate provincial capitals, and they had never been united within one administrative unit. The Ottoman Wilayat Suriyya with its capital of Damascus had extended from Hama to the Red Sea port of ʻAqaba. The Wilayat of Allepo ran north from Hama to east central Anatolia. The Wilayat of Beirut had encompassed the coastal regions from what is today the Turkish–Syria border to just north of today's Tel Aviv-Jaffa. In 1924 the region around Antakya and the historic port of Iskandarun were separated from Aleppo and became the autonomous Sanjak of Alexandretta. Alexandretta with its strategic location and mixed Turkish- and Arabic-speaking population was set aside as a future bargaining chip to be used in maintaining friendly relations with the emerging Turkish Republic.[60]

De Caix perceived the society of the region in simple terms melding sectarianism and French colonial interests seamlessly. The Uniate Christians were reliable "friends of France," and should be rewarded accordingly. The rural heterodox Muslims were isolated from the major cities and should remain so, governed by their tribal leaders with a strong guiding French hand. The major cities were the preserve of Muslim nationalist Sharifian extremists, who should be ruled directly, closely dominated, and kept from spreading their contagion of nationalism and fanaticism to other regions. De Caix saw urban Muslims and ex-Ottoman elites as what he called "nationalist extremists" and consequently potential clients of Great Britain, the imperial ally and rival that provoked endless official anxiety. French sponsorship of Arab Christians opposed to Arab nationalism fit neatly into this schema.

French Mandate policies and politics remained relatively constant in the first years of the mandate. Things changed, however, with the election of a leftist coalition in France in 1925 and the appointment of a leftist and anti-clericalist High Commissioner. After the costly and destructive suppression of the Great Revolt in 1926 and 1927, mandate policy came to be driven by fiscal retrenchment and the more indirect forms of rule over Aleppo and Damascus came to prevail, coupled with a fully militarized though somewhat remote structure of intelligence and repression. The more optimistic and ideological claims for mandate rule faded away.

Under Robert de Caix's guidance, the French mandates began as a more ideological undertaking than the British mandates. At the outset, mandate officials announced that they would institute a new legal system, regularize land tenure and survey all landed property, regularize taxation and customs, and build modern infrastructure. Direct rule and colonial ideology meant the wholesale rejection of much of the Ottoman governing apparatus. By the end of the mandate twenty-six years later, most of these plans had long been abandoned and forgotten, but some lasting changes had materialized. The mandate had been endowed with an authoritarian executive in the office of the High Commissioner, and an overriding legal structure of martial law and unchecked intelligence services answering directly to the High Commissioner.[61]

Infrastructural improvements had mostly served military ends in the form of paved roads, airfields, and other communication and transportation structures. Land tenure, taxation, and educational reforms had been mostly still-born. The announcement of such wholesale reform in 1920 took place in an atmosphere of ignorance and ideological self-delusion, ignorance of the existing Ottoman system, and self-delusion about the motives and capabilities of the colonial power.

The Mandate in Iraq and Transjordan

Iraq emerged a British-sponsored Hashimite monarchy and Transjordan a Hashimite principality in 1921. The deeply unpopular repression of the Iraqi revolt of 1920 led Colonial Secretary Winston Churchill to push through a plan to place Faysal on a hastily arranged Iraqi throne, and his brother Abdallah, already encamped in Amman, as prince of the newly created British protectorate, the principality of Transjordan.

The plan solved several vexing problems at once: the troublesome former wartime allies of the Hashimite family would be allowed to take some consolation from their loss of Syria and Arabia, and continue to serve the British Empire, and the impossible expense of direct rule would be decreased by a much cheaper structure of indirect rule. British strategic interests would be preserved, but at much lower cost from the treasury and with less political opposition in London. The overriding concerns of imperial security and communications between the Mediterranean, the Persian Gulf, and India, and petroleum concessions would be addressed by treaty. Both rulers would owe their position and loyalty to Britain. Churchill came to the point with customary crudeness, when he wrote, "Faysal will be a long time looking for a third throne."[62] Former Arab Bureau Director Kinahan Cornwallis conveyed the offer to Faysal and moved with Faysal to Baghdad, where he served as advisor to the new king and to the Interior Ministry, and as principal British architect of the Iraqi kingdom until 1936.

In Baghdad, King Faysal performed a difficult balancing act. He adapted to his dual role of Iraqi head of state and British-appointed monarch. The new state of mandatory Iraq comprised most of three dissimilar Ottoman provinces: Basra in the south, which had included British protectorate and principal port, Kuwait, Baghdad in the center, and Mosul in the north. Britain had sponsored the leading family of Kuwait since the end of the nineteenth century, and created a protectorate to dominate the Persian Gulf and counter pervasive fears of the Berlin–Baghdad Bahn. Ottoman control was briefly reasserted in 1914, and the British army launched its early wartime offensive from ships anchored just outside Ottoman waters a month later in early November 1914. Possession of Mosul was contested by the Turkish Republic and remained unresolved by the Lausanne conference. The desert sanjaq of Dayr al-Zur, was split between the Syrian and Iraqi mandates with undefined borders.

Faysal owed his crown and country to British support and had lost Syria when this support was withdrawn in 1920. Between 1922 and his premature death in 1933 he was generally successful in maneuvering between British demands and at least minimally satisfying the desires of the Iraqi public. Politicized and nationalist Arab–Ottoman army officers were his most important supporters and his most dangerous potential critics. Faysal could not run his government without such people, but except for those few such as Nuri al-Sa‵id, and Ja‵far al-‵Askari who had long attached their fortunes to Faysal and to Great Britain, the ex-Ottoman officers and provincial officials perennially opposed the British role in Iraq, and the king's role as mediator. The government was styled as a constitutional monarchy and the constitution was promulgated in mid 1925, and formed a bicameral chamber, with a lower chamber elected by male citizens, and an upper chamber appointed by the king. The High Commissioner and Faysal insisted on the right to dismiss the chamber, and the chamber won the right to dissolve the cabinet. British authorities resolved to control the country through the powers reserved for the king, confident he could be a reliable instrument of British policy.[63] His cabinet, however, was usually made up of a shifting cast of ex-Ottoman officers and a few civil officials, who often took a jaundiced view of British mandatory indirect rule.

The relationship with Britain was organized around a series of treaties. The first of several Anglo-Iraqi treaties was barely ratified after more than two years of negotiation in 1924. Peter Sluglett enumerates the goals of the treaty as the imperial air route to India, the oil fields, the RAF training ground, and British prestige and capital.[64] The securing of the treaty made way for other measures, and the following year the government signed a 75-year concession for the British-Foreign-Office-controlled Anglo-Persian Oil Company. The Iraqi concession became the Iraqi Petroleum Company in 1929. Deutsche Bank had owned shares in the original pre-war concession, but these were seized German property.

Faysal settled in at Baghdad, surrounded by a number of ex-Ottoman officers. Prominent among this group were Nuri al-Saᶜid, Jaᶜfar al-ᶜAskari, ᶜAli Jawdat al-Ayyubi, and Jamil al-Midfaᶜi. Most of them had been with him in Damascus, and some had passed through Transjordan or Anatolia on their way to Iraq. Those officers who became prominent politicians had local roots in the Ottoman provinces of Mosul or Baghdad. There was also, as in Syria and Palestine, a number of ex-Ottoman civil and political officials who assumed various offices in the mandatory state; most prominent in this group was Rustum Haydar, who had attended the peace conference with Faysal and hailed originally from Baalbak near Damascus. Others had remained in Ottoman service locally, and adapted their allegiance to the new government and arrangement. Yasin al-Hashimi and his brother Taha al-Hashimi, who had served the Ottoman army to the end of the war and beyond, formed a political opposition within the group, and criticized Britain and the treaties forced on the king.

After Faysal's death in 1933, conflict between the colonial power and its opponents re-emerged. Principal critic Yasin al-Hashimi became prime minister, and was overthrown in 1936. By early 1940, Yasin's allies returned to power and Britain invaded and overthrew their government in the so-called Anglo-Iraqi war of 1941. Still, both Iraq and Transjordan were places of relative freedom in comparison with Syria, Lebanon, and Palestine. And each state became a refuge for disaffected ex-Ottoman officials and officers. The meager independence enjoyed by King Faysal and his brother Prince ᶜAbdallah of Transjordan was enough that both states attracted unemployed and frustrated former Ottoman officers and officials. Many were wanted men in Syria and Lebanon and unwelcome in Turkey. Civilian politicians and activists often gravitated to Cairo, but the military men had limited financial resources and were unemployable in Cairo or Europe.

Transjordan, by contrast with the other mandates, had no large cities, little water or settled agriculture, and a sparse, and mostly nomadic population. The new state emerged as a colonial buffer zone between the British and French spheres, and a consolation prize for Amir ᶜAbdallah. Transjordan occupied a former frontier zone of the Ottoman province of Syria, and gained some importance with the extension of the Hijaz railway south of Damascus to Amman and south.[65] Embittered at the prospect of being out-maneuvered by Faysal and his British patrons for the throne of Iraq, ᶜAbdallah installed himself at the railway town of Maᶜan north of Hijaz in late 1920.

Transjordan had been nominally governed from Damascus between the armistice and the end of Faysal's Damascus government in July 1920. Thereafter it became an adjunct of the new mandatory government of Palestine under High Commissioner Herbert Samuel. As historian Mary Wilson has noted, ᶜAbdallah's march north was fortuitously timed. British intelligence worriedly reported he was in contact with insurgent leaders Ibrahim Hananu, Salih al-ᶜAli, and Mustafa Kemal, and menacing the settlement between Britain and France. ᶜAbdallah arrived in Amman ten days before the opening of Colonial Secretary Winston Churchill's Cairo Conference, where it was decided that he should be offered some kind of conditional governorship to keep him in Amman.[66]

Churchill traveled to Jerusalem where he met ᶜAbdallah. They agreed that ᶜAbdallah should take responsibility for Transjordan for six months, and Churchill suggested that, conditional on his ability to stop raids on the French-occupied region in Hawran south of Damascus, he might end up with more later on. On this meager suggestion, ᶜAbdallah became the custodian of the Transjordan portion of the British Mandate for Palestine, surrounded by a small group of otherwise stateless and unemployed ex-Ottoman civil servants and soldiers. The total population, settled and nomadic, was calculated at fewer than 250,000 people.

Conclusions

The Ottoman Empire and its realms were far more central to the 1914–18 war than historians of Europe or the Middle East generally acknowledge. The collapse and disappearance of the Ottoman state was furthermore far more a direct, and *intended*, result of the war than is usually argued. British wartime aims, strategies, and agreements envisioned Ottoman partition and imperial expansion into newly conquered territories as a central goal of the war.

For Britain, the Great War in the East emerged from fear of the alliance between Imperial Germany and the Ottoman state. The war dictated all manner of odd decisions and arrangements, including the search of an Arab caliph to help calm worries about Indian Muslims, and sponsorship and alliances with nascent Arab nationalism and Zionism. The eventual structures of rule in the post-war Middle East were haphazard and improvisational. In every case they were designed to meet immediate problems. As many historians have observed, the mandates were conceived as temporary arrangements. Colonial administrators rarely bothered to contemplate the long-term consequences of their policies and they were rarely punished for anything apart from embarrassing metropolitan politicians. Shortsightedness and reactive policy-making characterized the colonial state.

The end of the war was accompanied by a determination to dismantle the empires of the Central Powers into dependent small states governed under the "national idea." The League of Nations would help smooth relations between the victorious powers, and the various small nations, mandates, and protectorates. Representative government and ethnic-based nation-states had become ideas of wide acceptance. The states that emerged from the cataclysm of the war would be states based on the democratic ideals of consent, equal representation, popular national sovereignty, and theoretical equality of nations before the stage of the world. But the Ottoman state, like Germany and Austro-Hungary, had been constitutional monarchies with democratically elected parliaments.[67] The partitions and imposition of colonial rule on any of the defeated states of the Central Powers could hardly be based on the principal of consent, but only on a preponderance of power and coercion. There was discussion of League-of-Nation-administered plebiscites in territories separated from Germany and Austro-Hungary, but in most cases the referendums did not take place, and they were not proposed for the Ottoman realms in any case.

Both France and Britain based their claims of legitimate conquest on the liberation of oppressed subject peoples, as in the Greek Orthodox, Armenian, and Maronite Christians of Anatolia and coastal Syria. Arab Muslims were added to this list in 1916. The war's end brought various assertions of national rights and claims, many focused around the national rights and liberation of former Ottoman Christians. Such groups were in every case expected to become client populations of the respective victorious empire. Woodrow Wilson and the League of

Nations endorsed the tacit view that only Christian nations had legitimate claims to self-representation. Other, non-Christian, nations could conceivably receive acknowledgement, but the way was unclear, apart from the requirement to accept and endorse their subordinate status.

Conquest and partition of the Ottoman state was easier to contemplate if the inhabitants were defined as racially deficient non-Europeans in need of development, reform, and tutelage. In the speeches that accompanied Ottoman defeat and British victory, various nations had been liberated from "Turkish tyranny" and freed from the "Turkish yoke." France entered coastal Syria with promises of the immediate fulfillment of the *mission civilitrice*, especially for the purposes of bettering what was claimed to be the miserable lot of the Eastern Christians. The discourse of Middle Eastern post-world-war colonialism was based on racial, civilizational, and ultimately legal justifications for the League of Nations mandate system. The colonizing Great Powers' self-image represented everything the colonized population was claimed to lack: rationality, hygiene, modernity, moderation, and civilization itself. The League of Nations served as the principal support on which such claims to rule based themselves.

Notes

1. Shakib Arslan, *Sira Dhatiyya* (Beirut: Dar al-Ṭaliᶜa, 1969), p. 262. Quoted in William Cleveland, *Islam Against The West: Shakib Arslan and the Campaign for Islamic Nationalism* (Austin, TX: University of Texas Press, 1985), p. 40.
2. BNA CO 730/150/6, "Profiles and Assessments," "YASIN PASHA AL HASHIMI,"1932.
3. Interview with granddaughter-in-law May Ziwar al-Daftari, London, May 8, 2016, and May al-Daftari's forthcoming book, *Yasin al-Hashimi: Sira wa dhikrayat*. Ms. Al-Daftari conducted extensive interviews with Niᶜmat Yasin al-Hashimi al-Daftari in the early 1990s. Nuri al-Saᶜid, *Mudhakkirat Nuri al-Saᶜid ᶜAn al-Harakat al-ᶜAskariyya lil-Jaysh al-ᶜArabi fi al-Hijaz wa-Suriyya, 1916–1918: al-Fariq al-Rukn Nuri al-Saᶜid ᶜala tullab Kulliyyat al-Arkan bi-Baghdad fi Mayis 1947* (Beirut: al-Dar al-ᶜArabiyya lil-Mawsuᶜat, 1987); also see Phebe Marr, "Yāsīn al-Hāshimī: The Rise and Fall of a Nationalist (A Study of the Nationalist Leadership in Iraq, 1920–1936)," unpublished PhD dissertation, Harvard University, 1966, p. 71.
4. Eugene Rogan, *The Fall of the Ottomans: The Great War in the Middle East, 1914–1920* (London: Basic Books, 2015), p. 80. Rogan's new book on the Ottoman Great War now surpasses all earlier treatments.
5. Mustafa Aksakal, *The Ottoman Road to War in 1914: The Ottoman Empire and the First World War* (Cambridge University Press, 2008). Christopher Clark, *Sleepwalkers: How Europe Went to War in 1914* (London: Penguin, 2014).

6. BNA, Cabinet Office [CAB] 41/34, Asquith cabinet minutes, July 12, 1913.
7. The most relevant document is a secret report from Leo Amery to the Imperial War Cabinet, titled, "War Aims and Military Policy," BNA CAB 25/87, May 28, 1918. Earlier War Cabinet minutes echo these themes. CAB 29, April 12, 1917.
8. BNA CAB 19/1, 1917–18. The "Dardanelles Commission Report" principally blamed Churchill for the catastrophe.
9. Hasan Kayali, *Arabs and Young Turks: Ottomanism, Arabism, and Islamism in the Ottoman Empire, 1908–1918* (Berkeley: University of California Press, 1997).
10. Priya Satia, *Spies in Arabia: The Great War and the Cultural Foundations of Britain's Covert Empire in the Middle East* (Oxford University Press, 2008).
11. Mustafa Aksakal, *The Ottoman Road to War in 1914: The Ottoman Empire and the First World War* (Cambridge University Press, 2008), p. 16.
12. Elie Kedourie, *In the Anglo-Arab Labyrinth: The McMahon–Husayn Correspondence and its Interpretations, 1914–1939* (Cambridge University Press, 1976).
13. McMahon to Husayn, October 24, 1915. First published in the appendix of George Antonius, *The Arab Awakening: The Story of the Arab National Movement* (London: H. Hamilton, 1938).
14. The Husayn–McMahon correspondence has been the subject of countless books and articles, some accusing British leaders of deceit, some exonerating them.
15. BNA CAB 25/87, "War Aims and Military Policy," June 15, 1918.
16. Matthew Hughes, *Allenby and British Strategy in the Middle East, 1917–1919* (London: Frank Cass, 1999), p. 91.
17. BNA CAB 23/2 WC 96, March 14, 1917. The "Proclamation of Baghdad" was written by the War Cabinet and sent telegraphically to General Maude for public declaration.
18. Lenin issued his "Decree on Peace," November 8, 1917, and it was published in *Izvestia* the following day.
19. *The Times*, November 23, 1917, "A Leninist Armistice." British elite opinion considered the Russian revolution a Jewish project.
20. *The Times*, November 9, 1917. Headlines on pages 6 and 7 read, "Turks Defeated on Two Fronts," "Palestine for the Jews," "Victory in Palestine," and "America and the War." Eugene Rogan makes the point about renegotiating Sykes–Picot, Rogan, *The Fall of the Ottomans*, p. 350.
21. The language is McMahon's. "We confirm our approval of the Arab Khalifate when it should be proclaimed. We declare once more that his Majesty's Government would welcome the resumption of the Khalifate by an Arab of true race." BNA FO 371/2486, 125293/34982 McMahon's dispatch no. 94, Secret, Cairo, August 26, 1915.
22. Woodrow Wilson, speech to a joint session of Congress, January 8, 1918.
23. Erez Manela, *The Wilsonian Moment: Self-Determination and the International Origins of Anti-Colonial Nationalism* (Oxford University Press, 2007), p. 41.
24. David Lloyd George, *The Truth About the Peace Treaties*, and Jean Martet, *Clemenceau: The Events of His Life as Told by Himself to his Former Secretary*

Jean Martet (London: Longman, 1930), p. 190. Both quoted in Hughes, *Allenby and British Strategy*, pp. 123–4.

25. The quote originates with Clemenceu's interpreter, but Lloyd George's flexible standards of testimony are amply attested. Paul Mantoux, *Les Délibérations Du Conseil Des Quatre* (24 Mars–28 Juin 1919) (Paris: CNRS, 1955) vol. I, p. 379.

26. BNA FO 371/4310, Preliminary Peace Conference, session of February 14, 1919.

27. Rustum Haydar, *Mudhakkirat Rustum Haydar* (Beirut: al-Dar al-ᶜarabiyya al-mausuᶜat, 1988), pp. 9–10.

28. "King–Crane report on the Near East," in *Editor and Publisher*, 55, 27. Oberlin College holds the extensive King–Crane Archive, owing to the role of Oberlin President Henry King as co-chair of the commission. Much of the collection is digitized. Thanks to Leonard Smith for this citation.

29. James Gelvin, "The Ironic Legacy of the King Crane Commission," in David Lesch (ed.), *The Middle East and the United States* (Boulder, CO: Westview Press, 1996), p. 14.

30. "Crane and King's Long-Hid Report on the Near East," *New York Times*, December 3, 1922.

31. Robert de Caix, "The Question of Syria," *The New Europe*, September 4, 1919. The next day the *Spectator* complained woefully that Britain kept its promises and certainly did not desire to add to its already heavy responsibilities. Besides, the fault lay with the incomplete work of the Peace Conference. *Spectator*, "France and Syria," September 5, 1919.

32. BNA War Office [WO] 32/5730, 107A, War Office to Allenby, November 27, 1919.

33. FO 406/41, Sir E. Crowe to Earl Curzon, December 3, 1919.

34. LN, Geneva, carton R16, "Mandate for Palestine, 1922."

35. Manela, *The Wilsonian Moment*, p. 39.

36. LN R13, November 7, 1919, Eric Forbes-Adam to Eric Drummond.

37. LN R13, 1919. Alfred Milner to Robert Cecil.

38. LN R14 contains drafts and material on the mandate treaties.

39. *Manchester Guardian*, "The Problem of the Mandates," January 29, 1920, in LN Mandates, carton R20.

40. Yuval Ben-Bassat, *Petitioning the Sultan: Justice and Protest in Late Ottoman Palestine* (London: I.B. Tauris, 2013), pp. 27–30.

41. LN mandate, carton R14, Husayni to director of mandate section, letters of December 18, 1920, and February 12, 1921.

42. Khayr ad-Dīn al-Zirikli, *al-Aᶜlam: qamus tarajim li-ashar ar-rijal wa'n-nisa min ᶜarab a'l-mustaᶜribin al-mustastriqin*, 8 vols., reprint of *c*.1950 (Beirut: Dar al-ᶜIlm lil-Malayin, 1990), vol. VII, p. 326.

43. Cleveland, *Islam Against the West*, pp. 49–50.

44. LN R15, January 11, 1921, Rappard to Drummond.

45. LN R15, September 23, 1921, Drummond to Rappard. Emphasis in original.

46. LN mandates, R39, Congres Syrio-Palestinien, Geneve, August 23–September 21, 1921. Appel adresse à la Deuxieme Assemblée générale.

47. LN R22, 14993, August 25, 1921, report filed by Rappard.

48. Susan Pedersen, "The Meaning of the Mandates System: An Argument," *Geschichte und Gesellschaft*, 32:4 (Oct–Dec. 2006), 560–82.
49. This reconstruction owes much to Susan Pedersen's various articles.
50. LN R17,October 10, 1925, committee report on petitions.
51. LN R2282, for one of hundreds of examples in many files.
52. LN R27 1926 testimony of de Caix.
53. LN R15, Jamal Husseini to Council of the League of Nations, June 20, 1922.
54. Following here Rashid Khalidi, *The Iron Cage: The Story of the Palestinian Struggle for Statehood* (Boston: Beacon, 2006), pp. xlv–xlvi.
55. LN R41, ARRETE no. 336, "Réglementant provisoiromont l'organisation administrative de *l'État* du GRAND LIBAN," September 10, 1920. September 27, 1921. Report from William Rappard from a meeting with Soliman Kenaan, representative member of the Ottoman administrative council for Mount Lebanon, protesting the French Mandate. He bore a petition signed by seven of the twelve members of the council, requesting independence for Mount Lebanon.
56. Engin Deniz Akarli, *The Long Peace: Ottoman Lebanon, 1861–1920* (Berkeley: University of California Press, 1993), pp. 148–9.
57. LN R41, "Copie de la déclaration en date du 10 Juillet 1920 du Conseil Administratif du Liban."
58. Philip Khoury, "'Abd al-Rahman Shahbandar: an Independence Leader of Interwar Syria," in Camille Mansour and Leila Fawaz (eds.), *Transformed Landscapes: Essays on Palestine and the Middle East in Honor of Walid Khalidi* (New York: American University in Cairo Press, 2009), p. 57.
59. Gérard Khoury, *Une tutelle coloniale – Le mandat français en Syrie et au Liban – Écrits politiques de Robert de Caix* (Paris: Belin, 2006).
60. Khoury, "'Abd al-Rahman Shahbandar," pp. 58–9, and Benjamin Thomas White, *The Emergence of Minorities in the Middle East: The Politics of Community in French Mandate Syria* (Edinburgh University Press, 2011), p. 11.
61. Jean-David Mizrahi, *Genèse de l'État mandataire: Service des renseignements et bandes armées en Syrie et au Liban dans les années 1920* (Paris: Publications de la Sorbonne, 2003).
62. BNA CO 730/21/18407, minute by Churchill, April 1922, quoted in Peter Sluglett, *Britain in Iraq: Contriving King and Country* (New York: Columbia University Press, 2007), p. 77.
63. Marr, "Yāsīn al-Hāshimī," pp. 98–9.
64. Sluglett, *Britain in Iraq*, p. 63.
65. Eugene L. Rogan, *Frontiers of the State in the Late Ottoman Empire: Transjordan, 1850-1921* (Cambridge University Press, 2002), p. 160.
66. Mary C. Wilson, *King Abdullah, Britain and the Making of Jordan* (Cambridge University Press, 1990), p. 48.
67. Hasan Kayali, "Elections and the Electoral Process in the Ottoman Empire, 1876–1919," *International Journal of Middle East Studies*, 27:3 (August, 1995), pp. 265–86.

3 Losing the War and Fighting the Settlement: The Post-Ottoman Middle East Takes Shape, 1918–1922

Events in the Former Ottoman Realms, 1918–1923

October 1, 1918	British with Faysal in Damascus
October 26, 1918	Kemal's withdrawal from Aleppo to regroup just north of Aleppo at al-Ra^{c}i on the rail line. The line becomes the armistice line and the eventual Turkish–Syrian border
October 30, 1918	Armistice of Mudros
December 1918	Armenian Legion lands in Mersin
January 1919	Committees of National Rights
February 1919	British evacuate Cilicia in advance of French–Armenian occupation
March 1919	French forces occupy Ottoman Black Sea coal ports
May 1919	British and French ships land Greek troops at Izmir
September 1919	Sivas Conference
October 1919	General Gouraud lands at Beirut
January 1920	Ramadan Shallash takes Dayr al-Zur on Euphrates Beginning of Iraq Revolt
March 1920	Syrian National Congress
April 4–7, 1920	Jerusalem uprising
April 23, 1920	Inaugural Assembly of the Ankara Government
April 25, 1920	San Remo Conference concludes, mandates announced
May 28, 1920	Kemal defeats French backed Armenians, comes to terms with French ceasefire agreement
May–October 1920	Iraq Revolt intensifies and spreads
July 1920	Battle of Maysalun and French occupation of Damascus
December 1920	Palestinian Congress-Haifa
March 1921	Churchill's Cairo Conference decides to offer Iraq to Faysal and Transjordan to ^{c}Abdallah.
May 1921	Palestine May Day Protests
October 1922	Mudanya ceasefire
November 1922	Sultanate abolished
November 1922	Lausanne Treaty conference commences

The Battle of Nablus and the End of
the Ottoman Empire

The Ottoman army made its last stand of the Great War in Palestine in 1918. British General Allenby's defeat of an Ottoman army at the battle of Nablus led to the surrender of the Ottoman state, but in marked contrast to the defeat of Germany and Austro-Hungary, the army did not collapse. In the other two Central Powers, the collapse of the state accompanied the defeat and collapse of the army. The Ottoman army, product of more than a century of reform, careful student of Prussian military doctrine, and unlikely survivor, was neither definitively defeated nor fully demobilized. Remnants of the Ottoman 7th army under the command of Mustafa Kemal Paşa, and the 4th army, under the command of Yasin al-Hashimi Paşa, retreated to a town near Aleppo with the intention of regrouping and re-engaging British forces. Al-Hashimi was wounded in combat and could not continue the march north. The armistice came before the battle resumed.

Ottoman statesmen, products of the both the military and civil state education systems, had entered the war four years earlier, hoping to reverse recent defeats in the Balkans and elsewhere.[1] Few in Britain or France expected to encounter serious resistance from the Ottoman forces, and the public of each country took the Ottoman entry into the war as something of a joke. Newspapers and cartoons mocked the proverbial backwardness and disorganization of the "Sick Man of Europe." The Ottoman state mobilized nearly three million men between 1914 and 1918. Contrary to the expectations of the French and British high command, the Ottoman military proved a formidable opponent, and the Entente powers suffered notable defeats in Iraq, Gallipoli, and elsewhere. The war led to the end of the Ottoman State, but the army and other state institutions survived.

Days after the Battle of Nablus, the British army and its allies of the Arab Revolt finally entered Damascus. The occupation of Greater Syria and the defeat of the Ottoman forces had required an eighteen-month march from Egypt. As the British occupied Damascus, Ottoman general Mustafa Kemal Paşa commanded the retreat from Damascus to Aleppo. By the beginning of November, the five most important Ottoman-Arab cities, Jerusalem, Baghdad, Damascus, Beirut, and Aleppo were all occupied by British forces. The inhabitants of these cities, and many smaller towns and villages, did not fully understand what had occurred. Ottoman State employees and officials, like their German and Austrian counterparts, reeled from the shock of the defeat and occupation. The civic elite of the towns of Anatolia, Syria

and Iraq stayed at their posts and attempted to adapt to the occupation administration. People like Musa Kazim al-Husayni in Jerusalem,
worked to serve their regional population, and maintain relations with
the military occupation authorities. Ottoman civil officials who hailed
from Istanbul or from the Anatolian regions of the Ottoman State,
typically left Greater Syria, Iraq, Hijaz, or Yemen, and returned by
any means available to Anatolia. Shakib Arslan, who had served as a
parliamentary deputy from the Hawran, south of Damascus, was in
Berlin serving as an envoy for the Ottoman government. Local
Ottoman politicians remained in their local posts, but politicians and
intellectuals resident in the capital faced a range of unappealing and
potentially life-threatening choices. The leading officers and politicians of the Unionist government fled abroad.

Serving Ottoman military officers faced a dilemma too, after the
defeat at Nablus. Some 30 percent or so of the Ottoman military
had been made up of conscripts from Arab regions. Arab units had
served with distinction on all fronts, including Galipoli and Russia.
Percentages of Arabs among Ottoman officers were only slightly lower
than among common soldiers. Most Ottoman soldiers were not literate
in any language, and most spoke the Turkish, Arabic, Kurdish,
Albanian, Circassian, Southern Slavic, or Greek dialect of their native
region. It was natural that at the end of the war, or under conditions of
demobilization, they would return to their regions of origin. Those who
took part in the retreat from Syria, however, usually stayed with their
units. Many on all fronts had already deserted and began the long walk
back to distant villages and towns.

Officers were in quite a different situation. Since the military education
system was intended to foster the emergence of a state elite, including
Ottoman Turkish literacy, transnational Islamic cosmopolitanism, and
identity with the Ottoman State, rather than any one region or area, officers had to choose. At least 15 percent of the officers who led the
Turkish War of Independence, and ended up drawing pensions from the
Turkish Republic, hailed from the Arab regions including greater Syria,
Iraq, Libya, or Yemen which were partitioned in 1918. Put another way,
a majority of military academy graduates who listed their origins in Arab
regions, eventually served in the army of the Turkish Republic. The minority who did not include: all who were killed in action, all who retired,
and all who deserted or joined the Arab Revolt. Graduating classes
between 1895 and 1913 had been large, typically 500 cadets, and many
of these men had come from regions under British military occupation at
the armistice at the end of October 1918.[2] Such veteran officers typically

gravitated toward either the Anatolian insurgency, or less frequently, the "independent" Arab government of Amir Faysal in Damascus. Some returned to their towns and villages and resumed life as civilians, but after a lifetime in uniform, spent away from native villages and neighborhoods, this option seems common only among the oldest officers, and *alaylı* officers commissioned through the ranks, or those wartime recruits among Ottoman civilians. Ottoman-educated *mektepli* officers produced in the military schools and academy, whether Turks, Arabs, Kurds, Greeks, Circassians, Bulgars, Bosniaks, or Albanians sought to continue their military service, their comradeship with brother officers, and their service to Islam and the independence of the former Ottoman lands.

Allenby and Faysal in Damascus

On October 1, 1918 the Ottoman governor of Damascus had surrendered to the forces of the British army and the Arab Revolt led by Faysal ibn Husayn. T.E. Lawrence, not yet famous, arrived in Damascus with Faysal's forces. He stayed only long enough to visit the tomb of Saladin before sailing for England. While the vast majority of Arab Ottoman officers had remained in Ottoman service through the war, a small number of former Ottoman officers had joined Faysal's revolt after capture by the British or Arab forces.[3] These officers bore the responsibility of organizing the guerilla forces of the Arab Revolt. But once the war ended and Faysal arrived in Damascus with his staff of Arab officers, he attracted other defeated and suddenly unemployed veterans. Many of Faysal's officer supporters only joined his government after the defeat of Ottoman forces in Syria.

Former soldiers, both comrades and adversaries, doubtlessly hoped that Faysal would be the person to salvage something from the disaster and wreckage of the war, as Ottoman officers were beginning to do in Anatolia. Among those who joined Faysal, there were certainly some who would have preferred to stay with Mustafa Kemal and their brother officers, particularly when the scope of the disaster of the partition became visible. It is noteworthy that the two highest military officials of Faysal's government, Yasin al-Hashimi and Yusuf al-ᶜAzma, had both remained in Ottoman service as decorated staff officers until the end of the war. Neither joined Faysal until *after* the armistice. This fact contradicts the usual story, originating with T.E. Lawrence and the Hashimites, about supposed mass defections of Arab officers to join the British-sponsored revolt of Faysal and Sharif Husayn. Most Ottoman soldiers neither deserted nor changed sides, and the Ottoman army defeat at Nablus came from Allenby's British army, recently reinforced with British units, freed up by the American entry into the war. The forces of the Arab Revolt played a minor role militarily, but as a propaganda weapon, the Arab Revolt was invaluable to British imperial aims. At the armistice, hundreds of thousands of soldiers began the long walk home to their villages and towns across a devastated and famine-stricken landscape.

> Large numbers of prisoners of war continue to return. There have recently arrived in Damascus amongst them four officers from the Yemen and eighteen from African Tripoli. These are all trying to get north with the Turks. They are professional soldiers and the only army which can offer them a career is the Turkish army; it would appear, therefore, that if the release of prisoners continued Mustafa Kemal is not likely to suffer from shortage of officers.[4]

Yasin al-Hashimi had certainly wished to remain in service to the Ottoman state. The circumstances of the defeat and his wounds in combat made such hopes impossible. In September 1918 he had been in command of an army corps at the Battle of Nablus, a 34-year-old major general who had spent twenty-five years in service to the state.[5] Al-Hashimi had been a member of several secret political organizations in the years before the war including the CUP, and al-ʿAhd, the grouping of young Ottoman officers later associated with the Arab movement.[6]

Yasin al-Hashimi escaped the British advance at Darʿa, near today's Syrian–Jordanian border at the end of September 1918. He was wounded on the 100-kilometer retreat to Damascus, and took refuge at the house of the al-Naʿiama family near Damascus' Suq al-Hamidiyya after the collapse of the defense. Yasin al-Hashimi's wounds forced him to remain behind while Kemal retreated north toward Aleppo. Nuri al-Saʿid, ʿAli al-Jawdat, and Jamil al-Midfaʿi were junior Ottoman officers from Iraq who had been captured by British forces. They had joined Faysal's revolt after their internment in prisoner-of-war camps in Egypt. When they learned al-Hashimi was in Damascus, they searched until they found him, and after long and difficult conversations, convinced him to join the new government of Amir Faysal.

Al-Hashimi had rejected many invitations to abandon the Ottoman forces and join the Revolt. In October of 1918, however, he was seriously wounded and in hiding in Damascus. His four young children and wife were present in the city too, and he had no income, no job, and no means to feed his family. Ottoman officials were facing arrest and trial by the allied occupation forces, and the only Ottoman forces he could rejoin were already hundreds of kilometers north behind the British lines, and across a country now occupied by enemy forces, actively seeking his capture. Having found al-Hashimi, his old comrades and adversaries still had difficulty persuading him to join them.[7] He sought assurances they had not come as instruments of a British plot to capture him. Eventually they succeeded, and upon visiting Amir Faysal, he named al-Hashimi military chief of staff and put him in charge of organizing the new army. Less officially and perhaps in contradiction to Faysal's wishes, al-Hashimi soon set about raising guerilla fighters to counter the looming French threat from Lebanon. Yasin al-Hashimi retained his suspicion and mistrust of British motives and he quickly ran afoul of Faysal and his British sponsors.

The retreating army dug in just north of Aleppo at the rail line. Mustafa Kemal learned of the ceasefire by telegraph from Istanbul. He traveled to Liman von Sanders' headquarters at Adana and took overall command of the army from Liman. Kemal also learned of the terms of the armistice, among which were disengagement at the last line of contact, and demobilization of the Ottoman forces and the withdrawal of forces from Cilicia. This meant that while the British and Ottoman armies would theoretically hold their lines running roughly east from Alexandretta and Aleppo, the Ottoman forces would be forced to withdraw and demobilize. The Ottoman army would consequently lose the ability to resist any additional territorial demand. Before Kemal had decided his reaction to the armistice agreement, his fears were confirmed when British forces landed at Alexandretta and demanded an Ottoman withdrawal from the port city.[8]

British troops landed at Alexandretta and marched inland to occupy positions at Aleppo. Kemal organized a retreat of Ottoman forces to the area north and east of the Taurus mountains. He moved all supply depots and arms caches as well. He intended to fortify his positions, but when Istanbul ordered him to capitulate to any demands of the British, he requested to be relieved of command and left by train from Adana to Istanbul. Kemal appointed Nihat (Anılmış) Paşa, a staff officer of Bulgarian origin, commander and ordered the continuation of preparations for eventual resistance against the occupation forces. Shortly before his exit from Cilicia, Kemal received Yasin al-Hashimi and Yusuf al-ʿAzma seeking to coordinate military operations against the British and French. All were decorated, high-ranking Ottoman officers still officially in Ottoman service, even though al-ʿAzma and al-Hashimi came as envoys of Faysal. Kemal received his comrades warmly, despite his well-founded antipathy to Faysal and his Revolt. Of course, neither al-ʿAzma and al-Hashimi had joined the Revolt.[9]

French forces claimed the territory promised in the Sykes–Picot accord of 1916. Allenby allowed a small French force to land in Beirut in November 1918. The same month, French forces, in collaboration with locally raised Armenian irregular forces, landed at Adana and occupied the city and surrounding area. The ports at Alexandretta, Mersin, and the vast fertile river delta of the Adana region, had been long coveted by French colonial interests in commerce and the army. As allied troops began to appear in more towns, Islamic defense committees began to form, meeting in Izmir, Adana, Kars, Aleppo and Damascus, among many other places. The *Müdafaa-i Hukuk Cemiyeti* have been written into history as the site of the emergence of Turkish nationalist resistance and the origin point of the war of independence, but the rights (*hukuk*) to be defended were those of Muslim Ottomans, and not of any ethnic grouping.[10] James Gelvin has demonstrated that committees formed in Damascus using identical language and aims at exactly the same time as in Anatolia.[11] As popular committees met, and French soldiers occupied the towns, sporadic armed engagements between Ottoman and irregular forces and French troops took place immediately.

Yasin al-Hashimi was chief of staff and Faysal appointed Yusuf al-ᶜAzma minister of war. Al-ᶜAzma was a rarity among Ottoman officers since he came from a prominent notable family of Damascus, rather than from the modest background more common among officers. Neither had joined the Revolt, but they far outranked in distinction and experience any officers who had joined Faysal earlier. As a decorated and loyal Ottoman general from Damascus, al-ᶜAzma was an obvious choice.

Damascus' big landowners and the Ottoman civic elite of the city viewed Faysal and his officer supporters with suspicion. Some of the Ottoman provincial administration had fled at the end of the war and others stayed in their jobs. Faysal and his supporters expected to displace such people. General Allenby tended to support the efforts of Faysal to rule the country. But Damascenes mistrusted Faysal and his officer supporters, and many grumbled about their rule immediately. Some saw Faysal as a traitor against the Ottoman caliphate, some worried that he and his officer followers would upset the status of the former Ottoman leading families in politics and economic life, and some considered him a stooge of the British with poor nationalist credibility. At least a few influential Damascenes quietly welcomed the French who came to end Faysal's short-lived government eighteen months later, by which time Yusuf al-ᶜAzma was dead on the field of battle, and no longer able to help Faysal calm the nerves of Damascus' leading citizens.[12]

Faysal's government, supported first by British subsidy, and second by ex-Ottoman officers and nationalist activists, quickly attracted the hostile attention of France. As Faysal scrambled desperately during 1919 to insure continued British support, and to mollify French government officials, his followers in Damascus and the wider region began to organize on the model of the resistance emerging in Anatolia. Popular Committees in opposition to French occupation and partition formed, echoing the organizing efforts of the Defense of Rights committees in Anatolia, and eventually focusing their ire on Faysal himself.[13]

Popular Struggle after the Armistice

During 1919 and 1920 Britain and France moved to partition and govern the post-Ottoman region through proxies. Still reeling from the human and financial cost of the world war, and the bare victory they had managed, both powers resolved to pursue their imperial policies in the Middle East by use of proxy forces and various types of quasi-colonial client states. Governing elites in both Britain and France feared the potentially revolutionary wrath of metropolitan citizens if securing war gains began to cost the lives of more young soldiers and consume the depleted contents of the state treasury. Starvation and influenza threatened people everywhere. As popular revolution had toppled the Russian government, and the German monarchy, so too could popular upheaval potentially upend victorious states.

At the end of 1918, a force of 15,000 Armenian irregulars with 150 French officers landed in Cilicia at Mersin.[14] The Armenian Legion troops occupied evacuated British positions at Adana and Alexandretta. In March 1919, French forces landed at the Black Sea ports east of Istanbul with an intention to seize and hold the Ottoman coal-mining region. In May 1919, 20,000 Greek troops disembarked from British and French naval ships at Izmir.[15] The same month, the Istanbul government sent Mustafa Kemal to the Black Sea coast to organize the demobilization of forces required in the armistice. As the familiar story goes, rather than organizing a demobilization of forces, Kemal coordinated a new mobilization of Ottoman soldiers. He called upon still-serving Ottoman officers and used the still-operative Ottoman military telegraph system, to call local popular defense committees to action.

The public in all combatant powers were exhausted by war, and angry with political leaders who seemed to have brought years of pointless suffering. Millions of sons and fathers were never coming home, and British and French politicians faced an inability to mobilize men or money to occupy and hold newly won colonial possessions. By necessity, proxies and deputized imperial client regimes could police the partition of the Ottoman realms, but some prizes were too valuable to be ruled by natives, at least at first. Istanbul and the straits were placed under direct British–French military occupation, and Iraq, its waterways, railroads, and oil fields were intended for direct British rule. Palestine, Egypt, and the Suez Canal, and the corridor between the Mediterranean and the Gulf, would likewise remain firmly under British control. There was some internal discussion of the difference between the emerging League of Nations mandates for Palestine, and Iraq, and the wartime proclamation of the British protectorate of Egypt. The Foreign Office, the cabinet, and the Colonial Office immediately agreed that any policy that served to diminish absolute British control over its imperial realms was a bad policy. Colonial Secretary Lord Milner objected strongly to any subordination of British control to native authorities, or the League of Nations, unless France agreed to even greater limits on its authority.[16] The strategic prizes of the war, imperial waterways, and control of the Persian Gulf, and its oil fields, would be ruled directly as possessions. Iran would remain an informal protectorate, and the Anglo-Persian Oil Company, majority-owned by the Foreign Office, would rule the south. This, anyway, was Prime Minister David Lloyd George's evolving plan in 1919.

Before the Paris Peace Conference, Lloyd George had promised Clemenceau he would have Syria and Cilicia up to the central Anatolian town of Sivas. Having made his promise, and having extracted a promise of Mosul and Kirkuk from Clemenceau, Lloyd George reconsidered his options. By early 1919 Lloyd George decided he wished to deny possession of Syria or South Eastern Anatolia to France. But hanging on to Palestine, Mesopotamia, and Mosul, might require French cooperation and goodwill. Lloyd George's commitment to Faysal and the integrity of Syria was slight. Faysal was a native client prince in a territory suddenly unimportant to Lloyd George's larger imperial and strategic goals.

By mid 1919, Lloyd George instructed Allenby to cooperate with the French in occupying Syria and Cilicia. Allenby had already resolved to withdraw from Syria in advance of France, because he feared an outbreak and wanted to avoid being forced to combat a nationalist insurgency alongside French forces. Among allied generals, Allenby had a well-developed appreciation for the Ottoman military. Allenby may have felt some lingering commitment to Faysal, and he counseled Faysal to attend the San Remo treaty convention on the post-Ottoman partition, and assignment of the mandates, and to negotiate directly with France. Allenby also intervened to extend the financial subsidy to Faysal as long as possible.

SECRET. Withdrawal from Syria now decided upon, expenditure in territory destined for France should be reduced to absolute minimum forthwith, and when territory is handed over, should cease entirely. The question of Faisel's subsidy is being referred to the Foreign Office.[17]

Allenby recognized that support for Faysal would help minimize the danger to the colonial settlement from nationalist insurgencies. As British forces withdrew to Palestine and Iraq, and before French forces could take their positions, armed revolts emerged in Cilicia in the area east of Adana, under the leadership of Kemal's successor, Nihat Pasha, in the ʿAlawi coastal region, under the leadership of Shaykh Salih al-ʿAli, and in the countryside of Aleppo under former Ottoman officer Ibrahim Hananu. Both Hananu and Salih al-ʿAli drew weapons and support from Anatolian insurgents and from the arms cached by Mustafa Kemal's never fully demobilized Third Army, and from officers in Faysal's government. Yusuf al-ʿAzma visited his former Ottoman officer comrades in the Cilicia before the fall of Faysal's government. French forces of the Armenian Legion occupied ʿUrfa and Maraş east of Adana. Armenian nationalists understood that France would sponsor an Armenian state in Cilicia, as Britain was sponsoring a Jewish state in Palestine, and France a Maronite Christian state in greater Lebanon.

Allenby was well apprised of British intelligence on the Ottoman nationalist movement in Anatolia, and was unsurprised by the spread of armed opposition. He was determined to consolidate and reinforce his positions in those occupied Ottoman territories considered vital to the interests of Britain. Allenby was frustrated by Lloyd George's willingness to abandon Faysal, not because he owed Faysal, but because he recognized the value of Faysal in calming patriotic outrage throughout the former Ottoman realms. But retrenchment and Lloyd George's calculations demanded France, Faysal, and the Hashimites would be on their own, and by late 1919 Allenby had suspended the subsidy to Faysal's government in Damascus and withdrawn his forces to Palestine.

Mustafa Kemal landed in Samsun in May 1919. The first "Societies for the Defense of National Rights" (*Mudafaʿa al-Huquq*) had already formed in various towns and regions under threat of partition, including Adana, Aleppo, Damascus, and many other places. Renegade Ottoman officers convened a series of congresses to organize resistance to the Allied occupation. The congresses and the successful armed resistance movement they fostered have been written into the official history of the Turkish Republic as marking both the birth of the Turkish nation-state and a break with the Ottoman past. Yet the proclamations, contemporary writings, and actions of many participants suggest nothing of the kind: the nation to be saved was a diverse collection of Ottoman Muslims under continuous threat from local and international forces of European imperialism. The emerging movement embraced *all* the Ottoman regions.[18]

The Sivas Conference convened in September 1919. Delegates came from all Ottoman regions and proclaimed their determination to struggle to resist the partition of what they called their "Ottoman fatherland." They noted their attachment to the Sultanate and Caliphate, but argued that the institutions of the state were under the foreign control of the victorious powers, and consequently did not represent the will of the Ottoman nation. The central government was powerless to defend the national rights of the Ottoman Muslim people in their "undivided Ottoman fatherland."[19] British and French proxies in Greek and Armenian armed movements had violated the Ottoman-controlled territory within the armistice lines of October 30, 1918. The congress members maintained their intention to insure the rights of non-Muslims within the national territory, but the Ottoman nation was a Muslim nation. While the specific grievance was the violation of ceasefire lines, the Ottoman national movement did not define the limits of its territorial intentions.

In October 1919, General Henri Gouraud arrived in Beirut as commander of the *Armée du Levant* and first High Commissioner for the French Republic in Syria. His secretary-general and chief strategist was Robert de Caix.[20] Premier Clemenceau's choice of Gouraud defined the character of the French mission. Gouraud was a devout Catholic and advocate for a Christian crusade in the holy land for the glory of France. Robert de Caix was the leading member of the *Parti Colonial*, and represented the commercial interests of Lyonais textile industries and the policy of favoritism for Oriental Christians and minorities. Both men were members of the so-called "revenge generation" steeped in the national trauma of the Franco-Prussian war defeat in 1870, and both left an indelible mark on sectarian division and conflict on Syria and Lebanon.

Two months after the Sivas Conference, in November 1919, Mustafa Kemal addressed a proclamation to the Syrians:

Respected Brothers,
    I speak to you with a beseeching voice, emanating from a heart full of sorrows, caused by the oppression, torment and treachery of the enemy, and the divisions between the sons of one religion ... Let us put an end to this misunderstanding, and point our arms towards the traitors who wish to tear up Islam ... Our Mujahidin [Muslim warriors] will very soon be the guests of their Arab brothers, and by their union they will conquer and destroy their enemies. Long live our brothers in religion and may the enemy be conquered.

The proclamations of 1919 reveal much about the durable appeal of liberation movements led by former Ottoman officers. Kemal repeated the familiar ideological pillars of the Ottoman military educational system in evoking the language of Ottoman patriotism and the duty to defend Muslim lands. A leaflet distributed in both Aleppo and

Damascus in late 1919 and attributed to Mustafa Kemal and the nationalist movement read in part:

We do not want to have a war with foreigners.

We do not want to have a foreign Government in our country.

We shall defend the rights of our nation until death, in order to avoid its fall into the hands of the foreigners.

We wish to join together the parts [of the Ottoman state] against Wilson's principles.

Let everyone keep to his work and business. Our aim is justice.

We shall put to death without mercy everyone who stands against what we have already mentioned, whether he be a Muslim or a Christian.

The Muslims who love our Sultan, have a right to the Caliphate. Our nation has taken up arms for this cause, from east to west ...[21]

The Anatolian Model and Hope for Salvation, 1920

The appeal of the Anatolian movement in Syria has been erased by seventy-five years of mutually antagonistic nationalist historiography.[22] But there is much evidence that the Anatolian movement electrified people in all the defeated Ottoman realms. As a creation of British imperial policy, now abandoned by his patrons, Faysal was ill-suited to lead a movement of armed resistance against the post-war British–French settlement. As veteran officers realized the limits of his position, he began to lose their support. Some later ridiculed Faysal and the Hashimites as fools for abandoning the Ottoman state and joining the British, because Ottoman rule, for all its miseries and injustices, had been better than partition and domination by the European imperialists.[23] As the Anatolian insurgency emerged and became known in Syria, the Syrian and Iraqi officers hoped to emulate the example. British intelligence officer, Colonel Richard Meinertzhagen reported:

Yasin Pasha, the leading spirit in Syria, is now known to be in correspondence with Mustapha Kemal, though actual proof could only be obtained in using violence on the disguised Turkish officers who act as carriers. Yasin is aiming at reinstating Turkish rule in Syria, not so much on national or pan-Islamic grounds, as on those of personal power: in this he is the open disciple of Jemal. There is little doubt that at the present moment Yasin's influence has replaced for the bad the more moderate and reasonable influence on Feisal. He now carries with him the army and the majority of the people ... Arab feeling has been changed from anti-French to anti-European. This is now noticeable in propaganda where hostile allusions are made to the English and friendly overtures made to Turkish and even Germans.[24]

Fawzi al-Qawuqji had been at a loose end in Tripoli in early 1919 when an envoy from Amir Faysal invited him to Damascus. He was thrilled to accept and happy to join what he later called the modern Syrian Arab army at the moment of its formation. Yasin al-Hashimi was the central organizational figure of the new army, and Qawuqji noted that it included Ottoman Arab officers like him and Hashimi who had served the Ottoman state throughout the war, and others who had only recently been fighting against them. They joined together to defend Syria. In his new role, Qawuqji fought against the French occupation and organized guerilla operations in the region of Zahle, not far from Rayaq in what would become Greater Lebanon.[25]

Wartime military governor Cemel Paşa had tried Saᶜid al-ᶜAs in 1917 for his pseudonymous journalism critical of the Ottoman government. He spent the final year of the war imprisoned in the citadel at Aleppo. As a highly educated and seasoned staff officer, he was probably a major or perhaps a colonel at the time of his sentence and imprisonment. He was released the day Faysal arrived in Aleppo, on October 26, 1918. Between 1918 and 1921, al-ᶜAs participated in battles all over the region that became southern Turkey and northern Syria. He fought first alongside Ibrahim Hananu, and then went to the mountain districts west of Damascus, where he helped to organize a popular war council and a guerilla campaign against the French occupation of Zabadani, Baalbek, and other areas in what became the State of Greater Lebanon. After Maysalun, he fled Damascus, and by 1921 he remained in Amman.

By the end of 1919, France's Armenian Legion was fighting Ottoman insurgents to maintain control of Cilicia. General Gouraud in Beirut was preparing to march on and occupy Damascus and inland Syria. Ex-Ottoman officer and Tribal School graduate Ramadan Shallash had left for the Euphrates region from Aleppo in late 1919. Yasin al-Hashimi had convened a war council, probably against the wishes of Faysal, and appointed Shallash military governor of the district of Raqa and the Euphrates.[26] Ramadan Shallash was a central figure in the early stages of the Iraq Revolt of 1920, and continued to attack British outposts until June 1920, when Faysal managed to send the perennial troublemaker as an emissary to ᶜAbd al-ᶜAziz al-Saud.[27]

Shallash met with Hananu in the countryside of Aleppo, and proceeded to defeat a British garrison and occupy the upper Euphrates town of Dayr al-Zur in January 1920. When Faysal, then seeking diplomatic support in Europe for his tottering government, was informed that the town had been captured in the name of the Arab government, he disavowed the action, and instructed his brother Zayd in Damascus to repudiate and initiate arrests against the "rebels."[28]

Shallash's capture of the garrison and the threat of a wider uprising led British authorities to arrest Yasin al-Hashimi. Allenby ordered al-Hashimi taken by train to prison in Ramla in the British-occupied zone in Palestine. Meanwhile, Yasin's wife and four young children had been living with him in Damascus, and they traveled by train to visit him.[29] Both French and British officials feared al-Hashimi could become the leader of an insurgency on the model of and in collaboration with Mustafa Kemal, but when the French refused to take custody of al-Hashimi, Allenby ordered his release, noting publicly that he was complying with a French request.[30] Once back in Damascus, both al-Hashimi and Yusuf al-ʿAzma complained bitterly that they faced an impossible task in organizing defense, made all the more difficult by Faysal's refusal to seriously contemplate and prepare for military confrontation.[31] While Faysal looked in vain to his British former patrons for help, the officers looked to the example of their brother officers in Anatolia.

In March 1920, the Syrian National Congress met in Damascus and proclaimed Faysal constitutional king of undivided natural Syria. The congress was timed to precede the San Remo Conference scheduled for April during which the post-Ottoman settlement would be decided. The congress proclaimed Faysal king almost in spite of himself. British intelligence noted his ambivalent attitude toward the declaration of independence. "Feisal is exerting every effort to prevent a breach between the Arabs and the allies." His efforts had evidently included secretly helping Allenby to detain Yasin al-Hashimi. Al-Qawuqji and his brother officers were deeply affected by the jailing of their leader, and realized that great power politics and perfidy could defeat all their efforts in defense of the new state of Syria.[32] Quwuqji remained in the army through the defeat at Maysalun, and unlike the Hashimi brothers and Faysal's other senior officers, he stayed in Damascus, eventually accepting employment as a cavalry captain in the French–Syrian Legion.

Nationalists attended the congress from Jerusalem, Beirut, Nablus, and Haifa, among other towns and cities. Members of the prominent Husayni family of Jerusalem attended, including Haj Amin al-Husayni, who would come to be the first British-appointed Mufti of Palestine. Iraqi activists held a joint session in Damascus declaring Iraq independent under the rule of Faysal's brother ʿAbdallah.[33] The Iraqi and Syrian congresses were reported widely in the press in Baghdad, Damascus, Aleppo, Beirut, and Jerusalem, and the program and determination to resist colonial partition was popular. Faysal had briefly returned to Damascus to attend the congress after begging for a resumption of British support and petitioning one European capital after another for help against increasingly truculent French demands. The congress, with a clear view of armed revolts and events in Anatolia, Syria, and Iraq, proclaimed a unified Syria, including Palestine, rejecting the claims of the Zionists, and calling for an end to the government of military occupation. Their actions were more radical than Faysal desired or than the French would tolerate.[34]

Allenby wrote repeatedly to the Foreign Office to urge official support for Faysal's position. He forecast war if Britain did not bolster Faysal among those who had planned the congress and who remained opposed to the settlement. The possibility of such endorsement drew protest from London, and Allenby was instructed to remind Faysal, "that the future of the countries ~~conquered~~ freed from the Turks by the Allied Armies could only be determined by the Allied Powers."[35]

San Remo and the Nabi Musa Demonstrations in Jerusalem

The Syrian National Congress had declared the Zionist colonization of Palestine illegitimate and Palestine an indivisible part of united Syria. Two weeks later, in the course of the Nabi Musa procession on Easter Sunday, April 4, 1920, battles broke out between Arabs and Jews in Jerusalem. British intelligence blamed an impassioned speech from ᶜArif al-ᶜArif for inciting the crowd. Al-ᶜArif was from a Jerusalem family and edited the nationalist newspaper, *Suriyya al-Janubiyya*, or *Southern Syria*. He had been educated in literature in Istanbul and served as a reserve Ottoman army officer during the Great War. In 1915 he was captured by the Russians in Eastern Anatolia, and spent three years in a Siberian prison camp where he published a newspaper and learned Russian and German.[36] As the Nabi Musa procession paused, he urged the crowd to resist the injustice of British and Zionist occupation and partition of their country. A portrait of recently crowned King Faysal was on display. Al-ᶜArif soon fled to Damascus, where he joined his fellow former officers Yasin al-Hashimi and Yusuf al-ᶜAzma in time for the Battle of Maysalun.

Military Governor Ronald Storrs accused Jerusalem mayor Musa Kazim al-Husayni of involvement in the demonstrations and dismissed him as mayor. In 1920, Musa Kazim al-Husayni was nearly 70 years old, and was acknowledged as the leading politician and patriarch of the leading family of Ottoman Palestine (Sanjaq al-Quds). He had spent decades in Ottoman public service and had served as provincial governor and member of parliament. Between 1920 and the end of his life he became an international advocate for the cause of Palestine in Europe, and petitioned and visited the Foreign Office and the League of Nations. In 1914, it was the European Zionists who were disadvantaged in their attempts to wrest territory for settlement from the Ottoman central government, but

after 1919, the tables had turned, and Chaim Weizmann and other
Zionist leaders enjoyed access to European politicians at the highest
levels. It is hard to imagine the changed world that suddenly confronted
Musa Kazim al-Husayni in his seventh decade of life.

The countryside and region generally was already in a state of unrest
and raids on Zionist settlements and British garrisons had taken place
in the area between the French and British zone. Fighting and demonstrations spread within the region and lasted several days. Raids took
place against British and French positions in Hawran, and the western
mountain areas. Both French and British forces responded with airplane patrols and bombing raids, but attacks continued and intensified.
British intelligence noted that Faysal did not support such activities,
and was opposed to military confrontation, but in his weakened political
condition, he could not oppose the militant demands of the Syrian
Congress, without running the risk of being "thrown out" by the members of the congress, who objected in the strongest terms to the division
of greater Syria into separate mandatory states, and who were suspected
of maintaining worrisome contacts with the Anatolian insurgents.[37]

British inquiries into the disturbances at Jerusalem reported that
while authorities had promised just rule, Palestinians were well aware of
Zionist intentions, expressed widely in newspapers in Europe and
reported in the Arabic press, to displace the indigenous populations
and take full possession of the country. A month before the uprising,
then-famous writer and humorist, Israel Zangwill proclaimed in a
widely publicized speech in London, "if you shirk exodus, you are confronted by Numbers. Palestine contains 600,000 to 700,000 Arabs ...
Are we literally to re-create Palestine, and then to be told it belongs to
the ignorant half-nomadic tribes who have planted their tent poles or
their hovels there?" Four days before the riots, the Zionist Executive
wrote to the Foreign Office about Zangwill. "We are aware that these
utterances, which cannot fail to obtain wide publicity, are likely to exercise a disturbing influence on the situation in Palestine."[38]

At the end of April 1920, newspapers everywhere announced the
results of the San Remo Conference. The conference confirmed the
Anglo-French partition of the Ottoman Arab east, and the nominal
supervision of the League of Nations mandates system. Representatives
of Italy and Japan attended, but there were no representatives from any
of the territories discussed. Allenby had urged Faysal to attend the conference, but Faysal argued that he could not agree to the separation of
Palestine from Syria, or to the terms of the Balfour Declaration, both of
which were preconditions the conference was meant to confirm. When
Faysal finally decided he should attend, the French government

informed him the invitation had been revoked, and if he insisted on appearing he would be dealt the humiliation of being banished to his hotel room and excluded from the proceedings.[39] San Remo represented the final Anglo-French deal over the partition of the region. The next conference, at Sèvres in August 1920, was supposed to dictate terms of surrender to the Ottoman State, define borders, and transfer title to the new colonial masters of the Middle East, but the ground had shifted beneath the Great Powers.

In Baghdad, news of Ramadan Shallash's capture of Dayr al-Zur in January barely preceded news of the Syrian and Iraqi National congresses in Damascus. The people of Baghdad were excited by both events, and outraged by the news from San Remo, but the protests did not immediately threaten British control. Beginning in May, a major revolt, inspired by events in Dayr al-Zur and other former Ottoman lands, and led by ex-Ottoman–Arab officers and war veterans, spread along the river towns from the north to the south of the country, nearly leading to a British evacuation, and to a major crisis of confidence in London. A secret telegram noted, "we now require an army to hold Mesopotamia as large as that required to take it from the Turks."[40]

Iraq in Revolt

British officials in Iraq had warned that the population would not long tolerate direct military rule. The British military authority had styled itself as a liberating force from "Turkish tyranny," and British colonial authorities were flummoxed and anxious over the declarations of independence of the Iraqi National Congress at Damascus in March 1920 on the one hand, and declarations of support among many in Iraq for a return of the Ottoman military to expel the British. The colonial authorities were unprepared for the Iraqi uprising that emerged in late May 1920, but those in Baghdad had been warning London of such a possibility for months.[41]

At the beginning of May, British reports noted that the pro-British Arab independence faction, made up of former officers close to Faysal and his brother ʿAbdallah, would only prevail if Britain granted some form of constitutional native rule. Otherwise, the pro-Ottoman camp would certainly prevail in winning the allegiance of the majority of the population, particularly since such sentiments were already popular. The Jewish leaders of Baghdad and the Shiʿi clerics of Najaf and Karbala were the most favorable to a resumption of Ottoman rule.[42] News from Damascus, Jerusalem, and Cilicia was in wide circulation, and outrage over the results from the San Remo Conference united opposition against the British occupation.

The month-long Ramadan fast fell in May during 1920. Nightly anti-occupation demonstrations took place in towns and cities after breaking the fast, and after prayers. In the first weeks, demonstrations featured patriotic poems and orations. British officials were astounded to learn that Sunni and Shi'i Iraqis celebrated the breaking of the fast together preceding these demonstrations, and responded by banning public assemblies. The ban had the effect of causing demonstrations to become larger and more raucous, as nationalist leaders began to systematically organize opposition.[43] British intelligence claimed all the nationalist agitators had been members of the Ottoman Unionist or CUP Party. By the second week in May, the more remote British garrisons were under frequent attack from Abu Kamal on the upper Euphrates to the Persian Gulf.

By June, the entire region was in a state of revolt. As elsewhere, ex-Ottoman officers led the main insurgent bands. Rebels defeated and captured most of the smaller British garrisons, and it was only by the use of airpower and the hurried dispatch of additional bombers and other aircraft from India and Egypt that the major towns could be defended. Iraqi revolt leaders presented a number of petitions to British authorities and to the League of Nations demanding independence and the right of self-determination for Iraq.[44] British politicians, from Lloyd George on down, cast about for a solution to the crisis, but renouncing British control was never considered. British newspapers criticized colonial administrators and politicians strongly and complained that the cost of suppression would exceed 40 million pounds sterling, and would result in many dead British soldiers. Public discussions questioned the need to maintain British control over Iraq, but *The Times* noted that a prominent former general, John Cowans, only recently retired, was scouting Baghdad for an oil company. The *New York Times* reported that Cowans had been named managing director of one of the world's largest oil companies, Royal Dutch Group, which expected to control the new oil fields of Mesopotamia.[45] Forces of the Government of India and the Royal Air Force eventually suppressed the insurgency, as "countless towns and villages were destroyed."[46] Air power served as the principal tool of counter insurgency and villages along the rivers were bombed and strafed from the air.[47]

Anatolia and Cilicia

As British forces came under attack in Iraq, the French Armenian Legion in Cilicia was nearing defeat. A major French force had been besieged and defeated at Maraş by a popular uprising of Ottoman Muslims in February, and had been further decimated during a retreat through snow-covered mountains toward the Cilician coast. The French left fifty wounded behind in the care of an American missionary school in Maraş.[48] According to historian Robert Zeidner, Mustafa Kemal had requested Ottoman officers and units to coordinate their efforts to expel the French from the region on both sides of the armistice line (today's Turkish–Syrian border).[49]

Three who heeded this call were well-known "Arab" nationalist heroes Salih al-ᶜAli and Ibrahim Hananu in Syria and legendary "Turkish" nationalist hero Ali Şefik Özdemir. Özdemir was born in Egypt, Hananu was born three kilometers south of today's border with Turkey, and Salih al-ᶜAli hailed from the ᶜAlawi mountains, which extend from today's coastal Syria north into Turkey. In April, French forces evacuated their positions at ᶜUrfa after engaging not only popular insurgents, but reconstituted Ottoman army units under command of Kemal himself. General Gouraud at Beirut initially requested reinforcements for Cilicia, but within two months, French commanders had decided that their commitment to their Armenian allies might foment a renewed alliance between Anatolian and Syrian insurgents.[50] French forces sought and received a ceasefire agreement from Mustafa Kemal in late May, agreeing to withdraw all French forces west to the Mersin–Adana line. The agreement was negotiated on French initiative, with representatives of Kemal claiming to speak for the Ottoman government, at both Beirut and Adana.[51]

The British Armenian Committee protested vehemently that France and Britain were again abandoning their countrymen in order to placate the Ottomans. *Erivan*, an Armenian newspaper in Istanbul, under British censorship, defied the censor and published a banned editorial, announcing the independence of Armenia in Cilicia, and proclaiming a war against the Turks.

The Armenians have been deceived by false promises. When the French came to Cilicia and hoisted their flag, the Armenians never expected that the future would bring such disastrous results. Now the French are hauling down their flag and leaving us alone in the hand of the Turks, whose sanguinary appetite has become keener.[52]

French forces needed to retrench in order to occupy and hold Syria. General Gouraud knew that a renewed Ottoman army presence in Syria would make French colonial objectives impossible.

With revolt in Iraq, France facing defeat in Cilicia, and armed insurrection in Syria, British and French observers feared they would be unable to retain control of the region. France reached accord with Kemal to withdraw from Cilicia, allowing General Gouraud to concentrate his forces on consolidation in Syria and Lebanon. In late June of 1920, after continuous guerilla fighting on the border with the French-occupied coastal region, soon to be named Greater Lebanon, a French army marched over the Lebanon mountains and east toward Damascus.

Syria and Maysalun

Gouraud had made a series of truculent ultimatums to Faysal. Faysal, without British support, without diplomatic allies in Europe, and without the effective military mobilization Generals al-ᶜAzma and al-Hashimi urged, conceded everything to Gouraud. Faysal wished to discuss Gouraud's demands with Allenby, but Allenby ignored him. Faysal eventually replied to the ultimatum, but Gouraud ordered the advance on Damascus without waiting. As the march continued, Gouraud conveyed his complaint to Faysal that the concession was insufficiently detailed, to which Faysal replied in more detail within the allotted time. Gouraud implausibly claimed later that he considered Faysal's reply a legal ceasefire, and that he ordered his troops to retreat, but before they could retreat from the plain of Maysalun in the mountains just west of Damascus, they were attacked by Arab bands, and thereby forced to counterattack and march on and occupy Damascus.

The British, in disavowing support for their former client, had become increasingly hostile, and sought to blame Faysal for his inability to placate the French. As the battle loomed, the quarters of Damascus had been emptied of young men as crowds walked west, some armed only with swords or sticks, to meet the mechanized French column. Chief of staff Yasin al-Hashimi warned Defense Minister Yusuf al-ᶜAzma there were only a couple hours worth of ammunition for the inadequate forces. Al-Hashimi noted, "Orders to fight for the sake of honor are easy for ministers, but hard for soldiers."[53] Tahsin al-ᶜAskari, brother of Jaᶜfar al-ᶜAskari, and Ramadan Shallash had left Iraq and returned to Damascus with other ex-Ottoman officers only days before.[54] French commanding General Goybet reported that the Syrian defenders had created impressive fortifications and a comprehensive defense given their meager resources. A French artillery burst killed minister of war Yusuf al-ᶜAzma, as he commanded the defense.[55] When the family of Yasin al-Hashimi heard the leader of the army had been killed they were seized with grief, only to learn, when he walked through the door, that Yasin had survived and Yusuf al-ᶜAzma was among the fallen. With the Battle of Maysalun, France occupied and claimed Syria. Ex-Ottoman officers like Yasin al-Hashimi scattered and went into hiding. General Gouraud visited the tomb of Saladin and gave a speech proclaiming victory not only over Syria, but over the Crusades, and Saladin himself.

The surrender and partition of the Ottoman state was supposed to be formalized in the Treaty of Sèvres in August 1920. Ottoman–German concessions and oil resources would be reconfigured to benefit the victorious allies. Existing Anglo-French commercial privileges would remain. The Middle Eastern mandates would follow the agreement of San Remo, with a close resemblance to the lines drawn in 1916 in the Sykes–Picot agreement. Western Anatolia would be given to Greece, South West Anatolia to Italy, an Armenian state would be formed in eastern Anatolia, and the French zone would extend to Sivas and east to Van. Istanbul and the straits would be under international (British) administration and the demilitarized Ottoman government would control a shrunken core including Ankara, Bursa, and some Black Sea coastline.[56]

But things did not go according to plan. The Ottoman army returned to the field, along with irregular elements everywhere, and the victorious powers lost the struggle to enforce their partition plan. By forcing the treaty on the sultan's government, they precipitated its final break with the nationalist movement in Anatolia. After Sèvres, the nationalist movement could credibly declare the sultan's government and the Entente Powers the enemy of the Ottoman homeland and people.

In September 1920 General Gouraud declared the creation of a new state called Greater Lebanon. The creation of the separate mandatory state was based upon an expansion of a special Ottoman administrative district of Mount Lebanon (*Mutasarrifiyya Jabal Lubnan*), and French desires to foster a loyal client population among the Maronite Christians. The Maronite community, which had long had ties to the French Catholic church, was a majority in certain mountain districts east of Beirut, stretching along the mountain range to the south and north. The French plan to create Greater Lebanon expanded this district to include areas where the majority population was Muslim, both of the Shi‘i and Sunni rite.[57] General Gouraud and his secretary, Robert de Caix, designed the new state in modest collaboration with a selection of pro-French former Ottoman politicians and Maronite clergy. Eighteen months later, Gouraud announced the sectarian electoral law for Greater Lebanon. The law was partly based on the principle of an Ottoman parliamentary representative for each 50,000 residents, but in an innovation of Robert de Caix, the seats were allotted by religious sect, with clear favoritism for Maronite Christians, based on the results of a likely-rigged recent census. The sectarian division in the administrative council, with seats reserved by religion, was a

French invention. The sectarian apportionment forms the electoral basis of Lebanese parliamentary politics until today, and has been long-criticized as a source of instability and electoral injustice.[58]

In late summer 1920, and after occupying Damascus and Aleppo, France resumed the fight in Cilicia. French colonial troops landed at Mersin to fight their way back to the towns of the interior. France abandoned support for the Armenians and brought thousands of *Armée du Levant* colonial troops. Desire to wrest a suitable settlement from the Anatolian nationalists, and secure Syria drove these policies. Having fomented a sectarian war in Cilicia with the Armenian Legion, France publicly abandoned the Armenians as a colonial client population. The president of the National Assembly argued in the chamber that the motives of France in the East were entirely altruistic: French colonies would bring civilization to all people, but France did not come for imperialistic motives. And yet, the president noted, the previous policy of support for minorities in the former Ottoman territories could not stand when those same minorities were unable to recognize the benefits and limits of French support. The Greeks and the Armenians could not stand in the way of friendly relations with a new Turkey, and France would not fight a major war in Anatolia on their behalf. It was necessary to negotiate with the Turkish leaders, who seemed to be, the president argued, reasonable people.[59] France could protect her interests and rest secure in the promises that non-Muslim minorities would be protected.

By December 1920 Mustafa Kemal was personally commanding a re-formed Ottoman army division at ʿUrfa and promising to advance into the French zone in Syria. French forces in the Taurus mountains were defeated and withdrawing to the coast. Ibrahim Hananu had defeated a series of French patrols in the region of Aleppo. The mandate government controlled a radius no more than eight kilometers from Aleppo, and the French controlled no areas of the surrounding countryside. Salih al-ʿAli in the ʿAlawi Mountains south of Antakya and along the coast and other regional rebels had likewise defeated a series of French patrols, and were collaborating with nationalist forces to the north.

The Anatolian nationalists were widely considered capable of capturing and occupying Aleppo at their pleasure. According to British intelligence reports, the prevailing opinion held that Kemal's forces would be in Homs by spring. Kemal himself was said to have promised to blow up the Homs–Beirut railway line by the end of February. British intelligence forecast a warm welcome for returning Ottoman military forces. The French administration had summarily fired all former Ottoman officials, and was consequently unable to assemble a functioning colonial bureaucracy. General Gouraud was increasingly desperate to seek

terms with Mustafa Kemal.[60] Meanwhile, British airpower had temporarily cowed Iraqi insurgents, though at great cost in lives and the
British public treasury.

Faysal was a refugee king, but the rebellion and costly suppression of
Iraq led to a British effort to draft him as king of Iraq, a job he evidently
welcomed after his expulsion from Syria.[61] Faysal's friend, and former
British army officer, Thomas Edward Lawrence, had become a major
celebrity in London, as "Lawrence of Arabia." Lawrence had begun a
well-publicized campaign against direct rule of Iraq, which happened to
coincide with the public outcry over the costly suppression of the Iraqi
Revolt. Lawrence knew the fiscal argument against direct rule was per-
suasive, and he began to agitate for a new role for Faysal. Two days
after General Gouraud brought an end to Faysal's government in
Damascus, Lawrence published a letter in *The Times*. The letter was
widely read and crossed many desks in England, France, and the
Middle East.

Freedom is enjoyed when you are so well armed, or so turbulent, or inhabit a
country so thorny that the expense of your neighbour occupying it is greater
than the profit. Feisel's government in Syria has been completely independent
for two years, and has maintained public security in its area.

The expense curve will go up to 50 million pounds in Mesopotamia this year.
Mesopotamian desire for independence grows. The government we have set up is
English in fashion, and is conducted in the English language. So it has 450
British executive officers running it, and not a single responsible Mesopotamian.
In Turkish days 70 per cent of the executive civil service was local. Our 80,000
troops there are occupied in police duties, not in guarding the frontiers. They are
holding down the people. In Turkish days the two army corps in Mesopotamia
were 60 per cent Arab in officers, 95 per cent in other ranks.[62]

Churchill Salvages the Settlement

In March 1921 Colonial Secretary Winston Churchill convened a conference at Cairo. Churchill wanted to formulate a policy to insure
British imperial control of the Middle East, while drastically reducing
the expense of direct rule. The Conference's immediate imperative was
the expensive and deeply unpopular military suppression of revolt in
Iraq. Former Arab Bureau chief Kinahan Cornwallis advocated Faysal,
and the attendees agreed that Faysal should become king of Iraq, and
that his brother Abdallah would receive a temporary governorship centered on the town of Amman, where he happened to be encamped.
Abdallah would thus become a cheap means of ensuring some order in
the zone between French-mandate Syria and British-mandate Palestine,

rather than a potential source of disorder along with his armed retainers. Lloyd George feared that the benefit from finally conceding the French occupation of Syria would be destroyed by French anger over renewed British sponsorship for Faysal and Abdallah on the borders. His fears were well founded, but Churchill successfully persuaded him that the plan's merits outweighed its dangers.

The conference's location in Cairo was an accident of convenience. But the choice of Cairo, dictated by its proximity to Palestine, Iraq, and London, had consequences on the British Protectorate of Egypt too. Egypt had been effectively apart from the Ottoman State throughout the nineteenth century, and state modernization was quite different in Egypt than in the Ottoman realms. The British occupation had been a fact since 1882, but the enduring fiction of Ottoman sovereignty over the country was severed in 1914 when Britain declared Egypt a protectorate under direct martial law. Egyptians opposed martial law and the imposition of the protectorate status. At the end of the war, Saad Zaghlul and other nationalist leaders citing Woodrow Wilson's Fourteen Points Speech, petitioned the High Commissioner to end the protectorate and allow a delegation to attend the Paris Peace Conference in early 1919.

The petition was denied and as the leaders of the delegation, or *wafd*, began to speak publicly throughout the country, a protest movement emerged in support of the delegation, and in opposition to British occupation. After the High Commissioner ordered the arrest and exile of Zaghlul, Egyptians began to attack symbols of British domination throughout Egypt. The British military killed thousands of Egyptians in suppressing the revolt, and eventually determined that the maintenance of British control required a political settlement with Egyptian nationalist leaders.

The political settlement emerged from a commission of inquiry report, coincidentally published as Churchill arrived in Egypt. As elsewhere, British fiscal strain dictated a low-cost façade of native rule, and in early 1922 Britain unilaterally declared Egypt independent, reserving a series of exceptions by treaty that insured the British High Commissioner ruled the country despite the presence of an Egyptian king and elected prime minister.[63] The treaty exceptions provided a template for Iraq a few years later. The British government reserved control of imperial communications, defense, foreign interests and minorities. In practice, the treaty removed most practical matters of sovereignty from the Egyptian government.

The eventual assertion of French and British mandatory rule made life harder and more dangerous for former Ottoman officers and guerillas. British airpower and ground troops had crushed the insurgency in

Iraq in late 1920 and ex-Ottoman officers and insurgents moved west toward Aleppo to join Ibrahim Hananu in his fight against France. Yasin al-Hashimi, Ramadan Shallash, and Sa^{c}id al-^{c}As, among others, joined Hananu and maintained close contact with Kemal and his forces nearby. A few of Faysal's most loyal ex-Ottoman officers, especially Nuri al-Sa^{c}id and Ja^{c}far al-^{c}Askari had followed him into exile and worked with Britain to find a role for their patron, but most went elsewhere and actively fought the emerging colonial settlement.

Palestine May Day Riots 1921

The war devastated much of the Ottoman realms, but the suffering of the Palestinian population was unique in its severity. Unlike most Ottoman regions, Palestine had been an actual battlefield between British and Ottoman armies for most of 1917 and 1918. The majority of the male population had been conscripted and were consequently unable to support their families. In 1915 there had been a locust plague, and in 1916 there was a drought, crop failure, and famine that continued until the end of the war, followed by the worldwide influenza pandemic. Mortality between 1914 and 1920 may have been upwards of 25 percent of the population.[64]

Throughout the nineteenth century, Palestine, like Lebanon, had been an arena of intense international scrutiny and involvement. The Ottoman state had established, both in Mount Lebanon and in Palestine, a special administrative regime to manage and prevent international intervention in Ottoman affairs in each area. Jerusalem had been a special administrative *Sanjaq*, or district, under a governor directly appointed and answerable to the central authority in Istanbul. Unlike other important provincial cities, Jerusalem did not house a permanent army command or military middle and preparatory schools. This meant that in Jerusalem, unlike Baghdad, Damascus, Aleppo, and the provincial capitals of Anatolia, there were comparatively few local men who had been educated within the Ottoman military system.[65]

The Ottoman Great War had ended with the Ottoman defeat at Nablus. The rout had meant that the Ottoman army had been in full retreat from Palestine, and the British army was in uncontested control of the country from September 1918 onward. By contrast, the Ottoman military never fully demobilized in Anatolia. Syria was under nominal control of Faysal and his ex-Ottoman officer followers. Iraq, with its vast expanses, was not fully pacified until early 1921, but Palestine was completely occupied and de-militarized, undermining in advance any attempts to challenge the imposition of mandate rule by armed resistance.

The San Remo Conference had confirmed the British Mandate for Palestine and the Balfour Declaration in April 1920, formally ending British military occupation. Unlike other wartime pledges, the British government had remained committed to the Balfour Declaration because of the popularity and influence of Zionism in Britain, and because of the expectation that Zionism would make British control over Palestine easier and probably cheaper. These expectations turned out to be dramatically wrong. Opposition in the form of demonstration in the cities and periodic armed clashes in the countryside had emerged in 1919 and 1920.

With the start of the mandate, British authorities attempted to formulate some kind of native governing arrangement including political representation and police forces. This attempt was notably unsuccessful. The British conception of native rule was based on parallel Zionist and Arab governments and institutions. The Zionists in Palestine and abroad embraced the notion that their movement deserved equal representation. The Arab leadership protested first the notion that an indigenous majority, then constituting 85 percent of the population, should share equally in state institutions with a small, but clearly ambitious and growing, immigrant minority, and second, the idea that there should be divided state institutions. They argued that there should be one police department, with officers from all religious groups, one executive, one government, and so on. Arab leaders understood that they, alone among the former Ottoman regions, were subject to a religiously validated movement of settler colonialism aiming to displace them, first from positions of power, and ultimately from the territory altogether.

The British learned quickly how complicated their support for Zionism would make colonialism in Palestine. When in 1921, the High Commissioner proposed to the Zionist leadership a gendarmerie made up of one part Jews and one part Arabs, coordinated by British officers, the Zionists expressed their agreement, insisting that it could not be more than half Arabs. The mandate authorities then brought the proposal to the Arab representatives, who argued that they could not possibly accept a force in which more than a third of the members were Jewish immigrants, and that it should be fully integrated, since a divided force was an obvious ingredient for civil strife. The Zionist movement and the British were committed to dual structures of native rule existing in subordination to a British mandatory superstructure. While this arrangement suited the aims of the Zionist movement, the Arab leadership opposed it and generally registered their opposition by non-cooperation. Since the Zionist leaders cooperated eagerly, representation of the two communities was further unbalanced.[66]

In March 1921 the Mufti, or head Islamic judge, for Jerusalem, Kamil al-Husayni, died in office. The British High Commissioner, Herbert Samuel, selected his brother, Haj Amin al-Husayni to succeed him. British Middle East policies favored dynasties and various types of noble families over democratic structures, and Samuel subverted the normal election process to select al-Husayni in April and styled him Mufti of Jerusalem and Palestine – a title he invented. The year before, when Samuel's predecessor, military governor Ronald Storrs, dismissed Musa Kazim al-Husayni as mayor, he had appointed a member of a rival family, Raghib al-Nashshashibi, in his place. When the leading candidate for Mufti emerged an ally of the Nashshashibi family, Samuel resolved to manipulate the results in order to prevent a concentration of political leadership in one Jerusalem family.[67]

Haj Amin al-Husayni eventually become the leading figure of Palestinian politics during the mandate. His biography resembled that of many of his Ottoman contemporaries. Haj Amin was born in Jerusalem in 1893. He had spent two years at al-Azhar in Cairo, where he met and studied with the famous Syrian scholar Rashid Rida. Al-Husayni volunteered for service in the Ottoman army during the Great War, and received officer training and a commission as a reserve officer in Istanbul in 1916. He served continuously as an Ottoman army officer between 1916 and 1919, mostly in Izmir. After the war he returned to Jerusalem, where he immediately became involved in politics and attended various congresses including the Syrian National Congress of 1920 in Damascus.[68] After the Nabi Musa events of April 1920, he fled to Damascus and was at the Battle of Maysalun in July 1920.

Zionist efforts to publicize the project of Jewish colonization in Palestine were widespread and sophisticated. Chaim Weizmann had been in continuous contact with Lloyd George, who was sympathetic to Zionism, as he was sympathetic to the dreams of non-Muslim people to establish nationalist states within the Ottoman realms generally. Weizmann lobbied tirelessly for the expansion of the Jewish national home to include the Hawran south of Damascus, and much of the coastal plain and southern mountains of what became Greater Lebanon. To bolster the case, Weizmann invoked the bible, ancient history, modern economics, and the geopolitical priorities of Britain.[69] Weizmann was also well received at the headquarters of the League of Nations in Geneva.

Despite the best efforts of diplomats in Europe, the Zionist project in Palestine was never smooth. On May Day 1921, riots between Communist immigrant Jews and Socialist immigrant Jews broke out in Jaffa. As the two groups battled, the Communists were driven back into the lanes of the Muslim quarter, whereupon the inhabitants of the quarter joined the fight. By the end of the day, 20 had been killed and 150 wounded. In the following days the High Commissioner barred the landing of some 300 additional Jewish immigrants en route on two ships. Villagers from all over the region organized themselves into groups, often armed, and began marching toward Jewish settlements and Jaffa. There were continuous battles between British troops and Arab Palestinians. A number of villages were bombed from the air and the British navy sent two destroyers to Jaffa to intimidate the population.

The eventual investigation found that Bolsheviks had incited the crowd in the first instance, and that rampant rumors of attacks on Arabs by Jews, increased immigration, and rumors of Arabs dispossessed of their homes and lands had caused the disorder. There had likewise been a rumor in wide circulation that the British intended to give al-Aqsa Mosque and the Dome of the Rock to the Zionists for their exclusive use as a temple. The rumor was claimed to have started from a New York newspaper publishing an illustration of the Dome of the Rock topped by a Zionist flag. British intelligence officers feared widespread Muslim opposition, and worried ceaselessly that France would not be able to stop the Turks from returning to Syria, at which point Ottoman forces would return to Dar^ca at the border with Transjordan and Palestine. The mandate authority temporarily halted Jewish immigration and proposed to create an Arab Agency to represent the indigenous population as the Jewish Agency represented the Zionist immigrants.[70]

In June 1921, rebel fighters ambushed the convoy of General Gouraud near Dar^ca in the Hawran between Jerusalem and Damascus. Gouraud was unharmed, though one mandate official traveling with him was killed and one was wounded. The attackers, Adham Khanjar and Ahmad Muraywid, fled south into the British zone ostensibly ruled by Amir Abdallah.[71] The French authorities protested vigorously to the British authorities in Transjordan, but the insurgents were not caught. A year later, Adham Khanjar was caught on his way to blow up the electrical power station in Damascus. Armed opponents of the mandates were not easily dissuaded.

During summer 1921, France confronted the limits of its post-war ambitions. Kemal's reconstituted Ottoman army units had forced French forces from the area north of the armistice line of disengagement. A series of the treaties between Britain and France, imposed on the remnants of the Ottoman Sultan's government, had partitioned greater Syria, Iraq, and Anatolia. By the time of the Treaty of Sèvres, in August 1920, the conceit of victory was already dissolving. France had claimed a sphere extending to the town of Sivas and nearly to the Black Sea. But the territory claimed by France in Anatolia was under nationalist control and it was becoming clearly impossible to occupy both Syria and southeast Anatolia. Recently elected Prime Minister Millerand realized voters would punish him for either a retreat from the Middle East, or a renewed call-up of metropolitan troops. To keep Syria, France would come to terms with Kemal's nationalist movement. French envoy Henry Franklin-Bouillon negotiated the Treaty of Ankara in October 1921. France withdrew from Anatolia and recognized Mustafa Kemal's national government in exchange for nationalist recognition of the French Mandate in Syria, and a secret promise of a return of Ottoman weapons from Syria. The ceasefire with France eventually led to a new comprehensive peace treaty with the Anatolian nationalist movement in 1923 in Lausanne.[72]

Faysal received the newly invented Iraqi throne in August 1921. The process was less smooth than Churchill and Lawrence had hoped. After the bloody suppression of the revolt, and the deaths of at least 6,000 Iraqis, most segments of Iraqi society wanted nothing to do with Britain and a British-selected king. Some considered Faysal a British stooge, or an opportunistic interloper, but the way was cleared by the British arrest and exile of his most formidable Iraqi rivals for national leadership. The High Commissioner appointed a Council of Ministers made up of twenty-one prominent citizens, which was intended to formally offer the throne to Faysal. Formation of the Iraqi army followed. British officials appointed Faysal's two most loyal lieutenants, Ja°far al-°Askari and his brother-in-law Nuri al-Sa°id, minister of defense and chief of staff respectively. The promotion of Nuri and Ja°far was noteworthy. Unlike the other ex-Ottoman officers, Nuri al-Sa°id and Ja°far al-°Askari had accompanied Faysal into exile from Damascus, and then rushed to Baghdad to lobby British officials for positions for Faysal and themselves. Both had been involved in the Arab Revolt from the beginning, and had been recruited by British intelligence officers after they had surrendered, foreclosing the possibility of remaining in Ottoman service. Their Ottoman rank at the time of their capture had been modest, but neither was accused of taking up arms against France or Britain between 1918 and the coronation of Faysal as king of Iraq.

A Council of Ministers resolution and rigged referendum preceded Faysal's coronation in August 1921. Kinahan Cornwallis engineered both operations. Faysal and his British advisors soon recognized that while they shared an interest in the stability and durability of the system they devised, their interests diverged in many other ways. Faysal had no original connection to Iraq, and he required some level of Iraqi consent for his rule. It was obvious that his legitimacy would potentially increase or decrease proportionally based on the distance he could put between himself and the British Mandate authorities in Iraq. The majority of Iraqis opposed the idea of a colonial mandate. Depending on individual political outlook, citizens of the new state viewed the British role with something between moderate and intense opposition. The "extremist nationalists," comprising much of the former Ottoman elite of the country, opposed anything short of full independence and legal equality between states. Faysal and his closest advisors, Nuri and Ja'far, were more compromising to British demands, but they pointedly asked for the deletion of the word "mandate" from whatever agreement would ensue.

The British Foreign Office rejected this request. According to historian Peter Sluglett, the British wished to avoid trouble with France by appearing more receptive to Iraqi demands than the French were to Syrian demands.[73] The situation was similar to Egypt where the *Wafd* Party and Egyptian population rejected the notion of a "Protectorate," and united in opposition to such an arrangement. First High Commissioner for Iraq, Sir Percy Cox, resolved that a treaty between the Iraqi government and Britain could best protect British interests. The notion of quasi-native rule by treaty was common to British colonialism at the time generally, and the Egyptian Revolution of 1919 had been suppressed and followed by a year of fruitless "negotiations" over the Anglo-Egyptian treaty. When Egyptian politicians refused to accede to the demands of Britain to control most aspects of the state, Britain unilaterally declared Egypt independent in February 1922 and imposed the treaty conditions without further discussion or agreement. Simultaneous treaty negotiations were equally unpopular in Iraq, but Faysal owed far more to Britain than the leaders of Egypt's *Wafd*. Treaty discussions dragged out over months, as Faysal faced the anger of the Iraqi public on the one hand, and the impatience of his British benefactors on the other.

Ibrahim Hananu Puts the Settlement on Trial

The withdrawal of French forces from Anatolia, and the removal of Anatolian nationalist support for the Syrians, was the end for Ibrahim Hananu's movement. In July 1921 he fled to Transjordan where he was arrested and returned to French custody by the British. The French authorities considered Hananu an outlaw and rebel leader, but in defining the mandate and its rivals, French authorities seriously underestimated Hananu. In 1921, Hananu was 53 years old, and had served as an Ottoman reserve army officer, prominent Aleppo politician, and Ottoman provincial official. He had received an Ottoman civil education in Aleppo's Sultani civil preparatory school, followed by study and graduation from the elite Mülkiye civil service academy in Istanbul and a certificate and license in Ottoman law. He had taught briefly at the Ottoman Imperial Military Academy in Istanbul. Hananu was in jail awaiting trial until early the following year.[74]

General Gouraud announced Hananu's prosecution by public court martial. Hananu turned out to be a skilled lawyer and orator and the trial was a disaster for the mandate authority. According to the British consul, the extradition of Hananu from British-mandate Transjordan caused intense criticism of the British, and when Hananu was tried, in mid March 1922, thousands of people gathered outside the courtroom. He was accused of organizing rebel bands, of engaging in brigandage, and atrocities, murder, and the destruction of state property. Hananu challenged the legality of his extradition, the legality of mandate martial law, and the French Mandate itself. The judge replied that the League of Nations had given the mandate to France. Hananu pointed out that the King–Crane Commission had already received full testimony of Syrian opposition to the French Mandate, and consequently the League violated its own charter to safeguard the wishes of the mandatory populations. Neither the court nor the mandate itself was a legitimate body, he argued.

Hananu declared that he was a patriotic politician and not a brigand. The Syrian population evidently agreed, and the British consul opined that the local police and gendarmes were considered to be his enthusiastic supporters, and were likely to release him to the embrace of the crowd whatever the outcome of the trial. Hananu noted that before the war he opposed Ottoman laws he felt limited the autonomy of his region, but after the war, France and Britain had partitioned the region, curtailed liberty, censored the press, and jailed sincere patriots.

Hananu opposed the settlement, and had been appointed diplomatic envoy to Syria by Mustafa Kemal and the Anatolian nationalists. He had papers to prove it. General Gouraud had considered Kemal's nationalist government sufficiently legitimate to negotiate and sign treaties with it. As a documented representative of that government, he was immune from French prosecution. Anyway, he had been merely a diplomatic envoy and the military operations were in the hands of serving Ottoman officers. "In response to the charge that he had always opposed the French mandate, he admitted this, but stated this was not a crime punishable by death."[75] After numerous witnesses attested to Ibrahim Hananu's good character, and patriotic heroism, the court acquitted him by a vote of three to two. His acquittal provoked joyful celebrations, not only in Aleppo, but throughout the region.[76]

Also in March 1922, French Mandate official Colonel Catroux fired well-known Damascus intellectual, journalist, and publisher, Muhammad Kurd ᶜAli, from his job as chief of public instruction. Kurd ᶜAli is a famous figure in the history of the Arab nationalist movement. He founded the Arabic Academy at Damascus in 1918, and is known for his multi-volume work on Damascus, *Kitab al-Khitat al-Sham*, and his publication of *al-Muqtabas*, the nationalist newspaper of record through the early mandate. In a surprising subversion of his Arab nationalism bonafides, Kurd ᶜAli was fired because he visited Germany and France, paid a cordial visit to the exiled former Ottoman governor of Syria, Cemal Paşa, in Berlin, and failed to visit Colonel Catroux while in Paris. Catroux considered his visit to Cemal, and his failure to call on him, symbolic of his refusal to recognize the legitimacy of the mandate.[77]

Two weeks after the end of Hananu's trial, in early April 1922, American businessman Charles Crane visited Damascus. Crane had been the president of the American mandates (King–Crane) commission appointed by President Wilson to survey the wishes of the inhabitants of the former Ottoman realms in 1919. The Syrian countryside was increasingly restive after Hananu's release and on the day of Crane's arrival in Damascus, seventeen French soldiers and one officer were killed outside Aleppo. Upon his arrival, Crane met his friend from his 1919 visit, Dr. ᶜAbd al-Rahman al-Shahbandar.

ᶜAbd al-Rahman al-Shahbandar was briefly Faysal's foreign minister in 1920. French authorities exiled him in 1920 and allowed his return in 1921, after which he became the leading nationalist political figure in Damascus. He had spent the early years of the war in Damascus, until he felt in danger from Ottoman governor Cemal Paşa, in 1916, and left for Cairo, seeking refuge for a time at the village of a Druze shaykh named Sultan al-Atrash, about a hundred kilometers south of Damascus.

Shahbandar welcomed Crane back to Damascus with a large picnic along the verdant Barada river gorge, a short train ride from Damascus. Crane gave a speech and noted that in Europe people assumed the Syrians welcomed France in their region. Crane pointed out that the League of Nations was the last forum available for Syrians to make their case to the world. After a series of meetings and dinners, Crane left by car for Beirut a couple days later. As Crane left from the square in front of the Victoria Hotel, Shahbandar gave a fiery speech in opposition to the mandate. Once Crane was out of sight, on the road to Beirut, French police arrested the nationalist leaders who had hosted him, including Shahbandar. The prisoners were immediately transferred to prison outside Damascus.[78]

Larger demonstrations followed on Friday in front of the main Umayyad Mosque. Shops were closed and concentrations of police and mandate soldiers met angry protesters who called for the release of Shahbandar and the other leaders. When the crowds refused to disperse, armored cars and mounted troops advanced, and police fired into the air. Scores more were arrested. Gouraud declared martial law, and imposed a curfew on the city. Mandate soldiers barricaded streets with machine guns and tanks. Mandate authorities determined not to repeat the mistake of Hananu's trial, and a closed military tribunal tried and sentenced the nationalists. This established a precedent of military trials for political prisoners, which lasted for the entirety of the French mandate in Syria until 1946. Syria's post-independent governments also reinstated martial law under the euphemism "emergency laws."

After the demonstrations and arrests of the first week, prominent women, several of whom were married to the jailed political leaders, led a march of thousands through the city. Shops were closed in protest. The mandate authority posted notices threatening shop owners with heavy fines if they failed to open for business. The notices were immediately torn down. The "Women of Damascus" presented a petition to the High Commissioner and the British consul, signed by the wives of the imprisoned nationalists, calling for the release of the prisoners and the institution of rule of law and freedom in Syria. The petition noted the imprisoned leaders had simply called for the freedom of their country. The military tribunal released most of the hundreds of people arrested, but Shahbandar, Sa'id Haydar, Hasan al-Hakim, and four others were sentenced to prison terms of up to twenty years.[79] (See Figure 3.1.) Circulars appeared in Damascus addressed to "the Syrian Patriot Brothers," and signed by the *Fida'in al-Filistin*, or "Patriots of

Figure 3.1.   Dr. Shahbandar Prison Postcard, 1922 (Lemke Collection)

Palestine." The circular noted that the jailed Damascenes had declared they preferred "prison to shame," and that the Syrians' fervent desire for freedom from occupation and against the colonizers would surely prevail. Mandate intelligence attributed this notice to Haj Amin al-Husayni and his nationalist friends.[80]

Meanwhile, events in Anatolia were widely known and greeted rapturously in Damascus, Jerusalem and many other places. French authorities had hoped jailing Damascus' most popular nationalist politicians would calm the population, but the atmosphere of ferment and excitement was inescapable. The press declared Mustafa Kemal "a new savior of Islam," and a "Hero of the Ottoman East," and people throughout the region publicly anticipated the return of Ottoman armies of liberation.[81] A month or so later, a group of prominent Damascus citizens, not already in jail, organized to agitate for renewed union with the Ottoman state. Among the members were a number of former supporters of both the wartime Ottoman governor Cemal Paşa, and Arab revolt leader Amir Faysal. They called themselves The Society for the Salvation of the Near Eastern Peoples, or *Jami'at lil-Takhlis al-Sharq*. They wrote and printed pamphlets, which were distributed throughout the cities of the Syrian Mandate, calling for union with the brother Turks, and resistance against the French. Weapons were supposed to be forthcoming from nationalist forces north of the 1918 armistice line.[82]

In July 1922, Adham Khanjar, the would-be assassin of General Gouraud of 1921, crossed the border between Transjordan and the Syrian Mandate. Khanjar and a band of guerillas were on their way to sabotage the Damascus electrical generating plant by means of explosives. Mandate police dispersed the band at the border, and with the French authorities in pursuit, Adham Khanjar sought refuge at the house of Sultan al-Atrash, a Druze shaykh and well-known enemy of the French mandatory government. Sultan al-Atrash was not in his village, and French officers captured and arrested Adham Khanjar. When Sultan al-Atrash learned that Khanjar had sought refuge at his house and had been captured, he protested that the prisoner was his guest and he was honor-bound to protect him until the authorities made a formal request for him, with which he promised he would cooperate.

Sultan al-Atrash sent a series of telegrams to the native and French authorities protesting the breach of customary law.[83] Sultan al-Atrash gathered his brothers and a few friends to launch an attack to free Khanjar. The group, several Ottoman army veterans, including Sultan al-Atrash, among them, blocked a roadway with stones at a blind curve and ambushed a French armored car convoy in dramatic fashion. Khanjar was not in the convoy, and French authorities hanged him in Damascus shortly after, but the news of the convoy's destruction was greeted enthusiastically throughout the region and Sultan al-Atrash become regionally famous. French forces responded to the destruction of the convoy by issuing death warrants for the rebels, and dispatching the full French Mandate air force of thirty airplanes to bomb villages and fleeing rebels. The High Commissioner ordered the destruction of Atrash houses, and the burning of the fields of Sultan al-Atrash and his brothers. With French warrants on their heads, the guerillas fled to Transjordan.[84]

From exile, Sultan al-Atrash wrote to the League of Nations Mandates Commission at Geneva. Shakib Arslan forwarded a translation. The petition addressed the League of Nations in resolutely secular terms on behalf of the Arab nation (*Al-Umma al-ᶜArabiyya*). The letter refers to the Syrian nation, which they note is a geographical entity under occupation. The petition complains of the "broken promises of the allies, the division of Syria into four states and more territories, the curtailment of liberties previously enjoyed, and the persecution of intellectuals, exiled, imprisoned and tortured in the name of the mandate." Two years had passed since France had entered Syria, and despite the League of Nations, and the fine words of the civilized world, Syria had still not obtained justice, or the right of "self-determination." The petitioners noted that the mandate required their consent, which they did not give, and that France had entered their country by military force. They consequently wanted an end to the mandate and the recognition of Syrian independence within its natural borders. They finally noted that the Syrian–Palestinian Congress spoke for them and protested the bombing of their towns and villages by French aircraft.[85]

Events in Anatolia

> I have never seen anything to beat the hatred of the Kemalist for the British. If Mustapha Kemal could have a pickled Englishman served up to him for breakfast everyday, he would certainly do so.
> M. Laporte, French Chief of Mission, Adana, September 1922 [86]

By fall 1922, the allied partition plan for Anatolia had plainly failed. The Anatolian nationalist movement under command of various former Ottoman officers had defeated a French invasion in southeastern Anatolia and a Greek invasion in western Anatolia. France had attempted to sponsor an Armenian state, and Britain had attempted to sponsor an Anatolian Greek state in the west. Both projects foundered dramatically and further imperiled the already dire prospects of the surviving Armenian and Greek Christians of Anatolia. In September 1922, Lloyd George, with minimal cabinet consultation, ordered British troops to protect the allied occupied Dardanelles straits and Istanbul from the advance of Mustafa Kemal's troops.[87] France, having already come to terms with Kemal over Syria, evacuated its positions. A popular outcry in Britain against the possibility of renewed war led to calls for a ceasefire, and eventually for Lloyd George's resignation.[88]

As the victorious powers retreated, the terms of the armistice and treaties imposed on the Ottoman state became obsolete. The Armistice of Mudanya in October 1922 assured the retreat of Greek forces from western Anatolia, and arranged for the renegotiation of the previous treaties. Prime Minister Lloyd George was punished for his determination to hold on to his Ottoman war prizes, and his government fell from power by the end of the month. The nationalist movement had won the right to renegotiate the settlement by force of arms, and the Ottoman government had, for practical purposes, ceased to exist. The victory of the Anatolian insurgency was greeted with tremendous enthusiasm in all former Ottoman regions, and since many realized the peace settlement would be renegotiated, Arab-Ottoman statesmen from greater Syria hastened to make arrangements to travel to Switzerland and attend the conference.

The Anatolian national movement had formed the Grand National Assembly at Ankara in April 1920. Mustafa Kemal Paşa had become assembly speaker and leading nationalist politician. After the ceasefire in October 1922, Britain invited representatives of the Ottoman government in Istanbul and the National Assembly in Ankara to attend peace talks at Lausanne, Switzerland. Shortly before the opening of the peace conference, Kemal persuaded the assembly to vote to abolish the sultanate and reduce the Caliphate to a ceremonial religious office with no role in government. The debate was difficult but the argument was simple: the right to self-determination had been won by force of arms against the efforts of both the imperialist powers and the sultan's government. Intentionally diluting the force of their victory to honor an office that had played no part in bringing it about would only weaken the nationalist position at Lausanne. The abolition of the Ottoman sultanate was strategically important but politically unpopular, and newspapers in all former Ottoman regions criticized the move.

Preceding the nationalist victory in Anatolia, French Mandate forces in Syria had shipped vast quantities of stockpiled Ottoman munitions and supplies to nationalist forces in Adana. A single shipment in July included huge quantities of ammunition, 160,000 military rifles, hundreds of trucks, scores of large caliber mobile cannons, three anti-aircraft guns, and at least a few airplanes.[89] British agents in Syria were deeply worried by this development, since they were contemplating with horror the likelihood that Kemal's forces would defeat Greece in western Anatolia, seize Mosul in the Iraqi Mandate, and perhaps continue southward. There was dawning recognition that the British government would be powerless to fight a renewed war in the Middle East to maintain its hold on Iraq.

When Lloyd George tried to challenge Mustafa Kemal in September, the result was the fall of his government. British officials were also perplexed by French willingness to deal generously with the nationalists, and seemed unable to understand that France had determined that appeasing the Anatolian movement was the only way to insure French control of Syria. Britain in Iraq was in a more delicate situation with the Anatolian nationalists.

Yasin Paşa Returns to Iraq

Yasin al-Hashimi had gone into hiding after Maysalun. He traveled to northern Syria and Cilicia, and over winter 1921–2 Yasin sought reappointment in the Ottoman army. His request was rejected on the face-saving grounds that too much time had lapsed since the armistice in October 1918. But certainly, Mustafa Kemal was already thinking about eliminating potential political rivals, and had no wish to invite the collaboration of another similarly distinguished Major General.[90] Shortly after Faysal's coronation as king of Iraq in August 1921, Yasin conveyed a request to return to Iraq. Doubtless owing to his criticism of Faysal and his British patrons, Faysal refused Yasin entry.

His younger brother, Taha al-Hashimi, had remained in Ottoman service, ending the war as a colonel in Yemen. Between 1919 and 1920, he traveled from Yemen to Beirut, Damascus, and Istanbul, back to Syria and to Istanbul, and spent 1920 through 1922 in the field between Mosul and Aleppo and to the north in Cilicia.[91] Taha served as liaison officer between Mustafa Kemal, Faysal, Yasin al-Hashimi, and Ibrahim Hananu.[92] By 1922 he was posted to general staff headquarters in Istanbul.

After his failure to join Kemal, Yasin al-Hashimi again sought permission from King Faysal to enter Iraq.[93] This time Faysal, perhaps despairing the lack of administrative talent and expecting Yasin to be sufficiently humbled, agreed. In Baghdad, Yasin spent a few months settling down and avoiding politics. Despite his modest Baghdad childhood, he had not resided in the city since he left for the Harbiye military academy more than two decades earlier. In May 1922, Faysal asked Yasin to serve as governor (*mutasarrif*) of the newly organized Iraqi desert province of Muntafiq. The post was a significant step down for a man who had ended

Figure 3.2.   Yasin al-Hashimi, Civilian Politician *c.*1920s (Courtesy al-Daftari Family)

the war a major general in command of a division, and who had last been offered (and refused) the office of Prime Minister of Faysal's doomed Syrian kingdom. Hashimi's biographer Phebe Marr notes that Rustum Haydar, Faysal's secretary, came with the king's request. Hashimi bowed his head and asked, "Is there no one in Iraq but Hashimi for this mission?" Like many ex-Ottoman officers, Yasin al-Hashimi was a man with few options. He agreed to the post.[94] (See Figure 3.2.)

Percy Cox had appointed the fist Iraqi prime minister, ᶜAbd al-Rahman al-Kilani, in 1920. Al-Kilani was an 80-year-old religious shaykh and scholar. He had significant popular legitimacy, and Cox was amazed that he agreed to accept. Al-Kilani had initially opposed the nomination of Faysal as king, and he opposed the terms of the Anglo-Iraqi Treaty imposed on Iraq also. As Cox called on Faysal to extend his congratulations on a year as king, in late August 1922, a crowd massed outside the palace jeered him. As Peter Sluglett recounts, Faysal immediately publicly apologized to Cox and was hospitalized with appendicitis, at which point Cox assumed the power of government. Al-Kilani tendered his resignation, and signed the treaty as public opposition to the treaty and the Middle East crisis generally came to a head. As ᶜAbd al-Rahman al-Kilani's government resigned in Baghdad, Lloyd George's government fell in London.[95]

In October 1922, King Faysal appointed ᶜAbd al-Muhsin al-Saᶜdun second Iraqi Prime Minister. Over the next seven years, until his supposed suicide, al-Saᶜdun would repeatedly serve as prime minister and critic of King Faysal, and opponent of the role of Britain in Iraq. In his new position, al-Saᶜdun became the leading rival to King Faysal, and principal opponent to the ratification of the treaty. He provoked Faysal's wrath by refusing to order mosques in Baghdad to say Friday prayers in his name, rather than in the name of the Ottoman sultan and caliph.[96] ᶜAbd al-Muhsin al-Saᶜdun Paşa was born in al-Nasiriyya in 1879. He attended the Tribal School and the Ottoman military academy in Istanbul and graduated an Ottoman officer. Along with his brother, ᶜAbd al-Karim, he served as a military aide-de-camp to Sultan Abdul-Hamid. Between 1908 and 1918, al-Saᶜdun was an elected Ottoman parliamentary deputy for Iraq.[97] In October 1922, he formed a new government, which for the year it lasted, refused to ratify the Anglo-Iraqi Treaty. Al-Saᶜdun, like everyone else, had his eyes on events in Anatolia.

Even before the Anatolian nationalists signed the Mudanya ceasefire in October 1922, French forces in the region of Aleppo had come under renewed attack from rebels. Bands had ambushed several French patrols, killing officers and at least fifty soldiers during August and September. French soldiers and citizens were unable to leave Aleppo without armed escort. To the consternation of British observers, French forces continued to hand over stockpiled Ottoman ammunition to nationalist forces in southern Anatolia. French intelligence insisted on labeling rebels operating in Syria bandits and brigands, though they called themselves nationalists and followers of Mustafa Kemal.[98] Rumors persisted that France would cede more territory, including Aleppo, to the nationalists in order to maintain friendly relations. British intelligence claimed this would set a dangerous precedent since there was "no doubt the mass of the Moslems would welcome the return of the Turks."[99]

Rapturous celebrations in Aleppo, Beirut, Damascus, Jerusalem, and Baghdad greeted the victory in western Anatolia. Shops were festooned with banners and flags and the newspapers were full of glowing reports. French authorities encouraged the widespread rejoicing and believed their support of the Anatolian movement would benefit their local positions. British intelligence reports were full of worry and anger over the anti-British tenor of the celebrations. Reports also claimed that French forces would be unable to hold out against any serious Kemalist offensive in the region of Aleppo. A Beirut newspaper, *al-R'ay al-ʿAmm*, reported, "the people are showing their joy at the great victory of the Ottoman army," and calling for demonstrations. The paper cautioned Beirutis to restrain from firing guns and waving flags, since this would "anger the state [Britain] that is the friend of the Greeks, and the enemy of our friends and brothers, the Turks."[100]

In Damascus, the mufti received a telegram from Mustafa Kemal requesting special prayers celebrating and thanking God for the Muslim victory. Many prominent Damascenes sent telegrams of congratulation to Mustafa Kemal. A collection committee received 10,000 gold pounds as presents for Mustafa Kemal Paşa and his soldiers.[101] French intelligence reported that Sultan al-Atrash had been sighted at the border with a band of heavily armed horsemen, and Ahmad Muraywid, comrade of recently executed rebel Adham Khanjar, had returned from Mecca with 800 rifles and ammunition, two 77-mm light cannons, and 130 shells.[102] General Gouraud informed London that unless Amir Abdallah in Transjordan arrested Sultan al-Atrash, France would begin aerial bombardment of his suspected hideouts in Transjordan.[103] Most of rural northern, central, and southern Syria was beyond French government control.

The Last Sultan

The Grand National Assembly in Ankara voted to abolish the Ottoman sultanate on November 2, 1922. The debate and vote was contentious. Ottoman generals, having wrested from Britain the right to renegotiate the Treaty of Sèvres at Lausanne, insisted that the sultan, whose government had surrendered, would not benefit from their struggle. Other delegates resisted vehemently the presumption that the assembly could separate the office of the sultanate from the Caliph of Islam. Mustafa Kemal Paşa delivered the *coup de grâce* in a decisive speech declaring the sultan a traitor to the nation, its people, and to Islam. The news of the abolition astounded Muslims within the former Ottoman realms and outside.

A bit more than two weeks later, the last sultan of the house of Osman fled Istanbul aboard a British naval ship with a few suitcases and the members of the royal family.[104] He died three-and-a-half years later in Italy. He is buried in an ordinary grave at Damascus. Like the Royal Houses of the Hohenzollerns, the Austro-Hungarian Habsburgs, and the Romanovs, the Ottoman monarchy did not survive the transformations of the long nineteenth century and the world war.

Conclusions

In November 1918, the future of the Ottoman state was in question and the state's servants had few options. Ottoman leaders, both military and civilian, had hoped the war would reverse recent defeats in the Balkans and solidify the Ottoman position as a strong power.[105] In this they differed little from other European military and civil elites who willfully took the steps leading to war.[106] But battlefield defeat, armistice, and enemy occupation, presented a dilemma to Ottoman elites in government and the military. Probably most attempted to preserve their attachment to the Ottoman state, and tried to make their way to Istanbul, or at least to the unoccupied regions of Anatolia. Shakib Arslan, to take only one example, immediately traveled from Berlin towards Istanbul via central Europe and the Black Sea. He aborted his journey when he learned the British would likely imprison him in the occupied capital, and he fled to what would become permanent exile.

Mustafa Kemal, Yasin al-Hashimi, and countless others among them, made similarly fateful decisions over the next few months. Most officer graduates of the military education system who survived the war probably became citizens, and eventually pensioners, of the Turkish Republic, including those born in regions that became Greece, Bulgaria, the Balkans, or the Arab regions. The Ottoman education system nurtured the growth of a military elite, including Ottoman Turkish literacy, transnational Islamic cosmopolitanism, and identity with the Ottoman State, rather than any one region or area, and most preferred to remain within the system they served and to protect Islam and the independence of the former Ottoman lands. Civilian functionaries and politicians were in less direct peril from the allied occupation, and were more likely to return to their places of origin.

Common soldiers tried to return to their families, towns, and villages. Some stayed with their units or settled in some new place, especially if their native region was impossibly distant, or under enemy occupation. In this way, uncounted thousands eventually became citizens of new states far from their places of birth. Floods of refugees also traversed the lands of the empire from east to west and west to east. Demobilized soldiers often returned to the field in popular defense committees in the next years. By late 1922 the Ottoman state was gone, but its living citizens, officers, bureaucrats, buildings, schools, roads, memories, habits, culture, archives, and offices remained.

Notes

1. Mustafa Aksakal, *The Ottoman Road to War in 1914: The Ottoman Empire and the First World War* (Cambridge University Press, 2008), Eugene Rogan, *The Fall of the Ottomans: The Great War in the Middle East, 1914–1920* (New York: Basic Books, 2015).
2. Mesut Uyar, "Ottoman Arab Officers between Nationalism and Loyalty," *War in History*, 20:4 (2013), 538.
3. Dr. Mesut Uyar, by a careful examination of formerly closed Ottoman military archives, has shown that officers of Arab origin comprised 20–30 percent of the officer corps and served throughout the war with distinction. Very few deserted. Sulayman Musa, *al-Murasalat al-Tarikhiyya: al-Thawra al-ʿArabiyya al-Kubra* (Amman: al-Muʾallif, 1973), p. 100, reproduces a letter sent from Cemal Paşa to Jaʿfar al-ʿAskari begging him to rejoin the Ottoman army, and pointing out the evidence of British deceit displayed in the leaked Sykes–Picot accord.
4. BNA FO 406/41, SECRET report n. 37, Damascus, October 15, 1919. This report must refer to Taha al-Hashimi.
5. BNA CO 730/150/6, "Profiles and Assessments," "YASIN PASHA AL HASHIMI," 1932. Sami Sabit (Karaman) Paşa was a general of Damascene origin who retreated north with Kemal, took part in the Anatolian insurgency, and served in the army of the Turkish Republic into the 1930s.
6. Phebe Marr, "Yāsīn al-Hāshimī: The Rise and Fall of a Nationalist (A Study of the Nationalist Leadership in Iraq, 1920–1936)," unpublished PhD dissertation, Harvard University, 1966, p. 68.
7. Interview with granddaughter-in-law May Ziwar al-Daftari, London, May 8, 2016, and May al-Daftari's forthcoming book, *Yasin al-Hashimi: Sira wa dhikrayat*. Ms. al-Daftari conducted extensive interviews with Niʿmat Yasin al-Hashimi al-Daftari in the early 1990s. Nuri al-Saʿid, *Mudhakkirat Nuri al-Saʿid ʿAn al-Harakat al-ʿAskariyya lil-Jaysh al-ʿArabi fi al-Hijaz wa-Suriyya, 1916–1918: al-Fariq al-Rukn Nuri al-Saʿid ʿala tullab Kulliyyat al-Arkan bi-Baghdad fi Mayis 1947* (Beirut: al-Dar al-ʿArabiyya lil-Mawsuʿat, 1987); also see Marr, "Yāsīn al-Hāshimī," p. 71.
8. BNA FO371/5043, "Intelligence on Mustapha Kemal," E1337 de Robeck to Curzon, February 14, 1920, and Robert F. Zeidner, "The Tricolor over the Taurus: The French in Cilicia and Vicinity, 1918–1922," PhD dissertation, University of Utah, 1991, p. 135.
9. Zeidner, "The Tricolor over the Taurus," pp. 137–8.
10. Erik-Jan Zürcher, "The Vocabulary of Muslim Nationalism," *International Journal of the Sociology of Science*, 137 (1999), 81–92.
11. James Gelvin, *Divided Loyalties: Nationalism and Mass Politics in Syria at the Close of Empire* (Berkeley: University of California Press, 1998).
12. Philip S. Khoury, *Syria and the French Mandate: The Politics of Arab Nationalism, 1920–1945* (Princeton University Press, 1987), p. 98.
13. James Gelvin, *Divided Loyalties: Nationalism and Mass Politics at the Close of Empire* (Berkeley: University of California Press, 1998), pp. 20–2.
14. Zeidner, "Tricolor," p. 150.

15. Ryan Gingeras, *Sorrowful Shores: Violence, Ethnicity, and the End of the Ottoman Empire 1912–1923* (Oxford University Press, 2011).
16. LN R13, Milner to Cecil, November 6, 1919.
17. BNA WO 32/5730, SECRET cipher. WO to G.H.Q (Allenby) 27.11.1919.
18. BNA WO 158/766 Central Staff Intelligence, "The Nationalist Movement in Turkey," October 28, 1919.
19. BNA WO 158/766, Central Staff Intelligence, appendices, A, B, C, proclamations and speeches of the nationalist congresses, November 1919.
20. Khoury, *Syria and the French Mandate*, pp. 38–9.
21. Circulars recovered in Aleppo. BNA FO 406/41, No. 191, December 2, 1919. Both were translated into English from the Ottoman original. Kemal's "misunderstanding" was surely the Arab Revolt.
22. Awad Halabi, "Liminal Loyalties: Ottomanism and Palestinian Responses to the Turkish War of Independence, 1919–22," *Journal of Palestine Studies*, 41:3 (Spring 2012), pp. 19–37.
23. Fawzi al-Qawuqji, *Mudhakkirat Fawzi al-Qawuqji*, reprint of both volumes of 1975 edition, edited by Khayriyya Qasimiyya (Damascus: Dar al-Numayr, 1995), pp. 15–20.
24. BNA FO 406/41, "Situation in Syria," Meinertzhagen to F.O., November 29, 1919.
25. Qawuqji, *Mudhakkirat*, pp. 70–1.
26. Jurj Faris, *Man hum fi calam al-ᶜArabi* (Damascus: Maktab al-Dirasat al-Suriyya wa-al-ᶜarabiyya, 1957), p. 344.
27. For al-ᶜAs, see Adham al-Jundi, *Târîkh al-thawrât al-sûriyya fi ᶜAhd al-intidâb al-fransî* (Damascus: Matbacat al-Ittihad, 1960), p. 254. For Shallash, see Eliezer Tauber, "The Struggle for Dayr al-Zur: The Determination of the Borders Between Syria and Iraq," *IJMES*, 23 (1991), 379.
28. British Government, *Review of the Civil Administration of Mesopotamia* (London: H.M. Stationary Office, 1920), p. 135.
29. Interview with granddaughter-in-law May Ziwar al-Daftari, London, May 8, 2016, and May al-Daftari's forthcoming book, *Yasin al-Hashimi: Sira wa dhikrayat*. Ms. al-Daftari conducted extensive interviews with Niᶜmat Yasin al-Hashimi al-Daftari, born 1915, in the early 1990s.
30. FO 371/5033 Allenby to FO, March 14, 1920, and FO 371/5034.
31. Satiᶜ al-Husri, *Yawm al-Maysalun: Safahat min Tarikh al-ᶜArab al-Hadith* (Beirut: Maktabat al-Kishaf, n.d. [c.1947]), p. 123.
32. Qawuqji, *Mudhakkirat*, pp. 80–1.
33. Husri, *Yawm al-Maysalun*, p. 83. BNA FO 371/5034, WO, E2338, March 26, 1920. File includes congress proceedings.
34. Khoury, *Syria and the French*, pp. 99–105.
35. BNA FO 371/5033, March 16, 1920. Parliamentary Debates, advice to prime minister. Corrections in original first draft. The word "freed" was added to replace "conquered."
36. BNA FO 371/5119, "Interim Report on the Events of 4th April 1920." Biographical detail on al-ᶜArif from al-Zirikli, *Qamus*, vol. III, pp. 245–6.
37. BNA FO 371/5119, "Military Situation in Palestine," May 7, 1920.

38. *The Jewish Chronicle*, February 27, 1920, "Zangwill on Weizmann," with cover letter from the Zionist Organization, in BNA FO 371/5117. Zangwill argued that immigration alone could never make a Jewish majority in Palestine, and that the only solution was the expulsion of the Arabs by force or persuasion. The article was evidently reported in Arabic translation.
39. BNA FO 371/5036, March 1920, Gouraud to Faysal.
40. BNA FO 371/5226, Iraq Revolt, August 1920.
41. BNA FO 371/5226, letter, from Nuri al-Saᶜid to Major Young, April 20, 1920.
42. BNA FO 371/5226, "Public Opinion in Mesopotamia in Regard to Future of Mesopotamia," May 5, 1920. See Orit Bashkin, *New Babylonians: A History of the Jews of Modern Iraq* (Stanford University Press, 2012).
43. Amal Vinogradov, "The 1920 Revolt in Iraq Reconsidered: The Role of Tribes in National Politics," *IJMES*, 3:2 (1972), 134–5.
44. LN R58, 1920–3. Relative to Syria and Palestine, Iraqis sent comparatively few petitions to the Mandates Commission.
45. *The Times*, "A Case for Frankness," June 15, 1920. *New York Times*, "British Make Oil Coup," May 4, 1920.
46. For the make-up of rebel forces, see BNA FO 371/5229, July 12, 1920, report of Lt. Col. Leachman, who was killed a month later near Falujah. Also see secret telegram on the cost of suppression, August 30, 1920.
47. BNA WO 33/969, "An Examination of the Cause of the Outbreak in Mesopotamia."
48. BNA FO 141/552/1, "Situation in Cilicia," Wratislaw to HC Egypt, February 19, 1920.
49. Zeidner, "Tricolor," p. 378.
50. BNA FO 608/278, San Remo Conference and Cilicia, April–May 1920.
51. BNA FO 608/278, "Copy of the Agreement between Mustafa Kemal and the French," May 29, 1920.
52. BNA FO 608/278, "Press Extracts and Report of Istanbul High Commissioner," July 1, 1920.
53. Interview May Ziwar al-Daftari, London, May 8, 2016, and May al-Daftari's forthcoming book, *Yasin al-Hashimi*. Ms. al-Daftari conducted extensive interviews with Niᶜmat Yasin al-Hashimi al-Daftari, born 1915, in the early 1990s.
54. BNA FO 371/5229, political officer, Ramadi to Office of the Civil Commissioner, Baghdad, July 18, 1920.
55. BNA FO 371/5037; see Husri, *Yawm al-Maysalun*.
56. LN R13, San Remo Conference official map, April 1920.
57. LN R41, 1920, Arrêté no. 336, "réglementant provisoirement l'organisation administrative de l'Etat du GRAND LIBAN," Gouraud, September 1, 1920.
58. BNA FO 371/7846, Lebanon electoral law and census results, March 9, 1922.
59. BNA FO 141/552/1, report on chamber debate, Paris, July 11, 1921.
60. BNA FO 141/522/1, Beirut Consul to FO, December 21, 1920.
61. BNA WO 33/969. SECRET, "An Examination of the Causes of the Outbreak in Mesopotamia," October 1920, p. 25.
62. *The Times*, letters, "Arab Rights: Our Policy in Mesopotamia, Colonel Lawrence's Views," July 23, 1920. Preserved in British, French, and League of Nations archives.

63. James Jankowski and Israel Gerhoni, *Egypt, Islam, and the Arabs: The Search for Egyptian Nationhood, 1900–1930* (Cambridge University Press, 1987).

64. Salim Tamari, *Year of the Locust: A Soldier's Diary and the Erasure of Palestine's Ottoman Past* (Berkeley: University of California Press, 2011), for wartime and postwar mortality in Palestine.

65. IU, *Salname-i Nezaret-i Maarif-i Umumiyye*, h1319. Administrative Yearbook of the Ministry of Education, 1901, pp. 966–77.

66. BNA CO 537/849, August 2, 1921, Secret report, Dobbs to Young.

67. Charles Smith, *Palestine and the Arab-Israeli Conflict: A History with Documents*, 5th edition (New York: Bedford/St. Martin's, 2004), p. 109.

68. Khayr ad-Dīn al-Zirikli, *al-Aᶜlam: qamus tarajim li-ashar ar-rijal wa'n-nisa min ᶜarab a'l-mustaᶜribin al-mustastriqin*, 8 vols., reprint of c.1950 (Beirut: Dar al-ᶜIlm lil-Malayin, 1990), vol. VI, p. 45.

69. LN R14, December 29, 1919, Weizmann to Lloyd George.

70. BNA FO 141/439, "Jaffa Disturbance." File includes telegrams and reports of injuries. "Diary of Events, May 1921," Samuel to Allenby, August 22, 1922.

71. Zirkili, *al-Aᶜlam*, vol. I, pp. 262–3.

72. *The Times*, "Concession to the Kemalists," November 4, 1921. Interestingly, the appellation "Kemalist" seems to have originated with British intelligence, not the Anatolian nationalists themselves.

73. Peter Sluglett, *Britain in Iraq: Contriving King and Country* (New York: Columbia University Press, 2007), pp. 74–5.

74. Zirkili, *al-Aᶜlam*, vol. I, p. 41. Keith Watenpaugh, *Being Modern in the Middle East: Revolution, Nationalism, Colonialism, and the Arab Middle Class* (Princeton University Press, 2012), pp. 175–7, is the best compilation on Hananu's life and career.

75. BNA FO 371/7846, Consul Aleppo to FO, March 24, 1922.

76. Adham al-Jundi, Târîkh al-Thawrât al-Suriyya fî ᶜAhd al-Intidâb al-Fransî (Damascus: Matbaᶜat al-Ittihad, 1960), pp. 101–12.

77. BNA FO 371/7846, Damascus Consul to FO, March 14, 1922. See also Ahmad Djemal Pasha, *Memories of a Turkish Statesman, 1913–1919* (New York: George H. Doran, 1922), p. 199.

78. BNA FO 371/7846, telegram, Consul Palmer to FO, April 8, 1922.

79. BNA FO 371/7847, petition in the name of the Women of Damascus, signed wives of Dr. Shahbandar, Hasan al-Hakim, Munir Shakyk al-ᶜArd, and Saᶜid Haydar, April 10, 1922.

80. BNA FO 371/7847, Damascus Consul to FO, "Anti-French attitude here," May 4, 1922.

81. Quoted in Awad Halabi, "Liminal Loyalties: Ottomanism and Palestinian Responses to the Turkish War of Independence, 1919–22," *Journal of Palestine Studies*, 41:3, Spring 2012, p. 28.

82. BNA FO 371/7847, Damascus consul to FO, June 27, 1922.

83. Hanna Abi Rashid, *Jabal al-duruz* (Cairo: 1925, reprint, Beirut: 1961), pp. 180–1. He reproduced the letters. The version of this event I recounted in *The Great Syrian Revolt and the Rise of Arab Nationalism* (University of Texas Press, 2005), is more dramatic, but less accurate.

84. BNA FO 371/7847, Damascus consul to FO, August 8, 1922.

85. LN R22, original Arabic petition from Sultan al-Atrash, with cover letter and French translation by Shakib Arslan, September 9, 1922.

86. M. Laporte, Chief of French Mission at Adana, quoted in BNA FO 371/7848, "Military Operations to FO," September 14, 1922.

87. *The Times*, "Entente Powers Agreed: Straits to be Defended," September 16, 1922.

88. *The Times*, "Stop the War: Labour Denounces the Premier," and "'Leave Constantinople': Sir C. Townshend on Peace in the East," September 21, 1922. M.P. Townshend was the general in command of the 1915 surrender to an Ottoman force at al-Kut. He had just taken a journey through Syria and Anatolia and met Mustafa Kemal. See BNA FO 71/7848, "Report of the Situation in Syria," September 14, 1922.

89. BNA FO 371/7848, "Report on the Situation in Syria," September 14, 1922.

90. This is a central argument of Erik-Jan Zürcher's *The Unionist Factor: The Role of the Committee of Union and Progress in the Turkish National Movement (1905–1926)* (Leiden: Brill, 1984), p. 119.

91. Taha al-Hashimi, *Mudhakkirat Taha al-Hashimi, 1919–1943* (Beirut: Dar al-Tali'a, 1967), pp. 66–9.

92. BNA CO 730/150/6, "Profiles and Assessments," YASIN PASHA AL HASHIMI.

93. BNA CO 730/150/6, "Profiles and Assessments," YASIN PASHA AL HASHIMI," 1932.

94. Khayri al-'Umari, *Shakhsiyat 'Iraqiyya* (Baghdad: al-Dar al-'Arabiyya li-l-mawsu'at, 2008, reprint of Baghdad, 1927), p. 109. Quoted in Marr, "Yāsīn al-Hāshimī," p. 116.

95. Peter Sluglett, *Britain in Iraq: Contriving King and Country* (New York: Columbia University Press, 2007), p. 78.

96. Sluglett, *Britain in Iraq*, p. 85.

97. Khayr ad-Dīn al-Zirkili, *al-A'lam: qamus tarajim li-ashar ar-rijal wa'n-nisa min 'arab a'l-musta'ribin al-mustastriqin*, 8 vols., reprint of *c*.1950 (Beirut: Dar al-'Ilm lil-Malayin, 1990), vol. IV, pp. 151–2. 'Abd al-Muhsin graduated first in his class in 1898. Eugene Rogan's article on the Aşiret Mektabi lists both brothers: "Aşiret Mektebi Abdülhamid II's School for Tribes (1892–1907)," *IJMES* 28, (1996), 89. Rogan's article is the best investigation of the Tribal School.

98. BNA FO 371/7848, Reports from Aleppo Consul to FO, September 1922.

99. BNA FO 371/7848, Beirut Consul to Curzon, October 31, 1922.

100. *Al-R'ay al-'Amm*, September 16, 1922.

101. FO 371/7848, Damascus Consul to FO, September 23, 1922.

102. FO 371/7848, French Intelligence Summary, October 4, 1922.

103. FO 371/7848, telegram, HC Samuel to CO, November 11, 1922.

104. *The Times*, "The Sultan. Angora Attack on The Porte. Violent Debate," November 3, 1922.

105. Mustafa Aksakal, *The Ottoman Road to War in 1914: The Ottoman Empire and the First World War* (Cambridge University Press, 2008).

106. Christopher Clark, *Sleepwalkers: How Europe Went to War in 1914* (London: Penguin, 2014).

4 League of Nations Hopes and Disappointments: the Return of Armed Struggle in the Post-Ottoman Era, 1923–1927

Events in the Former Ottoman Realms, 1923–1927

July 1923	Lausanne Treaty conference concludes
October 1923	Ankara government's National Assembly forms Turkish Republic
March 1924	Iraqi Constitution and Anglo-Iraqi Treaty ratified in Baghdad
July 1924	Yasin al-Hashimi forms first Iraqi government as prime minister
November 1924	General Maurice Sarrail appointed third High Commissioner for Syria and Greater Lebanon
February 1925	People's Party forms in Damascus
June 1925	Lord Balfour tours Palestine and Syria to mass protest
July 1925	Syrian Revolt begins in Hawran, south of Damascus
October–November 1925	French bombardment of Hama and Damascus
February 1926	League of Nations Permanent Mandates Commission, extraordinary session on Syria meets in Rome
1926–27	Intensive French counter insurgency campaign in Syria
Mid 1927	Final collapse of Syrian Revolt

> If the Turks have any thought for the real interests of their bankrupt
> country and its miserably depleted and exhausted population, they will
> hasten now to conclude peace on the generous terms already offered
> them by the civilized powers. Otherwise Turkey will go down in chaos
> and will become the prey of primitive barbarism.
> *The Times*, "Two Months at Lausanne," January 29, 1923

The years 1923 and 1924 were tranquil by comparison with the decade
preceding. The goal of nearly all politics remained opposition to the
post-war settlement, the colonial mandates, and Zionism, but after the
military victory in Anatolia, and the subsequent reopening of post-war
treaties, diplomacy held new promise to the people of the former
Ottoman lands. An opportunity for elite politics reappeared, and armed
confrontation receded, to widespread relief.

The struggle for the future of the Middle East and the former lands of
the Ottoman state shifted away from the Ottoman lands and toward
Europe. Ex-Ottoman politicians from Anatolia, Syria, Lebanon,
Palestine, and Egypt, traveled to Switzerland, Paris, and London to press
their case against the post-war settlement. A delegation of Ottoman officers and veterans of the Anatolian insurgency went to renegotiate the
terms of the 1918 armistice and resulting peace treaties and settlements,
including the San Remo Conference and the Treaty of Sèvres. From territories already under mandate, Shakib Arslan, Musa Kazim al-Husayni,
and Rashid Rida made the trip as delegates of the Syrian–Palestinian
Congress. Two Egyptian delegations attended, one representing the *Wafd*
Independence Party and one representing the pro-Ottoman National
Party.[1] Except for those who had won their rights by force of arms, they
were to return disappointed.

By summer 1922, the reconstituted Ottoman army had defeated
France in Cilicia and British-sponsored Greek forces in the west, and
forced Britain to re-open the settlement. Britain, Greece, and the representatives of the Ankara Government's National Assembly signed a new
ceasefire at Mudanya in October 1922. The Powers were unable to
enforce the terms of the post-war treaties they had imposed on the
Ottoman state. France, Britain, Greece, and Turkey negotiated the terms
of the Treaty of Lausanne from November 1922 until July 1923. The
new colonial states of Syria, Greater Lebanon, Transjordan, Palestine
and Iraq had already emerged as League of Nations mandates.

British and French politicians and journalists bemoaned the overly
conciliatory attitude of the rival power. *The Times* of London claimed
that France's conciliatory attitude toward the Anatolian nationalists
constituted a loss of prestige from which France would never recover.
Having conceded Syria to France, British politicians were outraged that
France would concede Anatolia to its Kemalist enemy, in order to hold

Syria. British policy-makers were obsessed that nationalist "Turks" still menaced the tenuous British position in Mesopotamia, threatened the retention of Mosul, and refused to accept that they were defeated and Britain had won the war.[2]

The Lausanne Conference

The Lausanne Treaty codified the birth of the independent Anatolian Republic. Mustafa İsmet Paşa (İsmet İnönü) was the chief negotiator for the nationalists. His Kurdish family hailed from the upper Euphrates town of Malatya and he had attended military middle and preparatory school in Sivas, and graduated from the military academy in 1903, and the staff college in 1906. İsmet Paşa ended the war at the Battle of Nablus, a colonel and deputy to Mustafa Kemal. He joined the march north and became famous for his victories during the Anatolian insurgency. He went to Lausanne in November 1922, and stayed till the signing of the treaty in July of 1923. He exasperated the British delegation with his stubborn refusal to compromise.

The last Ottoman parliament had issued the *Misak-ı Millî*, or the National Pact, in early 1920. İsmet Paşa used the pact as his negotiating document at Lausanne and it came to be the foundational document of the Turkish Republic. The first article stated that Ottoman regions with an Arab majority under British or French occupation should have their status determined by the free choice of the inhabitants by referendum, a position İsmet Paşa emphasized. He noted that the populations of Iraq and Syria had not been consulted about their wishes, and he accused the British of coveting the oil resources of Mosul.[3] Foreign Secretary Lord Curzon countered by claiming his government was bound by three pledges. First, the "Arab nation" would not be returned to "Turkish rule." Second, his government was bound by a pledge to the Arab king (Faysal) who, he claimed, was elected by the whole country. Finally, Great Britain was bound by a pledge to the League of Nations, which had assigned a mandate over the whole of Iraq. No territorial adjustments were possible without the consent of the League. "I hope that my argument will convince that it is quite impossible for my country, consistently with a due sense of honour, to run away from pledges it has given, to break its word before the world, to cut out the vilayet of Mosul from the mandates territory, and give it back to the Turkish delegation."[4] Invocations of British honor cannot have been impressive to Ottoman citizens, whatever their religion or ethnicity.

Several years earlier, in the midst of the war, Lord Curzon had prepared a memo for the war cabinet titled "British Policy in Mesopotamia." The memo, drafted shortly after the British capture of Baghdad, contained similar arguments to those offered at Lausanne, but unlike the public arguments, Curzon's memo revealed the depth of British imperial anxiety over the Turco-German alliance and noted frankly that even if defeat loomed, Britain could never reconcile itself to a resumption of German and Turkish control over Basra, the Persian Gulf, and the frontier of India. According to Curzon, the war's central issue and "the real dream of German world policy" was an empire "stretching through Europe and Asia Minor, and as far as the Persian Gulf, and is the weapon, with which, in a future war, the British Empire is to be struck down."[5]

The disagreement over Mosul was drawn out and Britain successfully framed the discussion based on the national idea and the identity of the population. British claims centered on the "Arab" character of the region. İsmet Paşa noted the Ottomans had ruled these places for centuries and knew who lived there, but the Anatolian nationalist movement had abandoned claims to speak for the Arabs. Adopting the language of ethnic nationalism as defined by Woodrow Wilson, Britain, and the League of Nations, İsmet Paşa argued instead that all places with a Kurdish- or Turkish-speaking population should be part of the Anatolian state. People could speak Arabic or Kurdish and still be Turks. In any case, Turks, Kurds, and Arabs had long lived together harmoniously. Having argued strenuously for an undivided "Turkish" Anatolia, İsmet Paşa's delegation could not do more, and those who spoke for other former Ottoman lands still under occupation, were on their own.[6]

At Lausanne, İsmet Paşa represented the Anatolian state and nationalist movement, but politicians and ex-officers from many parts of the Ottoman state attended. They wished to learn how events would affect the former Ottoman citizens of British-occupied Palestine and Iraq and French-occupied Syria. Musa Kazim al-Husayni led the Arab–Palestinian Congress delegation, organized under the umbrella of the Syrian–Palestinian Congress. The congress included Shakib Arslan, Amin al-Tamimi, and several other Istanbul-educated former Ottoman officials. The delegation demanded the independence of Syria, including Palestine and Lebanon, and the rejection of the Balfour Declaration.[7] They called on İsmet Paşa and their former comrades to lend support to their movement for independence from imperialism.

The outcome was a triumph for those who spoke for the Anatolian nationalist movement, but it was a bitter experience for those who represented former Ottoman regions under British or French occupation. The message to those left out of the settlement was the same as that Mustafa Kemal addressed to the National Assembly at Ankara: the right of self-determination could only be taken, and was never given. The Anatolian insurgency provided an example to follow, and a bitter warning to those left behind in Syria, Palestine, and Iraq.

King Faysal had determined his interests best served by obedience to British policy. Faysal dispatched Ja°far al-°Askari to attend the conference as Iraqi delegate. Al-°Askari had no official status since the British delegation negotiated the border between Turkey and the Iraqi Mandate without Iraqi consultation. The British delegation to the conference considered al-°Askari an inoffensive and loyal bystander in their wrangling with İsmet Paşa over Mosul.[8]

Faysal's brother, Amir Abdallah in Amman, had no reason to send a delegate and did not bother. The British government had recently decided to acknowledge Abdallah as ruler of Transjordan, subject to his compliance with a few points, most especially that he "place Britain in a position to fulfill its international obligations."[9] In 1924, the British government separated its Palestine Mandate from its Transjordan Mandate, and began considering Transjordan a separate mandate from Palestine.

The League of Nations Picks up the Pieces

After their disappointment at Lausanne, Musa Kazim and the Jerusalem delegation traveled on to the League of Nations at Geneva, and having been refused a meeting with Secretary General Drummond, they met instead with William Rappard. As in the earlier peace conferences, the League of Nations had played a minimal role, but the League was left to contend with the more unhappy results of the treaty. Rappard filed a report on their visit.

They wished to know the attitude of the League of Nations towards the Palestine Mandate under present conditions. As I had no information whatever, to give on this subject, the interview must have been very disappointing to them.
   The effort of the Delegation to secure a reversal of the [Jewish] national home policy had obviously not been successful at Lausanne. The Turks had told them they would insist on some form of referendum on the Arab provinces in accordance of Article I of the National Pact ... From the French they had received no assurance whatsoever. The British had told them they were very anxious not to offend the French, and therefore could not entertain relations with the Syrio-Palestinian Delegation on account of its intimacy with discontented Syrians ... The Delegation did not seem to have any clear plan of action.[10]

It is no wonder that, as Rappard noted, they did not seem to have a clear path before them and formidable adversaries faced them. Musa Kazim and the veteran politicians who made up the Syrian–Palestinian Congress had never abandoned the Ottoman State, but as they had just learned at Lausanne, the Ottoman State had abandoned them.

Several months before Musa Kazim al-Husayni came to Geneva, Chaim Weizmann, President of the World Zionist Organization, had visited Rappard at his League office. Weizmann was rather more impressive to

Rappard than al-Husayni had been. Weizmann was not only a politician and lobbyist, but also a famous scientist, and former professor at the University of Geneva, where Rappard himself had a faculty appointment. Rappard was a decent and thoughtful person, and he had received al-Husayni courteously and with some sympathy, but Weizmann was in a position to make a much stronger impression and both men enjoyed what Rappard described as a long and extremely interesting meeting.[11] While no mandatory citizens were ever able to meet Secretary General Drummond, or to address the League Council, or even the Mandates Commission, Weizmann was received by all three, and he had continuous access to British policy-makers and politicians at all levels. The Mandate Charter's Article 4 acknowledged the Jewish Agency as the representative of the Jews of Palestine. It was the only representative body so recognized for the duration of the mandates. The Zionist movement had powerful friends in Europe and abroad also. Albert Einstein wrote letters to the League of Nations supporting Zionism, as did US Supreme Court Justice, Louis Brandeis, and many others. Jewish groups the world over sent telegrams and letters to the League of Nations in support of Zionism in Palestine.[12]

The Treaty of Lausanne ended the state of war between the Ottoman state and Greece, Britain, and France in July 1923. The treaty represented a retreat from the expansive post-war ambitions of the victorious powers. Britain and France had sought to dismantle the Ottoman state, and partition its lands, fostering new client states run by Armenians, Greeks, Maronite Christians, and Zionist Jews, and reducing the Ottoman sultan to a domesticated captive under house arrest in some minor palace not claimed by allied occupation forces.

Instead, premier Clemenceau, prime minister Lloyd George, and Greek prime minister Eleftherios Venizelos had all been swept from power, each defeat based on the human cost of their post-war ambitions. Four-and-a-half years after the armistice, the reconstituted Ottoman army had defeated the two main client states, and the Entente powers gave up their claims to every territory not actually occupied by the British army at the time of the 1918 armistice. The colonial client states to emerge, Palestine and Lebanon, were both tiny and endlessly troublesome to their Great Power patrons.

The Lausanne Treaty codified the triumph of exclusive and violently enforced concepts of national identity. On the sidelines of the conference, and supervised by the League of Nations, Greece and Turkey agreed to the bilateral expulsion of two million people based on religious identity and their involuntary membership in mutually incompatible new nation-states: Turkey and Greece.[13] The League of Nations' first High Commissioner for Refugees, Norwegian diplomat Fridtjof Nansen, supervised and coordinated the exchange. The two new nation-states seized the property of their former citizen/subjects. Russia, France, Britain, and the Balkan states had repeatedly used Ottoman Christians as levers to justify intervention and war with the Ottoman State. From the perspective of ex-Ottoman statesmen, a homogenous state of Muslim "Turks" offered insurance against future intervention.

Former Ottoman Christians in the east of Anatolia found that the emerging model of Turkish citizenship actively excluded them and made migration to Iraq or Syria the best option. Certainly, thousands were former Ottoman soldiers, including many Christian officers, mostly, but not entirely, from the Ottoman medical corps. Many struggled for years to establish rights of residence or citizenship in the new states in which they found themselves. The League of Nations' archives contain thousands of poignant petitions seeking redress for lost citizenship, property, or rights of residence.

The Lausanne Treaty affected individuals in ways both tragic and ridiculous.[14] Many sought pensions previously paid by Ottoman State institutions. Mandate authorities were uninterested in pledges made by their defeated enemies and refused to pay. Hundreds sought access to property lost in the settlement. A large number of former Ottoman citizens of Palestine, resident in Latin America, learned they had lost both residency rights and their property in Palestine. Hundreds more sought help returning to family far from their last post serving a government that no longer existed, paid salaries, or issued travel documents. The League of Nations was the last and ultimately futile hope for such people. A Mandates Section notation in reference to similar petitions recorded, "Is there any point in adding these to the file? No action seems to be required. Further letters will be thrown away."[15]

Leon Effendi Baos of Basra in southern Iraq wrote dozens of idiosyncratic letters over five years between 1919 and 1924. Baos was born in Basra, the Greek Orthodox son of an Ottoman telegraph official, and grandson of an Ottoman army physician, who had moved his family to Iraq with the Ottoman army in the nineteenth century. Under the Ottoman capitulations, his father had been considered Greek, but during the Greek–Ottoman war over Crete in 1897, he had been required to formally take an oath of Ottoman citizenship to keep his state employment. In 1919, Baos wished to know how he could be forced to accept Arab nationality in the new state of Iraq. As a lawyer, he wished to know what international law code legalized the forced nationalization of a citizen. Neither mandate nor League officials had an answer.

He wished to take Greek citizenship, but the mandate officials refused to assist him, or admit his eligibility. If he could not be Greek, then he would prefer to have his old Ottoman citizenship, and if he could not have that, he would take Turkish citizenship. He wished to understand how exactly the High Commissioner could force him to become an Arab. And how exactly the High Commissioner and his government could create from scratch "Hedjaz, Mesopotamia, Transjordanie, Egypt, and Turkey and now force people to become subjects of these new born countries." According to his letters, there were hundreds of others known to him in similar circumstances in Basra and Baghdad. "It is not sufficient that I have suffered from the Turks while in Mesopotamia, now the British government, to back the Arabs [is] forcing me to become an Arab, when I am not!"[16] His case seemed to have been unresolved.

The End of the Caliphate

In October 1923, the National Assembly at Ankara unanimously approved the formation of the Turkish Republic and elected Mustafa Kemal first president.

In the preceding months, Kemal had formed a party marginalizing his rivals and critics, and called elections. The new party, emerging from local Defense of Rights Committees was called the (eventually Republican) People's Party, and won an overwhelming majority in the National Assembly. Kemal followed his streak of triumphs with the most controversial move yet. In early March 1924 the National Assembly voted to abolish the caliphate.

The Grand National Assembly at Angora has decreed the abolition of the Caliphate in the House of Othman, and ABDUL MEJID, the last of the long line, has been expelled from the Ottoman Dominions and conducted under escort to the frontier. Of all the vast changes wrought by the war—the downfall of the Hapsburgs, the Romanoffs, and the Hohenzollerns, the transformation of the maps of all three continents of the Old World, the resurrection of ancient States and the rise of States, unknown before the evolution of novel forms of government, and the emergence of new ideas and new feelings among mankind—no single change is more striking to the imagination than is this and few, perhaps, may prove so important in their ultimate results.[17]

Abolishing the caliphate astounded many of Kemal's admirers. But in the atmosphere of post-war trauma and crisis, his success in salvaging some independence insulated Mustafa Kemal from the worst criticism.

In an atmosphere of worldwide shock among Muslims, Sharif Husayn, one-time British-anointed king of the Hijaz, declared himself caliph. In this decision, as in his wartime decisions, Husayn exhibited unerringly poor timing and instincts, and he failed to realize that he had outlived his usefulness to anyone, most particularly his British former patrons. British war-planners had sought Husayn as an anti-Ottoman Arab caliph in 1915 in their effort to occupy the Ottoman eastern flank, but in 1924, British colonial officials were preoccupied with Kemal and retention of Iraq. He had rebuffed British efforts to declare him caliph during the war, but in 1924, to the extent the Arabian Peninsula captured British attention, it focused on the more romantic and mysterious figure of Ibn Saud (ᶜAbd al-ᶜAziz al-Saᶜud), and when Ibn Saud led his forces against Husayn in 1924, first at Ta'if, and then at Mecca, Husayn found himself alone against forces his former British patrons enthusiastically supported. Ibn Saud captured Mecca in 1925, making Husayn, like the Ottoman sultan he had served and abandoned, an exile. He spent the last years of his life a guest of his sons and was buried at Jerusalem, not far from the resting place of the last Ottoman sultan-caliph at Damascus.

Military Confrontation Eclipsed

The example of the Anatolian insurgency remained potent, but by the end of 1922, the prospects for armed struggle receded. International diplomacy and colonial rule had left many Ottoman Great War veterans unemployed and at a loose end.[18] The emerging colonial state identified its enemies and exiled or jailed them. During a period of a year or so after the armistice, many Ottoman soldiers and state civil servants had found it possible to flee and relocate to Anatolia. Such people had then been able to maintain Ottoman citizenship, and claim citizenship in the new republic as it emerged. Those who tried to later claim citizenship in the Turkish Republic found the door shut in the new age of exclusive national membership.[19] Mustafa Kemal busily sidelined, and eventually purged, many of his old officer comrades from the Great War, especially those who had claims to heroic status in their own right, as Yasin al-Hashimi had discovered earlier than most when he tried to rejoin his fellow officers in Anatolia early in 1922.[20]

Most "Arab" Ottoman officers who survived the war fought in the Anatolian war and became citizens of the Turkish Republic.[21] Damascus-born Sami Sabit Karaman was among the most prominent of such people, and upon his release from a British prison camp in 1919 he made his way to Istanbul and commanded a division in the Anatolian war. He was able to retire in Istanbul on a general's pension in 1931.[22] Certainly, continued service was equally appealing to Muslims who hailed from the Caucasus, Crete, Bulgaria, Albania, or other parts of the Balkans. In their case however, the Treaty of Lausanne, the League of Nations, and the new national governments had already declared them "Turks," based on their religious identity. It seems likely that no more than a plurality of the Ottoman officer pensioners of the War of Independence could have hailed from regions that eventually were part of the Turkish Republic,

Salonica-born Mustafa Kemal, obviously foremost among them. For those who did not or could not become Turkish citizens, exile in Hashemite Iraq or Transjordan was usually the best choice among limited options.

By the early 1920s, ex-Ottoman officers outside Anatolia accepted temporary defeat and made the best of the situation as the mandate states emerged. Necessity dictated similar arrangements among many less prominent former Ottoman officers. Ja'far al-'Askari was far luckier than most, and was rewarded for his loyalty and service to King Faysal. Upon returning from attending and observing the Lausanne Conference, in November 1923, Faysal appointed Ja'far al-'Askari prime minister for the first of several terms. By 1921, Sa'id al-'As was an overqualified police constable in the desert principality of Transjordan.[23] He fled the French Mandate after Maysalun and went to work for Amir 'Abdallah as a policeman in Amman. For al-'As the decade between 1913 and 1923 must have been unimaginably tumultuous and bitter, starting as an important officer and school director in a cosmopolitan and exciting provincial capital, followed by years of war, prison, defeat, a return to Damascus under Faysal, life on the run, exile, and finally a job as a policeman in a remote desert town.

Ramadan Shallash was another ex-officer turned trans-border insurgent forced to become a refugee in 'Abdallah's Transjordan. Ramadan Shallash had been a central figure in the early stages of the Iraq Revolt of 1920, and continued to attack British outposts until June 1920, when Faysal managed to send the perennial troublemaker as an emissary to 'Abd al-'Aziz al-Saud.[24] After Maysalun, he took up residence in Transjordan, a fugitive from the French Mandate.

Taha al-Hashimi, younger brother of Yasin, spent 1919 traveling from Yemen to Istanbul, where he arrived in late October. He left Istanbul in March 1920 and traveled to Damascus to join Faysal's government, where he became chief of general security. After Maysalun he returned to Istanbul, and received an appointment in military history in the Ottoman Staff. In February 1921, he left (official) Ottoman service, joined the insurgency, and returned to the upper Euphrates region, where he coordinated guerilla operations for the next three years. In late 1923, he received an appointment as a staff officer in the Iraqi army.[25]

Civilian Politicians in Damascus and Jerusalem

Ottoman civilian bureaucrats and politicians usually fared better under colonial rule than military officers. Until at least 1908, and probably 1913, most Ottoman government officials were civilians, trained in state civil academies, rather than the officers trained in the military academies. The civil system had included civil *rüşdiye* middle schools, and elite Sultani preparatory academies in the provincial capitals. Promising students from prominent families had often advanced to the Mülkiye civil service academy in Istanbul. Many studied law in the imperial law academy. Some had gone on to study in Paris. A few, like Dr. ʿAbd al-Rahman Shahbandar, Faris al-Khuri, and Jamal al-Husayani, had received an English-language missionary education at schools like the Syrian Protestant College in Beirut.

French Mandate authorities released Dr. Shahbandar from prison in summer 1924. He had served seventeen months of his sentence at the crusader-era island prison of Arwad off Syrian's northern coast, and then been exiled for nine more months. In exile he traveled to London, Paris, and America to publicize the cause of Syrian independence.[26] During his time abroad, Shahbandar coordinated his efforts with the Syrian–Palestinian Congress and maintained correspondence with Shakib Arslan, though they eventually quarreled and became enemies. Unlike Arslan, who thrived in exile, Shahbandar relished the daily life of a Damascus politician and orator.

French metropolitan politics gave Shahbandar his reprieve. In May 1924, French elections returned a leftist coalition, the *Cartel des Gauches* government. The new government appointed France's most famous leftist general, Maurice Sarrail, High Commissioner to Syria and Lebanon. The anti-clerical left was underrepresented in the French officer corps, and Sarrail immediately snubbed the Maronite priests in Beirut and antagonized the conservative Catholic colonial officers operating the mandate. He also lifted the ban on Dr. Shahbandar and legalized political parties in Syria.

Shahbander and a few other politicians and intellectuals organized a new party in February 1925. In April, international events thrust anti-mandatory politics to the forefront of discussion in Damascus. Lord Balfour, former foreign minister and author of the Balfour Declaration, began a tour of the mandatory states, starting in Palestine. Balfour gave an address to inaugurate Hebrew University in Jerusalem, and received honors and accolades from various Zionist dignitaries in his excursion through Palestine. Apparently unnoticed by Balfour or his hosts, the Arabic press in Jerusalem, Damascus, Beirut, and Aleppo marked his visit with a campaign of relentless criticism of the injustice that Balfour, his Declaration, and Anglo-French imperialism had brought to the people of the region.[27]

Balfour's visit in Palestine had been fairly tranquil, but when he arrived at Damascus, a large crowd of demonstrators awaited him. The British consul had anticipated and out-maneuvered the demonstrators by collecting Balfour by car at the al-Qadam station outside Damascus and allowing the train to proceed to the central Hijaz station without its notorious passenger. The next morning, however, a larger demonstration took place outside the Umayyad Mosque, and when the crowd learned Balfour would not tour the city and visit the famous mosque, the demonstrators marched through the covered Suq al-Hamidiyya, down Cemal Paşa Street to the Victoria Hotel where Balfour was barricaded under police guard. Balfour was forced to flee Damascus under cover of French riot police and gunfire, and spirited out of the city by car convoy with an escort of gendarmes and mandate secret police. In Beirut, French police took him directly to a British ship moored in the harbor. He received official visits on board ship, but did not again set foot on land before departing two days later.

The visit had been arranged between the offices of the two respective High Commissioners, Herbert Samuel and General Sarrail. The tour planners were ignorant of the press campaign ongoing against Balfour and the colonial settlement and they had not sought the advice of colonial political officers. The British consul in Damascus blamed politicized Damascene law students, and agitation from nationalist politicians, and hinted darkly at French encouragement to embarrass Britain. But he noted:

Lord Balfour was naturally much distressed at the tumult his presence had provoked. He did not understand why Syria should be so much interested in his historic declaration, and seemed not to have realized that from the foot of the Taurus Mountain to the edge of the Sinai Desert is one country physically, ethnically, sentimentally, economically, though now partitioned owing to the exigencies of world politics. And of this country Damascus is the heart.[28]

Neither Lord Balfour, nor the mandatory governments, nor the High Commissioners themselves seemed to appreciate the depth of feeling in opposition to the post-war partitions and occupation. French and British officialdom clung to the ideological arguments made to justify their post-war policy in the former Ottoman lands. For those colonial functionaries in daily contact with the people of the region, such self-delusion was more difficult.

When Dr. Shahbandar announced the People's Party a month later, in June 1925, the Damascus public was well-primed for a political challenge to the mandate. Within a few months, however, the challenge to the mandate took on an altogether more militant complexion, and sidelined the politicians, in favor, once again, of ex-Ottoman army officers, and armed struggle. For a few months in early summer 1925, however, the central role belonged to the People's Party. Dr. Shahbandar led the party and served as its chief orator and strategist. The opening celebration for the party took place on June 5, 1925 in the Abbasid Opera house and at least a thousand people turned up to hear a series of impassioned speeches from Damascus' best political orators, including Faris al-Khuri and Shahbandar.[29]

Party leaders professed goals of Syrian sovereignty, unity, freedom, civil rights, and protection for Syrian trade and industry. Dr. Shahbandar noted that the Syrians faced something similar to the tyranny of Sultan Abdul-Hamid II, and as the leaders of the Unionist Party (Committee of Union and Progress) had smashed the despotism of the sultan, so the Syrians could smash the unnamed despotism facing them. Despite euphemism, the People's Party existed to advance two related, and widely understood, goals: full independence and the unity of Syria within its natural borders, from al-ʿAqaba to the Taurus Mountain, under British and French Mandate in Transjordan, Palestine, Syria, and Lebanon.[30]

Independence was the central objective of the party, but the party did not stand for armed struggle against the mandate power. The party attracted many of Damascus' leading political activists. There were a number of distinguished Istanbul- and Paris-trained lawyers and law professors, among whom were Faris al-Khuri, Saʿid Haydar, and Hasan al-Hakim. Graduates of Istanbul's elite Mülkiye civil service academy were well-represented, but at first there were no ex-army officers among the party ranks. Dr. Shahbandar spoke of secularism and social justice, but any goal or program beyond independence risked disunity, and division, and mobilization was based on slogans and not on detailed programs. Party life was stunted by the day-to-day reality of military occupation and geographical partition, and the vague policies and lack of party formation around common interests were a symptom of colonial domination much less than political immaturity. A party based around the goals of social transformation would have been the site of contentious negotiations, while most segments of Syrian society could agree on independence and unity. Still, both aims, explicitly stated, were anathema to the mandate power, and Syrian political leaders knew well that to be effective they had to avoid exile and prison. In spring 1925, Shahbandar spoke in circumspect terms, but his caution would not be enough, and he would come to spend the years 1926 through 1937 in exile, under French Mandate death sentence.

Shakib Arslan in Exile

Shakib Arslan had no choice but to make the best of exile. In the panic-stricken final weeks of the war, Arslan hastily left Berlin to return to Istanbul. The sultan signed the armistice before he arrived, as he learned during his journey. In Ukraine, at a Black Sea port, Arslan met a group of Unionist Arabs fleeing the Ottoman capital. Association with the wartime government put one's life in obvious danger and Arslan turned around and returned to Berlin where he was soon joined by his friend and notorious wartime governor of Syria, Cemal Paşa, and the other leading Unionist politician Talat Paşa.[31] Berlin may have been safer than Istanbul for members of the wartime government wanted by the Allies. But it turned out to be dangerous nevertheless. An Armenian nationalist in Berlin assassinated Talat in early 1921, and another assassin killed Cemal in Tbilsi in 1922. Arslan's idol, Enver Paşa, was killed leading an insurgency for an independent state in today's Tajikistan against his former Red Army allies in 1922.

Arslan spent the next few years in homeless exile and tireless political activity. On the recommendation of his friend Talat, he was elected president of the Berlin Oriental Club in 1920. On the advice of Enver Paşa he traveled to Moscow to attempt to meet with Soviet leaders in mid 1921. Like his many attempts to gain the support of new post-war leaders, he seems to have been unsuccessful. He traveled between Berlin and Switzerland repeatedly, and organized the first meeting of the Syrian–Palestinian Congress in August 1921 to correspond with the first meeting of the League of Nations Permanent mandates commission on the Syrian Mandate. In late 1922, Arslan returned to Switzerland to attend and experience at bitter first hand the Lausanne Conference. The result of his experience at Lausanne was a potentially dangerous return to Istanbul in late 1923.[32]

Arslan had successfully fled for his life in 1918. The sultan's government under allied occupation sentenced Arslan and the wartime political leadership to death in absentia in July 1919. With the end of the Ottoman Empire after Lausanne, Arslan decided to risk a return in hope of convincing Mustafa Kemal to aid the cause of Syrian independence or reattachment to the Anatolian Republic. In Istanbul, Arslan learned he was yesterday's man; there was no longer a death sentence on his head, but there were no potentially disloyal Arab provinces to worry about either, and it seems unlikely he gained any sort of audience with Kemal. He still retained his Ottoman citizenship, however, and was able to remain in Turkey. Arslan moved to Mersin on the coast near the border with the Syrian Mandate in early 1924. Here he reunited with his wife and son, who he had not seen since 1918, and received a visit from his mother. Arslan evidently found Mersin insufficiently exciting, and took long trips to Switzerland and Berlin later in the year. At the outbreak of the Syrian Revolt in August 1925, Arslan moved back to Geneva, headquarters of the League of Nations, where he stayed for the next twenty years, calling himself the "Warrior of the East in the West."[33]

The Rise of Yasin al-Hashimi and the Anglo-Iraqi Treaty

Yasin al-Hashimi quickly rehabilitated his professional prospects in Baghdad. By 1923 he had passed from ex-officer exile to prominent civilian politician, a transformation many surely sought and very few managed in the wake of Ottoman collapse. In May 1922 he had accepted Faysal's appointment as governor of the Muntafiq province. The middle Euphrates district surrounding the city of al-Nasiriyya had played a central role in the 1920 Revolt and was still not fully pacified. A number of tribal shaykhs continued to oppose the mandate and Faysal's monarchy and periodically raided government garrisons. Meanwhile, British political officers had been busily signing over vast land grants and tax-collecting concessions to tribal shaykhs willing to declare their allegiance to Britain.[34] Hashimi immediately ran afoul of the British political agents when he revoked the grants to pro-British shaykhs and forged ties with those still in revolt. By August 1922, the High Commissioner Percy Cox had forced Faysal to demand Yasin's resignation.[35] His punishment was short-lived.

Yasin al-Hashimi won his way to power and influence in Iraq by talent and cunning. In November 1922 he was appointed Minister of Works and Communications in the cabinet of Prime Minister ʿAbd al-Muhsin al-Saʿdun. Like Saʿdun, Hashimi was a relentless critic of the mandate, and like Saʿdun, resigned his office in November 1923 and dissolved the cabinet over its refusal to support ratification of the Anglo-Iraqi Treaty.[36] While his government tenure had been short, and he had earned the distrust of the High Commissioner's office, which inevitably referred to Hashimi as an "extremist nationalist leader," he had also learned much about the contours of British Mandate governance. If tribal shaykhs in the countryside could become wildly wealthy by the British transfer of state lands, there was no reason sincere patriots should not benefit as well. As governor of Muntafiq, and Minister of Works, Hashimi observed ways in which the allocation of agricultural concessions, irrigation rights, control of former Ottoman State agricultural land, and public works projects could benefit him personally, and he proceeded to make the most of these opportunities, becoming enormously wealthy in short order, and in contrast to his penniless return to the city of his birth in 1922.

Capitalist self-interest did not make Hashimi a supporter of the mandate or monarchy, and British intelligence continually accused him of working to subvert both the mandate and the king and convert Iraq into a republic aligned with the Turkish Republic.[37] British intelligence claimed he was in continual contact with Mustafa Kemal, which, given the vexing negotiation over Mosul and its oil resources, made Hashimi an enemy of the mandate. Mandate officials worried ceaselessly about Hashimi and considered him the most dangerous and most talented politician in the country. Hashimi won a seat in the 100-member-elected Constituent Assembly for Baghdad in the election of March 1924, and in that position continued his opposition and criticism of the Anglo-Iraqi Treaty. The Constituent Assembly had as its task the ratification of the Iraqi constitution and electoral law and the Anglo-Iraqi Treaty.

In March 1922, Major Hubert Young, a wartime comrade of Lawrence, and colonial official, wrote a constitution for the Iraq Mandate. Young believed that the enemy "Turk" had ruled Iraq by an age-old mix of violence and corruption, and resolved to endow the Iraq Mandate with a liberal constitution, which would help to bolster British claims of altruism and enlightenment in London, with the Mandates Commission in Geneva, and in the negotiations over Mosul at Lausanne. Young appointed two distinguished ex-Ottoman statesmen, Sasoon Eskell, a Jewish Baghdadi educated at the Mülkiye Academy, who had been an elected member of the Ottoman parliament from 1908 till 1920, when he returned to Baghdad, and Naji al-Suwaydi, an Istanbul-trained lawyer. While the constitution established a constitutional monarchy, and a dual parliamentary system, it placed the balance of power in the king, and left the elected bodies in a subordinate position. Left out from the constitution was the obvious fact that the king would be subordinate to the High Commissioner. Sasson and al-Suwaydi caused Young a serious problem when they complained that the new constitution was less liberal and less representative than the 1908 Ottoman constitution it was meant to supplant. Foreign Minister Lord Curzon deflected this in predictable fashion by claiming the mandate would *honor* its constitutions; the Turks had failed to *honor* anything.[38]

The assembly barely ratified the treaty in the face of opposition in March 1924. The cabinet of Prime Minister Ja^{c}far al-^{c}Askari had been so damaged by its support of the unpopular treaty that it fell from power in July 1924. This time Yasin al-Hashimi accepted the brief as prime minister and minister of defense – a positively meteoric rise in the space of two years. His first premiership lasted less than a year, but it signaled his arrival, and permanent occupation, at the highest reaches of Iraqi politics. It also placed him in a difficult position; he had been the most prominent critic of the treaty, and now he was at the head of the government charged with enacting the treaty he had opposed. His opposition to the mandate never waned, however, and British officials remained obsessed with his surveillance, but he accepted his place within the world of Iraqi Mandate politics, and he did not return to the field of armed opposition to the colonial settlement.[39]

Armed Insurgency in the French Mandates

Between 1920 and 1922, Robert de Caix, secretary general to the first French High Commissioner General Gouraud, directed the further partition of the Syrian Mandate. De Caix designed the separation of the mandate territory into a series of religiously tinged micro-states, starting with Greater Lebanon, and including the states of Damascus and Aleppo, and the territories of Jabal Druze (Hawran), and the Alawites. De Caix imagined the great cities of Damascus and Aleppo to be hotbeds of "Sunni extremist opposition" to the French role, and prescribed direct military rule and isolation from other regions.[40] French colonial functionaries devised complicated color-coded ethnographic maps to help manage the mandate territory, breaking the population into the smallest sectarian components, but significantly not admitting the possibility of more inclusive national categories such as "Syrian," or "Arab."[41]

Lebanon was expected to be compliant and supportive of the mandate due to its Maronite Christian population. The territories of Jabal Druze and of the Alawites were intended to be quasi autonomous homelands for the esoteric Muslims who formed a majority in the regions. De Caix expected the Druze and Alawi to be grateful to the mandate authorities for liberating them from what he claimed was Islamic tyranny. De Caix signed autonomy agreements with cooperative local families in both territories. In Jabal Hawran, the de Caix Agreement sponsored the ascendance of a formerly secondary faction among the leading families, and thus split the local leadership. Some families signed the agreement, and others opposed it and refused to sign. Sultan al-Atrash rejected the autonomy agreement, and maintained that the Druze were Syrians and that Syria should be a united, independent state made up of all its people. In September 1922, Sultan al-Atrash sent a petition to the League of Nations, via Shakib Arslan, in protest of the de Caix agreement. He demanded in the name of the Syrian nation the right of "self-determination," an end to the mandate, and the preservation of Syria within its natural, pre-partition, borders.[42]

In Damascus, the anti-Balfour demonstrations in April and the People's Party rally in June brought a feeling of expectation, and as the weather heated up in early summer 1925, confrontations with the mandate government increased. Newspapers in Palestine, Iraq, Egypt, and Turkey followed events in Damascus closely, and next to Mustafa Kemal and Sa^cd Zaghlul in Egypt, Dr. Shahbandar became the most famous political figure of the day. High Commissioner Sarrail responded to anti-mandate agitation in the southern countryside by arresting several leading Druze shaykhs under the guise of an invitation to dine and discuss grievances in mid-July. A few days later, on July 19, a group of 250 horsemen fired on and shot down a French airplane, above the Druze mountain region, 100 kilometers south of Damascus. The horsemen then forced the surrender of a French garrison and occupied several villages.

The next day, Sultan al-Atrash led Druze fighters in the occupation of Salkhad, the second town of the Jabal Hawran region, south of Suwayda, the provincial capital. The following day, insurgents destroyed a French column of two hundred men sent to retrieve the pilots and restore order on the road to Suwayda. The rebels continued to the regional capital, occupied it, and besieged the government citadel. In early August a French punitive column of 3,500 troops, including trucks and artillery, under the command of a general, had arrived at the foot of Jabal Hawran. Owing to sabotage of the rail line, scorching mid-summer heat, water shortages, and rebel-damaged roads, the French march was exceedingly difficult. The column suffered continual harassment, but when the commanding general resolved to retreat rather than continue to march on Suwayda, the rebels attacked in force and destroyed the column, leading to the battlefield suicide of the second-in-command.

French officials attempted to keep the defeat secret, but Damascenes learned of the rout immediately, as remnants of the devastated column straggled back. News spread quickly, and newspapers in all the surrounding countries announced the dramatic French reversal. The rebels captured 2,000 rifles with ammunition and supplies, a number of machine guns, and some artillery. Experienced ex-Ottoman officers and veterans were soon operating the artillery and more sophisticated modern weapons. Much of the capital and the surrounding countryside joined the revolt. The revolt began as a local protest, and conformed to patterns established under Ottoman rule during the second half of the nineteenth century, when revolts in rural frontier regions had occurred regularly. But unlike earlier uprisings, the 1925 revolt spread to include nearly all the territories under French Mandate, and drew participants from neighboring regions.[43]

The revolt originated with the Druze. Several close to Sultan al-Atrash had attended the Ottoman Imperial Tribal School and gone on to the military academy and wartime service. Sultan had been conscripted into the Ottoman army and been sent to the Balkans in 1910 and 1911. The Druze of Jabal Hawran had fought against centralized Ottoman rule in their region repeatedly during the previous decades, but in 1925, several of the insurgent leaders were ex-Ottoman officers and had been in close and continuous contact with Dr. Shahbandar and other nationalist politicians in Damascus. They called the revolt "The Syrian Patriotic Revolution" (*al-thawra al-suriyya al-wataniyya*), and supported the uprising, particularly in its dramatic first months. Once the revolt began, and news of its early successes spread, war veterans and ex-Ottoman officers flocked to southern Syria to take part. Damascus members of the People's Party met secretly to discuss supporting and spreading the revolt.

Their goal was rejection of the settlement, and the independence and unity of greater Syria on the model of Anatolia. Mandate intelligence officers arrested the leaders of the People's Party on the night of 27 August, after the conclusion of a secret party meeting, including Christian lawyer Faris al-Khuri, and Najib al-Rayyis, the editor of the banned nationalist newspaper, *al-Muqtabas*.[44] The meeting roster listed mostly lawyers or ex-military officers, including several journalists and prominent merchants.[45] Shahbandar, along with several civilian politicians and a dozen ex-Ottoman army officers, slipped the police dragnet. Some of those who escaped had already taken part in attacks on mandate troops in Hawran and outside Damascus. They scattered in the early morning hours after the arrests, and most made their way to rebel areas in Jabal Hawran. The arrests did not pass unnoticed in Damascus. 28 August was a Friday and the bazaars were closed. Protesters converged on the area outside the Umayyad Mosque after noon prayers, and were met by police gunfire.

Madam Shahbandar assumed the mantle of her fugitive husband, and held a series of meetings with the wives of exiled and jailed Damascene nationalists and with other prominent women. She organized women's marches, and decried the lack of courage among the men of Damascus and the failure of merchants to close the markets completely.[46] Madam Shahbandar held meetings at her house and drafted petitions to the League of Nations dispatched to Shakib Arslan. Twenty or thirty women routinely attended and comprised the most accomplished and publicly visible Damascene women. They included several school and orphanage directors and teachers, and at least one lawyer. The women discussed the valor of the fighters in the countryside, the readiness for patriotic martyrdom, and the work of bringing the rebellion to all of the country. They met at the Shahbandar house and the house of a jailed merchant. They also met at the Damascus-American Girls' School.[47]

Saʿid al-ʿAs resigned his job as policeman in Amman and traveled to Syria. Ramadan Shallash, who had also been working as an emissary to bedouin tribes for Emir Abdallah in Transjordan, slipped over the border to Syria. There they met at least twenty other ex-Ottoman officers who certainly hoped to replicate the example of the Anatolian insurgency. At least a few hoped to be the Mustafa Kemal of Syria.

By mid 1925, Fawzi al-Qawuqji was a cavalry captain in the French–Syrian Legion. Like some of his lesser-known former army comrades, Qawuqji had managed to avoid exile and earn a livelihood within the colonial state. He had joined the legion, and had been sent to the French Military Academy *École Spéciale Militaire* at Saint-Cyr for advanced training. He was stationed in the central Syrian town of Hama. Qawuqji grew dissatisfied with his pragmatic choice of service to the mandate government, and began plotting an uprising during the summer of 1925. In early October, Qawuqji led a mutiny against the mandate and led his cavalry troop in an attack on the French garrison and government offices in Hama. Qawuqji had spent the previous weeks organizing citizens groups and surveying the French defenses. He reasoned that with the Rif Revolt in Morocco, and Syrian in revolt, French forces would be easily routed and forced to evacuate the mandate.

Qawuqji defeated the garrison and captured the town with the backing of its inhabitants. But Hama's wealthier citizens did not support the uprising, and were vindicated when the French, lacking reinforcements, subjected the town to a sustained aerial and artillery bombardment.[48] Qawuqji and his comrades withdrew from the town, after the French command threatened to resume a more intensive bombardment, and the mayor begged that they leave. French intelligence documents were self-congratulatory over the suppression.[49] Qawuqji and his men rode to the dense gardens surrounding Damascus and began what would be an ultimately futile two-year campaign against the mandate.

Ten days later, Ramadan Shallash and several former Ottoman officers led the ill-fated assault on Damascus. Some Damascenes initially welcomed the insurgents and celebrated their arrival. The garrison commander had expressed his hopes that "the Damascenes would give France a chance of dealing with them as the Hama rebels had been dealt with."[50] The bombardment commenced without warning and continued for 48 hours. Unlike Hama, foreign newspapers reported the bombing of Damascus and brought unwelcome international attention to mandate policy and embarrassed the League of Nations. A major section of the old city was destroyed so thoroughly the streets were redrawn when it was rebuilt.

The week preceding the bombardment, Damascenes had witnessed a series of public hangings in the central Marja square. Bodies had been left strung up for hours after morning executions, and signboards around the necks of the corpses described their alleged crimes. Mandate forces had repeatedly failed to flush out insurgents from the dense gardens around Damascus, but a few days before the bombing, an infantry patrol had returned with a column of pack animals loaded with twenty-six dead rebels, which were laid out in the square for public viewing. A large crowd gathered and the Damascenes claimed the dead had been ordinary peasants murdered in their fields, since mandate forces had been unable to engage any actual insurgents.[51]

Insurgents and their ex-Ottoman officer leaders returned to the agricultural gardens and villages surrounding the capital. In the hamlets of rural Syria they preserved an advantage and continued to engage the colonial army with typical guerrilla tactics till 1927. Each night insurgents fought mandate forces in the Damascus neighborhood of Maydan and the surrounding orchards and gardens. Many villages joined the uprising. In December two thousand rebels attacked the barracks and mainline Damascus rail station at Qadam, south of Damascus. Druze Ottoman military academy graduates and ex-Ottoman officers led this attack.[52] Rebel bands were organized and active in the area around Homs, Hama, the eastern and southern regions of Lebanon, north to Aleppo, and in the areas around the Turkish border.

Ramadan Shallash mobilized and led villagers from the mountain region west and north of Damascus. Bedouin horsemen and local peasants, some armed only with farm implements, accompanied them. Shallash began to call himself a commander of the National Army, which evoked dreaded French memories of the withdrawal from Cilicia three years earlier.[53] Shallash would call the villagers to arms by announcing that they were all engaged in a struggle like that of Ghazi Mustafa Kemal and their village was like Ankara in 1920. Such talk was popular, including among Christians.[54] Shallash, who had become literate in the Ottoman Tribal School, wrote letters to the leading rural citizens and big landlords demanding their contribution to the "national struggle." Shallash's appeal to villages mixed patriotism, popular religion, and class warfare against landlords. Many letters relied upon threats of violence. His letters bear striking resemblance to the calls to arms signed by Mustafa Kemal a few years earlier.

To the *mukhtars* and *shaykhs* of the village of Qutayfa,
  Greetings and blessings of God.
  We need you to gather your *mujahidin* and leave one part to guard your village from the [French] troops and bring the other part to Yabrud tomorrow for the greater glory of the religion of Islam. If you bring them late, you will be responsible before God and before the partisans. If you do not respond to this appeal, and assemble [the *mujahidin*] today, we will come and take them tomorrow.
  October 1925
  General Ramadan Shallash

France Salvages its Mandate

The international outcry and crisis that followed the bombing of Damascus led to the recall of High Commissioner General Maurice Sarrail. Sarrail was the most famous leftist general in France. And so upon the electoral victory of the leftist *cartel des gauches* in 1924, Sarrail had become High Commissioner early in 1925. The pro-Catholic Right had its own celebrated colonial general in Maréchal Hubert Lyautey, who, after the leftist electoral victory, and the embarrassing defeats during the Rif War rebellion in Morocco, was recalled to France, and resigned as Governor General of Morocco in September 1925. Lyautey's many admirers in rightist circles in Paris felt the new government had humiliated their hero, and when the revolt in Syria became news the same month as Lyautey's resignation, several newspapers attacked Sarrail with enthusiasm.[55]

Henry de Jouvenel was appointed as new High Commissioner to suppress the revolt and salvage the mandatory mission. De Jouvenel was the first civilian High Commissioner and a prominent and well-connected liberal journalist and politician, well-respected at Geneva. His open style contrasted favorably with Sarrail, but de Jouvenel soon made clear that colonial policy was inflexible. In London he declared that France would not give up Syria.[56] As de Jouvenel was embarking on his journey, the Mandates Section was daily receiving letters and petitions protesting French war crimes and calling for Syrian independence and self-determination. British and French officials agreed any external investigation was unwelcome, and de Jouvenel aligned his position with his British counterparts, and proposed that *he* constituted a commission of inquiry, in order to preempt calls for international action.[57]

Before his departure from Paris, de Jouvenel invited Shakib Arslan to come to Paris for a meeting. Shakib Arslan was flattered by the attention and felt himself qualified to negotiate rebel demands with de Jouvenel. The rebel leadership in Syria, most under sentence of death from French military tribunals, objected to Arslan's presumption, and so de Jouvenel managed by his modest cultivation of Arslan to fracture the internal and external political leadership of Syria.[58]

De Jouvenel made a still more important visit on his journey when he called upon Mustafa Kemal. Upon his landing in Istanbul, de Jouvenel told a Turkish newspaper: "Ghazi Mustafa Kemal Pasha is the outstanding genius of the present day."[59] His visit aimed to ensure the solidity of Franco-Turkish peace agreements over the border region of northern Syria and southern Turkey, and to gain assurances that Kemal would not supply weapons or assistance to his Syrian former compatriots.

When the Syrian rebels sought help from Kemal, they learned that de Jouvenel had already visited and evidently had more to offer than they.[60] De Jouvenel flattered Arslan by granting the attention he craved, and then turned to Kemal to ensure the Syrians would be unable to seek military help from their former comrades. 10,000 additional French troops arrived in Syria before de Jouvenel had completed his tour.

De Jouvenel approved the renewal of martial law before his arrival. Martial law had been in effect with few interruptions since the beginning of the mandate, and de Jouvenel's renewal preceded a series of new counterinsurgency decrees, the most notable of which was seizure of property and the destruction of houses connected to insurgents. Leading families in Damascus accused of connection to the insurgency found their homes and lands seized. Destruction of houses was a commonplace method of punishment and often houses of suspected rebels were bombed from the air as punishment. Rural villages were required to formally submit to mandate forces, and if they did not, the village and its property would be subject to seizure and destruction under martial law decrees. Collective punishment for suspected crimes against the authorities could include a fine of money, labor, or detention levied on a village or neighborhood. Male villagers were occasionally gathered together and executed randomly.[61]

Martial law decrees also allowed hundreds to be condemned without formal trial in military tribunals. The "military tribunals" were no more than lists compiled by mandate intelligence officers. Once a name was known to the mandate intelligence service, the individual would be listed as wanted, and eventually tried, and condemned. During 1926, the Damascus military tribunal sentenced, condemned, and executed 355 Syrians without legal representation or civil due process. Many were publicly hanged in the central square and left hanging for hours to intimidate the population. Hundreds were tried and sentenced to death in absentia. Scores more were sentenced to varying terms, including life at hard labor.[62]

Since 1920, all local police forces and civil authorities had been subordinate to the jurisdiction of the French military. The military authority claimed the right to search the home of any citizen, day or night, without prior notice or arrangement, to remove and detain suspects from their homes or from local jurisdiction without charge or explanation, to suspend rights of speech and of the press and of public association at will, and to seize the property of any citizen without explanation or compensation. The High Commissioner delegated to the military commander the right to detain, and kill, if necessary, any citizen at any time without judicial or administrative oversight or review.[63] French authorities actively prevented League of Nations Mandates Section efforts to learn about the functioning of martial law in Syria.

De Jouvenel's arrival in Syria brought a flurry of well-publicized offers and decrees. De Jouvenel met a delegation of prominent Syrians not involved in rebel activity. De Jouvenel replied to the delegation's moderate demands with studied vagueness, and the delegates returned from their meeting dissatisfied that he had agreed with nothing and disagreed with nothing.[64]

De Jouvenel sought to enlist Syrian elites in suppressing the revolt. But when he published his reply to their demands in the days after the meeting, he made clear his policy of no concessions before the country was fully pacified, whether by the surrender of the rebels, or by their complete defeat. He declared that restoration of peace was the condition under which amnesty and a constitution would be granted. A negotiated peace settlement between the insurgent leadership and mandate authorities was consequently impossible. Once the formalities of rhetorical conciliation were out of the way, a fully military counterinsurgency strategy prevailed, outside of international view, and after the bombardment of Damascus in October, away from the foreign residents and witnesses of the capital city.

Rebels controlled the countryside and villages surrounding Damascus. The train lines, roads, and telegraph lines to Beirut in the west and Palestine in the south were regularly severed.[65] Newly arrived soldiers were garrisoned in and around Damascus, to protect the city and prevent renewed rebel infiltrations. Forces were mixed, including a small force made up mostly of European Great War veteran Foreign Legionnaires, a somewhat larger force made up of French-officered colonial troops from Senegal, Algeria, and Morocco, and a shifting number of locally raised and trained irregular troops, mostly comprised of Armenian refugees. French generals established a defensive cordon around Damascus, and implemented a new doctrine of offensive operations.

The outlying sections of the city were cut off by means of barricades, barbed wire, and roadblocks. Mandate forces established permanent posts astride all the entries into the city, and between the surrounding villages. French military spotters could quickly call artillery fire from the citadel or other artillery batteries, or air strikes from bases just to the south-west of the city. Bands of rebels remained active in the city, but getting in and out was harder. Mandate forces punished neighborhoods where insurgents had been active.[66] After a neighborhood was bombed from the air and shelled from stationary artillery batteries, Foreign Legion troops in armored cars and tanks would drive along the larger streets. Memoirs of soldiers who took part noted that these punitive expeditions were not intended to actually engage rebels but to intimidate the population. General Charles Andréa ordered the summary execution of anyone found in possession of firearms.[67] After the armored sweep, colonial and irregular troops would move through the neighborhood on foot and enter houses. The irregulars were mostly Armenian refugees from Anatolia, and the use of Christian refugee troops to pacify Muslim neighborhoods provoked hand-wringing among the European consulates. At least a few revenge murders of Armenian refugees and Syrian Christians took place. Syrian petitioners accused the irregulars of the worst outrages, but from the perspective of the mandate commanders, they were considered sufficiently unimportant to risk in direct contact with the population.[68]

Pacifying the regions around Damascus was slow, and the French command resolved to launch a spring offensive through the region south of the city. The volcanic mountain region of Jabal Hawran remained the rebel stronghold and origin point of the revolt. Despite daily bombing raids, the region could only be subdued by a massive offensive across the plain of Hawran stretching 100 kilometers south of Damascus. Everyone expected French forces would march south in the spring.

William Rappard, the League of Nations, and France

> The situation is inconvenient for the League of Nations. What has happened and is happening in Syria is no longer a secret. Clouds of journalists from various parts of the world have descended on the country. The Syrians are making a determined effort to get a hearing at Geneva. No doubt they will fail, but their failure will not strengthen the authority of the League.[69]

In 1925, Robert de Caix had become Accredited Representative for the mandate authority to the League of Nations. In his description the uprising was the "Druze Revolt," and did not represent any form of unified Syrian movement or aspiration. In explaining the insurgency to the Mandates Commission, de Caix claimed that Syria comprised seventeen or eighteen separate, mutually antagonistic, religious sects. Without France they could be expected to annihilate one another. In explaining the mandate policy to arm and recruit Christian irregulars, de Caix claimed that Muslims killing Christians was endemic to the country. Only France could save them. "In cases of disorder in these countries, there is no need of any special resentment to explain a massacre of Christians." French colonialism was the solution, not the problem.[70]

Mandate policing and counter insurgency proceeded by the recruitment, arming, payment, and minimal training of those segments of the colonial populations considered friendly to the mandatory government. In the region of Lebanon and the mountains more generally, this meant arming Christian villagers. In the southern and northern regions it meant arming Bedouin, Ismaili, or ⁿAlawi Muslims. Some were concerned that such policies had the potential to ignite sectarian civil war, but the mandate faced continual crises of both indigenous opposition and insufficient finances. Sectarian conflict confirmed French prejudices about Syrian society and served as rhetorical support for the colonial mission. Middle Eastern governments in Israel, Syria, and Jordan have continued to recruit local minority troops for security duty. Such policies have the added benefit of fragmenting unified movements of national opposition, and insuring a loyal core of supporters.

In September 1925, Shakib Arslan left his unhappy exile in Mersin and moved to Switzerland permanently. The Syrian Revolt gave Arslan, and the Syrian–Palestinian Congress, a renewed chance to become the voice in Europe for the mandatory populations. Arslan wrote articles for the French-language and Arabic press, and collected innumerable petitions from inside the mandate states, translated them, and forwarded them to the Mandate Commission, thus circumventing British and French efforts to prevent protests from reaching Geneva.

The congress submitted a detailed report in response to the public claims of the mandate authority.

The French have done everything in their power to stir up religious antagonism and to favour one community at the expense of another. [In Ottoman times] the people were divided into two main categories – Moslems and non-Moslem. The new decree pronounced by the High Commissioner has divided the nation into fifteen religious communities, viz. Moslems, Chiites, Druses, Nosseris, Ismailians, Orthdoxes, Greek-Catholics, Latins, Protestants, Armenian-Catholics, Orthodox Armenians, Syrian-Catholics, Orthodox Syrians, Maronites, and Jews. The seats on the representative council are distributed between these communities. If a community has less than 6,000 members, it is regarded as a minority and is not entitled to representation.

At Damascus, a distinguished barrister, formerly an Ottoman parliamentary deputy and minister at Damascus, at present President of Corporation of Barristers, professor of law and member of the scientific institute, is not entitled to stand for the sole reason that he is a Protestant. All this goes on in Syria under cover of mandate, and yet article 8 of its terms is quite explicit on this point. "No discrimination," it says, "shall be made between different religious communities."

This is how France, the home of liberty and the proclaimer of the rights of man, applies her noble precepts in Syria and the Lebanon.[71]

The lawyer mentioned but not named was jailed People's Party leader and eventual Syrian Prime Minister and first Syrian UN delegate, Faris al-Khuri. The system of sectarian proportional representation, exactly as described, still operates today in Lebanon. Sectarian proportional representation is regularly denounced by Lebanese citizens of all religions.

By early February 1926, the revolt had dragged on for more than six months, and Syrians believed the League of Nations was their only hope. Both insurgents and ordinary Syrians were exhausted, the countryside was devastated, and everyone craved peace. As it became clear that no conciliation would be forthcoming from de Jouvenel, Syrian hopes for relief and justice shifted to the international community and the League of Nations. The Mandates Section announced an extraordinary session devoted exclusively to Syria, and the discussion of a comprehensive French report on the causes and suppression of the revolt in Rome in mid February.[72] The announcement of the extraordinary session provoked a wave of petitions and intensive press coverage. William Rappard had resigned from his post as director of the Mandates Section, but had agreed to continue to serve as a member of the Mandates Commission. The Commission met over the course of more than three weeks during February and March.

Shakib Arslan and Ihsan al-Jabri traveled to Rome and sent a formal request to address the Commission as representatives of Syria. Arslan had been told to submit his request only after the Commission had sat, and this he did on the fourth day of the session. Arslan pointed out that only by hearing from the Syrian people could the Commission hope to have the full truth of events in Syria. He argued that the truth required a League commission of enquiry to Syria to judge the claims and actions of France. He knew as well as anyone, however, that sending a commission was beyond the powers granted to the PMC and the League.

If the Commission feels unable to decide upon such an enquiry, it can at least grant an interview to the duly appointed delegates of the Syrian nation, who, failing such an enquiry, are alone able to explain and rectify the inaccuracies of the statements made by the representative of the mandatory power.[73]

After waiting in his hotel room for the next two weeks, Arslan received a short reply two days before the end of the session. "The Commission considers that circumstances do not permit it to accede to your request."[74]

Despite the terse dismissal, the discussion over Arslan's request had consumed many hours. Ernest Roume, former colonial administrator in French West Africa and Indochina, objected to Arslan's calling himself "a delegate of the Syrian nation." This, he opined, was "a qualification to which he had no right."[75] Roume represented the official French position: the uprising was much smaller and more marginal than reported or claimed by the Syrians, rebels were sectarian fanatics, common criminals, and a small number of foreign-inspired political instigators who sought to profit from the circumstances. It would serve no one's interests to give too much attention to such people. His more critical colleagues were unconvinced.

Rappard cut to the heart of the matter. Petitions and the right of representation had long preoccupied the Commission, he noted. The Commission had to somehow divide its responsibility between the mandatory power and the mandatory inhabitants. There was, however, a five-year precedent of denying such delegations. Furthermore, the Syrian–Palestinian Congress delegation had submitted voluminous petitions, which had been used in questioning Robert de Caix, the Accredited Representative, and some had even been quoted in the minutes. Most importantly, there was the matter of legal procedure.

The rules determined that a petition could not be presented to the Commission before the mandatory power had seen the petition and had a chance to respond to it. If, on the other hand, the Commission received a delegation of petitioners, it would be hearing information and charges unknown to the mandatory power. The only remedy would be to have the delegation appear before the Commission *together with* the Accredited Representative of the mandatory power. This, however, was an impossible prospect, because "it would place the mandatory on a footing of apparent equality with the petitioners, whereas the tutor ought to maintain a real position of authority, even as regards appearances, with respect to his pupil."[76]

Rappard had glimpsed the implications, and stepped back. If mandatory inhabitants could challenge their mandatory rulers on equal footing, from a position of equality, the entire mandate edifice sat on a foundation of sand. The mandates could only function in an atmosphere in which national and racial hierarchies were operable and claimed to be based on something other than a preponderance of force. The unspoken assumption existed that "advanced" European Christians had essential characteristics entitling them to rule other people without consent. The characteristics of self-rule might be transferable through education, or "tutelage," to the subordinate nations and in this the mandate blurred the lines separating its conception from earlier models of colonialism. The mandatory power would be charged with education, fostering development, and so on. But when the functions of education, development, and eventual self-rule suddenly seemed to require endless martial law, mass public executions, and tons of explosives dropped from airplanes, the Mandate Commission's more insightful members appreciated the problem they faced.

Shakib Arslan had compiled and submitted detailed lists of damages, including exhaustive tallies of Syrians killed and injured, and the time and place of their deaths. The congress composed sophisticated petitions, citing an array of League of Nations documents, and legal precedents, including the covenant itself. He and his colleagues collected and translated hundreds of signatures and endorsements from prominent mandate citizens from all religious communities and vocations in Syria and Lebanon.[77] They forwarded letters from Syrian politicians, repeating precisely the demands of the delegation that had met de Jouvenel in November. Arslan and the Syrian–Palestinian Congress provided the only copies of French Mandate martial law decrees received by the Commission. They documented decrees denying due process and dozens of cases of extra-judicial detentions, internal exile, seizure of property, and deportations. The French government had repeatedly ignored Mandate Section requests and reminders of its legal responsibility to provide such documents.

Several commission members were mystified by the lack of petitions originating in Syria.

The Commission had received a large number of telegrams and despatches from Cairo and from Syrian colonies abroad. There was one striking fact. The Commission did not receive petitions from the country itself … How did it happen that they did not endeavour to make themselves heard? … The Commission had received nothing at all.[78]

De Caix attributed this lack to lingering fear instilled by the "Turkish regime."[79] It is likely that none of the commissioners knew that the Ottoman archives contain uncounted thousands of petitions from Ottoman Syria, which had sent many deputies to the elected parliament in Istanbul. Former Ottoman parliamentarians, including Shakib Arslan himself, were among the most prolific petition writers protesting French rule in Syria.

Members of the Commission asked Robert de Caix specific questions based on things they had read in petitions or in the press. How, one asked, could he explain the policy of bombing villages for the crime of harboring rebels, when they had no means to resist the rebels when they appeared? Other villages were forced to pay a collective fine in rifles that they did not possess. These villagers were forced to purchase rifles to hand over to the mandate authorities, under threat of their village being bombed.

De Caix personally regretted the need to bomb villages forced to receive pillagers, but the facts were unclear. "In these countries things were much less certain. A village which did not refuse hospitality was in many cases a village which willingly accorded it." De Caix noted bombing from airplanes was better than sending a column, which would certainly have meant greater losses of soldiers. But why did de Caix claim the choice was between bombing and sending a column when the villages under discussion had not been accused of attacking mandate forces? De Caix replied to this line of questioning to say that the villagers were habitual liars. Furthermore, airplanes were the accepted method of counterinsurgency, as Great Britain had shown in Iraq.[80] Women and children might be killed, but more might have been killed if other methods were used, and airplanes could be heard from a distance, allowing villagers to take cover. The mandatory power considered the lives of its soldiers foremost, as any other country would under the circumstances.

Rappard noted that the mandate forces seemed to be made up of colonial troops, from territories "less advanced" than Syria, by which he meant African soldiers or troops with darker skin than Syrians typically possessed. De Caix pointed out that France could hardly be expected to recruit and send her own sons to fight colonial wars. Rappard asked how it was that the mandate could be called a guardianship of civilization if colonial troops were in charge of the educational process in other colonies? How, he asked, had "such exhibitions as the corpses on pack animals helped the guardian to develop in his ward the idea of human dignity?" Rappard claimed Syrians were known for their aversion to trouble, and yet "their exasperation must accordingly have been very great to encourage them to meet an army equipped with aeroplanes, guns, and tanks."[81]

De Caix claimed that the average Syrian supported France. Indeed, ordinary people had never fought against the mandate at all. "The colonial soldiers had not been sent to Syria to spread civilization, they were [there] for the necessary work of repression, and war was not an education enterprise." As far as the bombardment of Damascus was concerned, there were few troops available and the response was a moderate display intended to create a strong impression on the population. "If there had been a really effective bombardment, nothing would be left of the town." De Caix considered the exhibition of corpses as personally repugnant, but it had been in response to complaints of Damascenes that the mandatory was insufficiently serious about fighting the insurgency. The display was in keeping with what the natives understood and expected and was anyway "in conformity with the procedure under the former regime."[82]

The final report of the Eighth Session made clear the Commission's displeasure and embarrassment over events in Syria. The mandatory power had ignored the covenant of the League of Nations, ignored its responsibilities to the Mandates Commission, and ignored requests for martial law codes. It had brought negative attention both to the mandatory mission and the League of Nations itself. The promised comprehensive report was not comprehensive and did not discuss the causes of the uprising, or the methods of repression employed. The government had refused to respond to appropriately submitted petitions. Since France had not provided a report on its suppression of the revolt, the Mandate Commission could not make any comment on the methods employed in its report. It seemed likely that in this omission, at least, the Mandates Commission was relieved to avoid discussion of what had been done in Syria to protect the mandate.[83]

The Mandate Commission did not recount the bombardment of Damascus or similar episodes in its final report. French reticence made this easier. The Commission members wanted to know how France understood its mission as League of Nations mandatory power over Syria. Robert de Caix provided a statement of philosophical intent that the Commission endorsed enthusiastically.

In the view of the Mandatory Power, the independence of the country was recognized, but the exercise of the free rights accruing to a sovereign and independent nation was deferred until such time as it was able to exercise them. During this period it was in the position of a minor, and the guardian exercised powers of control as well as of advice and assistance. It was the duty of the guardian to hasten by all means in its power the time when the minor would be able to stand alone. The present discords in Syria and Lebanon showed that this time had not arrived.

The Commission and the Accredited Representative agreed that only by surrendering and cooperating with France and the League of Nations could the Syrians make any progress toward self-government. British Commission member Lord Lugard noted finally, "the commission has done what it can – and it has received every possible assistance and collaboration from M. de Caix, whose knowledge, ability, and goodwill it desires to bear testimony."[84] Meanwhile little had changed in Syria.

The End of the Syrian Revolt

In April the colonial army marched on Hawran, and a week later the Damascus quarter of Maydan was destroyed by a 22-hour artillery bombardment. By July 1926, the leading insurgents had all been sentenced to death in absentia, and the French army made clear the intention to accept nothing less than complete victory and surrender. Rebel bands led by Fawzi al-Qawuqji, Saᶜid al-ᶜAs, and others continued to enter the city and occasionally fire upon French forces. Insurgents attacked convoys and fired on armored vehicles outside Damascus. Telephone lines were cut and trains were attacked, and in late August rebels attacked and captured a convoy of provisions and ammunition near Damascus. French soldiers continued to be killed by snipers and attacks on isolated outposts. Two small bands, one led by Sultan al-Atrash, and one made up of ex-Ottoman soldiers, remained active until mid 1927, when the survivors scattered into exile.

In August 1926, public notices printed in the newspapers boasted of French victories. General Andréa reported that he had toured a number of Hawran villages accompanied by three battalions of approximately 1,500 soldiers. The notices claimed that everywhere notables and ordinary villagers had welcomed him and sworn their sincere fidelity to France. He awarded medals to colonial soldiers in public ceremonies, and collected submissions of eight machine guns, seven mounted guns, 2,935 rifles, and 3,175 Ottoman gold pounds.[85]

Damage Control at Geneva, 1926

In November 1926, the mandates commission finally received the promised comprehensive report. Robert de Caix appeared at Geneva, and spent three days discussing the report and answering questions. De Caix claimed that both peasants and large rural landowners had turned against the insurgency. He reported that peasants were now eagerly notifying mandate authorities of the presence of insurgents in their areas, a goal the army had been working toward all along. But Rappard noted that the written report documented mandate forces forcing villages to pay hundreds of gold pounds for the crime of failing to report rebels passing through their areas. He alone seemed to find the collective punishments levied on Syrians troubling. De Caix claimed the fines were calculated based on what villagers would understand and expect, and should not be judged by other standards.[86]

De Caix and the majority of the commission had synchronized their collective interests and the confrontational character of February's session did not return. The only hostile exchange concerned the tarnished reputation of the Mandates Commission. Months earlier, in a general assembly meeting of the League Council, High Commissioner de Jouvenel had publicly blamed the Mandates Commission for prolonging the revolt. Rappard and others complained vigorously about his statement and demanded an explanation.

De Caix explained patiently that extremist Syrians had somehow felt that the Commission would take their side against France. De Jouvenel was frustrated by the Commission's excessive receptivity to petitions produced by extremists. Taking such petitions seriously encouraged those who felt they could separate the League from the mandate power. De Caix explained gently that

Among a population like that of Syria, whose active imagination was not restrained by a sufficient knowledge of the elements of politics, it had been possible to maintain at certain moments that the mandates commission, or more exactly the League of Nations, would intervene in a sense hostile to the French mandate. It was clear that the Commission was not responsible for such a state of affairs.

After some discussion, the commissioners decided that de Jouvenel's remark had been a simple misunderstanding. In any case, Portuguese diplomat Freire d'Andrade pointed out, the Syrians had no idea how seriously the Commission took petitions since they could not read the report. The mandatory power had banned its distribution in Syria.[87]

The mandatory government had finally given a written accounting of a sample of the petitions submitted to it. The petitions alleged arbitrary destruction of property, widespread pillage, numerous acts of extra-judicial execution and murder, and torture of prisoners among other similar acts, all committed with the knowledge and implied approval of high-ranking French officers. Many of the petitioners claimed that the worst atrocities had been committed in revenge for the deaths of soldiers in the immediate neighborhood.[88]

De Caix deftly parried discussion of the petitions, though the Commission had lost its taste for tough questions. He repeatedly disputed the facts of petitions, noting that there was no proof that the events as described had happened, while acknowledging that unpleasant and regrettable things had surely occurred in individual circumstances. When petitions cited specific facts, de Caix explained that the individuals in question were involved in the insurgency and had brought events upon themselves. No one had been murdered, and no one had been punished without cause. Prisoners had not been tortured, but in fact had been treated very well. The unfortunate fact was that regrettable episodes were unavoidable under the circumstances of widespread disorder. And those charged with the restoration of order were certainly not responsible for the consequences of insurrection.[89]

Commission member Freire d'Andrade read an excerpt from a representative petition into the minutes of the session. The petitioner wrote, "No one in Syria has any doubt that the crimes mentioned have been committed with the approval and consent of the French authorities. The pillagers carried out their depredations under the protection of tanks and under the orders of French officers." A Colonel Raynal had written the report and vigorously disputed the charges made by petitioners.

Freire d'Andrade emphatically stated that the "Commission should believe the word of such a man as Colonel Raynal, whose courage and character were beyond doubt, and who was incapable of not stating the whole truth."[90] In response to multiple charges of murder, pillage, rape, and official corruption, the commission had this to say: "The French nation had accumulated sufficient glory and prestige in the history of civilization to make it impossible for anybody to think that in her policy she had had recourse in any respect to methods such as murder, burning, pillage and rape to satisfy the pleasure or mere caprice of her officials."[91] Freire d'Andrade did not exactly deny that such things could have happened, only that any official could be directly responsible.

Mandate martial law decrees had never appeared. The commission had repeatedly noted the absence of operative statutes and martial law decrees in French submissions. Texts of decrees and laws had been promised often to the commission, but when a list finally appeared, mid way through 1926, it only covered to the end of 1924, completely ignoring the period of the revolt. The suppression of the revolt had been carried out in conformance with decrees that formally legalized summary executions, public hangings, preemptive destruction of villages, and military courts. Such laws, all with a colonial pedigree, are still operative in all post-colonial Middle Eastern countries, including Israel. De Caix offered yet another excuse for the requested materials never arriving. The members of the Commission apparently nodded and murmured their approval.[92]

The rebellion was over and Syria had disappeared from the pages of European newspapers. The Commission could file its last report without public scrutiny. Damascus had been repeatedly shelled, several outlying neighborhoods had been flattened and rendered uninhabitable, and a massive offensive had moved through the southern countryside, driving the remaining insurgents and their families into Transjordan, and eventually into the new Sultanate of ʿAbd al-Aziz al-Saʿud. According to the standards of the mandate and the League of Nations, civilization had triumphed over barbarism.

The commission, after carefully examining the reports submitted by the mandatory power, considers that there is no reason to affirm that the suppression of the revolt was carried out in abnormal manner or was accompanied by reprehensible excesses. If there have been acts of harshness, if there have been distressing incidents, if there have been innocent victims, these events are unfortunately such as usually occur in the course of all forcible measures of this kind. The commission can only hope that such measures will never be necessary again and that a lasting state of peace will be established without delay.[93]

Aftermath of the Syrian Revolt

Mandate military courts sentenced most of the known rebels to death in absentia, including Dr. Shahbandar, and by 1927 there was no safe refuge within the French Mandate. Shahbandar, Sultan al-Atrash, and hundreds of other wanted rebels, many ex-Ottoman officers among them, often accompanied by wives, children, and extended family, fled first to al-Azraq in Transjordan. Within months Amir Abdallah's police and the British Mandate officials forced them to scatter to various places. Most of the Druze fighters and their families moved to Wadi Sirhan, the closest point to Syria and Hawran within the new sultanate of ᶜAbd al-ᶜAziz al-Saud. There they lived in tents and survived on donations collected and disbursed by the Syrian–Palestinian Congress.[94] Shahbandar eventually traveled to Cairo, where he practiced medicine and engaged in exile politics with his comrades among the Cairo members of the Syrian–Palestinian Congress.

The ex-officers traveled to one or another of the new kingdoms of Faysal, al-Saud, or ᶜAbdallah, where they sought work in the army, police force, or military academies. Fawzi Al-Qawuqji finally left Syria permanently in mid 1927 after traveling from one of the mandates to the other, and attempting without success to continue armed struggle. After fleeing to Transjordan, he eventually traveled to the new sultanate of al-Saᶜud, where he found work training the army of the new kingdom. He stayed for five years and earned a small pension that supported him in his retirement in the 1960s and 1970s in Beirut.[95]

Ramadan Shallash surrendered to the High Commissioner and denounced his comrades. He later claimed plots and tricks forced his surrender and he was detained in Beirut under a kind of house arrest far from his upper Euphrates region until the end of the mandate, twenty years later. His sons received scholarships from the French government, and Shallash was probably supported by modest French stipend in his internal exile.[96] Others paid more severely for their opposition to the mandate. Saᶜid al-ᶜAs returned to Amman and eventually rejoined the police force. He continued to work in Transjordan until he joined the Palestine Revolt in 1936. Dr. Shahbandar resumed his medical practice in exile. He cultivated a growing rivalry with Shakib Arslan, and was allowed to return to Damascus in 1937, when most rebels, including Sultan al-Atrash, were finally amnestied. Shakib Arslan returned briefly in 1937 and Fawzi al-Quwuqji never received amnesty.

Henri Ponsot succeeded Henry de Jouvenel as High Commissioner in late 1926. Like de Jouvenel, Ponsot was a civilian, and effectively managed the final stages of countering and suppressing the insurgency. The first few High Commissioners in Syria were generals, but its most durable legacies in sectarian politics, border creation, and political structures were the work of its civilian leaders such as de Caix, Jouvenel, and Ponsot. Ponsot began the process of political reconciliation with a series of amnesty decrees beginning in early 1928. The amnesties allowed the formation of a moderate nationalist leadership and a grouping that came to be called the National Bloc (*al-Qutla al-Wataniyya*) in 1928. Philip Khoury noted that the National Bloc politicians shared several traits that recommended them to mandate authorities, including significant financial stakes in stability, a lack of involvement in the revolt or armed struggle generally, and in most cases no ties to the Hashemites or Faysal's British-supported government. French officials remained obsessed with "*sharifians*" and British intrigues, and barred most leading rebels for more than a decade.

The Syrian uprising had significant and lasting consequences. It took as its inspiration and model the successful Anatolian insurgency of a few years before, and drew its leaders from similar, albeit less experienced and well-known, strata. Sultan al-Atrash was certainly an inspiring figure for Syrians, but the revolt may have been a greater threat to the mandate with cosmopolitan Ottoman staff officer leaders, like the people who led the Anatolian movement. A figure like the late Yusuf al-ᶜAzma or Yasin al-Hashimi may have had a better chance of organizing a mass movement, mounting a military challenge to the mandate, and managing a successful negotiated settlement. As it was, the revolt drew its leaders from rural notables and junior-ranking Ottoman officers, and there seem to have been few staff officer graduates among them. They had nevertheless fully absorbed the Ottoman tradition of militarism and involvement in politics.

The tactics and the appeal of armed insurgency and opposition to colonial rule set the stage for the Great Palestine Revolt ten years later, in which many former Syrian rebels participated. Later armed confrontations in the region harkened back to revolts of the 1920s and 1930s, but forgot the original Ottoman context. Mandate governance changed during the revolt as policies of martial law, pervasive surveillance, and permanent counterinsurgency took hold. The eventual post-colonial state inherited many such legal and military structures from the mandate. The League of Nations mandates had been introduced with an array of idealistic claims and promises, but came to endorse, and encourage, the cosmetic facades of mandate rule that emphasized "progress," "development," and institution-building for the edification of international observers, but not for the benefit of the colonized society.

In its violence and ultimate failure, the revolt served to undermine the legitimacy of civilian political elites to serve as national representatives in the colonial state. As in Turkey, military figures supplanted civilians as claimants to the mantle of national leadership, but in Syria, and later in Palestine, such leaders were finally exiled and sidelined, at least until the end of the colonial period. The compromises their civilian successors were forced to make with the colonial authority rendered civilian politicians permanently vulnerable to charges of venality, corruption, and collaboration. In this way, the mandate period served to valorize eventual military rule over the rule of civilians and civil institutions, an experience Turkey partly escaped.

The suppression of the uprising killed thousands and devastated the Syrian countryside. The mandate government ordered the aerial bombardment of two major cities, and countless towns and villages, and the revolt destroyed the careers of several leading French generals. It is likely that Damascus was the first major city subjected to intensive aerial bombardment in history, and the world press covered the city's bombing extensively. The negative attention caused a legitimacy crisis for the League of Nations, which predated the more widely known international crises of the Italian invasion of Ethiopia, or the rise of Hitler and the rearmament of Germany of the 1930s.

Conclusions: Colonial Anxieties and Imperial Rivalries

French politicians and mandate officials argued bitterly that British officials in Transjordan and Palestine encouraged the Syrian rebels. The High Commissioner's office accused the British Consul in Damascus of exaggerating all aspects of the revolt, most particularly the level of opposition to the mandate. French military officers were angered at their inability to pursue insurgents over the border into Transjordan, and they argued that Britain had created a haven for criminal enemies of their mandate. While French officials found it comforting to blame their colonial misfortunes on British intrigue and fanatical foreign-inspired sectarian extremists, British officials were guilty of frequent public gloating over their supposedly more enlightened and less turbulent rule in Palestine, Transjordan, and Iraq. Both regimes enthusiastically censored the press in the cities they controlled, and both allowed newspapers to cover and to criticize calamities and outrages in the adjoining mandate territory. Damascene journalists, like their counterparts in Jerusalem and Cairo, knew they could criticize the rival mandate power in print, but criticism of the ruling mandate power would land them in jail.

Relations between British and French colonial functionaries were better in Europe. In Geneva, the need to pacify the League of Nations brought mandate officials together in a way their competition in the region could not. British officials helpfully pointed out to their French counterparts that the Mandates Commission eagerly consumed voluminous reports, and each mandatory government was better served to provide too much information to the League than to ignore or refuse requests for reports and information. Great Britain had conquered and occupied the region in 1918 and British policy-makers were confident and unconcerned about League of Nations authority over their actions. They conceded to League requests knowing that such requests came without threat or compulsion and were most easily dealt with by mild compliance and casual misdirection.

French Mandate officials, by contrast, owed their regional position to post-war British goodwill and international concord, and there was a degree of insecurity at the core of French colonial claims in the Middle East. French Mandate officials regarded the League and Britain with frequent jealousy and suspicion, which the revolt and criticism from London and Geneva intensified. The British mandatory delegations learned immediately that lengthy and frequent reports on mandatory "progress" were the best way to keep Geneva satisfied and out of the business of the mandatory power. French officials learned this lesson more slowly, and spent half a decade underplaying the crises and disorder in Syria and Lebanon, and providing reports grudgingly, if at all. By the late 1920s both mandatory regimes and the Mandates Commission itself had become vast bureaucracies producing libraries full of official reports, surveys, and official commission findings.

British colonial functionaries considered themselves better, more able, and less ideological administrators than their French counterparts. But opposition to the mandate and Zionism in Palestine in the years after the Syrian Revolt provoked counterinsurgency tactics in Palestine little different from Syria, and shook British convictions of enlightenment. International crisis and the political and financial cost of Middle Eastern colonialism for both Paris and London led eventually to decolonization and disengagement from the region for both powers.

Notes

1. *Al-Ahram*, November 4, 1922.
2. *The Times*, "Lord Curzon at Lausanne. Turkish Claims Refuted. Our Pledges to the Arabs. Ismet Pasha's Statement," January 24, 1923.
3. *L'Echo de Paris*, "Mécontents du Règlement de la Conférence les Turcs n'ont pas Encore Parle," November 23, 1922.

4. *The Times*, January 24, 1923.
5. BNA CAB 21/61, "British Policy in Mesopotamia," memo from Lord Curzon on why Britain must keep Iraq, September 1917.
6. *The Times*, "Ismet Pasha's Statement," January 24, 1923.
7. LN, Carton R16, William Rappard, "Report of an Interview with Musa Kazim Pasha al-Husayni, Mr. Shibli Jamal, Amin Bey al-Tamimi." Rappard identified them as delegates of the "Syrian–Palestinian Congress," but in their petitions they called themselves members of the "Palestinian Arab Congress."
8. FO 371/10838, October 26, 1925.
9. LN Transjordan report, 1924.
10. LN R16, December 19, 1922, Rappard, "Report of an Interview with Mousa [*sic*] Kazim el-Husseini, Amin Bey Tamimi, Mr. Shibly Jamal, Syrio-Palestinian delegation."
11. LN R16, Rappard, "Record of Conversation with Mr. Weizmann," October 5, 1922.
12. LN, S226, "Palestine Disturbances." There are many letters and petitions supporting Zionism in the League archives, including many written and signed by famous people like Albert Einstein.
13. Bruce Clark, *Twice a Stranger: How Mass Expulsion Forged Modern Greece and Turkey* (London: Granta, 2006).
14. LN, many files. See, for example, R 4096, 1925–32. Many Arabic petitions from Louis Ghaleb, formerly Lebanese Ottoman, at the time of the letters a stateless resident of Yugoslavia, and R2307 "Mandate over Syria," claim that the mandate government should pay an Ottoman pension from the state telegraph company. See also R58, "Iraq."
15. LN R28, "Events in Syria," November 23, 1926.
16. LN R58, Iraq, many letters, 1919–1924. Letter quoted, November 10, 1923.
17. *The Times*, March 5, 1924, "The End of the Caliphate."
18. The main Damascus nationalist daily, *al-Muqtabas*, ran a weekly column during the 1920s titled "News from Istanbul," and in April and May 1926 *al-Muqtabas* ran an eight-part, serialized front-page feature titled "Mudhakkirat Mustafa Kamal."
19. LN. The League archives are full of aggrieved petitions from people who had lost citizenship rights and property, and sought some redress from the League as a last, and obviously futile, resort.
20. Eric Zürcher, *The Unionist Factor: The Role of the Committee of Union and Progress in the Turkish National Movement, 1905–1926* (Leiden: Brill Publishers, 1984).
21. Mesut Uyar, "Ottoman Arab Officers between Nationalism and Loyalty," *War in History*, 20:4 (2013), 538.
22. Personal correspondence with Mesut Uyar, August 1, 2014.
23. Fayiz Sara, *Saᶜid al-ᶜAs, 1889–1936: Hayatahu-Kifahahu* (Damascus: manshurat wazara al-thaqafa, 1993), p. 35.
24. For al-ᶜAs, see Adham al-Jundi, *Tarikh al-thawrat al-suriyya fi ᶜahd al-intidab al-fransi* (Damascus, 1960), p. 254. For Shallash, see Eliezer Tauber, "The Struggle for Dayr al-Zur: The Determination of the Borders between Syria and Iraq," *IJMES*, 23 (1991), 379.

25. Taha al-Hashimi, *Mudhakkirat Taha al-Hashimi* (Beirut: Dar al-Ta'li^{c}a, 1967–78), p. 8.
26. Philip S. Khoury, *Syria and the French Mandate: The Politics of Arab Nationalism, 1920–1945* (Princeton University Press, 1987), p. 142.
27. *The Times*, "Damascus Riots," April 13, 1925.
28. BNA FO 371/10838, April 24, 1925, Smart to Chamberlain.
29. Khoury, *Syria and the French Mandate*, p. 144.
30. ^{c}Abd al-Rahman Shahbandar, *Mudhakkirāt wa khutab* (Damascus: Syrian Minsitry of Culture, 1993), pp. 145–51. Speech for the opening ceremony of *Hizb al-sh^{c}ab*, June 5, 1925. Summarized in Hisham Nashabi, "The Political Parties in Syria, 1918–1939," unpublished M.A. thesis, American University of Beirut, 1952, pp. 95–6.
31. Shakīb Arslān, *Sīra Dhātiyya* (Beirut: Dar al-Tali^{c}a, 1969), pp. 264–5.
32. William L. Cleveland, *Islam Against The West: Shakib Arslan and the Campaign for Islamic Nationalism* (Austin, TX: University of Texas Press, 1985), pp. 41–2.
33. Cleveland, *Islam Against The West*, pp. 43–4. *Mujāhid al-sharq fī al-gharb*.
34. BNA CO, *Report on Iraq Administration*, April 1922–March 1923, p. 15; Marr, "Yāsīn al-Hāshimī," p. 117.
35. Marr, "Yāsīn al-Hāshimī," pp. 118–19.
36. BNA CO 730/150/6, "Profiles and Assessments," "YASIN PASHA AL HASHIMI," 1932.
37. BNA CO 730/150/6, "Profiles and Assessments," "YASIN PASHA AL HASHIMI," 1932.
38. I owe this insight to Toby Dodge, *Inventing Iraq: The Failure of Nation Building and a History Denied* (New York: Columbia University Press, 2003), pp. 51–2. And BNA CO 730/35, CO 15296, March 31, 1922.
39. Marr, "Yāsīn al-Hāshimī," pp. 140–1.
40. Robert de Caix, *La Syrie* (Paris: Sociéte de l'histoire nationale, Plon, 1931).
41. Benjamin Thomas White, *The Emergence of Minorities in the Middle East: The Politics of Community in French Mandate Syria* (Edinburgh University Press, 2011). White's book is now the best exploration of the mandate process of making minorities.
42. LN R22, Arabic petition with French translation and cover letter from Shakib Arslan, signed and sealed from Sultan al-Atrash, Ahmad Muraywid, and Mahmud Iqab, September 1922.
43. Michael Provence, "Druze Shaykhs, Arab Nationalists, and Grain Merchants in Jabal Hawran," in Kamal Salibi (ed.), *The Druze: Realities and Perceptions* (London: Druze Heritage Foundation, 2005).
44. Munir al-Rayyis, *al-Kitab al-dhahabi lil-thawrat al-wataniyya fi al-mashriq al-^{c}arabi: al-thawra al-suriyya al-kubra* (Beirut: Dar al-Tali^{c}a, 1969), pp. 190–1. BNA FO 371/4310, 13028/251, Smart to Chamberlain, August 29, 1925. Nashabi, "The Political Parties in Syria," p. 103.
45. Ex-Ottoman military officers involved included Sa^{c}id al-^{c}As, Muhammad ^{c}Izz al-Din al-Halabi, Fawzi al-Qauwuqji, Zaki al-Durubi, Yahya al-Hayati, ^{c}Adil and Nabih al-^{c}Azma, Zaki al-Halabi, ^{c}Ali al-Atrash, Ramadan

Shallash, Husni Sahkr, Mazhar al-Siba‎ᶜi, and Mustafa al-Wasfi, among many others. Among Damascene nationalist politicians of the last Ottoman generation, nearly all participated, or later claimed to have participated.

46. MAE-Nantes, carton 1704, BR 159, September 2, 1925, "Attitude de Mme. Shahbandar." Mme. Adib Affandi ᶜArab ᶜUqla passed this report to the intelligence service.

47. MAE-Nantes, carton 1704, BR 164, September 9, 1925. The meeting of September 7 brought together thirty-seven women at the house of Mme. ᶜUthman al-Sharabati.

48. LN R24, Syrian–Palestinian Congress, list of casualties and property destroyed, July 3, 1926. The congress compiled, from French sources, a list of 11,800 insurgent deaths between September 1925 and May 1926. The congress, which generally published figures lower than British newspapers, listed 3,509 civilian deaths in the period in the area surrounding Damascus. The total mandate population was under 2.5 million, and less than half that in the region surrounding Damascus.

49. Ministère des Affaires Étrangères, Archives Diplomatiques-Nantes [MAE-Nantes], carton 1704, *Bulletin de Renseignements* (BR) 189, October 10, 1925, «Opinion publique de Damas.»

50. BNA FO 371/10835, October 10, 1925. See Alice Poulleau, *À Damas sous les bombes: Journal d'une Française pendant la révolte Syrienne, 1924–1926* (Yvetot: Bretteville, 1926), p. 81. MAE-Nantes, carton 1704, BR 197, October 20, 1925. «19/10/25 16h.10 Un officier revenant de la citadelle signale le bombardement [text cut] partie de Souk est en feu. Résultat du bombardement, très effectif. Le bombardement continue méthodiquement.»

51. *La Syrie*, October 8, 1925, quoted in Poulleau, *À Damas sous les bombes*, pp. 80–1; *The Times*, "Parade of Corpses," October 27, 1925; *Le Temps*, October 24, 1925.

52. MAE-Nantes, carton 1704, BR 243, December 7, 1925, pp. 4–7. ᶜIzz al-Din al-Halabi and ᶜAli al-Atrash.

53. MAE-Nantes, carton 1704, BR 210, November 4, 1925.

54. MAE-Nantes, carton 1704, BR 213, November 7, 1925. This report was confirmed by interviews with elderly Christian villagers. Interview with Wadiᶜa al-Maᶜri, 87-year-old former *Mukhtar* (headman) of Saydnaya, August 10, 2002. His father was *Mukhtar* during 1925.

55. *L'Écho de Paris*, «Le Crime: Sarrail envoie au massacre la colonne Michaud,» October 5, 1925, *The Times*, September 29, 1925, "Marshal Lyautey Resigns, Maker of French Morocco, A Brilliant Career," and August 9, 1925, "Agitation Against General Sarrail."

56. *The Times*, "M. de Jouvenel and his Mission," November 9, 1925.

57. See, for example, Edward Mead Earle, *The Nation*, "Syria – An Acid test for the Mandate System," January 13, 1926. This article was read and distributed among the staff of the Mandates Commission in Geneva, and is in the archive there.

58. Philip S. Khoury, "Factionalism among Syrian Nationalists during the French Mandate," *International Journal of Middle East Studies*, 13:4 (November 1981), 456.

59. *The Times*, "M. de Jouvenel in Turkey," February 13, 1926.
60. These attempts are mentioned in Fawzi al-Qawuqji, *Mudhakkirat Fawzi al-Qawuqji*, reprint of both volumes of 1975 edition, edited by Khayriyya Qasimiyya (Damascus: Dar al-Numayr, 1995), p. 115.
61. BNA FO 371/11505, "Arrêté No. 53," "Confiscation of Rebel Estates," January 26, 1926. Also «Arrêté No. 97, *Arrêté règlementant le mode de perception et d'administration des amendes collectives imposeés pour faits de pillages et de banditisme*»; Bennett J. Doty, *The Legion of the Damned* (New York: The Century Co., 1928), pp. 172–5.
62. [*Service des Renseignements*] Haut-Commissariat du mandat français, *La Syrie et le Liban sous l'occupation et le Mandat français, 1919–1927* (Nancy: Berger-Levrault, 1929), p. 53. See the Great Revolt Mixed Court files at the Syrian National Archive (*muhakamat al-mukhtalifa*, Markaz al-Watha'iq al-Tarikhiyya), Damascus.
63. Haut-Commissariat de la Republique Française en Syrie et au Liban, *Recueil des actes administratifs du Haut-commissariat de la Republique Française en Syrie et au Liban*, vol. VI, 1925 (Beirut: Haut-commissariat, 1925), Arrêtés nos. 4/S and 5/S, pp. 6–11, and LN *Minutes of the Eighth Session*, p. 22.
64. BNA FO 371/11505, "Le délégation de Damas chez le Haut-Commissaire," Enclosure in no. 174, Consul Beyrout to foreign secretary, December 24, 1925, and Smart to Chamberlain, January 6, 1926.
65. Provence, *The Great Syrian Revolt*, pp. 108–24.
66. Général Charles Andréa, *La révolte druze et l'insurrection de Damas* (Paris: Payot, 1937), 82; BNA FO 371/11505, Smart to Chamberlain, January 11, 1926.
67. Doty, *Legion of the Damned*, pp. 172–5.
68. BNA FO 371/11506, Vaughn-Russell to Chamberlain, April 1, 1926. "Thus does the work of attrition ruthlessly proceed: the French policy is evidently to crush the rebellion by the maximum use of every mechanical contrivance and with the minimum use of French troops, whose lives are not risked when other troops (i.e. Circassian, Armenian, Kurdish or other irregular) can be employed."
69. BNA FO 371/11505, Smart to Chamberlain, January 20, 1926.
70. LN, *Minutes of the Eighth Session*, pp. 74–5, 151.
71. LN R24, reproduced in *Minutes of the Eighth Session*, annex iii, "Executive Committee of the Syrian–Palestinian Congress, Appeal Addressed to the Sixth General Assembly of the League of Nations," September 29, 1925, p. 181.
72. BNA FO 371/11505, Smart to Chamberlain, February 5, 1926. "As soon as all hope is lost of succor from Geneva, my informants believe the rebel resistance will collapse."
73. LN, *Minutes of the Eighth Session*, "Letter of Emir Shakib Arslan," February 20, 1926, p. 156.
74. LN, *Minutes of the Eighth Session*, p. 168; *The Times*, "The French Report on Syria," February 17, 1926.
75. LN, *Minutes of the Eighth Session*, p. 159.
76. LN, *Minutes of the Eighth Session*, p. 158.

77. See many examples in LN, R21, R22, R23, R24, R25, R26, and R27.
78. LN, *Minutes of the Eighth Session*, p. 165.
79. LN, R25, Eighth Session, "Comments Submitted by the Accredited Representative of France," p. 150.
80. LN, *Minutes of the Eight Session*, pp. 148–9.
81. LN, *Minutes of the Eighth Session*, p. 152.
82. LN, *Minutes of the Eighth Session*, pp. 150–3.
83. LN, *Report to the Council of the League of Nations on the Work of the Eighth (Extraordinary) Session of the Commission*, March 8, 1926.
84. LN R27, Lugard notes. I have cited the draft version from Lugard's notes, not the version that was published in the commission report. The Lugard draft seems a more illustrative, less edited, representation of the collective conception of the mandate.
85. BNA FO 371/11507, Vaughn-Russell, September 7, 1926, Enclosure, "Extract from *La Syrie*," August 3, 1926.
86. LN, *Minutes of the Tenth Session*, "Collective Fines in Gold," p. 136.
87. LN, *Minutes of the Tenth Session*, p. 129.
88. LN, *Minutes of the Tenth Session*, p. 140.
89. LN, *Minutes of the Tenth Session*, p. 141.
90. LN, *Minutes of the Tenth Session*, p. 140.
91. LN, *Minutes of the Tenth Session*, p. 146.
92. LN, *Minutes of the Tenth Session*, "Copies of Laws and Regulations," p. 120.
93. LN PMC, *Report on the Work of the Tenth Session of the Commission*, pp. 4–19, November 1926.
94. Several interviews with Mansour Sultan al-Atrash (1925–2006), in 1999 and 2000.
95. Laila Parsons, *The Commander: Fawzi al-Qawuqji and the Fight for Arab Independence* (New York: Hill and Wang, 2016), is a masterful reconstruction of the period of 1926 and 1927.
96. Jurj Faris, *Man hum fi ʿalam al-ʿArabi* (Damascus: Maktab al-Dirasat al-Suriyya wa-al-ʿarabiyya, 1957), pp. 344–5. Ramadan Shallash. Stipends for domesticated revolutionaries were a feature of French colonial rule in both North Africa and Syria.

5   Colonial Constitutions and Treaties: Post-Ottoman Militarism, 1927–1936

Events in the Former Ottoman Realms, 1927–1935

October 1927	Lebanese Constitution ratified
October 1927	Syrian National Bloc formed
February 1928	Britain recognizes Transjordanian Emirate
August 1928	High Commissioner Ponsot closes Syrian parliament and ignores new Syrian constitution
July 1929	Major Palestine Disturbances
March 1930	Shaw Commission Report on Palestine released
March 1930	Nuri al-Saᶜid forms Iraqi government as prime minister
June 1930	Anglo-Iraqi Treaty
Mid 1930	High Commissioner Ponsot unilaterally declares Syrian and Lebanese constitutions, including added clause devolving power to mandate High Commissioner
1931	*Hizb al-Ikhwa al-Watani* formed in Baghdad
1931	Iraq General Strike
October 1932	Iraqi independence and admission to League of Nations
March 1933	Nuri al-Saᶜid Cabinet resigns
March 1933	Rashid ᶜAli Prime Minister and Yasin al-Hashimi Finance Minister in first Iraqi post-independence government
June 1933	Faysal I state visit to London
July 1933	Assyrian Crisis
September 1933	King Faysal dead of heart attack at 48
March 1934	Palestine's Musa Kazim al-Husayni dead at 81
March 1935	Yasin al-Hashimi forms new Iraqi government as prime minister
1933–	Increased radicalization and Pan-Arab agitation
November 1935	Ibrahim Hananu dead of tuberculosis at 63

The Mandatory shall frame, within a period of three years from the coming into force of this mandate, an organic law for Syria and the Lebanon.
This organic law shall be framed in agreement with the native authorities
and shall take into account the rights, interests, and wishes of all the
populations inhabiting said territory. The Mandatory shall further enact
measures to facilitate the progressive development of Syria and the
Lebanon as independent states. Pending the coming into force of the
organic law, the Government of Syria and the Lebanon shall be conducted in accordance with the spirit of this mandate. The Mandatory
shall, as far as circumstances permit, encourage local autonomy.

Article 1, Mandate charter for Syria and Lebanon, August 1922[1]

By 1927, the regional scene had begun to solidify. In 1925, Syrian
rebels and nationalist politicians had rejected the mandate regimes,
partitions, and borders, and insisted on the unity and independence
of greater Syria, including Syria, Lebanon, Palestine, and
Transjordan. But by 1927, with the defeat of the revolt, the time to
reasonably challenge colonial borders and arrangements had passed.
While the successful movement in Anatolia had been the dream,
Syrian nationalists came to see the compromise in Iraq as a more realistic aspiration. Exiled insurgents conveyed woefully their willingness
to accept less than they had demanded. In greater Syria, the political
horizons drew ever closer, and even the arrangement in place in Iraq
seemed impossibly distant.

Eventually, civilian politicians of the major cities worked out variable
accommodations with the mandate powers, and carved out a breathing
space for limited political activity. The colonial governments and local
politicians realized they needed each other. The colonial state also
found it useful to allow civilian politicians to enrich themselves by the
acquisition and control of what the Ottoman State had considered
state property. Ex-Ottoman officer politicians in Iraq were working
toward independence, but had already discovered the mandate
High Commissioner was happy to buy their cooperation with state
assets.

Constitutions and Colonial Treaties: Iraq

Iraq had already received a constitution, electoral law, and treaty governing
the relationship with Britain. By early 1924, the 100-member elected
Constituent Assembly had ratified the three laws, but the Anglo-Iraqi
Treaty had been barely passed with a series of shady parliamentary maneuvers, and the government of Prime Minister Ja^{c}far al-^{c}Askari fell

immediately after passage. The constitution gave the king the right to select the prime minister, and dissolve the assembly, among other powers. And while the constitution placed the king in a position of power above the assembly, the treaty placed the High Commissioner above the king, who was required to consult whenever summoned. Britain maintained the right to intervene to protect British interests, however defined, and British subjects were immune from Iraqi law and taxation. King Faysal selected Yasin al-Hashim as prime minister in July 1924 and asked him to form the next government. When the treaty's greatest critic became its servant, British colonial officials congratulated themselves on their wisdom. The apparent success of the Iraqi constitution and treaty provoked similar moves in the other mandates.

Faysal served at the pleasure of the British government. In Baghdad there was a small group of about thirty ex-Ottoman officer and civilian officials. These men ran the government. Those who had been with Faysal during the Arab Revolt and in Syria comprised what was sometimes called the "King's party." Nuri al-Saᶜid and Jaᶜfar al-ᶜAskari were the most prominent in this group, but it included civilian politician Rustum Haydar, and a dozen other variable individuals. They stood for, along with Faysal, a pragmatic politics of cooperation with Britain. When Faysal needed to get some bit of controversial business transacted with Britain, in the form of the treaty, oil concessions, or entry into the League of Nations, he appointed Nuri or Jaᶜfar to lead the government. Yasin al-Hashimi led another group, generally called the opposition, which was made up of men who had mostly joined Faysal's government after the war, and generally rejected compromise with Britain. Nationalist lawyer Rashid ᶜAli al-Kaylani was probably the next most prominent, after Yasin, among this group. Yasin and his brother Taha had been higher-ranking Ottoman officers than Nuri or Jaᶜfar, or any of Faysal's other ex-Ottoman officers had been at the time they joined him. Those who had not joined the Arab Revolt had enjoyed more distinguished Ottoman careers, than those who had.

The leading Iraqi politicians were all products of the Ottoman system, and all were comfortable with, and probably committed to, an authoritarian, militaristic and elitist system. Some, like Faysal and Nuri, thought working with Britain would best serve their ends. Some, like Yasin, looked to Ankara, and argued an enlightened authoritarianism could serve Iraq only when it no longer had to serve Britain first. Faysal established a pattern of appointing Nuri to lead governments when he needed to satisfy the British, and appointing Yasin to lead governments when he needed to satisfy Iraqis. Kemal and the Anatolian republic were still the model.

Syria and Lebanon

In early 1926, French Mandate High Commissioner Jouvenel appointed a constitutional committee for Lebanon. The four members included three pro-French Christians, and one pro-French Muslim. In October 1927, the Administrative Council ratified the constitution, and codified the existence of the Lebanese Republic. Lebanon was to be legally dominated by Christians, and permanently and irrevocably separate from Syria. It would have a seventeen-member Chamber of Deputies (formerly the Administrative Council) and an elected president, subordinate to the High Commissioner. General Gouraud and Robert de Caix had created the Administrative Council by decree in September 1920, when they announced the existence of Greater Lebanon, and following their sectarian electoral plan.

The council was organized by religion and locale and Gouraud appointed its first fifteen members. Beirut received three seats: one Greek Orthodox, one Sunni Muslim, and one Maronite or other minority Christian. Muslims received a total of five seats, divided between Shiʿi, Sunni, and one Druze. The remaining ten seats were reserved for Maronites (five or six), Greek Orthodox (four), and Greek Catholic (one).[2] Mass protests and attacks on the French presence followed both the 1922 decree, and the ratification of the constitution, and led to the expansion of the Chamber of Deputies by two seats set aside for Muslims, to bring the total to seventeen, and a 58 percent Christian domination, instead of 66 percent.[3] After 1922 the Chamber was partly elected.

In 1920, General Gouraud had ignored the existing Ottoman Administrative Council and appointed his own council. The Ottoman state had arranged the special administrative district of Mount Lebanon after local conflict and French and British intervention in 1860. The Ottoman administration had included a Christian governor, always originating from outside Lebanon, and a loose representative structure in which each district was supposed to be represented on the Administrative Council by a member of the "dominant sect." Modifications could be made, and in practice the representatives came from the leading families of the districts.[4]

The members of the last pre-war Administrative Council resented their exclusion from the mandate council and objected strongly to the mandate. Seven of the twelve members wrote a petition to the League of Nations. They protested against the expansion of Lebanon, the French Mandate, and the denial of the full independence they felt they deserved. Among the signatories were the most prominent Christians in the country, including Saadallah Hoyek, the brother of the Maronite

Patriarch, Elias Hoyek, and leading pro-French figure, who was sometimes called the "father of Lebanon."[5] The Lebanese constitution and
the hardening of mandate arrangements it signified provoked a reaction
among regional politicians.

In October 1927, fifteen ex-Ottoman civilian politicians and lawyers,
from most of the major cities of Ottoman Syria, met in Beirut to plan a
program to oppose the mandates, and demand representation. They
couched their demands in terms of the "necessity of collaboration and the
reciprocity of interests" in running the country.[6] Their meeting and reap-
praisal led to the emergence of the National Bloc (*al-Kutla al-Wataniyya*),
which became the leading political configuration in Syria between 1928
and independence in 1946. Ibrahim al-Hananu had managed to stay out
of jail during the 1925–7 Revolt and came from Aleppo to attend the
meeting. Homs politician Hashim al-Atasi, like Hananu, a graduate from
the Imperial Maktab-i Mülkiye administrative academy and former
Ottoman governor, also attended, as did Damascus lawyer Faris
al-Khuri. The Bloc leaders termed their strategy "honorable cooperation."

Events in Iraq had made an impression on High Commissioner Ponsot.
The British Mandate government seemed to have achieved its goals
in Iraq by negotiation and treaty. Ponsot appointed a new Syrian prime
minister to preside over elections for a seventy-member Constituent
Assembly. Among the jobs of the new assembly would be the drafting of a
Syrian constitution, and approving a treaty with France. The elections
proceeded smoothly, and the new National Bloc dominated in Damascus,
Homs, Hama, and Aleppo. French intelligence had recruited rural
notables to run in the districts outside the urban areas, and while the rural
representatives were more numerous, making up about two-thirds of the
assembly, they were outclassed by Ottoman-educated urban nationalists,
who were already veteran politicians.[7] The High Commissioner considered the rural deputies his "moderate majority."

High Commissioner Ponsot gambled on elections and then gambled
that the constitution could be written without interference in a way
acceptable to France. The plan failed when prominent nationalists and
ex-Ottoman politicians were elected to head the assembly. Hashim
al-Atasi became the president of the assembly, and Ibrahim Hananu
became the head of the constitutional committee. Hananu's committee
and its three experienced legal scholars produced the constitution
quickly, but it was not acceptable to France, and the French press
attacked Ponsot with enthusiasm.[8] Rustum Haydar, Nuri al-Sa^{c}id, and
Yasin al-Hashimi visited Damascus ostensibly as representaives of King
Faysal to investigate if France might want to consider the services of a
friendly king. But Yasin visited his old friends and nationalist colleagues

also, probably to quietly explore the possibility of an Arab republic joining Iraq and Syria.[9]

The troublesome constitution should not have been a surprise to the
French. The drafters stipulated that Syria would be a parliamentary
republic governed by a single assembly elected every four years by
universal adult male suffrage. It guaranteed equality of citizens of all
religions, but stipulated that the president must be a Muslim. Secular-
leaning ex-Ottoman nationalists did not favor any mention of religion,
but the drafters, one of the three of whom was Protestant law professor,
Faris al-Khouri, considered it necessary to preserve majority popular
support for the process.[10] The constitution declared that Syria included
all the regions under mandate except Iraq, and was indivisible. The
Syrian republic should have its own army. The president could con-
clude treaties, receive ambassadors, grant pardons and amnesties, and
declare and suspend martial law. The president had the power to dismiss the assembly, but was required to call new elections if he did so.
The British consul expected the assembly to vote Ibrahim Hananu first
president of the republic. High Commissioner Ponsot warned the
assembly that the constitution was unacceptable to France, but the
assembly voted to accept the draft constitution as written anyway. In
response, Ponsot dismissed the assembly for a period of three months
in August 1928. He extended the closure thereafter, and closed the
assembly indefinitely in February 1929.[11]

In summer 1930 Ponsot signed decrees enacting the Syrian and
Lebanese constitutions. Amended to the Syrian document was a final
116th article that rendered the Syrian constitution meaningless: France
had the right to determine, in all cases, if the constitution violated its
"rights and obligations" as mandatory power. Mandate prerogative over-
rode the constitution at the will of the High Commissioner. A petition to
the League of Nations noted that the constitution in its final form was an
imposed document, that it left no authority to the Syrians, and that it
merely dressed up conditions of military occupation. Sultan al-Atrash
sent a telegram to the League of Nations from exile in Transjordan. The
imposed constitution had "shattered Syria's sacred unity," he wrote.[12]

Transjordan

In early 1928, Amir ʿAbdallah's Transjordan became a British-
recognized principality. The British "statement of policy" defined a formal, subordinate relationship for Transjordan, in place of a treaty, or a
more ostensibly equal arrangement. A few months later, a constitution
was announced that established a twenty-one-member Legislative

Council, which was partly elected and mostly appointed, met infrequently, and could, in any case, be ignored or dismissed at the Amir's pleasure. A group calling itself the Jordanian National Party protested the arrangement, constitution, and collusion between Britain and Prince ᶜAbdallah as a violation of mandatory promises of representation and democracy.[13]

Palestine: 1928 and 1929

The Balfour Declaration made the prospects for a constitution more complicated in Palestine than the other mandates. The mandate treaty recognized the Balfour Declaration, acknowledged the Jewish Agency as the representative of "all Jews who are willing to assist in the establishment of the Jewish national home," and codified a number of provisions explicitly facilitating the goals of the Zionist movement. The indigenous 80–90 percent of the population rejected both the Balfour Declaration and the mandate. In August 1922, High Commissioner Samuel promulgated a constitution, which proposed a twenty-three-member council made up of eleven mandate government officials, and twelve members freely elected from the population. Samuel's original idea had been for an advisory committee with near numerical parity between Arabs and Jews, but he recognized the folly of such a plan, and the 1922 proposal was supposed to comprise eight Muslim Arabs, two Christian Arabs, and two Jews.[14]

Despite the realistic proportions, participation required acceptance of the Balfour Declaration and the terms of the mandate, and a majority of Palestinian politicians refused this acknowledgement. The Palestinian population boycotted the election and the council was not convened. Later efforts to appoint members similarly failed. The design of the mandates required acceptance in exchange for participation. Put another way, the Mandates Commission and the powers demanded mandate citizens endorse the legitimacy of the colonial/mandate arrangement before they could participate or complain. Protests that considered the settlement itself unjust were thus automatically disqualified. Palestinian politicians could not accept the mandate's terms, most particularly the Balfour Declaration, and so they were rendered officially unrepresented.

The representatives of the Zionist movement found the terms of the Mandate and Balfour Declaration congenial and were consequently able to choose their representatives according to their collective preferences.[15] By the time the Arab leadership had come around to the idea of proportional representation, it was no longer on offer. In 1924, Jamal al-Husayni wrote, "We demand the establishment in Palestine of a

National Constitutional Government in which the two communities, Arab and Jewish, will be represented in proportion to their numbers as they existed before the application of the Zionist Policy."[16] The proposal, and its ratio of ten to one, was, by this time, out of the question from the perspective of the mandate and the Zionists.

Reasoned arguments based on justice and rights seemed to go nowhere. Musa Kazim al-Husayni and other ex-Ottoman civilian political leaders opposed the mandate and Zionism by recourse to rights, promises, and careful argument. Musa Kazim and Jamal al-Husayni made numerous visits to Geneva, and to London and wrote scores of petitions protesting the injustice of the situation in Palestine. By the end of the first decade of mandate rule, such arguments were proven ineffective, and different rhetorical strategies and leadership came to dominate the opposition.

The Western Wall of the Temple Mount, or al-Haram al-Sharif, is contemporary Judaism's holiest place, and the last remnant of the Second Temple (70 CE). On the platform above the Wall lies the Umayyad era (eighth century CE) Dome of the Rock and the al-Aqsa Mosque. The Wall was close along an alley between medieval houses of the Ayyubid era (eleventh to twelfth century CE) Maghribi quarter. Ottoman authorities had allowed prayer but no alterations or added structures or furniture to the area. The alley adjoining the wall and the quarter were owned by a *waqf*, or Muslim pious foundation, established in the early fourteenth century. Mandate officials followed the practice of enforcing the Ottoman status quo over religious sites, but Zionist leaders found the status quo of their holy places unsatisfactory and worked within the mandate administration to change the terms of access to the Wall.[17] Even before the Armistice in 1918, Zionist leaders began to collect international donations with a view to purchasing the adjoining neighborhood and clearing the structures there.[18] Jerusalem Military Governor Ronald Storrs had attempted to broker such a sale. The administrators of the *waqf* rejected all offers and during the late 1920s the area was on its way to becoming the symbolic center for the struggle over control of Palestine.[19]

During Yom Kippur in September 1928, a group of Jewish worshipers brought some furniture and screens to the Wall. After complaints from the director of the Muslim *waqf* that administered the area, mandate police ordered the screen removed. When it was not, they removed it forcibly the next day. Jewish protests were intense and considered the offense very grave, since the screen was used to separate male and female worshipers in keeping with traditional practice. The insensitivity of the mandate police was widely covered in the international press, and from the perspective of the Zionist movement, the basic right to free exercise of religious practice had been grievously violated. From the perspective of Arab and Muslim petitioners, the change of status symbolized a new claim and assertion of control over sacred territory they believed belonged to them. A petition noted:

> The wall belongs to the Great Mosque, the Muslim ownership of which is uncontested. It is the tradition of our faith to respect the religious beliefs of others and members of our faith have, out of pity for the Jews, always allowed the latter to come and wail at the foot of this wall. This is simply a matter of toleration, a mere concession, and has never implied any right of ownership or usufruct.[20]

Mandates Commission member William Rappard commented on the petitions received. Arab petitioners considered that the British government had broken its word in enforcing the status quo, and actively favored the Zionists. A British Land Expropriation ordinance decreed a few years earlier, making legal the seizure of property for undefined "public good" heightened the sense of foreboding. The writers feared the possibility that the government could redistribute land to benefit one community at the expense of another. In Rappard's words, they considered the land decree a weapon designed for future use against their community. Meanwhile, Zionist petitions asked the League of Nations to assist them in "securing fundamental rights to the site" of the Wall, and in enacting a more positive interpretation of the idea of enforcing the status quo.[21] The events of 1928 showed anyone who cared to note that Zionist aspirations were irreconcilable with what the indigenous majority considered their rights to the country.

In Jerusalem, Musa Kazim al-Husayni was 76 years old. Decades before, he had served as governor and in state administrations in the Balkans and Yemen, both Ottoman territories thousands of kilometers apart. Educated in Jerusalem and Istanbul, he had served the state, and traveled widely between far-flung posts. In the late 1920s he devoted his efforts to advocating the rights of the Arab population of Palestine in a small mandate of about 26,000 square kilometers. The mandate was larger than the special Ottoman administrative district of Jerusalem, or *Mutasarrifiyya al-Quds al-Sharif*, but far smaller than most Ottoman provinces. In 1928 and 1929 his younger relative, Amin al-Husayni, the British-appointed Mufti, increasingly became the leading Palestinian political figure. Amin al-Husayni focused his political efforts on mobilizing Palestinians, rather than on lobbying the mandate government, or League of Nations.

In October, the Mufti led an escalating series of protests against what he termed the granting of new rights for Jews to claim Muslim holy land. He used not the language of rights, law, treaties, and equal justice as Musa Kazim al-Husayni and other petitioners had done, but claims of religious injury and insult, displacement, and usurpation. Younger and more radical Zionists both in Palestine and in Europe made similar appeals and made clear their claims to the Wall, and even their wish to rebuild the temple where the al-Aqsa Mosque and Dome of the Rock stood. Chaim Weizmann often found himself explaining to the British government why such activities were not representative, and why Hatzohar, or the Revisionist Movement did not speak for Zionist goals or tactics.

In July 1929, several hundred Zionist youth marched to the Wall. Once there they sang the Zionist anthem, waved flags, and chanted "the Wall is ours." The following day, a Friday, after noon prayers, the Mufti, Amin al-Husayni, led a march to the Wall, during which marchers destroyed some Jewish property and injured a Jewish prayer leader. In the following days, intensifying attacks on Jewish and Arab individuals took place around Jerusalem. The inertia of heated sentiment was ominous.

On Friday July 23, after a week of escalation, Palestinian villagers from the areas surrounding Jerusalem came to the city, and during the afternoon began to attack individual Jews and Jewish property around the city. Rioters killed many Jews without provocation that afternoon, and by the evening mandate authorities had begun to arm Jewish "special constables" and ex-British soldiers among the Jewish population. Other community members were issued wooden clubs. During the course of the next week, rioters killed many members of the Jewish community in Hebron, and other villages, including twenty people in Safad. At the end of the week, 133 Jews had been killed, mostly by rioters, and 116 Arabs were killed, mostly by police.[22]

British forces failed to protect Jewish inhabitants. The police forces available were inadequate to protect and separate the communities. In many cases police were unsympathetic to the Zionists, and denied the scope of the troubles. While support for Zionism was mandate policy, Zionist leaders considered many individual British colonial functionaries hostile to their movement. The High Commissioner requested and received reinforcements from Egypt and Malta, and attempted to close the border with Syria, lest armed insurgents travel to Palestine.[23] Mandate authorities accepted no blame, but intercommunal conflict between Muslims and Jews was without precedent during centuries of Ottoman rule.

The High Commissioner had promised publicly that he would not bomb villages and neighborhoods. The Colonial Office objected, and wished to know why an administrator would rule out tactics of bombing villages and destroying houses. The Colonial Office ordered him to threaten bombing, and deliver, if necessary.[24] The High Commissioner explained that bombing would make the situation worse and prolong unrest, and he had already had appropriate legal decrees to levy heavy fines, make arrests, and hold trials. He could not "entrust the maintenance of internal order security of Palestine to aeroplanes and armoured cars without the support of infantry."[25] The High Commissioner's reservation was not based on humanitarian grounds, but was part a bureaucratic struggle for resources and increased funding for security forces. The financial costs of mandate counter insurgency provoked public opposition in London. Reinforcements suppressed the unrest within ten days.

British intelligence intercepted a telegram appeal from the Nablus Arab Congress, which was to be sent to twenty-seven institutional recipients in surrounding countries. The telegram claimed falsely that the Arabs had been disarmed and that the Zionists were killing them. Populations in the surrounding mandates, and further afield, paid close attention to events in Palestine, and demonstrations and angry newspaper editorials were commonplace. British officials and consuls sent a flurry of worried telegrams and dispatches about agitation, marches, and public meetings in Iraq, Lebanon, Transjordan, and Egypt. Demonstrations took place in Damascus immediately, but police dispersed them. A few months later, five Damascus National Bloc deputies declared a one-day general strike to protest the events in Palestine and the anniversary of the Balfour Declaration. The deputies sent a well-argued petition opposing Zionism to the consul, who attached a note to the Foreign Office.

They laid stress on specific promises made to King Hussein in 1915/1916 ... It is not my duty to trace the thread of the negotiations the Arabs carried out with the India Office or the Arab Bureau, or of the Sykes–Picot agreement: I need only say that in Syria, the opinion is universal that his Majesty's Government has failed to honour its signature, – an accusation which I at least find extreme difficulty in refuting.[26]

The Colonial Office hastily sent a commission of enquiry to investigate the events in Palestine. The Shaw Commission visited the mandate and produced another official report, which it published in 1930.[27] The Commission found that the unrest was unplanned, spontaneous, and directed at Jews, and not the mandate government. The immediate spark had been intemperate articles in both Jewish and Arab newspapers, the willingness of some to exploit popular fears, and the long series of incidents at the Wall. The Mufti was mostly blameless in instigating events. But not quite as blameless as the mandate government.

The fundamental cause is the Arab feeling of animosity and hostility towards the Jews consequent upon the disappointment of their political and national aspirations and fear for their economic future ... The feeling is based on the twofold fear of the Arabs that by Jewish immigration and land purchases they may be deprived of their livelihood and in time pass under the political domination of the Jews.

The Arab Executive elected a delegation to present their case in London. British officials advised them to visit after the publication of the Shaw Commission Report, and they arrived in early April. Musa Kazim al-Husayni was cautious and careful by nature, a veteran survivor of successive Ottoman governments, but the political practice of petitions and traveling delegations to the imperial capital, familiar from Ottoman times, was unsuited to British colonial politics.

Chaim Weizmann and the World Zionist Organization had regular access to successive prime ministers and cabinets. King George eventually rewarded King Faysal with a lavish royal state visit complete with military escorts, horse-drawn carriages, and state dinners. Musa Kazim al-Husayni's visit in the spring of 1930 by contrast was a modest and unsuccessful affair, which failed to affect policy or draw much attention in Britain. The welcoming committee at Victoria Station consisted of an unofficial group of three English ladies from the pro-Arab National Political League.[28] Mid-rank government officials granted the delegation a series of meetings. The women of the League were hospitable and sympathetic to their cause, but the official meetings offered nothing of substance.

In 1929, British newspapers protested mightily the expense of the mandate. *The Daily Mail* exclaimed: "Hand back the Mandates or the Middle East may be our ruin!" The same piece claimed the British government had spent 300 million pounds over the decade since the war, or "a cash present of £100 for every man, woman and child living in the ex-enemy territories of Palestine and Mesopotamia."[29]The financial pressure on the mandate was intense, and in the wake of the Shaw Commission Report, the Yishuv was exposed, insecure, and uncertain of continued British support.

The Shaw Commission Report had found Jewish immigration and land purchases had created "a landless and discontented class."[30] The findings of the Commission brought a storm of protest in London and put the Labour government on the defensive. The prime minister convened another committee to reconsider the issue, and temporarily suspended immigration. The committee issued a report in agreement with the Shaw Commission and the government issued the Passfield White Paper based on the previous reports in October 1930.

The White Paper was a partial repudiation of the Balfour Declaration. But British conservatives and Zionists protested the White Paper so vigorously that the survival of the Labour government was threatened. Chaim Weizmann resigned as head of the World Zionist Organization, and wrote that the changed policy would be "denying the rights and sterilizing the hopes of the Jewish people."[31] The prime minister wrote to Weizmann, and repudiated the White Paper, and met with him to formulate a policy statement acceptable to the Zionist movement – a level of access no Ottoman or Arab leader ever enjoyed. Immigration and unrestricted land sales resumed.

The 1929 events were different from military insurgencies that had occurred in Syria, Iraq, and Anatolia. The unrest was short-lived. There was no defined political program, and there was no leadership, either military or political. Palestine was unique in that it was the focus of a colonization program of settlement and intense scrutiny unlike any of the other mandates. The historical circumstances of late Ottoman Palestine were also unique. Anatolia, Iraq, and Syria, were all geographical areas comprising two, three, or more Ottoman provinces. The region of Jerusalem, like Mount Lebanon, had not been part of an Ottoman province, but a special administrative district. Late Ottoman statesmen had designed each separate region to limit Great Power involvement in local affairs, but after the war and settlement, the peculiar circumstances of each made intense British and French involvement more likely, not less. Each Ottoman province had had an army command, several military middle schools, and a military preparatory school in the provincial capital.

Palestine had none of this state infrastructure, and while Amin al-Husayni and a handful of others had been Ottoman reserve officers during the Great War, there seem to have been no Palestinians among the *mektebli*-school trained Arab Ottoman officers. So while Damascus, Aleppo, Baghdad, and many cities in Anatolia and the Balkans had military preparatory schools, and consequently at least a few experienced and trained ex-officers who might return after the wars, Palestine did not have such people. The political leadership was hobbled by its inability to compete with Zionist Europeans, and there was little indigenous military leadership. The country had been a battlefield in 1918, and the victorious British army had occupied it and pacified it more fully than any other Ottoman region.

Nuri al-Saʿid Delivers: The Anglo-Iraqi Treaty of 1930

As Peter Sluglett pointed out decades ago, Britain's interest in Iraq usually boiled down to oil. Sluglett also pointed out that it was long considered bad manners to say so. Publicly acknowledged or not, exclusive control of Middle Eastern oil was a British policy goal even before 1914. Mosul was expected to be as rich in oil as the southern Basra province, the region around Kuwait, and southern Iran, where the Anglo-Persian Oil Company owned the concession, and supplied fuel oil for the Royal Navy. Britain successfully managed to wrest the province of Mosul from the Turkish Republic with the help of the League of Nations in 1926. The League sent a commission to the region, which reached the somewhat predictable conclusion that the ethnic make-up of the region was insufficiently "Turkish" to find in favor of Turkey. Consequently, Mosul province, with its typically cosmopolitan Ottoman linguistic and sectarian demographics, including Kurds, Turkmen, and Assyrian Christians among others, was declared part of Iraq.

The Turkish Petroleum Company had been a consortium owned by Deutsche Bank, Royal Dutch Shell, and the British-controlled Ottoman Bank. After the war, the Deutsche Bank share became a seized enemy asset, and Britain and France divided up control of the concession. In early 1925, the Iraqi cabinet signed an oil-concession deal with the company that would become the Iraqi Petroleum Company, and which eventually became known as British Petroleum. The company was majority-owned by the British government until Iraq nationalized its oil in 1972. The British government remained the majority shareholder in British Petroleum until Prime Minister Margaret Thatcher privatized it in the 1980s.

In October 1927, massive quantities of oil were discovered near Kirkuk in Mosul province. The oil boom convinced British officials the existing Anglo-Iraqi Treaty was inadequate, but Britain could write a new treaty and "appear to relax control without actually doing so."[32] In summer 1929, British and Iraqi officials agreed on their mutual desires; Iraq would stop paying for the mandate administration, Iraq's relations with Britain would concern the Foreign Office, rather than the Colonial Office, and Britain would support Iraqi entry into the League of Nations. In early 1930 King Faysal appointed Nuri al-Sa°id to form a new government as prime minister, and Ja°far al-°Askari as defense minister. Nuri signed the treaty in June 1930. Britain would receive a new treaty guaranteeing Imperial communications, security of the oil concession, no foreign advisors apart from British and continued occupation of RAF airbases. During "wartime," Britain reserved access to all Iraqi infrastructure. On the cusp of "independence," Iraq was bound more closely to Britain than ever. Yasin al-Hashimi accused Nuri of "exchanging a temporary mandate for permanent occupation."[33]

Syrian Elections and Martial Law

High Commissioner Ponsot was tired of Syria, and Syrians were tired of him and his mandate. The French Foreign Ministry wished to extricate itself from Syria generally, and Ponsot wished to remove himself for a more tranquil diplomatic posting. In 1931, he took a long visit to Paris, and the Foreign Ministry decided to hold new elections for the Syrian parliament in December and January. Members of National Bloc vacillated between a full boycott and participation. The choice between collaboration or impotent opposition was difficult.[34] Meanwhile, brothers and rivals, ᶜAbdallah of Transjordan, and Faysal of Iraq, sent separate envoys to Damascus to explore possibilities to profit from French exhaustion. Questions of reuniting mandate territories and how best to achieve unity provoked debate. Some among the Syrian and exiled leadership, like Dr. Shahbandar in Cairo, favored a united Syria and Iraq under King Faysal. Among the ex-Ottoman officers and politicians not living in Iraq, some form of united republic was more appealing, and the example of Turkey remained compelling. At least some in Iraq favored a republic, too. Yasin al-Hashimi, probably like most of his ex-Ottoman staff officer comrades, former members of the CUP, favored a one-party republic, provided, of course, that they led the state and party.

Shakib Arslan occupied an odd place in this debate since he detested both Mustafa Kemal's secularizing program and republicanism. To Arslan, King Faysal of Iraq had, along with his father, betrayed his beloved Ottoman state, and Kemal had betrayed the Islamic religion as well as the glories of the Ottoman past, which left him to favor the new king of Arabia, ᶜAbd al-ᶜAziz al-Saᶜud (Ibn Saud), as candidate for unifying the region. Al-Saᶜud looked favorably enough on Arslan to send him modest monetary support, grant him citizenship, and give him the only passport he ever had, beside his Ottoman original.

After the Treaty of Lausanne, ex-Ottomans had to claim some new citizenship in one of the successor states. Arslan only conceded reluctantly, and tardily, and the French consul at Lausanne denied his request for Lebanese citizenship in late 1926.[35] Al-Saᶜud granted Arslan citizenship, providing the itinerant activist a passport, but al-Saᶜud did not want the role Arslan had scripted for him, and had no desire to be king of Syria, or Iraq, or apparently of anywhere beside the kingdom he had already won from Sharif Husayn in 1925. Perhaps al-Saᶜud saw the bleak prospects of overturning the settlement more clearly than most. More likely he was satisfied with his sparsely populated desert kingdom. Most Istanbul-educated politicians agreed that al-Saᶜud and his remote kingdom was not a serious option. Shakib Arslan never lived there.

Fawzi al-Qawuqji found refuge and employment in al-Saᶜud's new kingdom. He had abandoned the Syrian Revolt later than most and he spent spring of 1927 along the Turkish border in the north of the

Syrian Mandate. From there he traveled to Istanbul, where he arrived
in time to witness Mustafa Kemal's triumphant first return to the city
since 1919. Al-Qawuqji had been hoping to raise support for continued
fighting against the French Mandate among his former Ottoman comrades. Unsuccessful diplomatic mission aside, al-Qawuqji was on the
run, and both mandate powers had a price on his head. He traveled
with Sa^{c}id Haydar who had been a prominent founding member of
Dr. Shahbandar's People's Party, and a close relative of Faysal's chief
advisor Rustum Haydar. The trip to Istanbul was frustrating, and by
the end of the year, al-Qawuqji had relocated to Najd where he supported himself training cadets and policemen for al-Sa^{c}ud's army. His
friend Sa^{c}id al-^{c}As was back in Amman as as a policeman for Amir
Abdallah. Like Shakib Arslan, al-Quwuqji benefited from al-Sa^{c}ud's
generosity, and ended up in the 1950s and 1960s living in Beirut on a
small pension paid by the Saudi government. Al-^{c}As was killed fighting
the British army in Palestine in 1936.[36]

In Damascus, High Commissioner Ponsot returned from Paris in
November 1931, and found the city restive. It was an inauspicious time
for his return and for elections. Demonstrations and meetings had taken
place to protest the execution and mourn the death of the last insurgent
hero of former Ottoman Libya in September 1931. ^{c}Omar al-Mukhtar
had led a rural insurgency against the Italian occupation of Libya even
before the Ottoman withdrawal in 1912. He fought the Italians for two
decades from 1911 until his capture in 1931, by which time he was an
old man. Once captured, he was paraded in chains before photogra-
phers, tried hastily, and hanged three days after his capture. Al-Mukhtar
was widely mourned, and his execution presented another example of
the struggle against European occupation and injustice.

Syrian legislative elections took place in several stages between late
December 1931 and January. In Damascus the polls were heavily rigged
and accompanied by large demonstration and youth riots. The markets
were closed by three days of strikes, and several people were killed and
many wounded in the unrest.[37] The High Commissioner chose a range
of candidates in Damascus and engineered the results. After the rigging
was clear, people boycotted the polls. Results varied in the countryside,
Christian areas, and the cities of Homs, Hama, and Aleppo. Ibrahim
Hananu called a boycott and withdrew the National Bloc list entirely in
Aleppo. Mandate authorities arrested a number of high-school student
demonstrators on election day in Damascus, and in protest, their classmates declared a strike and refused to attend school for more than two
weeks. Ponsot's educational advisor negotiated an end to the strike and
promised no reprisals, but a number of so-called ringleaders were

imprisoned anyway.[38] Despite all the machinations, National Bloc candidates won seventeen out of sixty-nine seats in the parliament. High Commissioner Ponsot responded to the return of the striking students to class by issuing a new decree for the maintenance of public security.

The new decree was draconian even for the mandate. It prescribed terms of imprisonment of between two months and two years, including possible fines of thousands of Francs for a range of seemingly minor offenses. It declared illegal and punishable taking part in an unauthorized meeting, gathering, or procession; wearing a badge, flag or other emblem, "calculated to disturb law and order;" interfering with traffic; engaging in subversive speeches, cries, or songs; and publishing, writing, or spreading material, including cartoons, likely to disturb public opinion. Finally there was a penalty aimed at exiled activists. Those "remotely associated with a demonstration contrary to law and order, even if absent in person, are to be charged with an offense under this decree, and are legally responsible for offenses committed by others under their instigation. If resident abroad they will be charged under this decree upon their return."[39] The parameters of legal political activity in Syria seemed ever smaller.

In June 1932, the Syrian parliament elected Muhammad ᶜAli al-ᶜAbid first president of the Republic of Syria. Muhammad ᶜAli al-ᶜAbid was 65 years old, mostly apolitical, and supposedly the richest man in Syria. He had spent most of his life in Istanbul and was the son of Sultan Abdul-Hamid's most influential advisor, Ahmad ᶜIzzat Paşa al-ᶜAbid. He had been educated at the Galatasaray Sultani School, and studied law in Paris, and had served as Ottoman minister to the United States briefly in 1908. The al-ᶜAbid family fled Istanbul in 1908 with the fall of their patron, and spent the next decade in Europe. Muhammad ᶜAli only returned to Damascus, his birthplace, in 1919.[40] He was a compromise candidate, and his place at the head of government impressed few in Syria. His job was to deliver a treaty between Syria and France, but what kind of treaty became a complicated question.

Independent Iraq

The League of Nations admitted Iraq as a member state and independent country in October 1932. Independence was neither surprising nor especially welcomed. Britain had renounced the ability to intervene in purely domestic affairs, but the 1930 Anglo-Iraqi Treaty left the Iraqi government little scope for independent action. Iraq retained a large British administration in the ambassador and advisors who could, in practical terms, still force the king to act on their advice. The Embassy

controlled defense, in the form of the RAF and its bases, which operated completely outside Iraqi control. In the event of conflict, Britain
was permitted to reoccupy the country. Finally, there was oil, which
was completely under the direct control of the Foreign Office.[41]

King Faysal, the League of Nations, and the British Foreign Office
had long been committed to some form of independence, and there
were many discussions and reports prepared for the Mandate
Commission in Geneva. A secret report prepared in 1930 sought to
synchronize exactly how much "independence" the Mandates
Commission would expect, and exactly how much control the British
government would relinquish. Iraqi aspirations were of peripheral concern, based mostly on preventing the Iraqi government from dismissing
British advisors, which was claimed to be "contrary to the interests of
Iraq."[42] A related, undisclosed, worry was the continued salaries of
British functionaries in Iraq. British officials in every Iraqi bureaucracy
were paid well, with higher salaries than the Colonial Office paid for
similar postings elsewhere. There was some effort, ultimately abandoned, to try to force the "independent" Iraqi government to keep such
people on the Iraqi payroll at their mandate government salaries. Yasin
al-Hashimi, always willing to make British enemies, was the main obsta-
cle, since as former finance minister he made the sensible argument
that the new state could not afford to pay such salaries when Iraqi state
employees were available at a fraction of the cost.

For Faysal, independence was the symbolic acknowledgement he had
sought since the days of the war and the Arab Revolt. Independence
would bring a slight loosening of British control, but the difference was
mostly cosmetic. Faysal considered it a victory all the same, and he had
obviously reconciled himself to life as British-appointed king more than
a decade earlier. Independence had eluded him in Syria in 1920, but to
have achieved it in Iraq was a vindication. For the League of Nations,
Iraq's emergence as an independent state after twelve years as a League
of Nations Mandate was powerfully affirmative, and a rejoinder to the
many critics who found the Mandate Commission an apologist for colonialism and injustice. For the British government, Iraqi independence
secured important and long-standing imperial priorities at the lowest
cost possible, and seemed a significant triumph of patient diplomacy.

Iraqi Independence and its Discontents

Independence was not widely popular among Iraqis. In fact, protests of
various kinds had been continual in the months preceding. The nationalist opposition, led by Yasin al-Hashimi, opposed independence on the

basis of the treaty, and the conviction that it represented a phony, truncated independence. Kurdish nationalists in the north opposed it because they objected to the Arab cultural and linguistic domination policy they thought would follow, and wished to be guaranteed some autonomy. Assyrian Christians feared the removal of the British Mandate because they were insecure of their position within Iraq, and desired autonomy, or at least protection.

Yasin al-Hashimi, in opposition, renewed his criticism of the treaty and the British presence. Iraq's politicians were all ex-Ottoman elites, but in 1931 al-Hashimi appeared to succeed in broadening his base of support and embracing and exploiting economic and social issues of importance to ordinary Iraqis. Early that year, during the opening of the *Hizb al-Ikhwa al-Watani* (Party of National Brotherhood) Yasin and Rashid ⁽Ali al-Kaylani gave major public speeches. Each called for a new government and a renegotiation of the treaty. In mid summer, as Faysal went to Europe, a series of large strikes brought Baghdad to a halt.[43] The initial grievance was a trade tax increase, but the scope of complaint rapidly increased. Street demonstrations expanded beyond the hated tax and called for an end to the monarchy and the election of Yasin as president of a republic. Within a couple weeks the strike had spread to most of the towns north and south of Baghdad. British military aircraft overflew demonstrations as a display of force. Mandate police forces were rushed from one end of the country to the other.

Yasin al-Hashimi and the party leaders published a petition to the king in their party newspaper. "We did not throw off the yoke of Abdul-Hamid to suffer under the yoke of Faysal."[44] The most interesting element of the petition is the comparison between Abdul-Hamid and Faysal. Dr. ⁽Abd al-Rahman al-Shahbandar had made a strikingly similar argument a few years earlier in Damascus in opposition to French rule.[45] The recent Ottoman past was still fresh, and al-Hashimi seemed to still consider himself a member of the Ottoman Unionist Party (Committee of Union and Progress), since he shared credit for the overthrow of Abdul-Hamid in 1908 and 1909. His attacks on the treaty soon progressed to attacks on the king, and to the institution of monarchy itself. Faysal closed al-Hashimi's party newspaper, with the support, if not at the instigation, of the High Commissioner.

An independent Kurdistan had been briefly part of the post-war settlement. Between the San Remo conference in early 1920 and the Treaty of Sèvres in August, there was a vague and aborted plan for a referendum on a Kurdish state, perhaps under British Mandate, but by summer 1920 the prospects for such a partition, along with a similarly vague Armenian state in Anatolia, had been eclipsed by the Anatolian insurgency and the inability of Britain or France to conquer or occupy any more Ottoman territory. In the event, the Turkish Republic and the British divided the area drawn out as Kurdistan between themselves at the Treaty of Lausanne in 1923. Kurdish leaders became aware that a more independent Iraqi government would seek to extend its control and limit Kurdish autonmy and local control, and they began a campaign of petitions to the League of Nations and British government in London.[46]

Kurdish agitation was inconvenient for the British Government. The League of Nations, focussed as it was on ethnicities, nations, and minorities, was especially keen to extract guarantees of minority rights from the mandatory power. Moreover, Britain and France had legitimated their seizure of Ottoman territory as guardians of minority rights. Kurds protested that they had been promised their own state, and that the Iraqi and British governments had abused them. But the British government wanted to exit, and likewise wished to avoid discussion of the extent of Kurdish opposition to an end of the mandate, and more importantly the extent of periodic rebellion and repression in the Kurdish region. The British Accredited Representative to the Mandates Commission denied emphatically the charges and dismissed the petitioners. But in private correspondence British officials admitted that, having claimed in the annual reports that Kurdistan was without problems, further discussion was potentially "very embarrassing."[47]

The Assyrian population had even better reasons to oppose independence. Assyrian Christians, many of whom had fled as refugees or, like much of the Armenian population, had been death-marched south from Anatolia during the war, had settled among a few villages of co-religionists in the region north of Mosul. The British Mandate recruited the Assyrians for a rural police and security force called the Assyrian Levies, which was British-officered and used for internal repression of tribal and rural disturbances and tax protests. They also comprised the security force for all RAF bases. Like the other minorities, the Assyrians aspired to an independent or autonomous state, but their close association with the British army and the mandate caused them to be viewed with mistrust by other Iraqis. They numbered only about 40,000 refugees in the 1930s and they were correspondingly weak and easily subject to neglect or worse. The Assyrian Levies were, however, armed, trained, and paid directly by the British government. They were, by design, outside the control of the Iraqi government. The Assyrian leaders began a concerted effort to attract the attention of the Mandates Commission and the Assyrian Patriarch traveled to Geneva in 1932.[48] The British Accredited Representative assured the Mandates Commission the new Iraqi government would respect minority rights.

For its part, Nuri al-Sa°id's government, having just secured limited independence, had no wish to invite additional oversight. British loyalists or not, the Assyrians were on their own.

In keeping with the pattern, shortly after independence, Faysal dismissed Nuri and asked Rashid °Ali Kaylani and Yasin to form a government in March 1933. A few months later, Faysal traveled to Europe with Nuri and a few others for a lavish state visit with full honors to London as a guest of King George V.[49] The Royal Navy escorted their ferry across the channel with four destroyers and nine fighter planes overhead. A special train collected them at Dover and delivered them to Victoria Station where King George himself welcomed Faysal and rode with him by carriage to Buckingham Palace. As a mere politician, Clemenceau's visit at the end of the war in November 1918 was accompanied by far less ceremony. Faysal proceeded to Switzerland for rest and recuperation from the rigors of his efforts. Within a month, events forced a return to Baghdad.

Members of the Assyrian Levies had quit their units, taken their weapons, and moved their families to Syria. The French refused to allow them to remain, and they returned to Iraq, where they engaged in a gun battle with Iraqi army troops in August 1933. In the following week Kurdish irregulars and Iraqi army units under the command of an ex-Ottoman officer and Iraqi army general named Bakr Sidqi killed several hundred Assyrians, many of whom were unarmed villagers. Bakr Sidqi, himself of Kurdish origin, had been educated in the Ottoman military-school system, graduating from the Academy in 1908, and gaining admission to the Staff College after several years of service in the field. He graduated from the Staff College in July 1914, the last class before general mobilization, and like Yasin remained in the Ottoman army throughout the war.[50] He finished the war at a rank of probably senior captain, which he maintained in the Iraqi army, which he joined in 1921. Bakr Sidqi benefited from an unusual level of British official favor and was sent repeatedly for advanced training among British officers, first in India and then in 1932 at Sandhurst in the UK. The British considered him especially impressive and reliable as an instrument of mandate policy. Upon his return from Sandhurst he was promoted to general in the Iraqi army.

Faysal returned amid the crisis and unwanted international attention. The uprising and brutal repression of the Assyrians embarrassed the League of Nations, the British government, and Faysal. But the Assyrian massacres provoked outpourings of nationalist fervor among Iraqis and elevated Bakr Sidqi and the army as national heroes. Yasin's *al-Ikhwa' al-Watani* Party already included Bakr Sidqi as a member, and the party and the army enjoyed swelling popularity, particularly relative to the absent king. Faysal returned to Switzerland in late August to resume his rest and medical treatment. Within a week of his return to Bern, he was dead from a heart attack. He became, at the age of 48, one of the first of his generation of late-Ottoman transitional statesmen to pass from the scene. His early demise turned out to be commonplace among his contemporaries and many followed him in the next decade.

Ibrahim Hananu and a False Start for the Franco-Syrian Treaty

Upon his return to Syria in October 1932, ten days after Iraq became a member of the League of Nations, High Commissioner Ponsot proclaimed his intention to negotiate a treaty "more liberal" than that of Iraq.[51] Ibrahim Hananu and Hashim al-Atasi meant to hold him to his word, and hammered out a consensus among all the Bloc member deputies to demand Ponsot define his terms in writing before they would return to parliament. The session was scheduled to begin a week later, and the parliament opened without Ponsot's terms and without the Bloc deputies. A few days later, after acrimonious discussions, the Bloc members decided to return to the chambers and trust the High Commissioner.[52] Their hopes were soon dashed.

High Commissioner Ponsot spent as little time as possible in Beirut and Damascus, and a few weeks after his arrival, he left for Geneva without revealing the outlines of the treaty. Ponsot unveiled his plans for the treaty before the Mandates Commission in Geneva in December, and Syrians learned of it from the Mandate Commission minutes published in January 1934.[53] He proposed the Syrian Republic would be governed by treaty and separated from Greater Lebanon, the State of the Alawites, and Jabal Druze, which would each be governed differently. The Syrian Republic would thus have no seaport. It would pay 17 billion Francs in reparations for French military expenses since 1920. Each government department would include French advisors, and the Syrian Republic could not issue government contracts to any foreign entity without French consent. After a successful three-year probation, France would support Syrian entry into the League of Nations.

Petitions protesting Ponsot's proposal arrived quickly in Geneva. The petitions focused on the partition of Syria, and the question of "Syrian unity." The mandate authority had learned the lesson of 1925–7, however, and a number of petitions had been submitted to the Mandate Commission through French offices in Syria and Lebanon. In earlier years, French authorities had prevented the submission of petitions to Geneva, but now they had learned to solicit petitions supporting their policies on the one hand, and submit petitions attacking their policies with critical commentary on the other. In this way the accredited representative at the Mandates Commission was able to demonstrate support for mandate actions, and discredit indigenous critics in advance. Twenty-two petitions, some with hundreds of signatories, came from the major cities of Syria and Lebanon. Fourteen of the petitions, including one from Tripoli with over 600 signatures, protested in favor of "Syrian unity." Eight petitions came from Christians, Alawites, and Ismailis of the region around Latakia, mostly in favor of full independence for their autonomous statelets, and thus in favor of partition.[54]

William Rappard prepared a report that the Mandates Commission endorsed after some discussion. He noted the mandate authority had long favored a policy of minority autonomy, but had taken no definite position, leaving the negotiation to the High Commissioner. He opined that the Mandate Charter called for autonomous regions, and the protection of minorities, consequently the wishes of petitioners for a unitary Syrian state was "contrary to the fundamental charter of the mandate." He noted that the different rates of "political maturity" could call for different schedules for independence. Yet clearly the chief measure of "political maturity" was a favorable disposition toward French colonialism. The Mandates Commission, without irony, wished the mandatory power good luck in reconciling aspirations for independence with its obligation to guarantee the rights and interests of minorities.[55]

In 1933, Ibrahim Hananu was 63 years old and ailing from tuberculosis. He spent his waning energy maintaining discipline among the Bloc ranks. Hananu's position was simple: no treaty without Syrian unity. And no discussion of the treaty until the High Commissioner guaranteed the unity of the Syrian Republic. Discussions among the non-Bloc members of parliament continued through 1933 but without the Bloc members, the discussions went nowhere. High Commissioner Ponsot left for his summer holidays in France in July and was reassigned to Morocco. His tenure of seven years would be the longest of any High Commissioner, but his accomplishments were modest by any standard. The new High Commissioner would arrive in October 1933.[56]

Desperation in Palestine and the Death of Musa Kazim al-Husayni

By the mid 1930s the ground had shifted ominously in Palestine. Jewish refugees from Hitler's Germany were struggling to flee central Europe.

Between 1933 and 1935 the Jewish population of Palestine doubled. Tel Aviv-Jaffa nearly tripled in population over four years from 1931 to 1935. Palestine was rarely a first choice for refugees, but became, for many, a last resort. Increased immigration relieved the fiscal pressure on the British government and increased numbers brought new self-confidence to the Zionist leadership. The urgency of compromise with the Arabs receded.

British authorities established a legal preference for Jewish emigrants of significant financial means and special skills.[57] The mandate migration regime had three categories: "capitalists, skilled workers without means, and skilled workers with capital." The first category was unrestricted, but the British government requirements to be considered a "capitalist" were approximately $100,000 cash in 2016 values, and a certificate from the German government allowing the legal expatriation of the funds – this while the German government was daily devising new ways to seize the assets and curtail the rights of Germans Jews. Nevertheless, by late 1933 10,000 immigration permits had been granted under this category. The second category allowed 2,000 immigration permits in 1933, and the third was somewhat more open, but the capital requirements were at least $25,000 per person. The mandate administration found that the influx of immigrants, and the taxes and fees they paid, made the mandate completely solvent, and even with increasing demands for expensive military repression of the indigenous population, self supporting.[58]

In 1932 and 1933 the three most prominent Palestinian political leaders, Musa Kazim, Amin, and Jamal al-Husayni, all attempted to participate in the governing structure of the mandate.[59] After the White Paper in late 1930, the British government was increasingly convinced that support for Zionism could imperil other imperial priorities. In the Foreign Office, Colonial Office, and the Labour government, enthusiasm for Zionism as a part of a colonial strategy waned. In parliament, especially among the conservative opposition, and people like Conservative MP Winston Churchill, support for Zionism was intensifying, and provided a stick with which to beat political rivals. At the League of Nations and especially in the Mandate Commission, reaction to the persecution of German Jews increased support for Zionism among liberal internationalists like William Rappard.

Musa Kazim's son ᶜAbd al-Qadir al-Husayni had graduated from the American University of Cairo in 1932. ᶜAbd al-Qadir had been a constant companion to his father from the age of 12, and knew well the tortuous terrain of mandate politics. His youthful radicalism and impatience had an influence on his father and helped bring a mood of confrontation. In October and November 1933 the Arab Executive planned demonstrations in opposition to Jewish immigration and land sales.[60] The High Commissioner learned of planned protests and warned Musa Kazim al-Husayni and the Mufti Amin al-Husayni against illegal demonstrations, but the demonstrations took place anyway. The mandate authority did not sympathize with the argument that Palestinian politicians wished to retain credibility as representatives and defenders of their community. Police met the first demonstration in Jaffa with live fire, and eleven people, including one policeman, were killed and twenty injured. British observers described the deadly measures as "controlled rounds" in response to a mob charge on the police baton line.[61] Demonstrations took place in Haifa, Nablus, and Jerusalem in the following days, and a dozen or more people were killed. Musa Kazim al-Husayni himself was beaten to the ground by baton-wielding mandate police. Police arrested and detained Jamal al-Husayni.

The Arab Executive declared a three-day General Strike as protests took place in Damascus, and other cities.[62] The High Commissioner announced the restoration of mandate martial law decrees.[63] The *New York Times* correspondent in Jerusalem noted the new regime gave the High Commissioner "military and dictatorial powers."[64] The law was called the Palestine Defense Order in Council, and had been originally written in 1931. It legalized wide censorship, arrests without warrant, and detention without charge or representation, deportation without appeal, and secret military courts. Nearly a century later, the mandate martial law decrees remain a central part of Israeli law today, governing the Arab population of the West Bank, occupied by Israel since 1967.

Musa Kazim Paşa al-Husayni died five months later in March 1934 at the age of 81. Many believed injuries received from British police hastened his death, and he was widely mourned. He was the undisputed leader of the Palestinian Arabs, the patriarch of Jerusalem's most prominent notable family, and the highest-ranking ex-Ottoman statesman in Palestine. His funeral was the largest seen in Jerusalem since the nineteenth century and thousands attended.

Yasin al-Hashimi Retires and then Returns

In October 1933, a month after Faysal's death, the Rashid ꜥAli-Yasin government fell in Baghdad. The collapse was perverse. The cabinet members had tried to publicly assure Britain that they would honor Faysal's agreements, including the treaty. But the public outcry against the olive branch to the ambassador was so intense that Rashid ꜥAli called new elections and resigned his cabinet. Over the next eighteen months Iraq had four governments, a series of tribal revolts, which General Bakr Sidqi repressed with intensifying brutality, and an economy suffering in the worldwide depression. Yasin al-Hashimi retired from politics and went home.

Al-Hashimi had cultivated prosperous commercial interests in Iraq, but he also enjoyed family life and the company of his friends. He lived in a large courtyard house in Baghdad, and during the months out of power he worked on the house, attended to a cement plant he had founded, read, and wrote letters to his daughters, all away at school, played bridge, and chess, and received visitors. He often spent his evenings at the Iraqi Club, where he was sought after as one of Baghdad's best bridge players.

Yasin al-Hashimi was devoted to, and adored by, his three daughters, and involved himself intimately in their education and upbringing. His eldest daughter, Madiha, was among the first women to attend the American University of Beirut (AUB) – a big step for any forward-thinking father in 1934.[65] The college had begun admitting female students in 1922. Madiha thrived at AUB and she joined the al-ᶜUrwa al-Wuthqa Arab Culture and Politics club formed by famous Arab intellectual Constantin Zureiq, who was then a young instructor. Madiha's sister, middle daughter, Sabiha, attended the Beirut College for Women (BCW – today's Lebanese American University), and his youngest daughter, Niᶜmat, attended high-school classes at the American Community School, also in Beirut. In 1935, Sabiha transferred from BCW to Smith College in Massachusetts.[66] Yasin wrote frequent letters to his daughters individually and collectively and urged them to write one another when they were separated.

June 1935[67]

My daughter Sabiha,

I am busy with work these days.[68] And thank God my health is fine. Work on the house progresses. I pray for your good health and am happy to hear you have resolved to lose a little weight. I am also happy that you want to learn German. Maybe you can write to me in German and I can reply in what is left of my knowledge of the language.

[Your younger sister] Niᶜmat is doing fine. We have been working on the house, which now has a new roof. I hope they will begin the second floor soon. Your mother is not satisfied with the kitchen, but I will try to improve it to suit her.

The weather [in Baghdad] has been beautiful. I have been making a point to keep copies of interesting news articles for you. I wonder if there is any reason to send the Iraqi newspapers to you? I will anyway ask Mahmud to send you al-Bilad.

I trust that your finances are adequate. If you do not need all the money for tuition and expenses, save some for next term. If you have some left after next term, save some for your trip home, when you may stop in Paris. Though I know the long Atlantic crossing is bothersome.

Do you hear from [your former teacher?] Miss Molka? Give her our respects. The family are all well. [Your older sister] Madiha is slow in writing, and misses you very much. You should write to her often. I don't think Ni^{c}mat writes unless I remind her. Madiha won a Ministry of Education scholarship, and she and Lulu are now roommates.

Greetings, hugs, and kisses, from us all,

and *liebe grüße!*

Your father

Al-Hashimi's political allies visited often for lunch or evening discussions on the politics and events of the country. His friends relied upon his advice, as titular party leader, but he resisted their repeated calls to be drawn back into active political life. As various disorders embroiled the countryside, the calls became more insistent. Some thought that, as in 1920, it would be possible and useful to harness the rural uprisings to nationalist politics. Al-Hashimi counseled against this path, and urged his opposition colleagues to have patience with the rotating cast of politicians attempting, without much success, to run the country.

In January 1935, Yasin al-Hashimi changed his mind. He suddenly appeared without warning at a late-night planning meeting at Hikmat Sulayman's house between rural shaykhs and Ikhwa politicians. The plotters applauded his entrance and evidently felt their leader had finally signed on to the effort.[69] In late February the ^{c}Ali al-Jawdat cabinet resigned and al-Hashimi decided to end his retirement. Young King Ghazi asked him to form a cabinet as prime minister, but al-Hashimi set several conditions, among which may have been a suspension of the constitution and a minimum time in power of two years.[70] The king protested he could not agree to such an arrangement before consulting the British ambassador, who rejected al-Hashimi's conditions. A new cabinet under Jamil al-Midfa^{c}i formed but was unable to restore order. Several weeks went by, and as the country became more ungovernable, and the rural areas passed out of government control, the king and Midfa^{c}i called on Yasin al-Hashimi, Rashid ^{c}Ali al-Kaylani, and Hikmat Sulayman to assist in restoring order. All demurred.

Taha al-Hashimi, Yasin's brother, played the pivotal role in his assumption of power in 1935. Taha was first appointed army chief of staff shortly after resigning from the Ottoman army and returning from Istanbul in 1923. A year later, Faysal appointed him chief body guard and tutor of his eldest son, Prince Ghazi. During the following decade he occupied a number of important posts including director of state education, and Iraqi military academy instructor of military history and geography. He wrote and published widely, including seven volumes exhaustively covering the history of late Ottoman military campaigns, military training, and tactics.[71] In 1930 he returned to active service, was promoted to general, and became again, army chief of staff – a post with increasing power and importance as the mandate came to an end.[72]

As the rural insurrection heated up, Jamil al-Midfaʿi asked Taha al-Hashimi to send the army to restore order and take the field against the insurgents in the south. Taha al-Hashimi argued that he had insufficient forces to intervene decisively, and did not support direct military confrontation, frustrating al-Midfaʿi's wish for forceful action, and leaving the government to flail ineffectually. Taha's inaction weakened the government and strengthened his brother's hand. Finally in mid March 1935, al-Midfaʿi's government resigned, and the king asked Yasin al-Hashimi to form a new government.[73] Quite likely al-Hashimi insisted on the same agreement the British Embassy had rejected months before. Events conspired to deny him the two years in power he had demanded, though he received and used the free hand he sought.

Al-Hashimi's cabinet resembled the government of his ex-comrade on the Ottoman general staff, Mustafa Kemal, in Ankara.[74] Half were Istanbul-trained ex-officers, and the others were Istanbul-trained lawyers. Al-Hashimi brought an immediate and comprehensive reform of the Iraqi state on modern authoritarian grounds. The new government aimed toward centralization and control of all areas of Iraqi society. It emphasized nationalist education, military conscription, bureaucratic reform, and economic reorganization on statist principles. Unqualified or unreliable civil servants were meant to be dismissed.

Al-Hashimi's government and the army under the command of Taha brought the rural insurrection to a swift end. Yasin gathered the tribal and rural shaykhs together for a huge banquet in Baghdad in which he gave a welcoming speech. He reminded, and cautioned, the leaders that their interests lay with the state, which could readily reward them for their loyalty. He warned them subtly that misidentifying their best path would be costly.[75] Al-Hashimi had been dealing with Iraqi rural leaders since his days as a young Ottoman staff officer, and had served successfully as governor of troublesome al-Muntafiq province in his first appointment under Faysal. He artfully employed Ottoman statecraft, and in his banquet and mix of generous promises and quiet threats, succeeded in convincing the shaykhs to lay down their arms.

Yet the new government represented itself a modern centralized authoritarian state. Like the Turkish Republic, it was the culmination and final embodiment of a variety of goals and aspirations that had been central to the ethos and priorities of the Unionist Ottoman staff officer cadres since 1909. The spirit of modern authoritarian militarism was hardly unique to the former Ottoman lands, however, and enjoyed worldwide popularity. Former members of the Ottoman general staff retained their Germanophilia, but also studied the state-building models of Stalin, Franco, and Mussolini.

In the eighteen months in power the new government introduced and parliament passed more than a hundred laws. The state received a new penal code, new tax laws for income, land revenue, and customs, laws guaranteeing workers' rights, and the abolition of aristocratic titles like *bey* and *pasha*. Seventeen years later, Gamal ᶜAbd-al-Nasser's new Egyptian government similarly abolished titles, but while Nasser's reform is remembered, Yasin's is forgotten. New laws facilitated large public works projects on roads, irrigation systems, and bridges. The new government was popular, and managed to increase the total number of seats in the parliament from 88 to 108, which after elections helped advance Yasin's legislative agenda.[76]

The government issued a detailed program of progressive nationalist principles. Al-Hashimi announced the expansion of the military, conscription, and programs to organize and educate citizens, workers, and civil servants with a "spirit of sacrifice, duty, education, progress, and the system."[77] The government launched new postal banks, agricultural banks, mortgage banks, and insurance programs, including pensions for government employees, irrigation and village potable water and electrification improvements, hygiene and healthcare, and industrial projects and funding, especially to equip the military and provide building materials for government developments. The state proposed import substitution, and enacted laws to favor local production of various products. New industrial ventures received tax breaks and incentives. Al-Hashimi aimed to assert full state control over Iraq's people, economy, territory, borders, and natural resources. The British Embassy tittered nervously.

Fawzi al-Qawuqji in Baghdad

Fawzi al-Qawuqji had traveled from the Saudi Kingdom to Cairo and visited his old comrades in mid 1932. He spent time with various exiled rebels of the Syrian Revolt, including Rashid Rida and Dr. Shahbandar who were skeptical of al-Saᶜud, and opposed Shakib Arslan's admiration for the new kingdom. Al-Qawuqji conveyed his positive experiences with King ᶜAbd al-ᶜAziz al-Saᶜud. He had several meetings with Yasin al-Hashimi, who happened to visit Cairo. Al-Qawuqji wrote that in the course of his travels, it finally dawned on him that al-Hashimi was the "man of the hour to unify the Arabs, and he pledged himself to the cause." Ex-Ottoman army officers had emerged the leading men of new independent Turkey, and they agreed they should both seek the help and heed the example of their brother officers in Turkey. The fixing of the borders between mandates, especially Syria and Iraq, could only harm the cause of unifying the Arabs behind the leadership of their military officer vanguard.[78]

Fawzi al-Qawuqji traveled to Baghdad immediately after Iraqi independence in October 1932. He needed a job but he also wanted to serve the cause. Nominal independence had removed the threat of extradition from one mandate state to another, and al-Qawuqji was eager to work for the future he and Yasin al-Hashimi had discussed. French Mandate military courts had sentenced in absentia many Syrian rebels of the period 1925–7 to death or to long prison terms. Al-Qawuqji had mutinied along with the French Syrian Legion cavalry unit he commanded. He was at the top of the list of wanted men for the mandate authorities.

Baghdad was a bit too distant from Damascus for al-Qawuqji to be a celebrity, but he had friends from his years in the Ottoman army and in Damascus after the Great War. Taha al-Hashimi arranged for al-Qawuqji to work as an instructor at the Iraqi military academy. But teaching horsemanship at the military academy did not satisfy al-Qawuqji's hunger for action and politics. He began to consider Palestine as the next place for decisive confrontations with the Mandate Powers.[79] He sought support for an organized guerrilla campaign in Syria or Palestine from Yasin and Taha al-Hashimi, and others among his ex-Ottoman army comrades, and made two clandestine trips to Palestine to test the waters in 1934 and 1935.

Ibrahim Hananu Exits the Scene

Ibrahim Hananu was dying of tuberculosis. He never wavered in his opposition to a French-imposed constitution or treaty and he led the veteran nationalists by force of will, but younger activists were more impatient. A group of mostly younger men organized a secret meeting of nationalist activists in August 1933 in the Lebanese mountain town of Qurnayil, above Beirut. The young radicals criticized what they saw as the ineffectual efforts of the older generation, but in their radical pan-Arab aspirations, they did admire a few among their elders, especially Yasin al-Hashimi and Shakib Arslan.

The activists agreed to form a new group they called *Usbat al-ʿAmal al-Qawmi,* or the League of National Action. Damascenes were probably overrepresented, but there were members from most of the larger cities of Greater Syria and a prominent few from Baghdad. According to Philip Khoury, their average age was 29, and they had experienced the Great War as children or teenagers. They grew to adulthood during the emergence of the mandates and the revolts of the 1920s.[80] Few had been educated in Ottoman schools, and fewer still had been Ottoman politicians or military officers. In time they came to reluctantly, and temporarily, join forces with the older, more compromising, ex-Ottoman politicians of the National Bloc.

The New High Commissioner, Damien de Martel, arrived in Beirut in October 1933. Two weeks later, in early November, the National Bloc staged a large demonstration and called for closure of the bazaar in commemoration and protest of the Balfour Declaration. In Aleppo, Ibrahim Hananu refused to follow his Damascene comrades and argued that demonstrations would needlessly provoke the new High Commissioner. Hananu wished to give de Martel a chance to negotiate from a clean start. Months earlier, Hananu had forced Jamil Mardam Bey, the one National Bloc member of the cabinet, to resign, when High Commissioner Ponsot attempted to break National Bloc ranks and get the Franco-Syrian Treaty signed. Hananu traveled to Damascus to personally see that the slippery Jamil Mardam Bey resigned from the government.[81] Hananu arranged a march in honor of Mardam Bey to preserve the fiction that his resignation had been based on the principled opposition of the unified Bloc, rather than party arm-twisting.

As High Commissioner, De Martel tried a different tactic from Ponsot. President Muhammad ᶜAli al-ᶜAbid and Prime Minister Haqqi al-ᶜAzm still led the government. They were two of the richest men from the two most prominent families in Damascus, and posed no threat to the High Commissioner's program. Both had made their peace with the mandate regime immediately after the occupation in July 1920. As major owners of commercial, industrial, and agricultural property, their politics reflected their economic interests and they opposed any type of confrontation with the mandate power. De Martel persuaded Haqqi al-ᶜAzm, the prime minister, to quietly sign the Franco-Syrian Treaty on November 16.

The Syrian parliament convened to vote on the treaty a week later. Mandate officials had attempted to buy votes in favor of the treaty and had posted armed guards for the purpose of security and intimidation. Bloc members took their seats in parliament for the vote, and managed to bend the body to their will. The parliament voted to reject the treaty and the High Commissioner suspended parliament for four months starting in late November 1933.[82] High Commissioner de Martel left Beirut and returned to Paris for a long vacation and further instructions before the end of the year.

De Martel returned in March of 1934. Like much of Europe, France was embroiled in political conflicts between the left and right. Anti-British agitation in Iraq had eclipsed the positive example of the Anglo-Iraqi Treaty of 1930. Yasin al-Hashimi had just formed a new, popular, and pointedly anti-imperialist Iraqi government. The French mood for tentative conciliation with Syrian nationalists had passed, and de Martel resolved to clamp down forcefully. The Foreign Ministry ordered him to extend the closure of parliament another six months and dismiss the government of President Muhammad ᶜAli al-ᶜAbid and Prime Minister Haqqi al-ᶜAzm.[83] He was also ordered to appoint the unpopular toady Taj al-Din al-Hasani prime minister to form a government. Al-Hasani had been the one Syrian politician willing to accept the job as head of state in 1925 as French bombs fell on Damascus under High Commissioner Sarrail during the Revolt.

As the High Commissioner intended, the Taj al-Din al-Hasani cabinet did little and left de Martel unimpeded to run the mandate. After the expiration of the six months' closure in November, de Martel closed the Syrian parliament indefinitely. Various protests took place from time to time against the al-Hasani government and the mandate. Economic distress connected to the Great Depression and contraction of the agricultural economy brought people into the streets regularly. Jamil Mardam Bey appointed himself to visit Paris in October 1934, where he received, like the Palestinian delegation to London of 1930, a perfunctory reception with mostly low-ranking colonial officials.[84] Mardem Bey returned humbled and asked for, and received, forgiveness from his Bloc colleagues for breaking ranks with the nationalists.

Rural misery increased in Syria and Palestine as markets for produce shrank. Economic desperation affected rich landlords. Wealthy landowning families in Jerusalem, Beirut, and Damascus had quietly sold vast tracts of agricultural land in northern Palestine to the Jewish National Fund since the early 1920s. But with booming Jewish migration to the crowded cities of coastal Palestine, fertile farmland in the Hawran region of Transjordan and Syria became desirable for Zionist settlement. The population of Tel Aviv had doubled in a couple years, and land near the city quadrupled in price in the same period.[85]

National Bloc leaders like Shukri al-Quwatli organized protests against agricultural land sales to the Jewish National Fund.[86] The protests popularized the weapon of boycott for the National Bloc, and during 1934 and 1935 the Bloc organized a number of boycotts against products from Palestine in opposition to Zionism, against the French-financed electric tram in Damascus, and against a new tobacco concession monopoly in Lebanon and Syria. Organized boycotts against symbols of colonial domination did not indicate strength on the part of the National Bloc leadership, but rather an admission of weakness.

De Martel's closure of parliament and his unwillingness to engage Syrian politicians increased the pressure, and heightened their desperation to remain relevant. Sooner or later, young radicals and the ex-officers would seize the mantle of nationalist leadership.

Ibrahim Hananu succumbed to tuberculosis in late November 1935 at the age of 65. His funeral drew every aspiring nationalist politician from the mandate states, along with tens of thousands of ordinary people. People of all regions and religious communities attended Hananu's funeral and by their presence subverted the sectarian French narrative of Syria and the League of Nations mandate. Muslim and Christian clergy officiated, and Islamic and Christian symbols figured in the procession.

Conclusions

Ottoman-trained political leaders were rarely willing converts to armed insurgency. Given a glimmer of hope that mandate authorities were ready to deal equitably, they wrote petitions, formed delegations, and attempted, repeatedly, to offer reasoned arguments why their claims of self-representation and self-determination were just and fair. These efforts were notably unsuccessful through the two-and-a-half decades of the mandates. But civilian political leaders achieved a few victories in the mandates. King Faysal's Iraqi kingdom was never as independent as its skeptics hoped, but at least for a time, it appeared more independent and more free than other former Ottoman regions like Syria and Palestine. Other civilian politicians, like Shakib Arslan, and the members of Damascus' National Bloc, had moments of fleeting triumph. They had few options but to keep trying.

Ex-Ottoman army officers had experienced the British and French as deadly wartime enemies, and pre-war imperial rivals, and took different political lessons. The emergence of the Turkish Republic was a powerful example also. Some, like Fawzi al-Qawuqji, were talented officers but flawed politicians. Others, like Mustafa Kemal, Ibrahim Hananu, or Yasin al-Hashimi, were talented as both military officers and as politicians and were consequently far more threatening to the colonial state than their civilian fellows. Mandate authorities learned quickly who among their enemies and critics demanded to be taken seriously. During a time of violence and war, followed by military occupation and colonial rule, politics demanded a wide tactical repertoire, and arguably people like Hananu, al-Hashimi, and the leaders of the Turkish Republic were formidable because they straddled both worlds. The mandates combined a facade of international concord and legitimacy with a veiled structure of violence and coercion. The mandate's most formidable challengers knew speeches, petitions, and reasoned calls for rights, justice, and equality would achieve little.

Notes

1. LN, *Official Journal*, Geneva, August 1922.
2. LN R41, "Arrêté 336," September 10, 1920, p. 6.
3. Fawaz Traboulsi, *A History of Modern Lebanon* (London: Pluto Press, 2007), pp. 80–1.
4. Engin Deniz Akarli, *The Long Peace: Ottoman Lebanon, 1861–1920* (Berkeley: University of California Press, 1993), pp. 148–9.
5. LN R41, "Copie de la Déclaration en date du 10 Juillet 1920 du Conseil Administatif du Liban."
6. Edmond Rabbath, "Courte Histoire du Mandat en Syrie at au Liban," unpublished ms, n.d., p. 53, quoted in Philip S. Khoury, *Syria and the French Mandate: The Politics of Arab Nationalism, 1920–1945* (Princeton University Press, 1987), p. 248.
7. Khoury, *Syria and the French Mandate*, pp. 33–5.
8. *The Times*, "Draft of the Syrian Constitution," August 3, 1928.
9. BNA, FO 684/4, Consul Hole to FO, June 21, 1928. Yasin al-Hashimi's visit provoked both French and British anxiety, and the drafting of at least two secret surveillance reports.
10. BNA FO 684/4, Consul Hole to FO, June 28, 1928.
11. BNA FO 684/4, Damascus Consul Files.
12. LN R2307, "Mandate over Syria," Sultan al-Atrash telegram, July 9, 1930.
13. LN R2280, "Mandate over Palestine, 1929–32."
14. Weldon Matthews has written the best book to date on Palestinian politics and parties in Palestine during the mandate. *Confronting an Empire, Constructing a Nation: Arab Nationalists and Popular Politics in Mandate Palestine* (London: I.B. Tauris, 2006).
15. Charles Smith, *Palestine and the Arab Israeli Conflict*, 5th edition (New York: Bedford/St. Martin's), pp. 110–11.
16. LN R17, Report from Palestine Arab Congress, Jamal al-Husayni, Secretary General, October 22, 1924.
17. LN R29, Palestine Mandate, "Custody of Holy Places."
18. The Israeli government demolished the neighborhood and expelled the residents on June 10, 1967, immediately after the 1967 war, establishing a large plaza in front of the Wall.
19. LN R2281, Petition to the Mandates Commission signed by Shakib Arslan, Riad al-Solh, and Ihsan al-Jabri, December 11, 1928.
20. LN R2181, Petition, December 11, 1928.
21. LN R2181, Report by William Rappard, July 1929, and Government of Palestine, *Official Gazette*, March 1, 1924. "Ordinance no. 5."
22. UK Government, *Report of the Commission on the Palestine Disturbances of August 1929* (Shaw Commission Report), March 1930.
23. BNA FO 371/13752, Palestine Mandate 1929.

24. BNA FO 371/13752, telegram, no. 13, CO to HC, August 31, 1929.
25. BNA FO 371/13752, telegram HC to CO, September 1, 1929.
26. BNA FO 371/13756, Hole to FO, November 7, 1929, enclosure, "In the Name of the Syrian Population."
27. UK Government, *Report of the Commission on the Palestine Disturbances of August, 1929,* March 1930. LN R2283, Palestine Mandate, Shaw Commission, press extracts, correspondence, and minutes of the Mandate Commission.
28. *The Times,* "Arab Grievances. Delegates Plea for Equal Rights," April 11, 1930. Yehosua Porath, *The Palestinian Arab National Movement, 1929–1939: From Riots to Rebellion* (London: Frank Cass, 1977), pp. 24–5.
29. LN R2283, press clippings on Palestine, *Daily Mail,* Viscount Rothermere, "Hand Back the Mandates or the Middle East May be our Ruin," September 12, 1929.
30. UK Government, *Report of the Commission on the Palestine Disturbances of August 1929* (Shaw Commission Report), March 1930.
31. *The Times,* "Palestine: A Statement of Policy. Dr. Weizmann Resigns," October 21, 1930, and Smith, *Palestine and the Arab Israeli Conflict,* p. 128.
32. Sluglett, *Britain in Iraq,* p. 169.
33. Marr, "Yasin al-Hashimi," p. 189.
34. BNA FO 684/5, Damascus Consul files, "1930-32," no. 17, Hole to FO, February 11, 1932.
35. MAE-Série E, Syrie-Liban, 211, Lausanne Consulate to MAE, October 14, 1926. Quoted in William L. Cleveland, *Islam Against The West: Shakib Arslan and the Campaign for Islamic Nationalism* (Austin, TX: University of Texas Press, 1985), p. 65.
36. Thanks to Laila Parsons for the details of al-Qawuqji's travels after the Revolt.
37. Khoury, *Syria and the French Mandate,* pp. 366–7.
38. BNA FO 684/5, "Syria 1930–32," no. 17, Hole to FO, February 11, 1932.
39. "Arrêté 4," February 12, 1932. BNA FO, 684/5 "Syria 1930–32." This decree is certainly an ancestor and antecedent for the various similar Syrian "Emergency Law" decrees of the 1960s.
40. Zirkili, *al-Aᶜlam,* vol. VI, p. 304, Stefan Weber, *Damascus: Ottoman Modernity and Urban Transformation, 1808–1918* (Aarhus University Press, 2009), vol. I, p. 55, and Khoury, *Syria and the French Mandate,* p. 378.
41. Sluglett, *Britain in Iraq,* pp. 216–17.
42. BNA UK Treasury Office [TO] 161/1147, 27306/1 Iraq Political Situation, 1926-35, colonial secretary to prime minister, January 30, 1930.
43. Sluglett, *Britain in Iraq,* pp. 208–9. I base my reconstruction here on Sluglett's description.
44. *Jarida al-Ikhwa' al-Watani,* Baghdad, August 27, 1931. Quoted in Marr, "Yāsīn al-Hāshimī," p. 194.
45. Dr. ᶜAbd al-Rahman Shahbandar, *Mudhakkirāt wa khutab* (Damascus: Syrian Ministry of Culture, 1993), pp. 145–51. Speech for the opening ceremony of *Hizb al-shᶜab,* June 5, 1925.
46. LN R2316, Iraq Mandate, report from Rappard on a petition from Kurds of Iraq, March 28, 1931. Sluglett, *Britain in Iraq,* pp. 212–16.

47. LN R2316, "Mandate over Irak," and BNA TO 161/1147, 27306/1.
48. LN R2316, "Mandate over Irak."
49. *The Times*, "State Visit of King Feisel," June 20, 1933.
50. Zirkili, *al-Aʿlam*, vol. II, pp. 64–5. Bakr Sidqi, like most of the Iraqi officers, is usually claimed to have joined the Arab Revolt, but as was often the case, he did not join Faysal till after the war, in Damascus.
51. Khoury, *Syria and the French Mandate*, p. 382.
52. Khoury, *Syria and the French Mandate*, p. 384.
53. LN, *Minutes of the Twenty Second Session, Geneva*, November–December 1932. *The Times*, "The Future of Syria," January 4, 1933.
54. LN R4097, Syrian Unity Petitions, 1932–3.
55. LN, *Extracts from the Minutes of the Twenty-Fourth Session*, Geneva, October 27, 1933.
56. Khoury, *Syria and the French Mandate*, pp. 390–1.
57. *The Times*, "German Jews for Palestine: How Emigration is Regulated," October 5, 1933.
58. *The Times*, "Race Pressure in Palestine. The Jewish Influx. Congestion on the Coast," February 27, 1935. See also BNA FO 371/20030, Weekly Intelligence Survey, SECRET, August 28, 1936. Smith, *Palestine and the Arab Israeli Conflict*, pp.128–9.
59. Illan Pappe, *The Rise and Fall of a Palestinian Dynasty: The Husaynis, 1700–1948* (Berkeley: University of California Press, 2010), p. 249.
60. *The Times*, "Arab Demonstrations in Palestine," October 26, 1933.
61. *The Times*, "Arab Riot at Jaffa. Many Killed and Injured. Government Ban Ignored," October 28, 1933.
62. *The Times*, "Palestine Unrest. Disorders in Jerusalem. More Casualties. Three-Day General Strike Proclaimed," October 30, 1933. *New York Times*, "Arabs Riot Again; Palestine Unrest Spreading Outside: Demonstrations of Sympathy Held in Damascus, Baghdad and Transjordan Towns," October 29, 1933.
63. *The Times*, "The Peace of Palestine. Government's New Power. Order in Council," October 31, 1933.
64. *New York Times*, "Dictatorial Rule Set For Palestine: High Commissioner Proclaims Defense Order," October 31, 1933.
65. Elizabeth Burgoyne, *Gertrude Bell from her Personal Papers, 1914–1926* (London: Ernest Benn, 1961), p. 342. Marr, "Yasin al-Hashimi," pp. 288–9.
66. AUB special collections, *Al-Kulliya Review*, Commencement 1937, and *al-ʿUrwa*, no. 1, December 1936.
67. May al-Daftari's forthcoming book, *Yasin al-Hashimi: Sira wa dhikrayat*, reproduces family letters. Ms. Al-Daftari graciously provided me with a copy and a translation of this letter.
68. Written when Yasin al-Hashimi was in the third or fourth month of his second prime ministership.
69. Muhsin Abu Tabikh, *Kitab Mabadi wa Rijal* (Damascus: Matbaʿt Abu Zaydan, 1938), p. 39, and Muhsin Abu Tabikh, *Mudhakkirat al-Sayyid Muhsin Abu Tabikh* (Beirut: al-Mu'assasa al-ʿArabiyya lil-Dirasat wa al-Nashr, 2001), pp. 315–16.

70. US Dept. of State, Consular Dispatch, Baghdad March 6, 1935, 890g.00/322. Quoted in Marr, "Yasin al-Hashimi," p. 291.

71. *Al-Majala al-ᶜAskariyya*, 7 vols. (Baghdad, 1929–1941).

72. Taha al-Hashimi, *Mudhakkirat Taha al-Hashimi, 1919–1943* (Beirut: Dar al-Taliᶜa, 1967), pp. 6–7.

73. Marr, "Yasin al-Hashimi," p. 295.

74. The insight originates with Phebe Marr, "Yasin al-Hashimi," p. 301.

75. US Dept. of State, Consular Dispatch, April 4, 1935, 890g.00/326. Quoted in Marr, "Yasin al-Hashimi," p. 309.

76. Khaludun S. Husri, "Iraq from Independence to Coup d'Etat 1930–36," Unpublished PhD dissertation, American University of Beirut, 1972, p. 195.

77. ᶜAbd al-Razzaq Hasani, *Tarikh al-Wizarat Al-ᶜIraqiyya* (Sidon: Irfan, 1958), vol. IV, pp. 125–7.

78. Laila Parsons' life of al-Qawuqji, *The Commander: Fawzi al-Qawuqji and the Fight for Arab Independence, 1914–1948* (New York: Hill and Wang, 2016), based partly on private papers and family documents, vividly reveals this story. Also see Qawuqji, *Mudhakkirat*, pp. 172–3.

79. Qawuqji, *Mudhakkirat*, pp. 178–9.

80. Khoury, *Syria and the French Mandate*, p. 400.

81. Khoury, *Syria and the French Mandate*, p. 388.

82. Khoury, *Syria and the French Mandate*, p. 393.

83. Khoury, *Syria and the French Mandate*, p. 443.

84. Khoury, *Syria and the French Mandate*, p. 453.

85. *The Times*, "Race Pressure in Palestine. The Jewish Influx. Congestion on the Coast," February 27, 1935.

86. Khoury, *Syria and the French Mandate*, p. 447.

6 The Final Days of the Last Ottoman Generation, 1936–1938

Events in the Former Ottoman Realms, 1936–1937

January–February 1936	Syrian General Strike
March–September 1936	France–Syrian Treaty negotiations
April–October 1936	Palestine General Strike
August 1936	Fawzi al-Quwuqji arrives in Palestine from Iraq
August–October 1936	Iraqi chief of staff General Taha al-Hashimi travels to Istanbul, London, Berlin, Prague, and Ankara on a diplomatic and weapons-buying trip
October 1936	Bakr Sidqi coup in Baghdad overthrows Yasin al-Hashimi's government. Leading figures flee into exile. Coup occurs on eve of Taha al-Hashimi's return to Baghdad
November 1936–January 1937	Peel Commission in the Palestine Mandate
December 1936	Syrian parliament unanimously ratifies the Franco-Syrian Treaty
January 1937	Yasin al-Hashimi dead of apparent heart attack in Beirut at 53. Funeral and interment takes place in Damascus

General Strikes in Syria and Palestine

The Syrian People, who formed a part of the Ottoman Empire without any distinction between them and the Turkish people, in rights and obligations, enjoyed suffrage rights for all councils and assemblies, controlled revenue and expenditures, and levied taxes through their deputies in the Ottoman Chamber. Their Constitution was safeguarded, their resources protected, and their liberty was respected. There were no Customs barriers between themselves and other parts of the Empire. They engaged in trade, made profits, and came and went as they pleased.

At the present time Syria, which was united, has been turned into several States with various ministers and Governments. There is not a single Syrian department which has not at its side another French department, from the ministry to the local police station. Elections are abolished, the Constitution has been torn up, and the Chamber of Deputies has been suspended …

Petition from Dr. Tawfiq Shishshakli, Hama, February 4, 1936
to the High Commissioner[1]

Hananu's death coincided with a regional explosion of frustration and disappointment. Forty days after the funeral, in January 1936, National Bloc leaders in Damascus organized a march from the Umayyad Mosque, through the central market Suq al-Hamidiyya, along Jamal Basha street (today's al-Nasr Street) to Damascus University. Yasin al-Hashimi, Amir ʿAbdallah, the Greek Orthodox Patriarch, and the Maronite Patriarch sent eulogies and condolences that were read to the crowd. Faris al-Khuri's younger brother, also a lawyer and president of the Damascus Bar, Faʾiz al-Khuri, gave a fiery speech demanding the unity and independence of Ottoman Greater Syria, the cancellation of the Balfour Declaration, Pan Arab Union, and the legal equality of all citizens regardless of religion.[2] High Commissioner de Martel summoned al-Khuri and the Bloc leaders to register his displeasure with their insolence. De Martel remarked that he could readily order the Senegalese sentry at his office door to take Faʾiz al-Khuri away in chains. The British consul noted wryly, "teaching subservient races the languages of their alien rulers is a two edged sword."[3]

Mass demonstrations followed, beginning in Damascus and soon including other cities under the mandate. The demonstrations brought an impromptu strike, which was only belatedly adopted by the Bloc leaders. Mandate police met the demonstrations in Damascus, Aleppo, Homs, and Hama with mass arrests and live fire. Toward the end of January, mandate police killed four protesters, and 20,000 Damascenes marched in a funeral procession the following day for their funerals.[4] Cautious Homs politician Hashim al-Atasi had become National Bloc president. Deprived of Hananu's decisive and steadying influence, al-Atasi and the Bloc declared a general strike at the end of January, by which time the younger activists had long seized the initiative and shut down the mandate's cities. As in 1925, Syria's nationalist politicians found themselves scrambling to keep up with popular anger and opposition to the mandate. By mid February, mandate troops had killed scores of demonstrators and High Commissioner de Martel had declared martial law. Tension and popular outrage spread throughout the region. The example of independent Iraq under Ottoman and pan-Arab hero Yasin al-Hashimi was the new inspiration.

The General Strike continued in all Syrian cities for nearly two months. Unlike the Great Revolt of 1925–7, which began in Hawran, and did not spread north of Hama, the 1936 strike involved all the regions of the mandate, and paralyzed the normal civic and commercial activities of every town and city, including remote Dayr al-Zur, on the Euphrates, and border towns closer to the urban centers of Iraq and Turkey than to Damascus. Activists strung thick green cords across the entrances to the covered markets to symbolically close the *suqs*. Students, ranging from those in primary schools to those in universities, stayed home till the mandate officials capitulated and ordered the schools closed until further notice. Food became scarce, and people openly shared what little was available. Some hoarding and profiteering occurred, but the general feeling emphasized communal sacrifice and effort. The major cities of Greater Lebanon, Beirut, Saida, and Tripoli all struck in sympathy and support. Marches and demonstrations took place daily, culminating in the largest weekly protests on Friday.[5]

Damascus had long been the most important Ottoman–Arab city, and the principal focal point of Ottoman State modernization and infrastructure projects. Members of the politically engaged public in Iraq and Palestine customarily followed the news and trends from Damascus, and notice of the strike and demonstrations spread widely. Yasin al-Hashimi was the most famous Arab politician, and nominally independent Iraq the envy of politicized Arabs everywhere. The Baghdad press covered agitation in Syria and Palestine exhaustively and the Iraqi cabinet welcomed one Arab delegation after another to Baghdad.[6] In the middle of the Syrian General Strike in February, Yasin al-Hashimi sent thirty Baghdad University law students on an official political study tour of Syria and Palestine. Demonstrations and donation drives in Baghdad gathered food and money for the relief of striking cities in Syria.

Neighboring Palestinians struck in solidarity with the Syrians and demanded action from the political leadership. Shopkeepers and labor leaders had tried to shutter their shops and strike alongside their Syrian cousins, but British Mandate officials threatened striking laborers with their permanent replacement by Jewish workers.[7] They threatened merchants with closure of their shops and seizure of their goods. Demonstrations nevertheless took place in every city under mandate in Greater Syria,

including Transjordan. In Damascus, mandate authorities blamed opposition on nationalist troublemakers in the cities and "bandits" in the countryside. High Commissioner de Martel ordered the arrest, imprisonment,
or exile of the Bloc political leaders. De Martel publicly argued that
agitation and fear of nationalist violence kept ordinary Syrians from cooperating with the mandate and reopening their shops and returning to
work. But merchants and tradesmen protested his assertions vigorously
and refused the "protection" he offered. Mandate martial law courts
arrested, tried, and sentenced 3,080 people during January and February.[8]

Bloc president Hashim al-Atasi declared the nationalist program the
only solution to the impasse in Syria. "Seventeen years of the Mandate
had passed with continuous bloodshed, terror and harsh sanctions, which
had long suppressed the voice of justice." Syrians' demands remained as
they had at the beginning of the miserable ordeal: the unity and independence of the country, and a nation in control of its own destiny.[9] Two
days after the manifesto appeared in Damascus' al-Qabas newspaper, the
largest demonstration yet took place in Damascus. Police fired on protesters, killing four and wounding many. Most Bloc leaders had been jailed
or exiled to Turkey, but Hashim al-Atasi had seemed sufficiently non-
threatening to remain free. The prospect of growing unrest spurred De
Martel to dismiss the cabinet of notorious toady Taj al-Din al-Hasani and
appoint a new Syrian cabinet headed by 59-year-old Mülkiye-trained
Ottoman statesman ᶜAta al-Ayyubi, and including three Bloc cabinet
members. High Commissioner de Martel, under urgent orders from
Paris, invited Bloc president Hashim al-Atasi, new prime minister
al-Ayyubi, and members of the cabinet to Beirut for intensive negotiations
to end the strike.[10]After two days of closed discussions, De Martel ordered
the release of the Bloc leaders from jail, and Bloc president Hashim
al-Atasi declared an end to the strike at the beginning of March 1936.

De Martel announced immediate treaty talks in Paris. A National
Bloc delegation including Hashim al-Atasi, Jamil Mardam Bey, Faris
al-Khuri, and a few others, sailed from Beirut for France, and arrived
in Paris at the end of March 1936. Treaty negotiations opened as
before: French priorities included the permanent sectarian partition of
the country, the imposition of French governors, and French military
garrisons. But French elections loomed, and at the end of April, the
French centrist Radical government fell and a leftist coalition was
elected. The election of Léon Blum's Popular Front government res-
cued the treaty negotiations from complete breakdown, but also postponed their resumption till June. The delegation remained in Paris,
waiting for the new government to take office. Yasin al-Hashimi paid
their hotel bills.

The Palestine Revolt

At the same time that the Syrian delegation arrived in Paris, the British High Commissioner for Palestine invited a delegation of leading Arab politicians to negotiations in London.[11] The Palestinian press gave voice to fears that refugee Jews fleeing Europe would overwhelm and displace the Arab population, and popular anxiety pressured politicians to be more confrontational. The popular daily *al-Filistin* declared, "the English do not understand leniency and kindness, and we should therefore be most extremist and speak to them in a language they understand. The Arabs are otherwise doomed for annihilation in ten or twenty years thanks to the British and the Jews." The press also bemoaned the lassitude of the Palestinians while Syrians were seizing their national rights.[12] The Iraqi law-student delegation, on a government stipend from Iraqi prime minister Yasin al-Hashimi, visited all sizable Arab towns in Palestine during March and held public meetings and speeches, emphasizing Arab brotherhood and the need for collective struggle to free all the Arabs from colonial rule and form a united Arab state. British observers remarked sourly that independence had encouraged Iraqis to agitate everywhere they wished.[13]

As opposition simmered, British officials tried to advance directly to political negotiations, and avoid the intermediate stage of a Palestine General Strike.[14] The British Mandate authorities hoped negotiations could halt the inertia toward confrontation. But among Palestinians, the stark lessons of the Syrian General Strike and the Syrian Revolt a decade before showed that change would only come from militant action. A few months before the Syrian General Strike, in October 1935, British police had discovered a huge cache of smuggled weapons destined for Zionist paramilitaries in a cement shipment at Haifa's Port. The next month, police tracked and killed roving rebel band leader and fiery anti-mandate preacher ʿIzz al-Din al-Qassam outside a village in the Nablus district. In April 1936 Palestinian political leaders accepted the invitation to London and discussed the members and schedule of the delegation. Their efforts were too late to prevent an explosion.

In mid April 1936 armed men, calling themselves Brothers of Qassam (*Ikhwan al-Qassam*), set up an ambush on the main road outside Nablus.[15] They stopped a convoy of about ten trucks by means of piled stones in the roadway, and opened fire when the drivers emerged to inspect the roadway. In 1922, Sultan al-Atrash had employed identical tactics to destroy a French armored convoy in an unsuccessful effort to ignite an uprising. The insurgents killed one Jewish driver on the spot and injured others, at least one of whom later died.[16] The Syrian Revolt and General Strike provided the inspiration.

A day later, Irgun members killed two Arabs in retaliation. Their funeral turned into a battle as demonstrating Jews attacked Arabs, who retaliated and attacked first Jews involved in the original demonstration and then bystanders. Police intervened, truncheons swinging, and were driven back by stones thrown by both crowds, at which point they began firing, but evidently dispersed the crowds with few injuries.[17] As in 1929, rumors flew, usually claiming a massacre of Arabs by Jews.[18] The High Commissioner declared martial law, and within a few days, leading Arab citizens in every town and village formed local strike committees to organize and direct opposition activities. The Arab boatmen's guild evacuated 4,000 Jews from Jaffa via the harbor to adjoining Tel Aviv. Arab inhabitants of Tel Aviv got out any way they could. The political leaders canceled their trip to London.

As in Syria, the nationalist politicians asserted leadership well after events had progressed. Shops everywhere were shuttered and streets empty before politicians, including Jerusalem mayor Husayn al-Khalidi, and the Mufti, Amin al-Husayni, declared the General Strike and the formation of a new Arab Higher Committee toward the end of April. The new committee issued three demands: a halt to Jewish immigration, a halt to land sales to Jews, and the appointment of a representative national government. They resolved to maintain the strike until the British authorities met the demands. When the strike extended to the transport sector by late April, the entire mandate economy was threatened. Strikers spread nails on city streets to disable private cars breaking the strike. As painful as six weeks of General Strike in Syria had been, prospects for Palestinians were far bleaker; in Palestine a larger, better-funded, Zionist economy already existed alongside the more agrarian Arab economy. Hungry Jewish immigrants were ready to take the place of every worker and fill the void created by shuttered shops. Meanwhile the Higher Committee worked to keep the strike peaceful and non-confrontational.[19]

A Higher Committee delegation visited Amir Abdallah in Transjordan, who advised them to call off the strike and negotiate with the British government.

Large demonstrations continued during May in Jaffa, Haifa, and Nablus involving thousands of people. Police responded to stone-throwing with live fire and killed small numbers of demonstrators. Smaller demonstrations took place in Transjordan in Salt, Amman, and Maʿan. Small groups of Jews attacked individual Arabs and small groups of Arabs attacked individual Jews in incidents in Jaffa and Jerusalem. The Higher Committee tried to assert control over the uprising and preserve relations with the mandate authorities, but brutal police tactics, hunger, frustration, and desperation, especially in the countryside, undermined their efforts. By mid May, organized groups of armed men had attacked mandate army and police patrols in rural areas and outside the towns. By June, the urban strike had become a rural revolt. Mandate authorities clamped down on the political leadership and arrested nationalist lawyer ᶜAwni ᶜAbd al-Hadi of the Istiqlal party and detained him in a "concentration camp with common agitators" at Sarafand in an effort to humiliate him. Jamal al-Husayni left the country for England, and British intelligence considered the leadership disunited and disconnected from events in the countryside. Local village and town committees emerged to continue clandestine organization, and food and relief distribution. New British counterinsurgency laws called for death sentences for anyone firing at Mandate troops or disrupting communications.[20] By mid June there were daily attacks throughout the Palestine Mandate.

Insurgents nightly destroyed train lines, mined roadways with explosives, cut telephone and telegraph wires, and sniped at trains and vehicles. Over the course of the month, attacks became more brazen and involved larger numbers, becoming more organized and effective. Mandate counterinsurgency tactics, identical to those criticized so fiercely earlier by British officials in Syria, appeared immediately. The Palestinian press accused mandate forces of atrocities and pillage, and as his French counterpart in Syria had done, the High Commissioner closed the newspapers.[21] Senior Arab government officials submitted a memorandum to the High Commissioner pointing out that "the cause underlying the present disorders is the insufficient regard paid to legitimate Arab grievances," and that "it is impossible to continue to act as the useful link between the Administration and the population." RAF airplanes dropped leaflets on the population of the old city of Jaffa, giving 24 hours' notice, before the city was sealed, hundreds of structures demolished with explosives, and a 100-foot-wide corridor bulldozed through the rubble for counterinsurgency access. Authorities planned further demolitions and clearing for a ring cordon. A hundred thousand leaflets were printed to warn the populace against the strike and outline the consequences of opposition for airdrop throughout the mandate.[22]

During July, British infantry reinforcements and RAF aircrews arrived from Egypt and Malta. Armored patrols and airplanes shelled and bombed the rural areas day after day. British intelligence reported that the Mufti and other religious officials had begun to mix religious appeals and language with nationalist agitation in vocal opposition to the mandate and to Zionism.[23] Ambushes of British forces increased and Arab riflemen were increasingly disciplined, accurate, and numerous. Smaller British patrols were often pinned down and needed rescue from armored car and mobile machine-gun units, as well as airplanes.

Regional Arab newspapers followed events and the Iraqi paper *al-Istiqlal* proclaimed Arab unity in defense of Palestine and argued British brutality could provoke a general uprising of all the Arab countries.[24] The Iraqi Petroleum Company Oil pipeline from Iraq to Haifa ceased functioning as saboteurs damaged the line repeatedly. Mid July marked the hundredth day of the strike, and British intelligence remarked with incredulity that insurgent attacks remained tactical and disciplined with no sign of looting. Reports noted that military training was increasingly evident among the insurgents and ex-Ottoman veterans appeared among the bands. Counterinsurgency operations required continuous air cover and British forces were stretched thin.[25] Murders and reprisal killings between Arabs and Jews increased, but British forces and personnel were the overwhelming targets of insurgent attacks. London announced the formation and eventual dispatch to Palestine of yet another official commission of enquiry.

In early August the Arab workers of the Haifa railway terminus and workshops walked off the job and the remaining Arab workers of the Haifa port joined them. Arab employees of the Iraqi Petroleum terminal, and oil companies Shell and Saucony also joined the strike. Jewish workers replaced some striking employees, but the labor shortage forced mandate authorities to shut down rail service and non-essential parts of the port. British army personal ran essential trains and services.[26] British police sought, arrested, and transported striking workers to their workplaces in chains under armed guard.

Iraqi Foreign Minister Nuri al-Sa^{c}id appointed himself negotiator between Britain and the Palestinian Arabs and traveled to Palestine.[27] Nuri met the High Commissioner immediately upon his arrival, but hastened to call upon the Mufti Amin al-Husayni, ^{c}Awni ^{c}Abd al-Hadi, and other imprisoned members of the Higher Committee in detention in the concentration camp at Sarafand. Observers expected Nuri to strengthen the hand of the Higher Committee political leaders who sought a negotiated end to the strike. The Higher Committee accepted Nuri's offer of mediation, but armed rebels active in the countryside were unimpressed.[28] The Zionist press feared that Nuri's close ties to the British government would yield concessions that would threaten Zionist goals. Nuri's diplomacy showed the Palestine question involved all the Arabs, and could undermine the primacy of the Zionist position. Zionist leaders warned the High Commissioner that they had long suppressed militant elements in their community, owing to the more civilized habits of the Jews and their cultural sympathy with the mandate authorities, but serious negotiations with the Arabs would embolden those who wished to secure and protect Zionist rights to Palestine through violent means.[29]

Nuri returned for more substantive negotiations in late August 1936. Optimism for British concessions and a favorable end to the strike ran

high, but Nuri and the Higher Committee only announced their intention to pursue negotiations and continue the strike as long as necessary
to "safeguard and attain the rights of the nation." Mandate authorities
initially greeted Nuri's claim to speak for the Iraqi government and "the
Arab kings and princes" with public disdain and private worry. But
Nuri was a reassuring presence to British colonial authorities, and since
1920 had ably reconciled and served his own and British imperial goals.
His ostensible leader, and perennial rival, Iraqi prime minister Yasin al-
Hashimi, was much more threatening to British imperial priorities.

Nuri and King Ghazi sought to expand their influence with British
authorities and Palestinian "moderates," but prime minister Yasin al-
Hashimi and his brother, army chief Taha al-Hashimi, supported a covert force of military men with roots in the Ottoman army and post-war
insurgencies in Anatolia, Iraq, and Syria. With Yasin's blessing and
financing, Fawzi al-Qawuqji recruited, organized, and armed a group of
Arab professional soldiers in Baghdad.[30] Yasin told the British ambassador he had halted their advance, but their appearance in Transjordan
in August belied the story. As they traveled toward Palestine, Syrian ex-
soldiers in exile in Transjordan, like Muhammad al-Ashmar and Saᶜid
al-ᶜAs, and other veterans of the Syrian Revolt, joined them. Together
they crossed into Palestine with a force variously reported between 50
and 300 armed men, and at least a few machine guns.[31] Qawuqji issued
proclamations signaling his intent to drive the British and Zionists from
Palestine, and unite the Arabs. He styled himself the "Commander in
Chief of the Revolutionary Forces of Southern Syria." His adventures
received wide press coverage in Baghdad and Damascus.

The British Foreign Office ordered the regional consuls to prepare
detailed reports on the effect of the Palestine revolt on the region. Both
the Aleppo and Damascus consul claimed forlornly that other European
powers were hated far more than Britain, and British "prestige" remained
intact due to the honesty with which the treaties in Iraq and Egypt had
been concluded. But each noted the undimmed vitality of the pan-Arab
movement emanating from Baghdad under Yasin Paşa. The Aleppo consul attributed to his French counterparts a creeping fear that the Iraq
Treaty and earlier concessions had measurably weakened the powers in
the region. "We are faced with a very difficult situation in the Arab countries, and this will inevitably grow worse if the methods pursued against
us meet with apparent success ... It is clear that every point scored will
be exploited assiduously to excite further efforts to render the presence of
France and Great Britain in Syria and Palestine impossible."[32]

Increasing crisis and the prospect of regional Arab revolt provoked a
response from the Zionist movement and the British government. The

Zionist Executive, learning that the Colonial Office intended to halt Jewish immigration to help stop the revolt, hurriedly sent David Ben Gurion to London to supervise Chaim Weizmann, who was considered overly accommodating to the British government.[33] On September 1, the *Palestine Post* published a front-page story titled, "End of the Arab Strike: Terms of Surrender Proposed by Arabs," complete with leaked Arab demands to halt immigration. The same day, Weizmann wrote to the Colonial Secretary demanding clarification of the concessions to the Arabs. The following day a cabinet meeting took place to consider Weizmann's letter and formulate a response. The day after, *The Times* published an official letter signed by Lord Frederick Lugard, British Accredited Representative at the League of Nations Mandates Commission. Lugard, speaking for the cabinet, suggested the Arabs and the Zionists should negotiate together, rather than through the mandate authorities, an invitation Weizmann welcomed in a subsequent letter. Lugard noted darkly, though, that before any negotiation could take place, or any concessions be contemplated, law and order in Palestine had to be restored. Intransigence should not be rewarded. Martial law might be necessary. Further decisions would be made.[34]

On Monday September 6, the Colonial Secretary announced the cabinet resolutions, which appeared the next morning in the pages of *The Times*. The government ordered an army division sent to Palestine immediately and the enactment of martial law. The Cabinet appointed General John G. Dill overall commander of the mandate. "The Government express their regret that this action has been forced upon them, especially as friendship with Moslem peoples has been 'a constant aim of British policy,' but they cannot yield to violence and outrage."[35] That week's secret intelligence bulletin remarked that the change in policy had "taken the Arabs completely by surprise."[36] Massive British reinforcements embarked for Palestine.

Fawzi al-Qawuqji was the man of the hour in the short interval before the arrival of reinforcements.[37] Palestinian villagers greeted his proclamations jubilantly and he was reported to be everywhere, "as often as not in several locations at the same time."[38] On September 3, he organized and led a carefully orchestrated ambush near the olive and orchard farming town of Balᶜa in today's West Bank. The ambush went well for the insurgents and careful planning yielded dramatic results. British reinforcements sped there by road and air, but five aircraft were hit by fire from the ground and two airplanes were shot down. British intelligence thought the RAF had faced specialized anti-aircraft weapons, but Qawuqji had actually positioned a conventional machine-gun crew to cover the expected air attack. The British counterattack was intense, and the insurgent casualties brought bitter accusations between Palestinian fighters and their "foreign" guests. After the insurgents left the town, British collective punishment of the people of Bal^{c}a was especially brutal; troops looted the town, demolished a number of houses, and arrested many citizens. The relevant report claimed: "this form of punishment has proved very effective and has had a certain amount of moral effect on the villagers concerned. It is a quick and conclusive form of punishment and one that is understood by the Arab mind. The ruins of the house or houses stand as a lasting memorial of Government punishment."[39] The relevant martial-law code remains in use in the Israeli Occupied Territories.

Qawuqji and his comrades tried to keep up the pressure but the odds were stacked against his brand of armed struggle. The combined forces of professional insurgents and Palestinian volunteers engaged British forces repeatedly over the next two weeks, but without the dramatic results of al-Bal^{c}a. Al-Qawuqji, following Yasin al-Hashimi's popular mobilization policies in Iraq, called for youth conscription, and paramilitary organization and training. Many peasant youth heeded his call, and the ranks swelled, but weapons, ammunition, and professional leadership were in short supply. As in Syria in 1926, Qawuqji also organized revolutionary courts, which provoked controversy when he ordered the executions of at least a few "spies and traitors." Prosperous youth who declined to join the ranks of the insurgents found it unsafe to venture onto village streets, and a climate of militant polarization took hold in the countryside.[40] Al-Qawuqji styled himself the "Commander of the Arab Revolution in Southern Syria," which irritated Palestinian civilian politicians who had been struggling against the Palestine Mandate for almost two decades by 1936.[41]

By the middle of September, the British War Office had assumed overall control of the Palestine Mandate and at least 10,000 additional soldiers had entered the field, against a few hundred armed insurgents. Boycott, rebellion, and counterinsurgency had ruined the Palestinian agrarian economy, and without the fall harvest, mass hunger loomed. The Higher Committee leadership sought a face-saving solution, and for some, a way to safely facilitate the British counterinsurgency campaign.

By the end of the month of September, insurgent bands faced irresistible pressure from the British forces. Early in October, a group under the command of al-Qawuqji's long-time friend, Ottoman staff-officer, and like Qawuqji, perennial rebel against the post-war settlement, Sa^{c}id al-^{c}As, and Musa Kazim al-Husayni's son ^{c}Abd al-Qadir ambushed an armed train and military escort. The following day an RAF patrol sighted the band, pursued, and summoned British ground forces. The

insurgents retreated and took cover and Saᶜid al-ᶜAs was killed. ᶜAbd
al-Qadir al-Husayni was injured and captured.[42]

The ambush and death of al-ᶜAs damaged the miliatry prospects of
an already lopsided struggle. Military setbacks notwithstanding, the
insurgents had become celebrities and heroes among the Arab public.
In death their exploits were even more exalted and Saᶜid al-ᶜAs was
widely mourned. Famous poet and intellectual Amin al-Rihani
bemoaned his death and celebrated his struggle in an elegy of lament in
the pages of the Palestinian newspaper *al-Filastin*. Al-Rihani praised
al-ᶜAs as the peerless and noble "knight of the revolutions," who represented the best among the Arabs in a front-page commemoration forty
days after his death.[43]

Two or three days later, a Higher Committee emissary met al-
Qawuqji at his camp in the hills north of Nablus, and persuaded him to
temporarily leave the field and declare a ceasefire so negotiations could
take place. Exactly eleven years earlier, in the midst of the Syrian
Revolt, the leading notable citizens of Hama had persuaded al-Qawuqji
to leave the city after a French bombardment. Both times al-Qawuqji's
forces were probably on the cusp of total defeat, and both times, he
came to blame the retreat on the treachery of aristocratic politicians
who, in their zeal to preserve their positions, betrayed the people's
hopes and the Arab cause.

On October 12, Fawzi al-Qawuqji declared a ceasefire and the
Higher Committee called an end to the General Strike. In a leaflet distributed in Palestine and Damascus, he hailed the achievements of the
mujahidin, and called on them to obey the call of the Arab kings and
princes and the Higher Committee to halt combat, but to keep their
weapons at the ready to re-enter the field should negotiations not yield
expected results.[44] Al-Qawuqji pictured himself the guarantor of an
acceptable outcome for the Arabs. But General Dill had no intention of
allowing armed insurgents to remain, and he ordered the collection of
weapons and the expulsion of insurgents. Members of the Higher
Committee agreed, and negotiated an exit for al-Qawuqji to Transjordan.
He left with fewer than 200 fighters on the night of October 23. British
forces stood aside and allowed them to leave.[45]

Within a week, about half the force had left for Syria, an option not
available to Qawuqji or others still under French Mandate death sentence from their role in the 1925 revolt. British intelligence had
reported rebels selling their rifles and ammunition to the *bedouin* in
order to fund their exodus.[46] When Qawuqji arrived in Transjordan,
Amir Abdallah was on a state visit to Egypt, and in his absence Crown
Prince Talal had welcomed the insurgents. Once Abdallah returned on

October 31, he conspired with the British government to deport Qawuqji to Iraq, but events unfolding in Baghdad made it necessary to stall his exit. Encamped outside Amman, Quwuqji waited and received guests, while British intelligence worried, plotted, and planned.

The Franco-Syrian Treaty and Syrian "Independence"

While the Palestine strike became an armed revolt, the Syrian treaty delegation waited through spring 1936 in Paris. Yasin al-Hashimi's government continued to pay their bills, and in June the new left-wing French government took office and negotiations resumed and continued over the summer. By early September, they had reached an agreement and initialed the Franco-Syrian Treaty. Léon Blum's leftist government had accepted the National Bloc, and appeared to have succeeded after a decade and a half of failed negotiations. Regional instability and a threatening climate in Europe had dictated imperial retrenchment for Britain and for France. It was a moment to compromise with the nationalist critics of colonial empire.

"The Treaty of Friendship and Alliance between Syria and France" was modeled on the Anglo-Iraqi Treaty, but with clauses concerning Syrian sectarian minorities.[47] A similar treaty for Lebanon followed in November, but demonstrators in Beirut, Sidon, and Tripoli called for rejection of the treaty and demanded union with Syria. Like Britain in Iraq, France retained a security presence at two airbases in Syria and the sea ports. The large Ottoman-era rail junction and airbase at Rayaq in Lebanon's Biqaᶜ valley would allow France to militarily dominate both Lebanon and Syria, and would come to be the stronghold of Vichy French forces during the battles of 1941. The treaties were supposed to be ratified by the Syrian parliament, the French senate, and the League of Nations, and govern the relations between the newly independent republics and the former mandatory for twenty-five years. In the event, only the Syrian parliament fulfilled its role, and both the French Senate and the League of Nations failed to ratify the treaty. Anxiety over the prospects for European war and the strength of the European Right hobbled both bodies.

The question of Syrian unity remained contentious. Arab nationalists in both mandates objected to the separation of Greater Lebanon from Syria, but consoled themselves that once France was gone, the borders could be erased and Damascus might resume its place as regional capital. Unlike Lebanon, the separate autonomous regions for the Druze and Alawite minorities were to be absorbed into the Syrian Republic with clauses insuring minority rights. The Hawran Druze leaders mostly accepted the treaty. Their region had played a leading role during the 1925 revolt and had been thoroughly drawn into the world of national-ist politics in Damascus. The more remote and inward Alawite region, between Homs, the coast, and the Turkish border, was less accepting. The Permanent Mandates Commission received at least four petitions arguing strenuously against incorporation of the Alawites, Christians, and Ismailis into a state presumed to be dominated by urban Muslims.

The League of Nations Mandate Commission and the French Mandate claimed from the outset to be tutoring new nations and pro-tecting the rights of minorities. At Geneva, William Rappard struggled to reconcile the new French policy of conceding Syrian unity with the pre-vious French policy of social and geographical fragmentation in the name of the rights and privileges of Christians and other non-Muslims. In the Mandate Commission meeting he again confronted Robert De Caix, the original architect and ideologue of France's minority mandate strategy. "Could it be believed that minority rights had the slightest chance of being safeguarded when, in place of the mandate, there stood a Treaty concluded between two countries on equal footing – which was the only possible footing under international law? A choice must be made between two irreconcilable ideas – the emancipation of Syria and Lebanon, [or] the protection of their minorities."[48] Rappard's protest, like every other Mandate Commission proclamation, meant little in prac-tice. The League was powerless to confront Great Power priorities, and in the face of a looming European war, France's priorities had changed.

The National Bloc delegation returned to Damascus on September 29. In the brief period of early October 1936, the long-awaited dawn of independence seemed in view. Syrian politicians of the National Bloc marched triumphantly in Damascus and the cities of the mandate and nationalist youth fell in step behind them. News of Qawuqji's adven-tures in Palestine was still encouraging, and Yasin al-Hashimi in Baghdad seemed to be leading an ever-stronger Arab nation asserting its independence on the world stage. Radical youth marched side by side with the aged members of the last Ottoman generation, both antici-pating a future of self-determination and dignity.

Young nationalists of the ʿUsbat al-ʿAmal al-Qawmi, or the League of National Action, had emerged to prominence in Damascus. They had pushed those of their parents' generation toward confrontation with the mandate authorities, and been rewarded by the promise of indepen-dence. The older civilian nationalists of the Syrian National Bloc had been targets of youthful disdain in past years, and the younger Syrians admired military figures like Yasin al-Hashimi, Fawzi al-Quwuqji, and exiled politicians like ʿAbd al-Rahman Shahbandar and Shakib Arslan.

Syrian politicians who had managed to avoid exile or jail appeared less heroic and more compromised, and young activists criticized their cooperation with the mandate authorities.

A young lawyer named Munir al-ᶜAjlani had emerged as a leading figure of the League of National Action. ᶜAjlani joined the National Bloc, and during the period of the Syrian General Strike in the early months of 1936 he started a paramilitary youth movement called the Steel Shirts, or *al-qumsan al-hadidiyya*.[49] Yasin al-Hashimi had led the way in organizing a paramilitary nationalist youth movement after coming to power the year before, and al-ᶜAjlani followed the Iraqi model closely. The Steel Shirts recruited educated Syrian youth, received athletic and military training, wore splendid uniforms including the distinctive Iraqi army *sidara* hat, and marched and paraded throughout the cities and towns. Ex-Ottoman officers trained the young men and emphasized the ethos of the Ottoman Unionists: discipline, patriotism, and sacrifice.[50]

The Fall of Yasin Paşa al-Hashimi

Yasin al-Hashimi had become Iraqi prime minister in March 1935. He assumed the role as the most prominent independent Arab leader, figurehead of Arab unity, and a popular hero in the surrounding countries. In Baghdad, he focused on his ambitious reform program and wresting meaningful independence from the British Embassy. At first his skill, energy, and resourcefulness won admirers among British officials. But as the regional and international atmosphere of crisis intensified, and the extent of his ambitions and the consequences of his potential success became evident, both King Ghazi and his British patrons panicked.

Yasin al-Hashimi bent the Iraqi state to his will. His authoritarian and militaristic vision was in common with Mustafa Kemal, and probably most Ottoman Unionists of their generation. Yasin dissolved and reopened parliament after calling elections and reorganizing the chamber to include more deputies and a majority he controlled. He alternately tightened and loosened press censorship, and dismissed many officials for corruption, or resistance to his program. About a third of the remaining British advisors in the Iraqi government were up for contract renewal in May 1935. Al-Hashimi allowed the contracts to expire, thereby reducing the number of serving British officials by a third.

By these means, Yasin al-Hashimi dismissed the two most powerful British advisors in Iraq. General John Charles Bruce Hay was chief military advisor and liaison to the Iraqi army, and an enthusiastic supporter of Bakr Sidqi. Yasin allowed his contract to expire in late 1936.

Sir Kinahan Cornwallis had been the most influential British advisor over a decade and a half as chief British advisor to the Interior Ministry. Cornwallis had been director of the Arab Bureau, running British Middle East intelligence between 1916 and 1920, and oversaw the recruitment of Ottoman prisoners of war for the Arab Revolt. He played the central role in organizing the Iraqi monarchy, planning King Faysal's initial referendum in 1921. Cornwallis enjoyed a very high salary from the Iraqi treasury in his years in Baghdad, and he did not take his dismissal easily. He complained bitterly to the ambassador, and endeavored to mobilize his many friends in London against Yasin's government.[51] Yasin dismissed many other less prominent figures who similarly resented their loss of status and income, and the humiliation dealt by a once-vanquished enemy. When new employment offers for foreign advisors were tendered, Yasin cut salaries significantly and did not favor Britons, as the treaty required.[52] He was rumored to prefer Germans.

Yasin al-Hashimi was a product of the Ottoman military-school system. He rose from a modest background, fully availed himself of the social mobility offered in the military schools, distinguished himself at every level as a student, cadet, young officer, staff officer, field commander, general, and statesman. He believed in education and he believed in military discipline. In his first months in power the Ministry of Education introduced military training into the state boys' middle- and secondary-school curriculum. Military officers would visit each school weekly and teach physical fitness drills and military discipline, theory, and terms.[53] Boys were encouraged to join the youth military organization, called *al-Futuwa*. They were taught to use firearms, to handle and maintain weapons, to read maps, camp, read and understand military manuals, and survey geography. Recruits subjected themselves to strict discipline, but were rewarded, like their Ottoman cadet forebears, with splendid free uniforms, various privileges, and the opportunity to take part in parades and official ceremonies, and to be honored and lauded by the leaders of the nation in public displays, inevitably attended by Yasin al-Hashimi himself.

In May 1936, Ambassador Archibald Clark Kerr filed a long report based on several meetings with Yasin. Clark Kerr was among Yasin's admirers, and yet his report must have stoked fears that Iraq under Yasin was becoming less reliable and more hostile to British interests. Al-Hashimi noted that persistent armed smuggling from Kuwait forced him to increase military pressure on the neighboring British protectorate. Clark Kerr noted Kuwaiti fears that Iraq would annex their principality, and while Yasin expressed his allegiance to Arab unity, and aspirations for a single, large Arab state, he denied his wish to annex Kuwait. Yasin was well known for his measured speech and ambiguous language, and he noted mildly that some Iraqis did see annexation as a solution to the problem posed by unfriendly Kuwaiti behavior, and the possibility existed that such pressure and Kuwaiti misbehavior could force his hand.[54] British oil prospectors had become active in the Kuwait protectorate after 1934, when the shaykh signed an oil concession with Anglo-Persian. In 1937, they discovered vast quantities of oil.

Regional developments combined to instill a growing sense of dread in London, but collusion in Palestine decided the policy toward Yasin's government. The Foreign Office archives offer mostly bland and euphemistic exchanges, but the private correspondence files of Ambassador Clark Kerr reveal the rising tide of panic. Clark Kerr detailed German oil exploration and concession-seeking in a series of secret letters.[55] Various scandals, discussed in lurid detail in personal correspondence, had embroiled the royal family, and Yasin al-Hashimi had enhanced his own power at the expense of the diminished young king. Twenty-four-year-old King Ghazi would take orders from the ambassador, but events weakened his position. Yasin would not take orders and as the king sank, his position was strengthened. The ambassador himself, who counted as a leftist among British diplomats, suggested mildly that a republican system could solve Iraq's royal problems, but his Foreign Office counterparts reacted with great irritation, and complained that Clark Kerr had exceeded his brief.

Meanwhile, Baghdad newspapers praised Yasin al-Hashimi as the unifying defender of Arab rights and "Bismarck of the Arabs."[56] Needless to say, Bismarck was not beloved among British officials. Yasin publicized and advocated the cause of the Palestinians in their struggle against Britain and Zionism and announced a national holiday called "Palestine Day" in May 1936.[57] In August, British intelligence accused Yasin of covertly supporting the Palestinian revolt with weapons and money, sending Fawzi al-Qawuqji to command the insurgent forces, and sending Iraqi state funds directly to Haj Amin al-Husayni for the purposes of prolonging the General Strike and armed revolt.[58] The Foreign Office considered these unforgivable transgressions, and urged the Embassy to abandon their friendly attitude toward Yasin. The ambassador and the Counsellor, Charles Bateman, argued against drastic moves against the government in Baghdad, but George Rendel, head of the Foreign Office Eastern Department, pointed out that policy was made in London, where the whole picture was visible. Dismissed advisor Kinahan Cornwallis was by this time back in London, where he reported extensively to his Foreign Office colleagues. Rendel noted

British moves in Palestine were likely to be so unpopular in Baghdad that the stability of all British positions were imperiled, and policy retrenchment was required in ways still under discussion.[59] "A special cabinet committee is actively going into the whole matter in the hope of bringing the present difficulties to an end."[60]

In early August, army chief of staff Taha al-Hashimi departed for Istanbul to investigate Turkish views on the possible unification of Syria and Iraq, and went on to Britain to buy weapons and aircraft. The Anglo-Iraqi Treaty stipulated that Britain would supply the Iraqi military with arms, but as the al-Hashimi brothers asserted their influence, and war loomed in Europe, the British government delayed Iraqi weapon requests and stalled existing orders. Not coincidentally, Taha al-Hashimi made several alarming detours on the way back to Iraq to buy weapons and renew old friendships. He traveled directly from London to Berlin, where he visited armament and airplane factories and surveyed German military capabilities. From Berlin he visited Czechoslovakia and contracted weapons purchases from the Skoda works, after which he proceeded to visit old comrades in Ankara.[61] In view of the last war and the war looming, both Germany and Turkey retained their power to worry British imperial strategists. In Taha al-Hashimi's absence, Bakr Sidqi fatefully served as commander of the armed forces. Taha al-Hashimi was due to return and resume his command as chief of staff, on October 30, 1936.

At dawn on October 29, 1936 Iraqi RAF airplanes dropped leaflets over the capital announcing the overthrow of the government. The leaflets addressed the nation and claimed "your sons in the Army had lost patience with the present government, and been compelled to act, signed, General Bakr Sidqi." Early that morning Hikmat Sulayman delivered a letter to the king from Bakr, inviting the king to dismiss the government and appoint Hikmat prime minister. King Ghazi immediately telephoned British ambassador Clark Kerr, who raced to the palace and advised him to do whatever necessary to avoid the entry of soldiers to the capital.[62] Months before, King Ghazi had complained of Yasin's ambitions, and said that if Iraq was to have a dictator, he wished it to be Nuri al-Saᶜid, a sentiment the Foreign Office certainly shared.[63]

The evidence of British foreknowledge and collusion in the first coup in the modern history of the Arab world is strong. Influential British advisors, like General Bruce Hay and Kinahan Cornwallis, had lost their Iraqi government positions and high salaries from Yasin's reforms. The Foreign Office was increasingly anxious over the appeal and power of Yasin's ambition to unite the Arabs and assert actual independence. He actively supported politicians and armed insurgents in both Palestine and Syria, and he flaunted with impunity elements of the

Anglo-Iraqi Treaty he found unappealing. Yasin al-Hashimi enjoyed durable friendships with leading Turkish and German officers and Great War comrades. British policy-makers had many reasons to want Yasin and Taha out.

Four-and-a-half years later, in 1941, British RAF airplanes dropped leaflets over Baghdad in precisely the same way, shortly after the return of Kinahan Cornwallis as ambassador. The leaflet-drop in 1941 announced the coup and invasion known as the Anglo-Iraqi war of 1941, and the specifics are in the archives for the perverse reason that the leaflets, printed in Cairo, were dispatched to Air Headquarters Iraq by regular British Airways commercial freight. When British authorities in Iraq realized the leaflets were sitting on a loading dock, waiting for Iraqi customs inspections, a covert diplomatic and intelligence crisis erupted with much finger-pointing and angry correspondence.

A consignment of other pamphlets addressed to Wing Commander Jope-Slade, Habbaniyah, by Brigadier Clayton, under commercial bill of lading reached Habbaniyah Airport by British Airways yesterday and was then transported to Baghdad in usual way for Customs examination. We fortunately got wind of this and managed to abstract pamphlets without knowledge of Iraqi authorities. If we had not been successful, irreparable damage to our cause would have been done.[64]

In 1936, things evidently went more smoothly.

Yasin and Nuri arrived at the palace while the king conferred with the ambassador. Yasin had already convened a cabinet meeting and attempted to reach Bakr Sidqi by phone that morning before going to the palace. The ambassador left the room, and according to Iraqi historian ʿAbd al-Razzaq Hasani, al-Hashimi asked the king if the coup plotters should be met by force.[65] The king answered with silence, which proved al-Hashimi's suspicion that the king approved the coup. He offered his resignation. Moments later, in the presence of the ambassador and king, Yasin reported that he had spoken that morning by phone with Bakr Sidqi who claimed his coup had the backing of the king. The king visibly winced when confronted with the evidence of his collusion with the plotters.[66]

At 1pm, the king had Yasin al-Hashimi's letter of resignation, and he ordered Hikmat Sulayman to form a new cabinet, which was announced the following morning, and included reformers and only one ex-Ottoman officer, ʿAbd al-Latif Nuri, as Minister of Defense. Hikmat Sulayman was born in Baghdad in 1889, the much younger brother of Ottoman Grand Vezir and post-1909 leader Mahmud Şevket Paşa. Hikmat Sulayman was educated in the Ottoman civil system, and attended the Imperial College, later known as Istanbul University, at which time his brother was already a senior staff officer. ᶜAbd al-Latif Nuri was, by comparison with Hikmat Sulayman, Nuri al-Saᶜid, or the al-Hashimi brothers, a minor figure who had joined the Arab Revolt from a prisoner-of-war camp in Egypt, He had served Faysal and his family faithfully since 1916, and he was Bakr Sidqi's second-in-command in the plot.[67]

At about the same time, King Ghazi sent Jaᶜfar al-ᶜAskari to deliver a letter to Bakr Sidqi. Ghazi wished to inform Bakr that his demands had been met, and there was no need to continue the march on the capital. An escort from Bakr of three soldiers and an officer named Ismaᶜil al-Tuhallah met Jaᶜfar al-ᶜAskari about 15 kilometers outside the capital. Al-Tuhallah executed Jaᶜfar al-ᶜAskari alongside the road with a revolver and had his men bury his body in the desert.[68] Upon the news reaching Baghdad during mid afternoon on the same day, Yasin and Rashid ᶜAli Kaylani went into hiding in the city. Nuri al-Saᶜid went to the British Embassy and refused to leave the safety of the ambassador's house, where he spent the night, and waited for the ambassador to arrange an RAF airplane to fly him to temporary exile in British-occupied Cairo.[69]

Chief military advisor General Charles John Bruce Hay wasted no time in embracing the new regime. The morning after the coup, Bruce Hay called on the barracks to publicly congratulate and pledge his support to Bakr Sidqi. Bruce Hay's zeal to celebrate Yasin's fall annoyed the Foreign Office and his colleagues in Baghdad and Clark Kerr remarked, "Many of the mission feel the general would have been better advised not to rush in quite so quickly, and I am bound to say I share their view." At least a few of his subordinate British officers threatened to resign their positions, though it is not clear whether the complaint was Bruce Hay's behavior or the coup itself. Bruce Hay surely resented Yasin al-Hashimi's cancellation of his contract, since in the weeks before the coup he had been casting about, somewhat desperately, for employment opportunities. Clark Kerr added that at least Bruce Hay did not yet know that Jaᶜfar al-ᶜAskari had been killed. And indeed, the Foreign Office tied itself in knots trying to convey its disapproval of the killing of Jaᶜfar, who had been a loyal client to the Embassy, without souring the relations with its new clients.[70] George Ward of the Eastern Department later lamented, "we might have had a shot at removal of [Jaᶜfar 's killer] from the Iraqi army, if not from this life. But it is probably too late now."[71]

New prime minister Hikmat Sulayman visited the British Embassy even before Nuri al-Saᶜid had made his escape from Baghdad. Hikmat had proclaimed immediately, in private, on the day of the coup, his "categorical and apparently sincere assurances of close and friendly relations with His Majesty's Government, and his desire to have the help and guidance of the Embassy."[72] Visiting the Embassy a few days later, he promised that the new government would cease "grandiose pan-Arab schemes," which meant involvement in politics in Syria and Palestine and the annexation of Kuwait, and he indicated his intention to break up large tribal estates, which provoked a handwritten comment in the margin, probably by Head of the Eastern Section, George Rendel, in London, "I suppose this doesn't include Kuwait!"

Hikmat promised his government would concern itself with Iraqi internal affairs, as distinct from the worrisome pan-Arab political program of Yasin, and ensure the rights of the minorities. He complained, moreover, that British parliamentary debates, especially comments from foreign secretary Anthony Eden, reported in the Baghdad press, made it seem as if the new Iraqi government had been installed by, and was taking its orders from, the Embassy.[73] Iraqi Interior Ministry advisor Cecil Edmunds wrote a long report, widely admired and read in London, detailing his efforts to influence the new government, and Hikmat's attempt to draw him into the conspiracy before the coup had taken place.[74] Edmunds expressed relief at avoiding being drawn in. The ambassador noted repeatedly in his dispatches that General Bruce Hay was pleased with Bakr Sidqi, and considered him capable and reliably friendly to Britain.

Meanwhile Fawzi al-Quwuqji had been forced out of Palestine and waited in Transjordan, ceremoniously burnishing his reputation with press interviews and guests to his camp. The entry of Qawuqji's forces to Iraq had to wait for the overthrow of his main patron in Baghdad. Once the government of Yasin al-Hashim had been overthrown and Yasin had left the country in the opposite direction, toward Damascus, Qawuqji was finally allowed to leave Transjordan for Iraq at midnight on November 3, in a twelve-vehicle convoy of Nairn Company cars.[75] The coup plotters could not risk the possibility that Qawuqji and his forces could join with Yasin and his army supporters to re-take the capital and restore the government. Anxiety at the highest levels of the British government, including foreign secretary Anthony Eden himself, focused on Qawuqji until late January, when Clark Kerr confirmed that Bakr Sidqi had banished him to Kirkuk, very far from the action and under close watch.[76]

Yasin Paşa in Exile among the Syrians

Yasin al-Hashimi, Rashid ᶜAli al-Kilani, and Jamil al-Midfᶜai, with their families, departed Baghdad by Nairn car for Damascus and arrived on the afternoon of October 31. Arriving in Damascus, Yasin spoke to the press and declared that Iraq would prevail in winning and preserving its independence. He concluded his remarks saying "no fear for Iraq." Jamil al-Midf'ai and Yasin also met British consul Colonel Gilbert MacKereth, during which encounter Yasin accused King Ghazi of instigating the coup, a veiled accusation of British collusion.[77] The consul offered Yasin a rest and a meal, but he declined, and proceeded that evening directly towards Beirut. French intelligence reported the coup and the arrival of the exiles in Damascus, and noted that while Arab nationalists viewed Britain with deep suspicion, the better-informed officers of the French intelligence bureau considered the coup a British operation. "British official policy is implicated in the movement in question," the Damascus intelligence chief remarked obliquely.[78] The exiles spent the night at the house of Georges 'Abdini in the Lebanon mountain town of 'Alayh. The next morning they continued to Beirut, to the house of Riyad al-Sulh, where the National Bloc delegate welcomed them and invited them to an elaborate lunch.[79] French intelligence surveilled them closely.

Only four days earlier the National Bloc President Hashim al-Atasi had finally published the Franco-Syrian Treaty alongside a manifesto for the future of the Syrian Republic. Al-Atasi had referred forcefully to the events of the day in Palestine and Iraq and proclaimed the need for Arab brotherhood. National Bloc members were busily preparing for two-stage parliamentary elections for the middle and end of November,[80] but several Bloc politicians turned up to greet the Iraqi exiles on the afternoon of their arrival at Baramka station in Damascus. French intelligence reports noted that Damascenes, many of whom remembered Yasin al-Hashimi from his role as an Ottoman Great War general, chief of staff of Faysal's short-lived Syrian kingdom, and comrade of Yusuf al-'Azma, regretted his overthrow intensely, and believed he was the victim of British intrigues against Arab unity.[81] Palestinians likewise widely mourned the fall of pan-Arab hero Yasin al-Hashimi and feared for a future without his support.[82]

In Beirut, al-Hashimi rented a house near the American University of Beirut campus in Ras Beirut, where his eldest daughter Madiha was a student. In Beirut, Yasin received friends and admirers and drew the devoted and somewhat obsessive attention of the French intelligence services.[83] He renewed his always keen and devoted interest in his daughters' education and intellectual pursuits. Visitors from Damascus, Baghdad, Palestine, and Turkey called on him and discussed politics and events in their regions. He stewed on the turn of events in Baghdad and his health suffered. He had bouts of depression and he had frequent bitter arguments with his wife.[84]

On the day of the coup, Taha al-Hashimi was in Ankara, enjoying the final day of his long trip before returning to Baghdad.[85] He spent the afternoon at the Anatolia Club dining with old friends from the Ottoman general staff, swapping memories of school days and wartime adventures. When he returned to the Iraqi legation he found a telegram informing him of the change of government. The Czechoslovak Embassy telephoned to ask him how the coup would affect the arms contract. In his memoirs he wrote that he eventually learned King Ghazi had been part of the plot to force Yasin's government out, but Ghazi had not planned for bloodshed or an army revolt; these were Bakr Sidqi's work. Late that night, Naji Shawkat, head of the legation, called on Taha and brought news of the armed uprising and Bakr Sidqi's role in the events. It seemed unwise to proceed to Baghdad, and he stayed in Ankara.[86] Like most of his Ottoman brother officers, he preferred life in the ancient capital, and once it became clear he was not returning to Iraq, he went back to Istanbul, tried to keep in touch with unsettled events in Baghdad, corresponded with his brother in Beirut, worried, and waited.

During the middle of November 1936, Charles Bateman, Counsellor of the British Embassy at Baghdad, had occasion to pass through Beirut. Bateman had heard that Yasin al-Hashimi was in seclusion owing to fears of assassination. He nevertheless contacted him by note and was surprised when Yasin replied quickly by phone and proposed to visit Bateman at his hotel. The meeting was cordial. Yasin artfully probed the depth of British government involvement in his overthrow by asking if British loans might be forthcoming for the plans of the new government. Such loans had long been stalled for Yasin's far more ambitious development programs. Bateman missed the elliptical query and lectured Yasin pedantically that the British government did not make loans, but could only advise British banks to loan money, or alternately, the Ministry of the Treasury could block loans on behalf of the government. Apparently loans might be forthcoming for Hikmat Sulayman's new regime. All of this was information already known to Yasin, as ex-Iraqi finance minister, and author of at least one published treatise on international finance.[87] Yasin mentioned that he had good evidence, including from the French High Commissioner, that "certain army officers" wished to assassinate him, and that Rashid ʿAli had fled to Istanbul for this reason. He preferred to stay with his wife, and perhaps travel to Palestine, but he understood British determination to oppose such travel.[88] They discussed the inoffensive possibility of Cyprus as a new home for Yasin al-Hashimi. Bateman was enthusiastic.

Syrian elections concluded on November 30, and by early December the Bloc was triumphant and in the process of forming a government. The most prominent members of the new government traveled to Beirut to call on Yasin al-Hashimi shortly after the election.[89] Confidential French intelligence sources reported that new prime minister Jamil Mardam Bey, Ihsan al-Jabri, and other Bloc members spent an hour with Yasin at the Saint George Hotel and pledged that the new Syrian government would oppose Hikmat Sulayman's government, maintain their pan-Arab stances, and exert their influence on the Damascus press. They expressed their gratitude for Yasin's support during the Franco-Syrian Treaty negotiations in Paris. Yasin had ordered the Iraqi legation in Paris to pay their expenses and provide them every assistance. Moreover, they knew and appreciated his promise of men, money, weapons, and ammunition if negotiations failed and armed revolt in Syria became necessary. French intelligence recorded that an agreement had existed between the parties, but noted with self-congratulations that the fall of Yasin's government foreclosed the threat of armed revolt in the Syrian Mandate. Meanwhile, Hikmat Sulayman's government tried to pay Damascene journalists, probably through the British Consul, for favorable coverage of the new government.[90] A month later, the new Iraqi consul invited the Bloc leaders to a lavish dinner at Damascus' Umayyad Hotel. The consul wished to foster positive relations between the new Iraqi government and Syrian leaders and to dispel rumors about Iraqi disinterest in common Arab affairs. Munir al-ᶜAjlani attended and insisted on the importance of Arab unity, and the forthcoming Arab Congress, which Yasin al-Hashimi was expected to attend.[91]

The Franco-Syrian Treaty was not universally popular among politicized Syrians. Exiled politicians and members of the League of National Action registered their protest. Dr. Shahbandar from exile in Cairo voiced his opposition to the continued French military presence and Munir al-ᶜAjlani made similar arguments. It seems likely that such protests were based not on the terms of the treaty, which appeared likely to finally deliver both Syrian unity and independence, but on the writers' hurt feelings of exclusion from the negotiations. Even in exile, Shahbandar was among the most popular Syrian political leaders, and an authentic hero of the Great Revolt. He was perennially threatening to the more compromised members of the National Bloc, who were, however, in control of the government, and on December 26, 1936, the Syrian parliament ratified the Franco-Syrian Treaty with a unanimous vote.

The Death and Funeral of Yasin al-Hashimi

At the beginning of January, Rashid ᶜAli al-Kilani advised Taha that Yasin was ailing and under the care of doctors at the AUB hospital. Mutual friends suggested he might be best able to oversee the care of his brother, who was depressed and mostly refusing to rest or take medical advice. Taha al-Hashimi left from Istanbul Haydarpaşa Terminal and traveled two days by train through Anatolia, via Aleppo, to Tripoli in the Lebanese Mandate. From Tripoli, Taha al-Hashimi traveled by car to Beirut.[92] In Beirut, Taha found Yasin surrounded by family, including his wife, Rafiqa, and daughters Madiha and Niᶜmat, who had recently arrived from Baghdad with her new husband, Ali Mumtaz al-Daftari. His second daughter, Sabiha, remained at Smith College in the United States. Despite his weakness, he continued to receive visitors.

Back in Baghdad those close to Yasin's government were in danger. Several ex-cabinet minsters and high officials fled the country on hastily arranged official leaves. Rustum Haydar, who had recently served as King Ghazi's private secretary, left for Damascus. Mosul deputy and chief cabinet secretary Dhia al-Din Yunis had been dismissed by prime minister Hikmat Sulayman in the days after the coup. On the evening of January 20, as he was taking a nightly walk near his house in the Baghdad neighborhood of al-Batawin, a car carrying two men and a driver came to an abrupt stop. The two passengers emerged, and each fired several pistol rounds at Yunis before speeding away. British ambassador Clark Kerr filed a report on the assassination in which he noted that the bullets that killed Yunis were fired from a new model of British service revolver that had been issued in very small quantities. He suggested this could only implicate Iraqi security officials who had access to British stores. He did not mention the possibility of any direct British role. Clark Kerr noted, "It is difficult to say what motive there was for this crime, but it is commonly believed that Dhia Younis had been in correspondence with Yasin al-Hashimi and he had paid for this indiscretion with his life."[93] No arrests were made.

The next morning at 9am, Yasin al-Hashimi died in Beirut. His wife, brother, and two daughters were with him. His eldest daughter, Madiha, was in her final year of studies at AUB and would graduate in June 1937. His youngest, and only married daughter, Niᶜmat, and son-in-law ᶜAli Mumtaz al-Daftari, who had been Iraqi director-general of revenue, had fled Baghdad weeks before. Niᶜmat's baby, born in September 1937, would have been Yasin's first grandchild. They named the baby Yasin for his grandfather. Taha recorded that his fatal heart attacks had followed a particularly heated argument between

Yasin and his wife Rafiqa. Exile had been stressful, and Yasin had been under the care of physicians at the AUB hospital. Heart attack was the official cause of death, but many in Iraq, Palestine, Syria, and Lebanon questioned the claims of natural causes, and many noted Yasin al-Hashimi's heroic stature and many powerful enemies. At the age of 53 he was young and had been apparently healthy until his exile. British officials sought to quash such rumors and intimations of foul play. The Beirut consul noted that his death was a great surprise and the heart affliction, from which he had been ailing in Beirut, was not generally known. The Foreign Office instructed the consul and Baghdad ambassador to speedily counter any claims that there might be "something fishy" about the death of Yasin.[94]

Attending physicians immediately announced al-Hashimi's death. They telegramed National Bloc leaders in Damascus, Haj Amin al-Husayni, Amir Abdallah, and King Ghazi requesting permission for transport and burial to Baghdad, as well as other Arab governments.[95] Riyad al-Sulh, Beirut National Bloc delegate, visited the house in mourning and before King Ghazi or the new Iraqi government could reply, proposed a funeral in Damascus. AUB doctors embalmed the body for travel. A banner headline in Damascus' *al-Qabas* read, "Calamity of the Arab Nation: Yasin Pasha al-Hashimi."[96]

Hikmat Sulayman and Bakr Sidqi denied requests of the family for a funeral and burial in Baghdad. Yasin al-Hashimi was less a threat dead than alive, but was undoubtedly still a threat. The Iraqi army's loyalty to the new regime was notably unsteady, and the Embassy, Bakr, Hikmat Sulayman, and Ghazi trod carefully. A few weeks earlier, during the month of Ramadan, King Ghazi had invited the Iraqi General Staff to an *Iftar* dinner. Only coup leader General Bakr Sidqi and fewer than a quarter of the invited senior officers bothered to respond or attend; a Cairo newspaper reported the "affront to the King has caused a sensation in political circles."[97] Bakr Sidqi was assassinated while visiting the Mosul officers' club eight months later.[98] The Iraqi government finally agreed to Yasin al-Hashimi's burial in Baghdad, but demanded a small ceremony devoid of politics, and explicitly banned Taha al-Hashimi's entry into the country with his brother's body. By then the specifics of the funeral and burial in Damascus had been set.

The National Bloc in Beirut and Damascus rose to the pan-Arab occasion. Uniformed youth, Steel Shirts, and AUB students carried the coffin out of the house where Yasin had died. According to Peter Wien, the uniforms had special significance as they echoed Arab folk dress, and the *kuffiya* headdress that had come to symbolize the Palestinian rebels and their struggle. They placed the deceased in a bier atop an open truck adorned with flags and flowers, and led the procession to its first stop at Beirut's central al-ᶜUmari Mosque for early morning prayers. The convoy proceeded over the mountains and in many places the road was lined with mourners and admirers of the late statesman.

The procession traveled slowly over the course of the morning hours along the Damascus road past mountain villages, across the floor of the fertile Biqa valley, and up the eastern mountains. In Maysalun, it made a ceremonial stop at the tomb of Yasin's martyred comrade Yusuf al-ᶜAzma, cementing the link between the two military heroes of the Great War and Faysal's Damascus government. The convoy dropped into the Barada river valley and followed the road and river to Damascus. Upon the foothills of the city, the valley opened up, and the procession skirted the river to the city's outskirts, near today's Umayyad Square, and the municipal gardens across from the ancient mosque complex of Ottoman Sultan Suleyman, and more recent government and administrative buildings, including the elite Tajhiz preparatory school, the Ottoman Teachers' College, and Damascus University law school.

Thousands of Damascenes had assembled at the city gardens and the daily *al-Qabas* reported the crowds as the largest the city had ever seen.[99] By the time the procession reached the garden, about 1pm, uniformed Steel Shirts lined the street and dozens of dignitaries, both Damascenes and visitors, walked behind the bier and at the front of the crowd as the procession crossed the Barada at Victoria bridge, up the street past the Orient Palace hotel, in front of the Hijaz railway station, and along Jamal Paşa Street, past the Ottoman military preparatory school where he had taught as a young staff captain, into the covered Suq al-Hamidiyya, and finally into the courtyard and prayer hall of the Umayyad Mosque. New Syrian president Jamil Mardam Bey delivered the eulogy and celebrated Yasin al-Hashimi as a hero of Arabism.

Yasin's return to Damascus symbolized a return to the birthplace of the Arab nation two decades earlier. The traces of the Great War and Ottoman modernity, and the formative struggle against the colonial domination the war's victors imposed was obvious. Yusuf al-ᶜAzma was dead, King Faysal was dead, and now Yasin al-Hashimi had joined them. At the age of 36, in November 1918, he had been a decorated Ottoman staff officer, equal in rank and experience with Mustafa Kemal, Yusuf al-ᶜAzma, and a handful of others, but like them, defeated, and with no army or state left to serve. He and his fellows eventually came to serve whatever successor polity seemed available or possible. In January 1937, his corpse and funeral procession made a similar journey, past the tomb of Yusuf al-ᶜAzma, past all the monuments of modern, late

Ottoman Damascus, including the road and railway made under Sultan Abdul-Hamid, the Barada river water project similarly inaugurated, the university, colleges, and schools, the ancient mosque named for Sultan Süleyman, which first cemented and symbolized the Ottoman present and future of the great city, and had served, since 1926, as the final resting place of the last, exiled Ottoman sultan, the glorious train station built with funds raised by Ottoman subscription, and opened months after Yasin and his brother Ottoman officers forced Sultan Abdul-Hamid to accept their dominant role in government, state, army, and society in 1908, the processional street laid out and named for Ottoman officer and wartime governor Jamal Paşa, and finally through the modern covered market named for Sultan Abdul-Hamid.

The processional route was not an accident. It did not pass through Marja Square, in front of the Ottoman Saray and colonial mandate administration, or past the official Damascus residence of the High Commissioner at the ʿAzam Palace a couple hundred meters from the Umayyad Mosque, and down the covered market named for Ottoman governor Midhat Paşa. Or past any administrative structure now dominated by the mandate government, but no one could ignore the ever-present links with the recent Ottoman past. The body of Yasin Paşa al-Hashimi was laid in state in the prayer hall, of the Umayyad Mosque, which had been restored by the Ottoman government while Yasin was a schoolboy. In the following days, the Syrian government and Yasin's family attempted to have him buried in Baghdad. Neither Hikmat Sulayman's Iraqi government, nor British or French officials, wanted the political attention on Yasin al-Hashimi to continue and they blocked the return of his corpse to Baghdad, the city of his birth. He was finally buried in the small garden just next to the tomb of Saladin.

Conclusions

The success of Yasin al-Hashimi in Baghdad, the Syrian and Palestine general strikes, the Franco-Syrian Treaty, and the uprising in Palestine gave rise to a mood of hope and optimism in summer 1936.[100] Former Ottoman Arabs could believe they were emerging from the long nightmare that began in 1911 and 1912. They could believe that Yasin Paşa was about to lead their region into a new era of unity, justice, freedom, and dignity equal to that enjoyed by their Turkish former compatriots. These hopes came crashing to earth with the Iraq coup, the death of Yasin al-Hashimi, the failure of Syrian independence, and the end of the Palestine revolt. The Arabs were confronted by ominous forces outside their control.

On the same day as Yasin al-Hashimi's flight to Syria, November 1, 1936, Mustafa Kemal gave a speech to the National Assembly in Ankara in which he announced his intention to claim the region of the port of Aleppo at Iskandarun, and its surrounding Sanjaq for the Turkish Republic. Negotiations with France had been ongoing for more than a decade. Atatürk enthusiastically embraced the League of Nation's language of ethnic nationhood when he proclaimed the matter concerned the whole of the Turkish people, owing to the region's "purely Turkish character." Thus crisis piled on crisis, the remaining threads of Ottoman brotherhood were finally severed, and İsmet İnönü's advice to Musa Kazim al-Husayni at Lausanne in 1923, that the Ottoman Arabs were on their own, came to its logical conclusion.[101]

Notes

1. LN, R4101, Syria, 1936. Excerpted in PMC Report by M. Palacios, November 15, 1937.
2. *Oriente Moderno*, Anno 16, no. 2 (February 1936), 61. Much of this reconstruction is based on Philip S. Khoury, *Syria and the French Mandate: The Politics of Arab Nationalism, 1920–1945* (Princeton University Press, 1987).
3. BNA FO 684/9, Damascus Quarterly report, January–March 1936, Damascus Consul to FO, p. 3. Of course, al-Khuri had learned French in Ottoman schools, including the Istanbul law college, and studied in Paris *before* the war. Jurj Faris, *Man Huwa fi Suriyya 1949* (Damascus: Maktab al-Dirasat al-Suriyya wa-al-ᶜarabiyya, 1950), p. 155.
4. Khoury, *Syria and the French Mandate*, p. 458.
5. BNA FO 684/9, Syria, Syria File, February 10, 1936, Damascus Consul to FO, and Damascus Quarterly report, January–March 1936, Damascus Consul to FO. LN R4101. Petition from Dr. Shishshakli comparing Ottoman enlightenment to French despotism.
6. BNA FO 684/9, Embassy Baghdad to FO, February 24, 1936, on pan-Arab agitation.
7. *The Times*, "Palestine Quiet: Arabs Fail to Extend Strike," April 25, 1936.
8. Figures from the official newspaper *Les Echos*, and cited in FO 684/9, Damascus Quarterly report, January–March 1936, Damascus Consul to FO.
9. *Al-Qabas*, "Hashim al-Atasi: Bayan Hizb al-Watani," February 10, 1936.
10. *L'Écho de Paris*, "Replâtrage Syrien," March 2, 1936. Khoury, *Syria and the French Mandate*, p. 461.
11. The recent dissertations of Charles W. Anderson and Steven Wagner are now the most comprehensive works on the Palestine revolt. See Charles W. Anderson, "From Petition to Confrontation: The Palestinian National Movement and the Rise of Mass Politics, 1929–1939," unpublished PhD dissertation, New York University, 2013, and Steven Wagner, "British Intelligence and Policy in the Palestine Mandate, 1919–1939," unpublished DPhil dissertation, University of Oxford, 2014.

12. BNA FO 371/20030, E2054, Monthly Intelligence Survey, SECRET, March 31, 1936. Press extracts.
13. BNA FO 371/20030, E2054, Monthly Intelligence Survey, SECRET, March 31, 1936.
14. BNA FO 371/20030, E2890, Monthly Intelligence Survey, SECRET, April 29, 1936, p. 1.
15. Gudrun Krämer, *A History of Palestine: From the Ottoman Conquest to the Founding of the State of Israel* (Princeton University Press, 2008), p. 271.
16. *The Times*, "Racial Riots in Palestine," April 20 , 1936. *The Palestine Post*.
17. BNA FO 371/20030, E2890, Monthly Intelligence Survey, SECRET, April 29, 1936, p. 3.
18. BNA FO 371/20030, E2890, Monthly Intelligence Survey, SECRET, April 29, 1936, p. 3.
19. BNA FO 371/20030, E3723, Monthly Intelligence Survey, SECRET, June 3, 1936.
20. BNA FO 371/20030, E4041, Weekly Intelligence Survey, SECRET, June 17, 1936. Weekly Intelligence Survey, SECRET, June 17, 1936. Intensity of activity brought a change from monthly to weekly intelligence summaries.
21. *Mira't al-Sharq* and *al-Filistin*, in press extracts, in BNA FO 371/20030, E4041.
22. BNA FO 371/20030, E4245, Weekly Intelligence Survey, SECRET, June 24, 1936.
23. BNA FO 371/20030, Weekly Intelligence Survey, SECRET, July 1, 1936.
24. BNA FO 371/20030, E4848, Foreign Arab press extracts, Weekly Intelligence Survey, SECRET, July 17, 1936.
25. BNA FO 371/20030, Weekly Intelligence Survey, SECRET, August 18, 1936.
26. BNA FO 371/20030, Weekly Intelligence Survey, SECRET, August 18, 1936.
27. *The Times*, "Parley in Palestine," September 1, 1936.
28. BNA FO 371/20030, Weekly Intelligence Survey, SECRET, August 28, 1936.
29. BNA FO 371/20030, Weekly Intelligence Survey, SECRET, "Jewish Affairs: Reactions to the Pasha's Visit," August 28, 1936.
30. Hazim Al-Mufti, *Al-ʿIraq bayn ʿAhdayn: Yasin al-Hashimi wa Bakr Sidqi* (Baghdad: 1990), p. 25.
31. BNA FO 371/20030, E5854, Weekly Intelligence Survey, SECRET, September 2, 1936.
32. BNA FO 684/9, "Memorandum on the Interdependence of the Outbreaks in Syria and Palestine during 1936," Aleppo consul to Eden, August 20, 1936, and Damascus consul to Eden, August 21, 1936.
33. Michael J. Cohen, "Origins of the Arab States' Involvement in Palestine," *Middle Eastern Studies*, 19:2, April 1983, 249.
34. *The Times*, "Arab and Jew: The Deadlock in Palestine, Lord Lugard's Proposal," September 2, 1936.
35. *The Times*, "Cabinet and Palestine. Full Statement of Policy. More Decisive Policy. A Reluctant Step," September 7, 1936.

36. BNA FO 371/20030, E5996, Weekly Intelligence Survey, SECRET, September 11, 1936.
37. Al-Qawuqji's leaflets are reproduced in ᶜAbd al-Wahhab al-Kayali, *Watha'iq al-muqawama al-Filastiniyya al-ᶜarabiyya didd al-ihtilal al-Britani wa-al-Sahyuniyya (1918–1939)* (Beirut: Mu'assat al-dirasat al-Filastiniyya, 1988), pp. 433–53.
38. BNA FO 371/20030, E6151, Weekly Intelligence Survey, SECRET, September 19, 1936. Laila Parson's work on Qawuqji is the best illustration of his romantic charisma and controversial actions.
39. BNA FO 371/20030, E 5854, Weekly Intelligence Survey, SECRET, September 2, 1936.
40. Anderson, "From Petition to Confrontation," p. 739.
41. See the correspondence reproduced in the Institute for Palestine Studies compilation, Bayan Nuwayhed al-Hout (ed.), *Watha'iq al-haraka al-wataniyya al-Filastiniyya 1918–1939, min awraq Akram Zuᶜaytar* (Beirut: Mu'assat al-dirasat al-Filastiniyya, 1984), pp. 453–4.
42. Saᶜid al-ᶜAs, *Safahat min al-ayyam al-hamra': mudhakkirat al-qa'id Saᶜid al-ᶜAs, 1889-1936* (Jerusalem, 1935, reprint Beirut: al-Mu'assasa al-ᶜArabiyya lil-Dirasat wa al-Nashr, 1988). Fayiz Sara, *Saᶜid al-ᶜAs, 1889–1936: Hayatahu-Kifahahu* (Damascus: manshurat wazara al-thaqafa, 1993), p. 35. *The Palestine Post*, "Battle Near Bethlehem," October 9, 1936.
43. Al-Filistin, "Saᶜid al-ᶜAs: Ritha' al-Rihani l-faris al-thawrat," November 26, 1936.
44. *Watha'iq al-haraka al-wataniyya al-Filastiniyya 1918–1939*, p. 461, and BNA FO 371/20031, RAF Intelligence, E6747, Weekly Intelligence Survey, SECRET, October 16, 1936.
45. *The Times*, "An Arab Leader Got Rid Of: Army's Tact in Palestine. Allowed to Escape," October 27, 1936. Fawzi al-Qawuqji, *Mudhakkirat Fawzi al-Qawuqji*, reprint of both volumes of 1975 edition, edited by Khayriyya Qasimiyya (Damascus: Dar al-Numayr, 1995), p. 241.
46. BNA FO 6371/20031, RAF Intelligence, E7084, Weekly Intelligence Survey, SECRET, October 30, 1936. Quwuqji, *Mudhakkirat*, p. 251.
47. Khoury, *Syria and the French Mandate*, p. 467. See Albert Hourani, *Syria and Lebanon: A Political Essay* (Oxford: Royal Institute of International Affairs, 1947), Appendix A, pp. 314–33, for a full text.
48. LN, *Minutes of the Thirty-Fifth Session*, p. 84, and LN R4102, Syria Petitions, 1936. Rappard to PMC Commission, November 2, 1938.
49. Keith Watenpaugh, "Steel Shirts, White Badges, and the Last Qabaday: Fascism, Urban Violence, and Civic Identity in Aleppo under French Rule," in Nadine Méouchy (ed.), *France, Syrie et Liban: Les ambiguïtés et les dynamiques de la relation mandataire* (Damas: IFEAD, 2002), pp. 325–48.
50. *Oriente Moderno*, Anno 16, no. 5 (Maggio 1936), p. 265, and Khoury, *Syria and the French Mandate*, p. 473.
51. BNA FO 800/298, Private Papers of Sir Archibald Clark Kerr. Cornwallis' aggrieved letter complaining of Yasin runs to twelve handwritten pages, April 16, 1935.

52. US Dept. of State, Consular Dispatch, December 16, 1936, 890g.01/5. Quoted in Marr, "Yasin al-Hashimi," p. 323.
53. Marr, "Yasin al-Hashimi," p. 346.
54. BNA T161/1147, E 3233/38/91, Clark Kerr to FO, May 20, 1936.
55. BNA FO 800/298, private papers of Sir Archibald Clark Kerr.
56. *Jarida al-Bilad*, June 26, 1936. Quoted in Marr, "Yasin al-Hashimi," p. 351.
57. BNA FO 371/20016, Iraq correspondence, 1936.
58. BNA FO 800/298, private papers of Sir Archibald Clark Kerr, Bateman to Rendel, September 30, 1936.
59. BNA FO 800/298, private papers of Sir Archibald Clark Kerr, Rendel to Clark Kerr, October 8, 1936.
60. BNA FO 371/20017, Rendel to Bateman, September 29, 1936.
61. Taha al-Hashimi, *Mudhakkirat Taha al-Hashimi, 1919-1943* (Beirut: Dar al-Talica, 1967), pp. 132–4. Taha al-Hashimi's memoir is a daily recounting of his visits and activities. Mohammad Tarbush, *The Role of the Army in Politics: A Case Study of Iraq to 1941* (London: Kegan Paul International, 1982), p. 128.
62. *The Times*, "Coup D'État in Baghdad. Cabinet Turned Out. Bombs on Baghdad," October 31, 1936, and BNA T161/1147, telegram no. 265, Clark Kerr to FO, October 29, 1936.
63. Phebe Marr recounts this story, which she seems to have heard at third hand, "Yasin al-Hashimi," p. 310.
64. BNA FO 371/27066, cypher telegram, Baghdad to Cairo, April 17, 1941. Additional secret correspondence from the War Office reads, with handwritten corrections, "It was certainly ~~most careless and stupid~~ crazy to have sent these pamphlets to Iraq under commercial bill of lading." BNA FO 371/27066 WO to FO, April 28, 1941. Strike outs in original.
65. ʿAbd al-Razzaq Hasani, *Tarikh al-wazirat al-ʿIraiyya* (Sidon: Matbac al-ʿIrfan, 1953), vol. IV, p. 85.
66. BNA T161/1147, E7145/1419/93, November 16, 1936. Clark Kerr to Eden. This is the full report on the coup. Hazim al-Mufti, *Al-ʿIraq bayn ʿAhdayn: Yasin al-Hashimi wa Bakr Sidqi* (Baghdad: 1990).
67. BNA T161/1147, telegrams no. 266, 267, and 268, Clark Kerr to FO, October 29, 1936.
68. *The Times*, "The Coup D'État In Iraq. General Jafar Shot," November 2, 1936.
69. Majid Khadduri interviewed Nuri in the 1940s or 50s when he claimed King Ghazi told him he wanted Yasin out. Nuri's version sounds self-serving, especially considering the other witnesses were all dead. It is worth noting that Ghazi was 24 years old, while Nuri was a veteran politician near 50. Majid Khadduri, *Independent Iraq: A Study in Iraqi Politics Since 1932* (Oxford University Press, 1951), p. 69. BNA T 161/1147, telegram No. 269, Clark Kerr to FO, October 30, 1936.
70. BNA FO 800/298, private papers of Sir Archibald Clark Kerr, Clark Kerr to Oliphant, "Personal and secret," November 2, 1936.
71. BNA FO 371/20014, J.G. Ward, handwritten notation on Clark Kerr to Rendel, November 18, 1936.

72. BNA T161/1147, telegram no. 268 to FO, October 30, 1936.
73. BNA T161/1147, telegrams no. 276, Clark Kerr to FO, November 4, 1936.
74. BNAFO 371/20015, Cecil Edmunds, "Narrative of Events," October 29, 1936.
75. BNA FO 371/20013, Iraq correspondence, and RAF Intelligence, E7203, Weekly Intelligence Survey, SECRET, November 6, 1936.
76. 800/298, private papers of Sir Archibald Clark Kerr, Clark Kerr to Vauchope, January 25, 1937.
77. Extract from *al-Ahrar*, November 2, 1936, in BNA FO 684/9 (DSC05915).
78. MAE-Nantes, BOX 1SL/1/V/1906, Renseignements et Presse, Information Sureté Générale, Année 1936.
79. MAE-Nantes, BOX 1SL/1/V/1906, Renseignements et Presse; Information Beyrouth Sureté Générale, no. 4192, November 3, 1936.
80. Khoury, *Syria and the French Mandate*, p. 469.
81. MAE-Nantes, BOX 1SL/1/V/1906, Bulletin d'Information, November 5–11, 1936.
82. Filistin, "Asbab al-Inqilab fi al-ʿIraq," published in eight parts, front-page, and written by Yusuf Hanna between late November and December 1936. FO 684/9 E7203, Weekly Intelligence Survey (Palestine. Misfiled in Damascus files), SECRET, November 6, 1936.
83. MAE-Nantes, many files in: BOX 1SL/1/V/1892. Renseignements et Presse; Information Sureté Générale, Année 1936.
84. al-Hashimi, *Mudhakkirat*, p. 171.
85. al-Hashimi, *Mudhakkirat*, p. 134.
86. al-Hashimi, *Mudhakkirat*, pp. 135–6.
87. Yasin al-Hashimi, *Radd al-Hashimi ʿala taqrir al-sir Hilton Young al-iqtisadi* (Baghdad: Matbaʿat al-Najah, 1930).
88. BNA FO 371/20015, Iraq coup, Bateman to Clark Kerr, November 30, 1936. In 1941, Ambassador Kinahan Cornwallis arranged to detain, or perhaps assassinate, another Iraqi minister during a stay in hospital in Beirut. BNA T161/1147, Secret cypher telegram, Cornwallis to MilPal, October 1, 1941. "Referring to reports that Mohammad Hassan Salman, Inspector of Education in Rashid Ali's Government, may now be in Hospital in Beirut. If this report is true, can you arrange his detention pending decision regarding further action." Salman was brother of Golden Square Col. Mahmud Salman.
89. MAE-Nantes, BOX 1SL/1/V/1893, Renseignements et Presse; Information Sureté Générale, Année 1936, no. 4799, "Relations Bloc Nationaliste avec Yassine Pacha el Hachimi," December 4, 1936, and no. 5038, December 18, 1936.
90. MAE-Nantes, BOX 1SL/1/V/1893, Renseignements et Presse; Information Sureté Générale, Année 1936, no. 4652, November 25, 1936.
91. MAE-Nantes, BOX 1SL/1/V/1893, Renseignements et Presse; Information Sureté Générale, Année 1936, no. 4617. Sureté Kammechlie, November 20, 1936.
92. al-Hashimi, *Mudhakkirat*, p. 167.

93. BNA T161/1147, Iraq Treasury files. Clark Kerr to Eden, February 14, 1937.

94. BNA T161/1147, Iraq Treasury files, several letters between S.D. Whaley, Bank of England, Baghdad ambassador Clark Kerr, and FO Eden, to insure no assassination rumors circulated, February 1937.

95. al-Hashimi, *Mudhakkirat*, p. 176.

96. *Al-Qabas*, "Faj^ca al-Umma al-^cArabiyya bi-Yasin Pasha al-Hashimi," January 22, 1937, *Al-Ayyam*, "Mata al-Hashimi," January 22, 1937, quoted in Peter Wien, "The Long and Intricate Funeral of Yasin Al-Hashimi: Pan-Arabism, Civil Religion, And Popular Nationalism In Damascus, 1937," *IJMES*, 43: Special Issue 2, May 2011, 271. Peter Wien has written a thorough and outstanding analysis of the episode, which this section draws from.

97. *Egyptian Gazette*, "Iron Hand in Iraq," December 9, 1936. Also *Manchester Guardian*, December 9, 1936, with long, irritated commentary in FO 371/20015, complaining of "wild exaggerations" and asking for intervention with the editors, against reports "that can only do harm."

98. BNA T161/1147, no. 342, Clark to Eden, August 30, 1937. The same report noted that no Baghdad paper expressed regret at his death. The widow of Ja^cfar al-^cAskari threw a party.

99. *Al-Qabas*, quoted in Peter Wien, "The Long and Intricate Funeral of Yasin Al-Hashimi," p. 279.

100. The spirit of optimism is amply attested in all the extant Arab press sources. See *al-Ayam, al-Qabas, al-Jam^ciyya al-^carabiyya*, etc.

101. LN R4103, "First White Book on the Question of Alexandretta and Antioch," in League of Nations *Official Journal*, January 1937.

7 Epilogue and Conclusions

Events in the Former Ottoman Realms and the Middle East Mandates, 1937–1939

January 1937	France concedes to Turkish demands in the Sanjaq of Alexandretta
January 1937	Syrian prime minister Jamil Mardam Bey travels to Geneva and Paris, seeking clarity on the Alexandretta Crisis and ratification of the Franco-Syrian Treaty
February 1937	League of Nations Committee of Experts, including Robert de Caix, prepares Sanjaq Report
May 1937	General Amnesty for Great Syrian Revolt veterans
July 1937	Peel Commission Partition Plan published
September 1937–1939	Palestine Revolt resumes
July 1938	Sanjaq Alexandretta elections return 60 percent Turkish delegates
September 1938	Munich Agreement allows German annexation of Czechoslovakia borderlands
November 1938	Mustafa Kemal dead at 57
May 1939	British House of Commons approve McDonald White Paper repudiating Balfour Declaration and support for Jewish National Home in Palestine
June 1939	Penultimate Mandates Commission Meeting finds Britain and France in violation of Mandates Charter
June 1939	Turkish Republic annexes Sanjaq Alexandretta with French acquiescence
September 1939	German invasion of Poland
December 1939	Last Mandates Commission Meeting at Geneva

Saladin's Companions and the Beginning of the End for Anglo-French Colonialism in the Middle East

The death and funeral of Yasin al-Hashimi overshadowed the other momentous events of fall and early winter 1937.[1] But historical judgment is changeable and the sensation and symbolism of Yasin al-Hashimi's death are forgotten today among the events of 1936 and early 1937. In the immediate period surrounding his death, the Great Palestine Revolt faltered, both Syria and Lebanon seemed to finally achieve treaties promising independence, one enshrining sectarianism and minority rule, the other eschewing it, and France, Britain, and the League of Nations confronted the consequences of the rules they had brought to the region. In 1936, the Turkish Republic declared the protection of an oppressed Turkish population compelled it to intervene in the Syrian north coastal province of Iskandarun, including Aleppo's historic port, in an episode that came to be called the Alexandretta Crisis. At about the same time, the Peel Commission, destined to bring the first partition plan to the conflict over Palestine, began its work. The League of Nations, weakened and diminished by the various crises and contradictions at the core of its mission, endorsed the increasingly perverse outcomes of the settlement of 1920 and the mandates system.

Within days of al-Hashimi's elaborate funeral, news emerged that France had been negotiating the fate of the north coastal region of Iskandarun with Turkey and the League of Nations. By the time of the announcement of the Franco-Syrian Treaty in September 1936, the Turkish Republic had been a fully independent country under the presidency of Mustafa Kemal for thirteen years. Syria, in contrast, was only beginning its emergence as a nominally independent state, contingent upon the French Senate's ratification of the treaty. France had occupied the region in 1918, committing to be the "Protector of the Oriental Christians" and the champion of minorities against the claimed tyranny of Muslim rule. French colonial functionaries had envisioned the development of several friendly Christian nations among the former Ottoman realms.

Lebanon had just received a treaty as a nominally independent state constituted as the homeland of a Christian Maronite minority. The League of Nations had officially recognized and still clung to the Palestine Mandate as the "national home for the Jewish People," an immigrant minority uncomfortably placed amongst an indigenous former Ottoman majority. Syria, by contrast, had apparently wrested the hard-won principal of Syrian unity within mandate borders and presumed majority rule from French Mandate officials. The unity of Syria included the cosmopolitan Sanjaq of Iskandarun, but the Turkish Republic protested to the League of Nations against the claimed oppression the Turkish population suffered among the Sanjaq's diverse population.[2]

The Alexandretta Crisis

By January of 1937 the logic of French colonialism, minority national rights, and the League of Nations mandates regime had turned on itself. At the end of January, Hitler had declared his intention to overturn the Treaty of Versailles in part because of the claimed oppression of German minorities living outside German borders. Months before, the leftist French government of Léon Blum had wished to conciliate the Syrian National Bloc and finally grant nominal independence to the mandate, but in 1937, as crisis in Europe loomed, the government needed to placate the French right, maintain its hold on Middle Eastern and North African colonies, and prepare for war. The French Senate declined to ratify the treaties with Lebanon or Syria, and the Foreign Ministry slowly determined that placating Turkey over Alexandretta was a higher priority than maintaining the territorial unity of the Syrian Mandate. The flexible and flawed idealism of the mandate regime proved dispensable. Few outside Geneva noticed the contortions of mandate apologists.

The Sanjaq of Iskandarun and its principal town of Antakya had remained bastions of Ottoman cosmopolitanism. The population included sizable numbers of Arabic-speaking Orthodox Christians, Arabic-speaking Alawi Muslims contiguous with their co-religionists in the former French *territoire des Alaouites*, Turkish- and Armenian-speaking Armenians, Kurds, and Turkish- and Arabic-speaking Sunni Muslims, among Jews, Catholics, and a few Protestants. By the end of January, France had agreed to separate the Sanjaq from Syria under a special joint Turkish–French Mandate regime, subject to supervision from the League of Nations, and the findings of a League-appointed Committee of Experts. The Committee of Experts proposed elections based on proportional sectarian representation like the French Mandate regime implemented in Lebanon, and only averted in Syria by the upheaval of the Great Revolt a decade earlier. Before the elections could take place, the various sectarian communities listed had to register to determine their numbers and proportions in the new government. Robert de Caix, first mandate secretary general under General Gouraud, and inventor of Greater Lebanon and its sectarian system, led the French delegation on the Committee of Experts.[3]

Vigorous Arab protests ensued in the Sanjaq. (See Figure 7.1.) Shakib Arslan in Geneva organized and led a petition collection drive. Dr. ͨAbd al-Rahman Shahbandar, still in exile in Cairo, organized exile

جماهير من العرب المسلمين، والمسيحيين، والعلويين واليهود ،
والأرمن، تهتف بحياة اللواء العربي السوري في مدينة الاسكندرونة

Figure 7.1. Demonstration in Iskandarun, 1936, reads, "A demonstration of the Arab Muslims, Christians, Alawites, Jews, and Armenians acclaiming the Syrian Arab flag in the town of Iskandarun." From *al-Mussawar*, November 6, 1936 (author's collection)

opposition, and scores of aggrieved petitions arrived in Geneva. A group calling itself the Congress of Arab Students wrote:

People of the Arab World have not ceased since the World War to appreciate the ability of Turkish Nationalists to rebuild out of a tottering Empire a living and vigorous nation.

We see in our neighbors what we lack in various measures: an inflexible nationalism blended with practical idealism. It grieves us, however, to say that the attitude taken lately by the Turkish government over the question of Alexandretta and Antioch arouse our anxiety and stimulates our apprehension. Least of all has it been thought that the country whose example we appreciate would be a source of undue vexation to the Arab World.[4]

By the time the elections finally took place in mid summer 1938, voters registering as Turks had increased dramatically to 60 percent of the population of the Sanjaq. The elections returned an absolute majority of Turks, as opposed to all others. Within a year of the election, Turkey had annexed the independent Sanjaq, and created ten of thousands of new refugees streaming toward Aleppo and points south. Turkish officials suggested another League of Nations supervised population exchange, but the prospects for an exchange were bleak, and the population movement amounted to an expulsion; the refugees were mostly non-Muslims and came only from within the newly expanded borders of the Turkish Republic. The new regime allowed them to keep whatever property they could carry.

Mustafa Kemal himself had played a central role in the Alexandretta crisis. Kemal had fully embraced the racial and national theories that underlay the League of Nations and its mandates. He was anxious to demonstrate to the Anatolian population and the world that the Turkish nation was racially pure and historically significant. Like the Maronite and French scholars of Lebanon who claimed the Maronite Christians were descended from the original Phoenicians, and Zionists who argued they were the rightful inheritors of ancient Israel, Kemal argued the Sanjaq was the homeland of the Hittites, the forebears of the Turks, who thus had an unbroken racial link to the region stretching back into antiquity.[5] But as in Lebanon or Palestine, untangling the imperatives of international politics from racial theory was difficult, and Kemal underscored again the powerless position of the colonized Arabs, and demonstrated to his former Ottoman compatriots that only violence, or the credible threat, received respect among states. A few months later, at the end of 1938, he died in Istanbul at the age of 57.

The Peel Commission and the End of the Palestine Mandate

In late 1936, just as Yasin al-Hashimi fled west and Fawzi al-Qawuqji fled east, another British commission of enquiry arrived in Palestine. The Peel Commission stayed in the mandate two months until January 1937 and published its report in July 1937. The Arabs mostly boycotted the Commission and the Zionists mostly cooperated. The findings of the Commission were nevertheless new and damning for the supporters of both the mandate mission and Zionism. The Commission found that the one million Arab inhabitants were in "open or latent" rebellion against the 400,000 Jews. The Arabs desired "a free and united Arab

World." The Jews desired to show "what the Jewish nation can achieve when restored to the land of its birth."[6] British officials had long consoled themselves that Arab opposition was focused on Zionism, but this time the fiction was dropped. The report called the revolt "an open rebellion of the Palestinian Arabs, assisted by fellow-Arabs of other countries, against British mandatory rule."[7] The prospect of armed revolt throughout the region remained the singular fear of the mandate governments.

The solution to this state of affairs was abandonment of the mandate, and partition of the country. The report recommended the end of the mandate, the division of the territory under mandate, the conclusion of treaties, and population and territory exchanges on the model of the Greek and Turkish exchanges.[8] The report concluded forlornly, "partition seems to offer at least a chance of ultimate peace. We can see none in any other plan."[9] As Gudrun Krämer has pointed out, the report opined that the Arabs of Palestine were certainly generous enough to bear the sacrifice of helping to solve the "Jewish Problem." They would thus "earn the gratitude not of the Jews alone, but of all the Western World."[10]

But both Arabs and Zionists hated the idea of partition, though the Zionists opposed it more quietly, and within months the rebellion resumed. The British government arrested, jailed, and deported all the Arab political leaders they could catch. Amin al-Husayni escaped to Lebanon, Baghdad, and eventually Berlin, with fateful consequences for his reputation and legacy. Jamal al-Husayni fled to Baghdad but was eventually arrested and spent the war years in prison in what was then the British colony of Southern Rhodesia. British forces repressed the uprising during 1938 and early 1939 and in May of 1939 British Colonial Secretary Malcolm McDonald announced a new White Paper designed to limit Arab and Muslim colonial opposition to Britain in view of the anticipated war. The White Paper capped Jewish immigration at 75,000 over the following five years (1940–4), and only allowed immigration thereafter with Arab acquiescence, restricted Jewish land purchases, and proposed a binational state to last ten years till ultimate independence. The White Paper was widely understood as a renunciation of the Balfour Declaration, Zionism, and the mandate, and as a desperate move to defend British colonialism and the empire.

General Amnesty in Syria

In February 1937, with the Franco-Syrian Treaty ratification stalled in Paris and the Alexandretta Crisis looming, Syrian Prime Minister Jamil Mardam Bey went to Paris. There he learned the Blum government was unwilling to seriously oppose Turkish designs on the Sanjaq, or to expend effort in the Senate to ratify the Franco-Syrian Treaty. The mandate authorities were, however, willing to grant a general amnesty to most of the remaining exiles condemned during the Great Revolt. The return of the legendary heroic figures cannot have pleased Mardam Bey, and served to further undermine his government, unable as it was to enact the treaty or protect the Sanjaq. Among those finally amnestied were Sultan al-Atrash, Shakib Arslan, Dr. ʿAbd al-Rahman Shahbandar, and the remaining rebels of 1925–7. Fawzi al-Qawuqji was among a small handful still deemed too dangerous to allow to return.

The exiles returned home to rapturous public receptions. Sultan al-Atrash returned to his village, and mostly retired from national politics, but Dr. Shahbandar and Shakib Arslan each toured the country separately, meeting well-wishers and giving speeches. Apart from a short visit to Palestine in 1934, Shakib Arslan had not been home since Ottoman minister of war Enver Paşa had dispatched him to Berlin in summer 1918 on a supposedly brief mission.[11] Both Shahbandar and Arslan made gestures of loyalty toward the National Bloc government, but both enthusiastically criticized its failings and each other. Shahbandar emphasized a secular liberal perspective; Arslan emphasized the need for Islamic union. He was especially eager to denounce the Godless treachery of Mustafa Kemal. Neither had anything good to say about Jamil Mardam Bey.[12] When Arslan temporarily left Syria for Egypt and Europe in late 1938, the mandate authorities decided to bar his re-entry. He spent the war years back in Switzerland, and only returned to Syria in the last months of his life in 1946. Shahbandar was assassinated in a public market in Damascus in July 1940 at the age of 60, by which time he had reclaimed his position as the most popular and formidable nationalist politician in Syria.[13] His followers accused Jamil Mardam Bey and mandate intelligence agents of colluding to murder their hero. Shahbandar was the last person buried in the garden next to Saladin's tomb. He lies next to the grave of Yasin al-Hashimi.

The End of the League of Nations Mandates

The last two meetings of the Mandates Commission took place in Geneva in 1939, in June and December. The final meeting was brief and poorly attended and the Commission noted that present circumstances (the German invasion of Poland and the European declarations of war), made it impossible to schedule further meetings. Everyone knew the League of Nations had passed into final irrelevance. The grand buildings on the shores of Lake Geneva emptied, the staff scattered to the winds by the world war. The Axis soon surrounded neutral Switzerland.

The second-to-last meeting, by contrast, in June 1939, was long and detailed and focused on the effective end of the French Mandate over Syria and Lebanon, and the end of the British Mandate for Palestine. Shakib Arslan, an exile once again, was still denied an invitation to speak, but mandate citizens had finally been convinced of the futility of reasoned appeals to justice. Petitions still arrived, but the leading intellectuals and political figures had long given up on Geneva.

The British government sent Colonial Secretary McDonald to explain the practical renunciation of the Balfour Declaration and the mandate itself. In keeping with British practice, McDonald delivered a lengthy speech to the Commission that echoed closely the 400-page-long Peel Commission Report. Rappard asked how the mandate proposed to reconcile the contradictory promises of the Balfour Declaration. McDonald argued that they had not been promises exactly, or what had once been understood as promises. Rappard pointed out that the "Commission had always done its best to approve the actions of the Mandatory Power and had been almost acrobatic in its attempts to agree with fluctuations in policy."[14] Nevertheless, "M. Rappard could not help finding very great difficulty." He noted that the British government could hardly claim its pledges to uphold the "civil and religious rights of the existing [Arab] communities" made it now necessary to seek the approval of the Arabs for Jewish immigration when the Arabs had never been consulted before, and in fact had been entirely consistent during the previous twenty years in their opposition to the Balfour Declaration, the mandate, and Jewish immigration. Rappard noted in 1939 the Arabs desired the same they had desired in 1918: liberty and independence in their own county.[15]

McDonald admitted that from the perspective of 1939, the British government could only defend the Jewish National Home by massive and continual military force against the resistance not only of the Palestinian Arabs but of the Arabs generally. Overthrowing Yasin al-Hashimi's government and repressing the Palestine Revolt had failed to eliminate opposition. Conciliating the Arabs, and thus protecting the empire, was suddenly more important than the conciliation (or by implication, the survival) of European Jews.[16] The equation had been the reverse in 1917.

The Commission was concerned with the fate of European Jews. Thousands had fled Germany, Austria, and Czechoslovakia penniless and under the most difficult circumstances, often in leaky boats at the mercy of smugglers. McDonald expressed his sympathy, but not all were equally worthy of sympathy; "many came from Poland, and Roumania and were not refugees at all." The British government could hardly allow every ship full of illegal migrants to disembark in Palestine.[17] The Commission did not discuss evacuation of European Jewish refugees to Britain or some other country. The Commission knew they were unwelcome in Britain.

In the following days, the Commission turned to the Syrian and Lebanese mandates. William Rappard and Robert de Caix represented the Mandates Commission and France respectively, as they had at the first Mandates Commission meeting seventeen years earlier in 1921. De Caix had been the first secretary general of the mandate in Syria and Lebanon and the original architect of its sectarian legal and political structures, but in 1939 he smoothly explained that changing circumstances made it necessary to ignore the previous two decades of official policy and his own theories about Oriental minorities, claims to be the protector of the Eastern Christians, and governing the mandates. Rappard questioned de Caix with his customary energy and incisiveness over the aborted treaty, and the abandonment of the Sanjaq.

Robert de Caix addressed the French failure to ratify the treaties with Syria and Lebanon. He attributed the Senate's refusal to old worries about the minorities and new fears arising from the changed security situation.[18] He alluded to an unstable political atmosphere in Paris. Rappard, jousting once again with de Caix, wanted to know exactly why the minorities needed the protection of France. And why was the democratic process not enough to ensure their voice and rights? De Caix had become an advocate of Syrian unity and yet he had been the architect of minority fragmentation. But France, like Britain, found endless engagement in the Middle East an unappealing and dangerous prospect, and so the calculation had changed. Both British and French Mandate officials complained bitterly of their costly sacrifice in the mandates, and de Caix himself had remarked before the Commission that "Syria, with the outlay involved, was not really a paying proposition."[19]

The Commission came to the matter of Alexandretta and Rappard noted that he had received the thankless task of rapporteur for all the Sanjaq petitions. His efforts led him to assert that ceding the territory to Turkey was a "flagrant violation of article 4 of the mandate," which clearly prohibited mandate powers from ceding or leasing any part of the land under mandate.[20] Robert de Caix deflected deftly and attributed the renunciation of the mandate to a threatening international scene. Such matters were beyond their control and there was really nothing more to be said. The Commission closed its final session on the Middle East mandates by agreeing unanimously that both the McDonald White paper on Palestine and the ceding of Alexandretta violated the terms of the League of Nations Mandate charter.[21] Rappard was characteristically to the point when he addressed Alexandretta:

> The guardian, in an interest which was essentially his own, had abandoned to a third party a part of the ward's inheritance, after having been entrusted with its defense. [M. de Caix] would certainly say that what had been done was in the interest of the ward ... but it would require all the gifts and persuasive talents of M. de Caix to make one believe that there had not been a violation of the mandate.[22]

The Mandate Inheritance in the Arab East

To those colonies and territories which as a consequence of the late war have ceased to be under the sovereignty of the States which formerly governed them and which are inhabited by peoples not yet able to stand by themselves under the strenuous conditions of the modern world, there should be applied the principle that the well-being and development of such peoples form a sacred trust of civilisation and that securities for the performance of this trust should be embodied in this Covenant.

There was no dramatic ending to the League of Nations' former Ottoman mandates. The colonial mandates outlived the League of Nations and they all reverted to the status of military colonies during the war. In May and June 1941, Free French and British forces, including the Zionist Palmach Brigade, marched on Syria and Lebanon and fought the Vichy French. High Commissioner Henri Dentz, one-time chief of mandate intelligence, was eventually sentenced to death for colluding with the Axis Powers. British forces invaded Iraq through the corridor of Transjordan at the same time and overthrew the nationalist government of Rashid ʿAli Kaylani, Yasin al-Hashimi's old comrade. Even the nominal independence of Iraq was curtailed for the duration of the war. The mandate powers left after the World War II, diminished and made poor by the cost of holding their empires and the European war. No one among mandate or League officials really granted independence, and no one among mandate politicians really won independence.

In 1920, the League of Nations Mandates charter and the ideological foundations of the mandates demanded that colonial rule combine with paternalistic structures of liberal rule. But the colonial state could only take power if the wishes and consent of the population were ignored, as people like Shakib Arslan and Musa Kazim al-Husayni immediately pointed out. Both Britain and France temporarily resolved the contradiction by promising power and influence disproportionate to their numbers to various individuals, families, or sectarian groups in return for consent and support. In this way, each mandate power served to guarantee eventual sectarian conflict and civil war, and to enshrine the need for political factions to draw on outside support to prosecute their internal political struggles. A stunted politics that eschewed compromise was built in.

Britain and France lacked the popular legitimacy to derive consent from the majority population. As mandate citizens proclaimed repeatedly, Ottoman rule had delivered an imperfect but superior semblance of rights, justice, and representation to the majority of the population and petitioners viewed the Ottoman state as more legitimate and representative than the colonial regimes that replaced it. The Mandate state was afflicted by an immediate crisis of legitimacy, and continual opposition and challenges to its authority required violent suppression of the population.

But recourse to violence contradicted the altruistic claims of the mandate charters. Bloody counterinsurgency campaigns covered in newspapers all over the world damaged the reputation and international standing of the League of Nations also. To satisfy the League of Nations Mandates Commission, and metropolitan critics, mandate authorities erected facades of liberal rule, including constitutions, parliaments, elections, and law courts. But the structures of liberal rule were not designed to deliver consent, rights, equal justice, or participation, and were instead designed to console external critics and as innovative mechanisms to shroud colonial rule and military occupation.

The mandates regimes undermined the appeal and credibility of civilian rule and civilian political leadership. Each mandate developed extensive mandate martial law codes to routinely limit the rights of citizens and allow unrestricted use of state power to punish opposition. Each mandate state maintained an executive High Commissioner who had absolute power, including denial of rights to property, liberty, and life, without judicial process or oversight over every mandate citizen. The High Commissioners were always able to overrule any decision made by councils, parliaments, judges, or elected prime ministers. The executive implemented policy through large, and sometimes competing, military and intelligence bureaucracies, which were similarly without review or oversight. These features re-emerged in the post-colonial state.

The mandates gave the region its most enduring conflicts. The two states explicitly designed to favor minorities, Israel and Lebanon, have been involved in decades of intermittent civil and regional war. All three of the smallest former mandates, Israel/Palestine, Jordan, and Lebanon, have been dependent upon, and often at the mercy of, larger regional and international powers. The two larger mandates, Syria and Iraq, endured various varieties of military rule nearly from the moment of independence, and each military regime built upon the structure and habits endowed by the mandate regime to continue a dictatorial executive structure implemented through security agencies without oversight. Each preserved a cosmetic facade of democratic elections, a powerless legislative body, and a judiciary with no power to challenge the state or its various martial law codes. Both Syrian and Iraqi post-colonial politicians fixated on escaping the influence of powerful neighbors and on efforts to dominate less powerful neighboring states. These tendencies were built into the structure of the colonial state, with its odd boundaries and pervasive security anxieties, and were inherited directly by the post-colonial state.

No one can say what might have happened if the Ottoman state had continued to rule the Middle East. And no one can say how the region might be different today if its people had prevailed in their struggles to rule themselves after the World War I. Ottoman State modernization campaigns and pervasive international crisis elevated army officers in society and politics and tended to undermine the role of civilian and representative bodies. War and mass mobilization brought terrible state crimes against groups considered disloyal, and terrible suffering to the population generally. Violence brought more violence, and new mutually exclusive claims on identity divided people just as war, partition, and occupation divided them. Many resisted their involuntarily inclusion or exclusion. When former Ottoman army officers took power in Turkey or Iraq, they ruled as authoritarians shaped by their education and experiences and not as democrats or liberals. But perhaps, over the past century in the Middle East, the happier outcomes, and more satisfactory arrangements for the people of the region, have come to the people most able, by luck, circumstance, and struggle, to seize the greatest freedom of choice and independence from those outside and within the region who would deny it. It cannot be said that the people of the Middle East freely made the world they are forced to inhabit, but it may be that those most able to determine their own conditions and destinies have survived the events of the last century with greater success and happiness than their less fortunate neighbors.

In 1941, on the eve of the British invasion and military occupation of nominally independent Iraq, British ambassador Kinahan Cornwallis held a banquet in Baghdad. Cornwallis had been the deputy director of the Arab Bureau between 1916 and 1918 when it helped run the Arab Revolt against the Ottoman state. In 1918 he went to Damascus with Faysal, and in 1921 he went to Baghdad, where he engineered the referendum that preceded the installation and coronation of King Faysal. He spent the next fourteen years as chief British advisor to the Interior Ministry. Shortly after coming to power, Yasin al-Hashimi dismissed him in April 1935. In 1941, with the British Empire again at war with Germany, and Iraq again a crucial strategic interest, he was back in Baghdad. After the death of Bakr Sidqi, Yasin al-Hashimi's widow and daughters had returned to Baghdad also.

At the banquet, Cornwallis met Niᶜmat al-Hashimi, Yasin al-Hashimi's 26-year-old youngest daughter, accompanied by her husband, finance minister ᶜAli Mumtaz al-Daftari. The ambassador engaged Niᶜmat in conversation, and asked, "What would your father, Yasin Paşa, say if he were still alive today and could see me back here in Baghdad?" She replied, "If my father were still alive, you would not be back here in Baghdad."[23] Cornwallis left Baghdad at the end of World War II. Niᶜmat al-Hashimi al-Daftari spent most of her life in Baghdad until another invasion of Iraq, in 1991, took her to London, where she spent her last years in exile.

Notes

1. Peter Wien, "The Long and Intricate Funeral of Yasin Al-Hashimi: Pan-Arabism, Civil Religion, and Popular Nationalism in Damascus, 1937," *IJMES*, 43: Special Issue 2 (May 2011), pp. 271–92.
2. This is the central point of Sarah Shield's outstanding *Fezzes in the River: Identity Politics and European Diplomacy in the Middle East on the Eve of World War II* (Oxford University Press, 2011).
3. Majid Khadduri, "The Alexandretta Dispute," *The American Journal of International Law*, 39:3 (July 1945), 420.
4. LN R4103, Sanjak Alexandretta petitions, "A Request from the Executive Committee of the Congress of Arab Students to the League of Nations." The file contains at least forty petitions, mostly from Christians of the Sanjaq and Muslims of Aleppo, Damascus, Jerusalem, Beirut, and other cities.
5. Şükrü Hanioğlu, *Atatürk: An Intellectual Biography* (Princeton University Press, 2013), p. 166.
6. *Palestine Royal Commission Report* [Peel Commission] (London: H.M. Stationary Office, 1937), p. 370. Also quoted in Gudrun Krämer, *A History of Palestine: From the Ottoman Conquest to the Founding of the State of Israel* (Princeton University Press, 2008), p. 280.
7. *Palestine Royal Commission Report*, p. 104.
8. *Palestine Royal Commission Report*, p. 390.
9. *Palestine Royal Commission Report*, p. 370.
10. *Palestine Royal Commission Report*, p. 395, quoted in Gudrun Krämer, *A History of Palestine: From the Ottoman Conquest to the Founding of the State of Israel* (Princeton, 2008), p. 283.

11. William L. Cleveland, *Islam Against The West: Shakib Arslan and the Campaign for Islamic Nationalism* (Austin, TX: University of Texas Press, 1985), p. 39.
12. BNA FO 684/10, Damascus Quarterly Report, April–May 1937.
13. Khoury, *Syria and the French Mandate*, p. 588.
14. LN, *Minutes of the 36th Session*, 1939, p. 105.
15. *Minutes of the 36th Session,* p. 104. The quote is from the Balfour Declaration.
16. *Minutes of the 36th Session*, p. 117.
17. *Minutes of the 36th Session*, p. 132. McDonald's testimony.
18. *Minutes of the 36th Session*, p. 208.
19. *Minutes of the 35th Session*, p. 90.
20. *Minutes of the 36th Session*, p. 222.
21. *Minutes of the 36th Session*, pp. 249 and 278.
22. *Minutes of the 36th Session*, p. 222.
23. Interview with May and Mazin Ali al-Daftari, son of Ni^cmat Yasin al-Hashimi, London, May 7, 2016.

Select Bibliography

Archives

Syria
Asad Library
Markaz al-Watha'iq al-Tarikhiyya
Archives of the Syrian Arab Republic Ministry of Education

Turkey
Istanbul University Archival Collection
Archives of the Turkish Republic Military Museum
Archives of the Turkish Republic Prime Minister, Istanbul
Yıldız Saray Photo Archive, IRCICA

Lebanon
National Archives
American University of Beirut, Jafet Library
Periodical Collection
Special and Archival Collections

Switzerland
Archives of the League of Nations Permanent Mandate Commission, Geneva

Germany
Staatsbibliothek zu Berlin
Zentrum Moderner Orient Library

France
Archives Diplomatiques de Nantes, Nantes
Archives Ministère de la Défense, Armée du Levant, Vincennes
Bibliothèque nationale de France

United Kingdom
British National Archives, Kew
Imperial War Museum, London

United States
Library of Congress, Abdul-Hamid collection

Press Sources

Alif Bâ', Damascus daily newspaper, various dates
L'Echo de Paris, Paris daily, various dates
al-Muqtabas, Damascus daily paper, various dates
Jamᶜia al-ᶜArabiyya, Jerusalem daily, 1927–
L'Humanité, Paris daily, various dates
al-Fata al-'Arab, Damascus daily, various dates
The Times, London daily, various dates
Jarida al-Bilad, Baghdad daily, various dates
Al-Qabas, Damascus daily, various dates
Al-Ayyam, Damascus daily, various dates
Egyptian Gazette, Cairo weekly, various dates
Manchester Guardian, Manchester daily, various dates
Al-Mussawar, Cairo weekly, various dates

Published Primary Sources

Abi Rashid, Hanna, *Hawran al-damiyya* (Cairo, 1926, reprint, Beirut: Maktabat al-Fikr al-'Arabi, 1961)
  Jabal al-duruz (Cairo: 1925, reprint, Beirut: Maktabat al-Fikr al-'Arabi, 1961)
ᶜAli, Tahsin, *Mudhakirrat Tahsin ᶜAli 1880–1970* (Beirut: al-Mu'assasa al-ᶜArabiyya lil-Diraset wa al-Nashr, 2003)
al-ᶜAs, Muhammad Sacid, *al-Tajarib al-harbiyya fi harb al-thawra al-suriyya* (Beirut, 1990)
Andréa, Général Charles Joseph, *La révolte druze et l'insurrection de Damas* (Paris, 1937)
Arslan, Shakib, *Sira Dhatiyya* (Beirut: Dar al-Talic a, 1969)
al-Askari, Jafar, *A Soldier's Story: From Ottoman Rule to Independent Iraq: The Memoirs of Jafar Pasha Al-Askari (1885–1936)*, trans. Mustafa Tariq Al-Askari (London: Arabian Publishers, 2003)
de Caix, Robert, *La Syrie* (Paris: Sociéte de l'histoire nationale, Plon, 1931)
Carbillet, Capitaine Gabriel, *Au Djébel Druse, choses vues et vécues* (Paris: Éditions Argo, 1929)
Coblentz, Paul, *Le silence de Sarrail* (Paris: L. Querelle, 1930)
Djemal Pasha, Ahmad, *Memories of a Turkish Statesman, 1913–1919* (London: Hutchinson, 1922)
Doty, Bennett J., *The Legion of the Damned: The Adventures of Bennett J. Doty in the French Foreign Legion as Told by Himself* (New York: Century Co., 1928)
Dowson, Sir Ernest, *An Inquiry into Land Tenure and Related Questions* (Letchworth, England: printed for the Iraqi government by Garden City Press, 1932)
al-Faris, Jurj, *Man hum fi al-ᶜalam al-ᶜarabi* (Damascus: matbaᶜ al-ahali, 1957)
  Man huwa fi suriyya 1949 (Damascus: matbaᶜ al-ahali, 1950)

Gibb, Sir Alexander and partners, *The Economic Development of Syria*, report commissioned by the Ministry of Public Works and Communications, Republic of Syria (London: Knapp, Drewett and Sons, 1947)

von der Goltz Colmar, *Das Volk in Waffen* (Berlin: R. V. Decker, 1883)

al-Hasani, ʿAbd al-Razzaq, *Tarikh al-wizarat al-ʿIraqiyya*, vols. I–III (Sidon: Matbaʿ al-ʿIrfan, 1953)

al-Thawra al-ʿIraqiyya al-Kubra (Sidon: Matbaʿ al-ʿIrfan, 1952)

al-Hashimi, Taha, *Mudhakkirat Taha al-Hashimi* (Beirut: Dar al-Taʾliʿa, 1967–78)

al-Husri, Satiʿ, *Mudhakkirati fi al-ʿIraq, 1921–1940*, 2 vols. (Beirut, 1967–8)

Yawm al-Maysalun: Safaha min tarikh al-ʿarab al-hadith (Beirut: Maktabat al-Kishāf, 1947)

League of Nations Permanent Mandates Commission Minutes (League of Nations, Geneva: various dates)

Maarif Nazereti Salnamesi (Istanbul: AH 1318 [1901])

Mekatibi Askeriyye Sakirdanınım Umumi, *Imtihanlarınım neticelerini* (Istanbul: AH 1318 [1901])

Midhat, Ali Haydar, *The Life of Midhat Pasha* (London: J. Murray, 1903)

Mühlmann, Carl, *Die deutsche Militär-Mission in der Türkei* (Berlin: W. Rothschild, 1938)

Deutschland und die Türkei 1913–1914: die Berufung der deutschen Militärmission nach der Türkei 1913, das deutsch-türkische Bündnis 1914 und der Eintritt der Türkei in den Weltkrieg (Berlin: W. Rothschild, 1929)

Poullea, Alice, *À Damas sous les bombes: Journal d'une Française pendant la révolte Syrienne, 1924–1926* (Yvetot: Bretteville, 1926)

al-Qadi, Niqulaws, *Arb'aun 'aman fi Hawran wa Jabal al-Duruz* (Beirut, 1927)

al-Qawuqji, Fawzi, *Mudhakkirat Fawzi al-Qawuqji* (reprint of both volumes of 1975 edition, edited by Khayriyya Qâsimiyya, Damascus: al-Tawzi, 1995)

al-Rayyis, Munir, *al-Kitab al-dhahabi lil-thawrat al-wataniyya fi al-mashriq al-ʿarabi: al-thawra al-suriyya al-kubra*, vol. I (Beirut: Dar al-Taliʿah lil-Tibaʿah wa-al-Nashr, 1969)

al-Kitab al-dhahabi lil-thawrat al-wataniyya fi al-mashriq al-ʿarabi: thawra Filastin ʿam 1936, vol. II (Beirut: Dar al-Taliʿah lil-Tibaʿah wa-al-Nashr, 1969)

al-Kitab al-dhahabi lil-thawrat al-wataniyya fi al-mashriq al-ʿarabi: harb al-ʿIraq ʿam 1941, vol. III (Beirut: Dar al-Taliʿah lil-Tibaʿah wa-al-Nashr, 1969)

al-Saʿid, Amin, *al-Thawra al-ʿarabiyya al-kubra* (Beirut: Dar al-katib al ʿarabi, reprint, n.d.)

al-Saʿid, Nuri, *Mudhakkirat Nuri al-Saʿid ʿan al-harakat al-ʿaskariyya lil-jaysh al-ʿArabi fi al-Hijaz wa-Suriyya, 1916–1918: al-Fariq al-rukn Nuri al-Saʿid ʿala tullab Kulliyyat al-Arkan bi-Baghdad fi Mayis 1947* (Beirut: al-Dar alʿArabiyya lil-Mawsuʿat, 1987)

al-Shahbandar, ʿAbd al-Rahman, *al-Thawra al-Suruyya al-Kubra: Mudhakkirat al-duktur ʿAbd al-Rahman al-Shahbandar* (Beirut: 1967, reprint, Damascus: manshuratwazara al-thaqafa, 1993)

Mudhakkirat wal-khutab (Beirut, 1967, reprint Damascus: manshurat wazara al-thaqafa, 1993)

Salname-i Nazaret-i Maarif-i Umumiyye (Istanbul: Matbaa-i Amire, AH1316 [1899])

Salname-i Nazaret-i Maarif-i Umumiyye (Istanbul: Matbaa-i Amire, AH1319 [1901])

al-Zirikli, Khayr ad-Dīn, *al-A^clam: qamus tarajim li-ashar ar-rijal wa'n-nisa min ^carab wa'l-musta^cribin al-mustasthriqin*, 8 vols., reprint of *c.* 1950 (Beirut: dar al-^calam al-malayin, 1990)

Unpublished Dissertations

Abu Fakhr, Fandi, "Tarikh liwa' Hawran al-ijtima^cal-Suwayda'– Dar^ca-al-Qunaytra – ^cAjlun, 1840–1918," self-published PhD dissertation, Damascus University, 1999

Ajay, Nicholas, "Mount Lebanon and the Wilayah of Beirut, 1914–1918: the War Years," unpublished PhD dissertation, Georgetown University, 1972

Anderson, Charles W., "From Petition to Confrontation: The Palestinian National Movement and the Rise of Mass Politics, 1929–1939," unpublished PhD dissertation, New York University, 2013

Bailony, Reem, "Transnational Rebellion: The Syrian Revolt of 1925–1927," unpublished PhD dissertation, University of California, Los Angeles, 2015

Dalati, Aziz Amin, "The Ghouta of Damascus," unpublished B.B.A. thesis, AUB, 1938

Griffiths, Merwin, "The Reorganization of the Ottoman Army under Abdül-Hamid II 1880–1907," unpublished PhD dissertation, UCLA, 1966

Marr, Phebe, "Yasin al-Hashimi: The Rise and Fall of a Nationalist (A Study of the Nationalist Leadership in Iraq, 1920–1936)," unpublished PhD dissertation, Harvard University, 1966

Méouchy, Nadine, "Les formes de conscience politique et communautaire au Liban et en Syrie à l'époque du mandat Français 1920–1939," unpublished Doctorat en Histoire dissertation, Université de Paris, 1989

Mufarrij, Fuad K., "Syria and Lebanon under French Mandate," unpublished MA thesis, AUB, 1935

Nashibi, Hisham A., "The Political Parties in Syria, 1918–1939," unpublished MA thesis, AUB, 1952

al-Qaysi, Abdul-Wahhab Abbas, "The Impact of Modernization on Iraqi Society During the Ottoman Era: A Study of Intellectual Development in Iraq, 1869–1917," unpublished PhD dissertation, University of Michigan, 1958

Rustum, Asad, "Syria Under Mehemet Ali," unpublished PhD dissertation, University of Chicago, 1923

Sanagan, Mark, "Lightning Through the Clouds: Islam, Community, and Anti-Colonial Rebellion in the Life and Death of Izz al-Dīn al-Qassām, 1883–1935," unpublished PhD dissertation, McGill University, 2016

Tomeh, Ramez George, "Landownership and Political Power in Damascus: 1858–1958," unpublished MA thesis, AUB, 1977

Steven Wagner, "British Intelligence and Policy in the Palestine Mandate, 1919–1939," unpublished DPhil dissertation, University of Oxford, 2014

Secondary Sources

Abu Husayn, Abdul-Rahim, *Bayn al-markaz wa al-atraf: Hawran fi al-watha'iq al-ʿUthmaniyya* (London: Druze Heritage Foundation, 2015)

ʿAbd al-ʿAziz Muhammad ʿAwad, *al-Idara al-ʿuthmaniyya fi wilayat suriyya, 1864–1914* (Cairo: Dar al-macruf, 1969)

Agha Kassab, Sawsan and Tadmori, Omar, *Beirut and the Sultan: 200 Photographs from the Albums of Abdul Hamid II (1876–1909)* (Beirut: Beirut Municipality, 2002)

Akarli, Engin Deniz, "Abdülhamid II's Attempt to Integrate Arabs into the Ottoman System," in David Kushner (ed.), *Palestine in the Late Ottoman Period* (Jerusalem and Leiden: yad Izhak Ben-Zvi/Brill, 1986)

The Long Peace: Ottoman Lebanon, 1861–1920 (Berkeley: University of California Press, 1993)

Aksakal, Mustafa, *The Ottoman Road to War in 1914: The Ottoman Empire and the First World War* (Cambridge University Press, 2008)

Antonius, George, *The Arab Awakening: The Story of the Arab National Movement* (London: H. Hamilton, 1938)

Batatu, Hanna, *The Old Social Classes and the Revolutionary Movements of Iraq* (Princeton University Press, 1978)

Syria's Peasantry, the Descendants of its Lesser Rural Notables, and their Politics (Princeton University Press, 1999)

Beinen, Joel and Lockman, Zachary, *Nationalism, Communism, Islam, and the Egyptian Working Class, 1882–1954* (Princeton University Press, 1987)

al-Bi'ayni, Hasan Amin, *Duruz suriyya wa lubnan fi ʿahd al-intidab al-fransi, 1920–1943* (Beirut: al-Markaz al- 'Arabi li-al-Abhat wa-alTawtiq, 1993)

Bokova, Lenka, *La confrontation franco-syrienne à l'époque du mandat, 1925–27* (Paris: L'Harmattan, 1990)

Burke, Edmund III, "The Sociology of Islam: The French Tradition," in Malcolm Kerr (ed.), *Islamic Studies: A Tradition and its Problems* (Malibu, CA, 1980), pp. 73–88

"A Comparative View of French Native Policy in Morocco and Syria, 1912–1925," *MES*, 9 (May 1973), 177

"Understanding Arab Protest Movements," *Arab Studies Quarterly*, 8:4 (1987), 333–45

Chatterjee, Partha, *The Nation and its Fragments: Colonial and Postcolonial Histories* (Princeton University Press, 1993)

Commins, David Dean, *Islamic Reform: Politics and Change in Late Ottoman Syria* (Oxford University Press, 1992)

Dawud, Ahmad Yusuf, *al-Mujahid Saʿd al-ʿAs* (Damascus: Dar al-Mustaqbal, 1990)

Deringil, Salim, "The Invention of Tradition as Public Image in the Late Ottoman Empire, 1808 to 1908," in *Comparative Studies in Society and History*, 35 (1993), 3–29

The Well-Protected Domains: Ideology and the Legitimation of Power in the Ottoman Empire, 1876–1909 (London: I.B. Tauris, 1998)

Doumani, Beshara, *Rediscovering Palestine: Merchants and Peasants in Jabal Nablus, 1700–1900* (Berkeley: University of California Press, 1995)

Evered, Emine O., *Empire and Education under the Ottomans: Politics, Reform and Resistance from the Tanzimat to the Young Turks* (London: I.B. Tauris, 2012)

Faris, Basim (ed.), *A Postwar Bibliography of the Near Eastern Mandates*, 5 vols. (Beirut, 1932)

Fawwaz, Leila Tarazi, *A Land of Aching Hearts: The Middle East in the Great War* (Cambridge, MA: Harvard University Press, 2014)

Findley, Carter, *Ottoman Civil Officialdom: A Social History* (Princeton University Press, 1989)

Firro, Kais M., *A History of the Druzes* (Leiden: Brill, 1992)

Fortna, Benjamin, *Imperial Classroom: Islam, the State, and Education in the Late Ottoman Empire* (Oxford, 2002)

Frevert, Ute, *A Nation in Barracks: Modern Germany, Military Conscription, and Civil Society*, trans. Andrew Boreham (Oxford: Berg, 2004)

Gelvin, James L., *Divided Loyalties: Nationalism and Mass Politics in Syria at the Close of Empire* (Berkeley: University of California Press, 1998)

"The Social Origins of Popular Nationalism in Syria: Evidence for a New Framework," *IJMES*, 26 (1994), 645–61

Handan, Nezir-Achmeşe, *The Birth of Modern Turkey: The Ottoman Military and the March to World War I* (London: I.B. Tauris, 2005)

Hanioğlu, Şükrü, *Atatürk: An Intellectual Biography* (Princeton University Press, 2013)

Hanna, ʿAbdallah, *al- ʿAmmiyya wa al-intifadat al-falahiyya (1850–1918) fi jabal Hawran* (Damascus: al-ahali, 1990)

al-Haraka al-ʿummaliyya fi suriyya wa lubnan: 1900–1945 (Damascus: dar dimashq, 1973)

al-Qadiyya al-ziraʿiyya wa al-harakat al-fallahiyya fi suriyya wa lubnan (1820–1920), vols. I–II (Beirut: dar al-Farabi, 1975 and 1978)

Hanssen, Jens, *Fin de Siècle Beirut: The Making of an Ottoman Provincial Capital* (Oxford University Press, 2005)

Himadeh, Sa'id (ed.), *Economic Organization of Syria* (Beirut: AUB Press, 1936)

Hobsbawm, Eric, *The Age of Empire: 1875–1914* (New York: Vintage, 1987)

Hourani, Albert, "Ottoman Reform and the Politics of Notables," in William Polk and Richard Chambers (eds.), *Beginnings of Modernization in the Middle East: The Nineteenth Century* (Chicago University Press, 1968)

Syria and Lebanon: A Political Essay (Oxford: Royal Institute of International Affairs, 1946)

Hughes, Matthew, *Allenby and British Strategy in the Middle East, 1917–1919* (London: Frank Cass, 1999)

"A Very British Affair? The Repression of the Arab Revolt in Palestine, 1936–39 (Part One)," *Journal of the Society for Army Historical Research* 87:351 (Autumn 2009), 234–55

Hull, Isabel V., *Absolute Destruction: Military Culture and the Practices of War in Imperial Germany* (New York: Cornell University Press, 2006)

al-Jundi, Adham, *Târîkh al-Thawrât al-Suriyya fi ʿAhd al-Intidâb al-Fransî* (Damascus: Matbacat al-Ittihad, 1960)

Kasmieh, Khairieh (al-Qasimiyya, Khayriyya). *al-Hukuma al-'arabiyya fi damashq bayn 1918–1920* (Cairo, 1971)

Kawtharani, Wajih, *Ittijahat al-ijtimaʿiyya al-siyasiyya fi Jabal Lubnan wa-al-Mashriq al-ʿArabi, 1860-1920* (Beirut: Maʿhad al-Inma' al-ʿArabi, 1978)

 Dawlah wa-al-khilafa fi al-khitab al-ʿArabi abbana al-thawrah al-Kamaliyya fi Turkiyya (Beirut: Dar al-Taliʿa, 1996)

Kayali, Hasan, *Arabs and Young Turks: Ottomanism, Arabism, and Islamism in the Ottoman Empire, 1908–1918* (Berkeley: University of California Press, 1997)

Keydar, Caglar and Tabak, Faruk (eds.), *Landholding and Commercial Agriculture in the Middle East* (New York: SUNY Press, 1991)

Khadduri, Majid, "'Aziz 'Ali al-Misri and the Arab Nationalist Movement," in Albert Hourani (ed.), *Middle Eastern Affairs*, no. 4 (St. Antony's Papers, no. 17) (London, 1965)

Khalidi, Rashid, *British Policy Towards Syria and Palestine, 1906–1914: A Study of the Antecedents of the Hussein – the McMahon Correspondence, the Sykes–Picot Agreement, and the Balfour Declaration* (Oxford: Ithaca Press, 1980)

 Palestinian Identity: The Construction of Modern National Consciousness (New York: Columbia University Press, 1997)

Anderson, Lisa, Muslih, Muhammad, and Simon, Reeva (eds.), *The Origins of Arab Nationalism* (New York: Columbia University Press, 1991)

Khalidi, Tarif (ed.), *Land Tenure and Social Transformation in the Middle East* (Beirut: SAUB Press, 1984)

Khoury, Philip S. *Syria and the French Mandate: The Politics of Arab Nationalism, 1920–1945* (Princeton University Press, 1987)

 "A Reinterpretation of the Origins and Aims of the Great Syrian Revolt, 1925–1927," in Atiyeh, George N. and Oweis, Ibrahim M., *Arab Civilization: Challenges and Responses: Studies in Honor of Constantine K. Zurayk* (Albany: State University of New York, 1988)

Kitchen, James E., *The British Imperial Army in the Middle East: Morale and Military Identity in the Sinai and Palestine Campaigns, 1916–18* (London: Bloomsbury, 2014)

Köroglu, Erol, *Ottoman Propaganda and Turkish Identity: Literature in Turkey During World War I* (London: Palgrave Macmillan, 2007)

Latron, André, *La vie rurale en Syrie et au Liban* (Beirut: Impr. Catholique, 1936)

Lewis, Norman, *Nomads and Settlers in Syria and Jordan, 1800–1980* (Cambridge University Press, 1987)

Longrigg, Stephen H., *Iraq, 1900 to 1950: A Political, Social, and Economic History* (Oxford University Press, 1953)

 Syria and Lebanon under French Mandate (Oxford University Press, 1958)

MacCallum, Elizabeth, *The Nationalist Crusade in Syria* (New York: Foreign Policy Association, 1928)

Makdisi, Ussama, *Faith Misplaced: The Broken Promise of U.S.-Arab Relations, 1820–2001* (New York: PublicAffairs, 2010)

Matthews, Weldon, *Confronting an Empire, Constructing a Nation: Arab Nationalists and Popular Politics in Mandate Palestine* (London: I.B. Tauris, 2006)

Mazower, Mark, *No Enchanted Palace: The End of Empire and the Ideological Origins of the United Nations* (Princeton University Press, 2009)

Méouchy, Nadine and Sluglett Peter (eds.), *The British and French Mandates in Comparative Perspectives/Les Mandats Francais et Anglais dans une Perspective Comparative* (Leiden: Brill, 2004)

Mundy, Martha and Smith, Richard Saumarez, *Governing Property, Making the Modern State: Law, Administration and Production in Ottoman Syria* (London: I.B. Tauris, 2007)

Nezir-Akmese, Handan, *The Birth of Modern Turkey: The Ottoman Military and the March to WWI* (London: I.B. Tauris, 2005)

Parsons, Laila, *The Commander: Fawzi al-Qawuqji and the Fight for Arab Independence 1914–1948* (New York: Hill and Wang, 2016)

"Soldiering for Arab Nationalism: Fawzi al-Qawuqji in Palestine," *Journal of Palestine Studies*, 36:4 (Summer 2007), pp. 33–49

Pederson, Susan, *The Guardians: The League of Nations and the Crisis of Empire* (Oxford University Press, 2015)

Qarqut, Dhuqan, *Tatawwur al-haraka al-wataniyya fi suriyya, 1920–1939* (Beirut: Dar al-Tali'a, 1975)

Rafeq, Abdul-Karim, "Land Tenure Problems and their Social Impact in Syria around the Middle of the Nineteenth Century," in Tarif Khalidi (ed.), *Land Tenure and Social Transformation in the Middle East* (Beirut: AUB Press, 1984)

The Province of Damascus, 1723–1783 (Beirut: Khayats, 1966)

Sluglett, Peter and Weber, Stefan (eds.), *Syria and Bilad al-Sham under Ottoman Rule: Essays in Honour of Abdul Karim Rafeq* (Leiden: Brill, 2010)

Ramsaur, Ernest E., *The Young Turks: Prelude to the Revolution of 1908* (Princeton University Press, 1957)

Reilly, James A, "Property, Status, and Class in Ottoman Damascus," *JAORS*, 112: 1–2 (1992), pp. 9–21

Reynolds, Michael A., *Shattering Empires: The Clash and Collapse of the Ottoman and Russian Empires, 1908–1918* (Cambridge University Press, 2011)

Roberts, Stephen H., *History of French Colonial Policy, 1870–1925*, vols. I–II (London: P.S. King & Son, 1929)

Rogan, Eugene, "Aşiret Mektebi Abdülhamid II's School for Tribes (1892–1907)," *IJMES*, 28 (1996), 83–107

The Fall of the Ottomans: The Great War in the Middle East, 1914–1920 (London: Basic Books, 2015)

al-Safarjalanî, Muhi al-Din, *al-Tarikh al-thawra al-suriyya* (Damascus, 1961)

Salibi, Kamal, *A House of Many Mansions: The History of Lebanon Reconsidered* (Berkeley: University of California Press, 1988)

Sara, Fayiz, *Sa'id al-'As, 1889–1936: Hayatahu-Kifahahu* (Damascus: manshurat wazara al-thaqafa, 1993)

Schäbler, Birgit, *Aufstände im Drusenbergland: Ethnizität und Integration einer Ländlich en Gesellschaft Syriens vom Osmanischen Reich bis zur Staatlichen Unabhängigkeit, 1850–1949* (Gotha: Perthes, 1996)

Schayegh, Cyrus and Arsan, Andrew (eds.), *The Routledge Handbook of the History of the Middle East Mandates* (London: Routledge, 2015)

Schilcher, Linda, *Families in Politics: Damascene Factions and Estates of the Eighteenth and Nineteenth Centuries* (Stuttgart: F. Steiner, 1985)

"Railways in the Political Economy of Southern Syria 1890–1925," in Thomas Philipp and Birgit Schaebler (eds.), *The Syrian Land: Processes of Integration and Fragmentation in Bilâd al-Shâm from the 18th to the 20th Century* (Stuttgart: F. Steiner, 1998), pp. 97–112

Schölch, Alexander, "The Emergence of Modern Palestine (1856–1882)," in Hisham Nashabe (ed.), *Studia Palaestina: Studies in Honor of Constantine K. Zurayk* (Beirut: Institute for Palestine Studies, 1988), pp. 69–82

Seale, Patrick, *The Struggle for Syria: A Study of Post War Arab Politics 1945–1958* (New Haven, Yale University Press, 1986)

Seikaly, Samir M., "Pacification of the Hawran (1910): The View From Within," *Essays on Ottoman Civilization: Proceedings of the XIIth Congress of the Comite international d'etudes pre-ottomanes et ottomanes* (Prague: Academy of Sciences of the Czech Republic, Oriental Institute, 1996)

"Land Tenure in 17th-Century Palestine: The Evidence from the Fatâwâ al-Khairiyya," in Tarif Khalidi (ed.), *Land Tenure and Social Transformation in the Middle East* (Beirut: AUB Press, 1984)

Shambrook, Peter A., *French Imperialism in Syria, 1927–1936* (Reading, UK: Ithaca Press, 1998)

Sluglett, Marion Farouk and Sluglett, Peter, "The Application of the 1858 Land Code in Greater Syria: Some Preliminary Observations," in Tarif Khalidi (ed.), *Land Tenure and Social Transformation in the Middle East* (Beirut, 1984)

Sluglett, Peter, *Britain in Iraq: Contriving King and Country* (New York: Columbia University Press, 2007)

Somel, Selçuk Akşin, *The Modernization of Public Education in the Ottoman Empire, 1839–1908: Islamization, Autocracy and Discipline* (Leiden: Brill, 2001)

Tamari, Salim, *Year of the Locust: The Great War and the Erasure of Palestine's Ottoman Past* (Beirut: Institute for Palestine Studies, 2008)

Tanenbaum, Jan Karl, *General Maurice Sarrail: The French Army and Left Wing Politics* (Chapel Hill, NC: University of North Carolina Press, 1974)

Tejel, Jordi, Sluglett, Peter, Bocco, Riccardo, and Bozarslan, Hamit (eds.), *Writing the Modern History of Iraq: Historiographical and Political Challenges* (Singapore: World Scientific, 2012)

Thomas, Martin, *Empires of Intelligence: Security Services and Colonial Disorder after 1914* (Berkeley: University of California Press, 2007)

Thompson, Elizabeth, *Colonial Citizens: Republican Rights, Paternal Privilege, and Gender in French Syria and Lebanon* (New York: Columbia University Press, 2000)

Justice Interrupted: The Struggle for Constitutional Government in the Middle East (Cambridge, MA: Harvard University Press, 2013)

Tibawi, Abdul-Latif, *American Interests in Syria, 1800–1901: A Study of Educational, Literary and Religious Work* (Oxford: Clarendon Press, 1966)

A Modern History of Syria Including Lebanon and Palestine (New York: St. Martin's Press, 1969)

Trumpener, Ulrich, *Germany and the Ottoman Empire 1914–1918* (Princeton University Press, 1968)

"German Officers in the Ottoman Empire, 1880–1918: Some Comments on their Backgrounds, Functions, and Accomplishments," in Jehuda L. Wallach (ed.), *Germany and the Middle East: 1835–1939* (Tel-Aviv: Nateev-Press, 1975), pp. 30–44

ʿUbayd, Salama, *al-Thawra al-suriyya al-kubra: 1925-1927 ʿala dawaʾ wathaʾiq lam tunshar* (Beirut: dar al-ghad, 1971)

Uyar, Mesut "Ottoman Arab Officers between Nationalism and Loyalty," *War in History*, 20:4 (2013), pp. 526–44

Uyar, Mesut and Erickson, Edward, *A Military History of the Ottomans: From Osman to Atatürk* (Santa Barbara: Praeger Security International, 2009)

Warriner, Doreen, *Land Reform and Development in the Middle East* (Oxford University Press, 1962)

Weber, Stefan, *Damascus: Ottoman Modernity and Urban Transformation, 1808–1918* (Aarhus University Press, 2009)

Weiss, Max, *In the Shadow of Sectarianism: Law, Shiʿism and the Making of Modern Lebanon* (Cambridge, MA: Harvard University Press, 2010)

Weulersse, Jacques, *Paysans de Syrie et du Proche-Orient* (Paris: Gallimard, 1946)

White, Benjamin Thomas, *The Emergence of Minorities in the Middle East: The Politics of Community in French Mandate Syria* (Edinburgh University Press, 2011)

Wilson, Mary, *King Abdullah, Britain and the Making of Jordan* (Cambridge University Press, 1990)

Wright, Philip Quincy, "The Bombardment of Damascus," *American Journal of International Law*, 20:2 (1926), pp. 263–80

Zeine, N. Zeine, *The Struggle for Arab Independence: Western Diplomacy and the Rise and Fall of Faisal's Kingdom in Syria*, 2nd edition (New York: Caravan, 1977)

Zürcher, Erik-Jan, "The Vocabulary of Muslim Nationalism," *International Journal of the Sociology of Science*, 137 (1999)

"The Ottoman Conscription System in Theory and Practice, 1844–1918," *International Review of Social History*, 43 (1998)

(ed.), *Jihad and Islam in World War I: Studies on the Ottoman Jihad on the Centenary of Snouck Hurgronje's "Holy War Made in Germany"* (Leiden University Press, 2016)

Index

al-ᶜAzm, Haqqi, 220, 221
al-ᶜAzma, Yusuf, 33, 34, 35, 36, 73,
    91, 104, 106, 107, 110, 114,
    115, 120, 165, 182, 248, 253

Baghdad, 12, 21, 23, 24, 25, 30, 32,
    36, 38, 43, 59, 65, 66, 93,
    94, 102, 106, 114, 117, 118,
    120, 125, 129, 137, 138, 139,
    147, 149, 154, 161, 162, 190,
    192, 202, 208, 210, 214, 215,
    216, 217, 218, 219, 227, 229,
    235, 239, 240, 241, 242, 243,
    244, 245, 246, 247, 248, 249,
    251, 252, 254, 266, 272, 273,
    278, 279
Balfour, Arthur, wartime British
    Foreign Secretary,
    declaration, 1925 mandate
    tour, 66, 67, 73, 78, 82, 83,
    86, 87, 88, 116, 126, 147,
    150, 157, 158, 163, 196, 200,
    201, 220, 228, 261, 266, 268,
    280
Balkan Wars, 59, 60
Bateman, Charles, Councellor British
    Embassy Baghdad, 243, 244,
    249
Bedouin, 89, 167, 172
Berlin, 2, 9, 11, 12, 35, 43, 44, 48,
    57, 79, 86, 93, 103, 132, 141,
    159, 160, 227, 244, 266, 267,
    278, 279
Bismarck, Otto von, 19th century
    German Chancellor, 11, 12,
    243
Blum, Léon French Popular
    Front Premier, 230, 239,
    263, 266
Borders
    of the mandatory states and
    "micro-states," and nationalist
    opposition to, 7, 45, 71, 72,
    93, 117, 124, 135, 159, 163,
    191, 218, 219, 239, 262, 263,
    265
Boycotts, in Palestine, and Syria,
    204, 205, 221

Britain
    colonial martial law, 124, 236
    Damascus consul, 131, 157, 158,
        195, 228, 248
    intelligence, 44, 45, 95, 110, 112,
        114, 115, 116, 118, 122, 128,
        129, 139, 140, 161, 200, 233,
        234, 236, 238, 239, 243, 279
    policy in Ottoman lands, 59, 66,
        68, 94, 148, 150, 184, 202,
        236, 245
Bruce Hay, John Charles, British
    general and Iraqi Army
    adviser, 241, 244,
    246, 247

de Caix, Robert, French League of
    Nation delegate, 83, 90, 91,
    111, 163, 175, 176, 178, 179,
    180, 240, 269
Caliphate, abolition, Arab Caliph, 5,
    39, 62, 139, 140, 154
Cartel des Gauches, 157
Cemal Paşa Ahmad, Ottoman
    wartime military governor, 18,
    33, 38, 39, 42, 44, 45, 47, 48,
    104, 132, 134, 158, 160
Christians
    Greek Catholic, 193
    Maronite Catholics, 47, 85, 89, 90,
        96, 110, 121, 152, 157, 163,
        193, 228, 262, 265
    Orthodox, 96, 153, 172, 193, 228,
        263
Christians, French policy of arming,
    171
Churchill, Winston, British
    Statesman, 11, 56, 61, 62, 92,
    93, 95, 101, 123, 124, 129,
    213
Cilicia, region in S.E. Anatolia, 56,
    60, 68, 71, 72, 73, 101, 106,
    108, 109, 110, 113, 117, 118,
    119, 122, 137, 148, 167
Clark Kerr, Archibald, British
    Ambassador to Iraq, 242, 243,
    244, 245, 246, 247, 249, 251,
    252